LAWRENCE *of* ARABIA ON WAR

OSPREY
PUBLISHING

LAWRENCE
of ARABIA
ON WAR

THE CAMPAIGN IN THE DESERT
1916–18

ROB JOHNSON

OSPREY PUBLISHING
Bloomsbury Publishing Plc
PO Box 883, Oxford, OX1 9PL, UK
1385 Broadway, 5th Floor, New York, NY 10018, USA
E-mail: info@ospreypublishing.com
www.ospreypublishing.com

OSPREY is a trademark of Osprey Publishing Ltd

First published in Great Britain in 2020

A catalogue record for this book is available from the British Library.

ISBN: HB 978 1 4728 3491 1; PB 978 1 4728 3492 8; eBook 978 1 4728 3489 8;
ePDF 978 1 4728 3488 1; XML 978 1 4728 3490 4

20 21 22 23 24   10 9 8 7 6 5 4 3 2 1

Maps by Bounford.com
Index by Zoe Ross

Typeset by Deanta Global Publishing Services, Chennai, India
Printed and bound in Great Britain by CPI (Group) UK Ltd, Croydon CR0 4YY

Front cover: Talbots and a Rolls-Royce armoured car in support of Arab irregulars.
(Marist Special Collections, B&W glass plate 1264.2)
Back cover: Dorsetshire Yeomanry crossing the desert. (TopFoto)

Imperial War Museums Collections
Many of the photos in this book come from the huge collections of IWM (Imperial War Museums)
which cover all aspects of conflict involving Britain and the Commonwealth since the start of the
twentieth century. These rich resources are available online to search, browse and buy at www.iwm.org.
uk/collections. In addition to Collections Online, you can visit the Visitor Rooms where you can explore
over 8 million photographs, thousands of hours of moving images, the largest sound archive of its
kind in the world, thousands of diaries and letters written by people in wartime, and a huge reference
library. To make an appointment, call (020) 7416 5320, or e-mail mail@iwm.org.uk
Imperial War Museums www.iwm.org.uk

Osprey Publishing supports the Woodland Trust, the UK's leading woodland conservation charity.

To find out more about our authors and books visit **www.ospreypublishing.com**. Here you will find
extracts, author interviews, details of forthcoming events and the option to sign up for our newsletter.

Contents

CONTENTS

Preface

T. E. Lawrence 'of Arabia' is an iconic figure, not only in studies of the First World War, but in the historiography of guerrilla warfare. Since there are so many excellent biographies of Lawrence, this book does not seek to retrace the story of his extraordinary life. Instead, it is concerned with three things: first, Lawrence's ideas on the nature and practice of war; second, the conduct of his insurgent operations which gave him experiences that modified his theories; and third, how both his ideas and his conduct have been instrumentalized by others since the First World War.

The centenary of the conclusion of the Great War in 1918 stimulated much reflection, not only on the outcomes and costs of that conflict, but also the extent to which it shaped the world thereafter.[1] Lawrence was but one figure in that global struggle, though his peripheral campaign took on a greater significance in the subsequent fortunes of the Middle East. His ideas had even more impact on the attempts to understand irregular warfare as it reappeared throughout the twentieth century and into our own times. This presents us with an opportunity to reappraise how theoretical ideas about war are used, but also, when taken out of their context, how they can generate potentially misleading deductions.

This study shows the relative significance of Lawrence's guerrilla operations, which were dependent on the concurrent military campaign conducted by General Edmund Allenby, the commander of the Egyptian Expeditionary Force (EEF). It was the EEF that checked, then defeated the Ottomans in the Levant, and facilitated the Arab forces in the Hejaz, providing us with an instructive example of how conventional armed forces work with local irregular and regular units. This book offers some insights on the reactions of the Ottoman Empire to guerrilla war, explaining the calculations that determined the outcome of Lawrence's campaign. These elements are often overshadowed by studies of Lawrence himself, but they are vital if we are to understand the achievements, and the setbacks, of this remarkable man.

From the outset it is important to emphasize that this is a work that seeks to explain Lawrence's ideas on war and their significance: it is a critical study of warfare and the manner in which Lawrence, and others, made their assessments of what was changing, what was distinctive, and what was unique to guerrilla operations, to the desert environment, and to the character of war in that period. The intention is to convey the significance of 'hybrid warfare' (that is, guerrilla actions, combined with psychological warfare and other unconventional methods, alongside conventional military operations), and the distinctive complexion of the desert campaign, to reveal the relative importance of local forces in it.

Acknowledgements are due to a great many friends, supporters and scholars. I would especially like to thank, for their inspiration on the region, the conflict, and the geography of place and mind, not least in the workshops, conferences, field-trips and archival marathons that I have engaged with them in: Professor Eugene Rogan, Dr James Kitchen, Dr Neil Faulkner, Dr John Peaty, the late Jeremy Wilson, Eran Tearosh, Dr John Nagl, Dr Justin Fantazzo, Professor Margaret MacMillan, Professor Sir Hew Strachan, Dr Metin Gurcan, Professor Himmet Umunc, Professor Mesut Uyar, Dr Tuncay Yılmazer, Dr Saul Kelly, Dr Adrian Gregory, Dr Todd Greentree, Professor Yakov Ben Haim, Dr Eado Hecht, Dr Eitan Shamir, Dr Rod Bailey, Dr Johnny Fennell, Professor George Joffe, Daryl Green, Group Captain John Alexander, Professor Charles Townshend, Professor Sir Lawrence Freedman, Dr Jonathan Boff, Dr David Murphy, and Professor Gary Sheffield.

I would particularly like to thank Dame Vivien Duffield who has been an incredibly generous supporter for several years, and together we have assisted a very special team for whom this book was always intended. I am deeply grateful also to the Gerry Holdsworth Trust for their generosity in funding, at last minute, part of this project, without which I would not have been able to make a crucial return trip to the Middle East. Sadly, the civil war in Syria precluded the opportunity of reaching some of the sites concerned with Lawrence's campaign, particularly Deraa, but I am very grateful for all the efforts friends and colleagues made to get me to the other locations. The Ax:Son Johnson Foundation supported me as a researcher and as Director of the Oxford Changing Character of War Research Centre throughout the period in which I wrote this work, for which I am immensely grateful.

I should also like to thank the various collections, museums, libraries and archives that have given me permission to read, consult, study and reproduce material in this volume. Particular thanks are due to the Middle East Centre Archive at St Antony's, Oxford, the Bodleian Library, and the Ashmolean Museum, as well as Magdalen College, my former college, All Souls, and my own college, Pembroke. Illustrations appear from several collections, for which I am immensely grateful, including the Imperial War Museum, the National Portrait Gallery, the Library of Congress and the Marist College Special Collection of New York.

I am also hugely grateful to the many friends and comrades of the United States Army and the United States Marine Corps who have shown such interest in, and support for, this project, and protected me along the way. I also want to express very special thanks to the Royal Air Force who not only had an important role to play in the campaign in the Middle East, but who have been very generous, informative and supportive in furthering my research.

This book is dedicated to Marianne. As you know, the mind is everything.

Rob Johnson, Oxford, 2019

List of Illustrations

The Hejaz in 1917

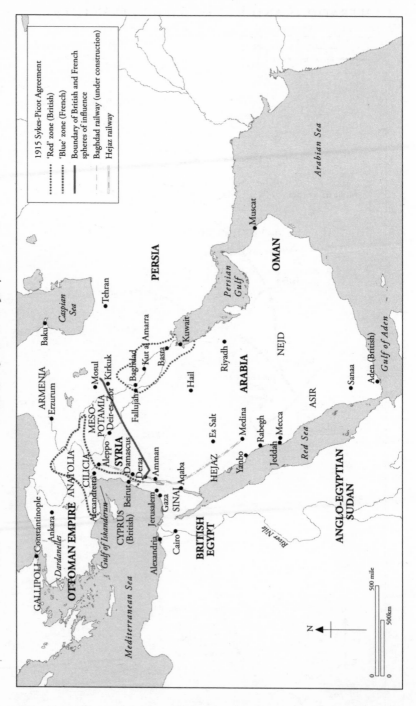

Operations and Raids in the Levant, 1917–18

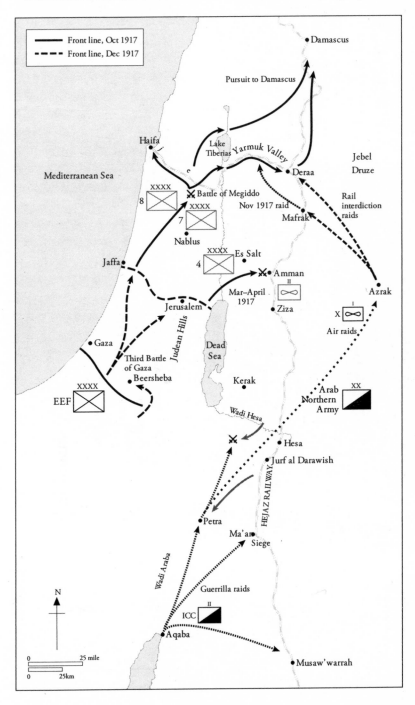

Front line, Oct 1917
Front line, Dec 1917

Damascus

Pursuit to Damascus

Haifa

Lake Tiberias

Yarmuk Valley

Jebel Druze

Mediterranean Sea

Battle of Megiddo

XXXX
8

XXXX
7

Nablus

Nov 1917 raid

Deraa

Mafrak

Rail interdiction raids

Azrak

XXXX
4

Es Salt

Jaffa

Amman

II

Mar–April 1917

Ziza

X I

Jerusalem

Judean Hills

Air raids

Gaza

Dead Sea

Third Battle of Gaza

Beersheba

EEF
XXXX

Kerak

Wadi Hesa

Arab Northern Army

XX

Hesa

Jurf al Darawish

HEJAZ RAILWAY

Petra

Wadi Araba

Ma'an

Siege

N

Guerrilla raids

ICC
II

Aqaba

Musaw'warrah

0   25 mile
0   25km

13

The Final Operations, 1918

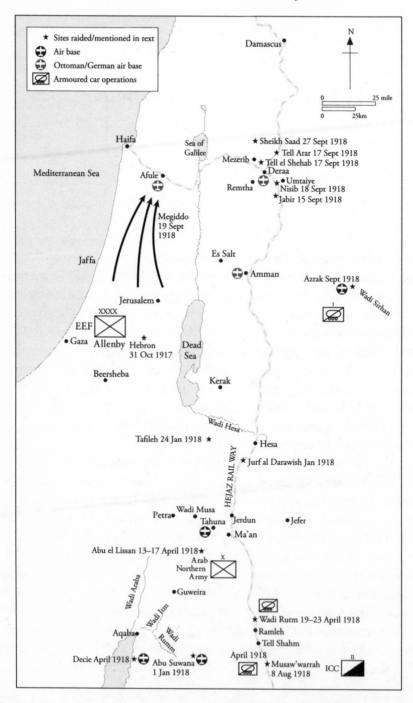

Sites raided/mentioned in text
Air base
Ottoman/German air base
Armoured car operations

N

0   25 mile
0   25km

Damascus

Mediterranean Sea

Haifa

Sea of Galilee

★ Sheikh Saad 27 Sept 1918
★ Tell Arar 17 Sept 1918
Mezerib ★ Tell el Shehab 17 Sept 1918
★ Deraa
Remtha ★ Umtaiye
Nisib 18 Sept 1918
★ Jabir 15 Sept 1918

Afule

Megiddo
19 Sept
1918

Jaffa

Es Salt

Amman

Azrak Sept 1918 ★
Wadi Sirhan

Jerusalem

EEF
XXXX
Allenby
Gaza   Hebron
31 Oct 1917

Dead Sea

Beersheba

Kerak

Wadi Hesa

Tafileh 24 Jan 1918 ★

HEJAZ RAILWAY

Hesa

★ Jurf al Darawish Jan 1918

Petra
Wadi Musa
Tahuna
Jerdun
Ma'an
Jefer

Abu el Lissan 13–17 April 1918 ★

Arab
Northern
Army
X

Guweira

Wadi Araba

Wadi Itm

Wadi Rumm

★ Wadi Rutm 19–23 April 1918
Ramleh
Tell Shahm

Aqaba

Decie April 1918 ★   Abu Suwana
1 Jan 1918

April 1918
★ Musaw'warrah
8 Aug 1918
ICC
II

I

T. E. Lawrence and Contemporary Ideas on War

The iconic image of Thomas Edward Lawrence is of a young Western man, dressed in the robes of a prince of Mecca. To draw a greater distinction with his surroundings and the local population, this enigmatic figure was described as 'blond as a Viking', a man whose achievements could be compared with those of Raleigh, Drake, Clive and Gordon, and perhaps Ulysses, King Arthur or Richard Coeur de Lion.[1] According to his greatest advocate, the American publicist Lowell Thomas, his significance was that he 'brought the disunited tribes of holy and forbidden Arabia into a unified campaign against their Turkish oppressors ... which caliphs and sultans had been unable to accomplish in centuries of effort'.[2]

On the other hand, his detractors have poured scorn on such hyperboles, arguing that Lawrence was a failure. Walter Lacquer, an analyst of guerrilla warfare and terrorism, saw Lawrence's contribution to war as purely a literary one.[3] Critics state that his magnum opus, *Seven Pillars of Wisdom*, is riddled with errors.[4] They argue some of the journeys he claimed to have made are not physically possible in the time he says they took place.[5] One or two ideas in this post-war memoir contradict despatches he wrote at the time to his headquarters in Cairo.[6] The Arab Revolt, one critic states, was no more than 'banditry'.[7] It is maintained that the revolt he led, or rather supported, was never the pan-Arab movement that it seemed. Efraim and Inari Karsh argue that the Hashemite Arabs were a self-interested clan who managed to co-opt, for a brief period, a handful of other groups. This was not, they maintain, an 'Arab Revolt', but merely a dynastic one.[8] There are others who assert that the significance of Lawrence's operations are exaggerated, and that he gained the reputation he did because of Lowell Thomas, his literary fans, and film makers.[9]

Undoubtedly, his legendary status was partly a consequence of his skills as a writer, since *Seven Pillars* is generally considered to be an outstanding work of literature.[10] There is no doubt that he remains one of the most recognizable figures of his age.[11] His celebrity was also due to popular appetite: the British public were eager to believe that an individual could still change the course of history in an era where mass and industrialism seemed to deluge every aspect of war, and to a large extent the post-war peace. In the mid-twentieth century, at the height of the Cold War, there were many Western writers who believed the success of guerrilla resistance was an inevitability.[12] But Lawrence confessed that he had structured *Seven Pillars* to amplify the 'excitement' for the reader when conveying his final triumph, and this made it seem 'inevitable'.[13]

Supporters of Lawrence see him as ahead of his time, a visionary for Arab liberation who was broken by his unfulfilled dreams. Basil Liddell Hart, the prolific and outspoken British writer on strategy in the inter-war years, felt Lawrence had created a new understanding of strategy, one which would avoid the mass killing that had characterized the European fronts in the First World War. He ranked him alongside some of the greatest generals of history.[14]

Lawrence has many biographers, and they find him a fascinating subject because of his literary and military reputation, his unusual life, and, perhaps most importantly, because of his personality.[15] He was, and remains, an enigma. His background in British Intelligence, his shyness and search for anonymity, his virtuosity as a writer, and his profound sense of shame all stimulate our curiosity.[16] Certainly his recklessness commands admiration, although his ruthlessness, when judged out of context, seems equally appalling.

The critics have plenty of ammunition, thanks to Lowell Thomas. In Thomas's account of Lawrence's career, there is, for example, a vivid description of the battle of Petra in 1917.[17] Prior to the action, Lawrence is depicted in his headquarters, in the old palace of the ancients, summoning the women of the area who encourage their men to arms with wild ululations. The Ottomans are described moving in towards Lawrence's intrepid fighters in several converging columns, and the odds are stacked against the rebels. Yet, standing tall, in the thick of the fight, there is Lawrence, orchestrating the battle from a mountain top, surrounded by loyal acolytes who serve as runners. The ridgeline is defended in what appears to be an epic struggle and the Ottoman troops are driven off.

The only problem with Lowell Thomas's account is that Lawrence wasn't actually there. The battle, if it can be called that, was no more than a brief skirmish and was conducted by the Arab sheikh, Maulud. At the time, Lawrence was in Aqaba, where he scornfully noted that Lowell Thomas appeared only briefly, for no more than a few days, and never accompanied the Arab fighters into the desert.[18]

Do these erroneous accounts or the accusations of the critics make Lawrence less or more significant as a military theorist? What effect do they have on his well-known ideas about guerrilla war? On the one hand, we may retain some faith in the 'primary actor theory' that suggests that the ideas of individuals do have the capacity to change events, even in the midst of a global war. We would need to acknowledge, however, that industrial warfare created a strong desire for human agency, and Lowell Thomas amplified a public appetite for the heroic and romantic individual in a deeply impersonal war. Lawrence himself evoked a lost chivalric and heroic age. Indeed, he took to heart the Crusader iconography, both for professional and personal reasons.[19] He craved a cause, and found it championing the liberty of the Arabs from Ottoman imperial domination. His aspiration for Arab emancipation was 'simple and romantic', according to one biographer, 'to bring freedom and dignity to the peasant villagers of Syria, a population which had for centuries been exploited by corrupt Turkish administrators'.[20] Crucially, he felt that the Arabs deserved a reward for fighting alongside Great Britain. It is a sentiment one can find amongst British and American military personnel in the early twenty-first century, particularly 'embedded advisors', who fought alongside Iraqis and Afghans as part of a long war against violent Jihadist groups.

The Arab revolutionaries had launched their revolt against the Ottoman Empire in June 1916, but it was a campaign in danger of failure from the start. Poorly armed, badly organized, and faced with a seasoned enemy, their leader, Emir Hussein, the Grand Sharif of Mecca, had implored the British for military assistance. The British were initially reluctant to intervene. The Arabs of the Hejaz, ostensibly still aligned with the enemy, were hardly a priority in a war spanning the globe and which was exhausting every resource of the British Empire. Instead of deploying a large Western force that might cause affront to Arabs by its proximity to the Holy Places of Mecca and Medina, a handful of selected officers, with a small contingent of Muslim regulars, were sent to advise and assist the Arab revolutionary cause.[21] Their objective was to further the British war effort, by, with, and through local forces. During the campaign, these advisors introduced new technologies, primarily air power, high explosives and armoured vehicles, to enhance the effectiveness of Arab guerrilla operations. This 'combined arms' campaign, utilizing psychological operations, deception techniques, air attacks and highly mobile local forces alongside conventional troops, is today known as 'hybrid warfare'.

Given the early twenty-first century interest in the use of modern technology in support of local forces, and the partnerships of 'advise and assist' missions, it seems appropriate for us to re-examine the assumptions, and functions, of the approach which appeared in its first modern form in this theatre. The counter-insurgents' perspective (in this case, the Ottomans) reveals much about the setbacks they were able to inflict upon the Arab guerrillas, and helps explain why it was necessary to significantly upgrade the capability of the Arab forces through 1917–18. The Ottomans and their German allies made increasing use of air power, for example, to locate and strike the small, mobile insurgent groups. The campaign highlights the vulnerability of insurgents and their relative military weaknesses, and hence why it was that Lawrence emphasized a dual strategy: one, to have the insurgents avoid combat in favour of strikes against the material fabric of his enemy; and two, to develop a political strategy that would render military operations irrelevant.

The enduring significance of Lawrence's war lies within the framework of military theory, and the tactical or strategic aspects of insurgency, so these are drawn out through specific chapters and ideas.[22] This book offers an appreciation of the distinctive features of irregular warfare. It tells us about the politics of insurgency, including the critical importance of legitimacy and cohesion for insurgents; the negative effects of reprisals on popular backing for the guerrilla cause; the demoralizing effect of tactical failures and casualties; and the centrality of concealment and mobility as the important 'ways and means' of a successful irregular campaign. The decisive element, though, was the constant 'presence' of the insurgent amongst the population, constituting both a threat to the enemy and an encouragement to the population on whom security and supplies depended. Moreover, Lawrence reveals the centrality of psychology in the conflict – building the confidence of his partners while at the same time demoralizing his enemy.

This book explains how Lawrence's thinking on war has been instrumentalized by recent theorists and military personnel. Lawrence's ideas were invoked at regular intervals in the twentieth century as a source of wisdom on irregular warfare, and his ideas continue to be used in the twenty-first century by those countering insurgency, as an authority on irregular operations, and as a justification for partnerships with local forces. These, and other examples, illustrate the continuing relevance of Lawrence's approach to the study of war.

Lawrence's war in the Middle East was a struggle primarily against the environment, and it involved great nerve against a more numerous and better-armed adversary. This was a conflict that highlighted the importance of morale, where there was no 'home front' or front line, and where meagre resources, water supplies and intelligence were critical to survival. Crucially, Lawrence and his revolutionary Arab allies could not be entirely certain of the allegiance of the people. The Ottomans attempted to undermine the revolt, largely by recruiting Arab partners of their own and by references to Islamic obligations such as loyalties to the Caliph. Alignments in the campaign were thus fluid.

Lawrence later claimed success for his approach, arguing that, in time, even without the British operations in Palestine, the Arabs would have taken all of the Hejaz and the Levant. This is almost certainly an exaggeration. His greatest triumph was in July 1917, when the Arab force under Feisal, the son of Sharif Hussein, emerged from the greater hinterland of Arabia's desert and seized the port of Aqaba, an event which seemed to indicate that this hitherto insignificant revolt had great potential. Yet the autumn of that year was a bitter disappointment. Lawrence's missions from Aqaba into Syria faltered. That winter, the Arab cause was in danger of fragmentation and morale was at a low ebb. Consequently, the entire revolt lost momentum. Worse was to follow. At Amman in the spring of 1918, their British allies suffered a significant operational setback.[23] The subsequent defeat of the Arabs at Ma'an created another crisis of confidence.[24] Lawrence turned instead to the British Imperial Camel Corps, armoured car companies and the Royal Air Force.

Nevertheless, returning to guerrilla operations, with more 'regularization' of Arab troops through training, and supported by the hybrid combinations of irregular fighters, air power and mobile armour, British and Arab forces continued to harass peripheral Ottoman lines of communication. The Turkish authorities responded with a variety of measures, but exasperated soldiers inflicted reprisals against Arab civilians. These raised further dilemmas for the insurgency, and the insurgents struggled to sustain backing for the revolt. More deliberate Ottoman counter-offensives created even greater anxiety. From an operational point of view, the Ottomans could hold settlements against Arab raiders, leading to a protracted conflict that the insurgents could only sustain with external financial and material backing.

Following military victories at Gaza, Jerusalem and the Judean Hills, the British and Imperial forces, led by General Allenby, finally broke the impasse at the battle of Megiddo in September 1918, and this aided the sudden recovery of the Arab cause. While the Arab forces in the south maintained their blockade of the Ottoman Medina garrison, the Arab Northern Army, spearheaded by Lawrence, severed crucial rail links, made assaults on key railway junctions and then attacked the retreating Ottoman forces in the final stages of the campaign.

Despite the less-than-glittering operational record for the insurgency, Lawrence's ideas are of much interest to us. Many are drawn to the spirit and atmosphere of the campaign in his subsequent written works in which he related the textures of the Arabian and Syrian landscapes, conveying their alien and disconcerting qualities to a Western audience, and the uncertain, fickle dedication of the people. His work was popular because he created a literary escape, a travelogue and a war narrative, with a modern twist of irony, for a weary public. The Arabia Lawrence described fitted with an image many wanted to believe existed, namely a distant and unmodern realm, coloured by a form of Orientalism that was untainted by the savagery of modernity. For Lawrence, and those with whom his ideas resonated, there was disquiet with a world that had produced the killing fields of France and Flanders.

But these works were more than literary achievements. Some of Lawrence's human observations indicate an acute obsession with assessing the character of those he met, a form of 'human intelligence', and a concern to understand the psychology and behaviour of those he encountered. His suggestions on the advisory role of a foreign contingent to local forces, and his honesty about their reactions to the nature of war, make for valuable reading. For all his flaws, and there were many, Lawrence would still be listed as one of the most insightful thinkers on the human dimensions of war.

His most significant contribution was arguably his observations on war itself. Lawrence's approach was analytical and critical; his desire was for modern military officers to acquire a thorough yet creative professional education. While an amateur himself, he advocated a dedication to knowledge and understanding, not a model of mechanistic training. One of the most succinct summaries from Lawrence in this regard came in the form of a letter to Basil Liddell Hart in June 1933. In it he asked, 'Will you (if you agree with my feeling) ... strike a blow for hard work and thinking?'[25] He laid out the idea that intuition, vital for making decisions under crisis conditions, comes with experience, but that must be founded on a dedication to learn, and immersion in study:

I was not an instinctive soldier, automatic with intuitions and happy ideas. When I took a decision, or adopted an alternative, it was after studying every relevant – and many an irrelevant – factor. Geography, tribal structure, religion, social customs, language, appetites, standards – all were at my finger-ends. The enemy I knew almost like my own side. I risked myself among them a hundred times, to learn.[26]

Lawrence applied the same idea, of intense study, to tactics:

The same with tactics. If I used a weapon well, it was because I could handle it. Rifles were easy. I put myself under instruction for Lewis, Vickers, and Hotchkiss [machine guns] (Vickers in my OTC [Officer Training Corps] days, and rifles, and pistols). If you look at my article in The Pickaxe you will see how much I learned about explosives, from my R.E. [Royal Engineers] teachers, and how far

I developed their methods. To use aircraft[,] I learned to fly. To use armoured cars[,] I learned to drive and fight them. I became a gunner at need and could doctor and judge a camel.

Referring to his study of war across history, he concluded: 'The same with strategy. I have written only a few pages on the art of war – but in these I levy contribution from my predecessors of five languages.'[27]

Lawrence was eager that, if Liddell Hart was going to use the desert campaign as an exemplar in war studies, he should emphasize the importance of intensive military education, to enhance leadership: 'Do make it clear that generalship, at least in my case, came of understanding, of hard study and brain-work and concentration. Had it come easy to me I should not have done it so well.' He continued:

> If your book could persuade some of our new soldiers to read and mark and learn things outside drill manuals and tactical diagrams, it would do a good work. I feel a fundamental, crippling incuriousness about our officers. Too much body and too little head. The perfect general would know everything in heaven and earth. So please, if you see me that way and agree with me, do use me as a text to preach for more study of books and history, a greater seriousness in military art. With 2,000 years of examples behind us we have no excuse, when fighting, for not fighting well. [28]

Therefore, in the spirit of Lawrence's rallying cry, this book is about Lawrence's ideas on war and his career that shaped those ideas. It is not about Lawrence's life and personality per se. It is, of course, impossible to separate them entirely, and it would be somewhat misleading even if one could. It was Lawrence's life experiences, education and personality that shaped his thinking. He admitted, for example, that he was a dreamer, and famously warned that men like him, who dreamt while awake, were dangerous. Eyewitnesses testified to his puckish sense of humour, but he was clearly a serious and driven man.[29] He possessed great conviction in his beliefs. He was willing to endure considerable pain, and he was often trying to prove himself. He was also aware of his shortcomings and agonized over them. But, if we read beyond the man, we'll see that he bequeathed some fascinating ideas on war, and it is to these we now turn.

LAWRENCE'S EARLY INFLUENCES

Lawrence's work is peppered with pen portraits of those he encountered. He judged all categories of men on a moral spectrum.[30] This was in part a common feature of the period, but character and honour were constant themes in Lawrence's motivation, and he recognized their power and vulnerability in other men. Shame was an even stronger element in Lawrence's identity, which had begun in his early life. His father was T. E. Chapman, a man who had left his wife for another woman and therefore earned the censure of a morally conscious society. Lawrence moved home six times, as his father sought to avoid being recognized by his former associates. The young 'Ned', as he was known, and his five brothers led a life in secret from the start. This fact may have fuelled his fascination with the fantasy, in a pre-Raphaelite fashion, of medievalism, which was popular in Britain before the Great War. His desire to experience the redeeming spirit of the Crusades or to live by the honour code of the knights of Malory's *Morte d'Arthur* certainly stayed with him all his life.[31]

His father eventually moved the family to Oxford and Lawrence was educated at the Boys School in George Street, which now houses the History Faculty of the University of Oxford.[32] He did not enjoy school, but he read avidly in military history, from Sennacherib to Moltke, including the examples of irregular warfare which appeared in Xenophon and Caesar. Lawrence became interested in medieval fortification architecture, desiring to understand its construction. At the time, Oxford was undergoing one of its frequent pulses of building, and the exposure of many archaeological remains fuelled Lawrence's imagination.[33] He then toured the Welsh castles before developing a keen interest in the Crusader fortifications of the Near East.[34] His obsessions seemed to indicate he was set on a career in antiquities.

At Oxford University, his tutor noted that he liked unusual texts and he tended to dwell on particular lines or sections, as if meditating on them. As he told Basil Liddell Hart in later years, he read mainly medieval work, but did consume some more modern history, including R. M. Johnston's *The French Revolution*, which may have given him some indication of how revolutionary movements were sustained.[35] Lawrence chose Military History and Strategy as his final year subject, a new option introduced in 1908, which indicated his developing interests. Unusually for an Oxford student, Lawrence spent little time indulging in college life or its sporting activities. His parents built a bungalow for him to study in at the bottom of the garden of their home in No. 2 Polstead Road, which gave him the silence he craved, and he practically lived in it for two years. Here he read avidly, and widely.

Lawrence was also keen to hone his body for anticipated challenges, and, to some extent, in emulation of his idealized notion of the chivalric knights of his studies. In this way he was to develop, later, the idea of freedom through intense self-discipline. In his first year at Oxford, he combined his studies with feats of physical endurance. One summer, he made a long cycling and sketching tour of French castles, which formed the basis of assessed work. In autumn 1908 the Oxford University Officer Training Corps was formed and Lawrence was amongst the first of its 626 volunteers. He had already been in the St Aldate's Church Lads' Brigade and knew some of the rudimentary aspects of military drill and turnout.

Alongside his epic cycling tours, it was at Oxford that he discovered another opportunity to combine his desire for physical prowess and the study of the past. In that same autumn of 1908, he visited the Ashmolean and was given the idea of travelling to the Levant to see the Crusader castles for himself.[36] For his undergraduate thesis he conducted a walking tour, covering hundreds of miles in two years.[37] While visiting the holy land he began to conceive of a new aspiration. When he got back to Oxford, he changed his mind about the final paper for the examination from the military history subject, which was due to be on the well-trodden Waterloo Campaign, to the First Three Crusades. In his studies, Lawrence now augmented his readings with travel guides on Arabia and Syria.[38] His appetite for physical endurance was therefore matched only by this genuine, deep, and developing knowledge of the archaeology of the Middle East. He graduated with a specialism in medieval pottery, a critical register for dating evidence, and he managed to join the British Museum expedition to Carcamesh: it was a life-changing experience.

Lawrence had not, however, entirely abandoned his interest in modern strategy and military history. While he was at Oxford, in 1909, the Chichele Chair in Military History was formed, and the first professor was Spenser Wilkinson, the influential writer and journalist on the *London Morning Post* who, in that year, had just written *Britain at Bay.*[39] Wilkinson had studied the German strategist Clausewitz who famously emphasized the value of the application of maximum force to achieve a decisive victory. Lawrence would have been aware of the developing tensions in international relations between Germany and Britain that Wilkinson articulated, and his ideas on war.[40]

In one of his lectures at Oxford, Wilkinson had delineated the differences between Clausewitz and Baron Antoine de Jomini in their respective assessments of Napoleon and perhaps, had sown the seeds of how a 'national' or people's war could succeed. Wilkinson had stated:

> When the French forces came under the control of Napoleon, the overthrow of the old monarchies was inevitable. But the pressure of the French Empire upon the populations then aroused such bitter resentment that the nations one after another rushed to arms, and thus the overthrow of Napoleon was as much predetermined as had been his unprecedented conquests.[41]

Wilkinson's treatise dissected the relative importance of the study of generals, and the origins of the theories which were being studied so intensely, which identified the requirements of a national uprising:

> Scharnhorst attributed the success of the French to the energy and unity of the French nation, and the failure of the Allies to their discord and their inadequate efforts. ... The subsequent exertions of Prussia in and after 1813 confirmed Clausewitz in his view of the importance of the distinction between national and dynastic war.[42]

A war between the peoples of Europe was becoming a distinct possibility in the 1910s. There was a growing consciousness, shared across the country, of German militaristic rivalry to Britain. On his archaeological expedition in Syria, Lawrence observed German efforts to gain influence over the Ottoman Empire, not least through the construction of the so-called Berlin–Baghdad railway and its southern branch, the Hejaz line.[43] Lawrence contrasted the German sense of privilege and exceptionalism against his own notions of winning allegiance. He developed a close association with the Arab workforce. They shared his interest in the archaeological work and the structures being unearthed, and Lawrence spent time with them, getting to know their language, culture and beliefs. This coincidence of interests developed into an impish desire to persuade the Germans and their Ottoman partners that he was a spy. According to his colleague, Leonard Woolley, he even confronted the Germans over their high-handed treatment of the local labour force and threatened to have one of them flogged in public.[44]

THE CONTEMPORARY UNDERSTANDING OF WAR

To appreciate the distinctive contribution Lawrence made, some sense of the landscape of professional and popular writing about war before 1914 is valuable. It is, moreover, an antidote to historicism or anachronism. Trying to separate any author from their context is problematic, and can create misleading generalizations, but given Lawrence's tendency for wit and parody, one can easily misunderstand the strengths and weaknesses of his ideas. This has important implications.

In the early twenty-first century, there has been a desire amongst many professional military officers of the Western world to grasp the insights Lawrence had to offer on guerrilla warfare and on partnering with local forces. The need to understand the Arab mind, to assimilate its constraints in order to avoid giving offence, and to appreciate its aspirations, was at the forefront of the campaigns in the Middle East in the 2000s. But the broad definitions of 'cultural understanding' used by Coalition armies, while laudable, missed the detail and difference of the great variety of groups that constitute 'the Arabs', and, of course, all the other peoples of the region. It was precisely this level of detail and variation that Lawrence insisted upon. He would emphasize, frequently, the importance he attached to studying the groups that he accompanied. He would listen to their concerns, dialects, accents, and learn their prejudices, rituals, and manners. All this took time: a contrast to the generic 'cultural understanding' sought by military personnel who lacked this one precious resource.

In the twentieth century, Britain's empire meant there was widespread contact with Middle Eastern, Asian and African populations. The British authorities had developed strategies to co-opt, pacify and delegate, despite considerable armed resistance. Prior to the First World War, the British had been confronted by a serious conflict in South Africa. In 1899, Afrikaners of the interior, fearing British occupation, had declared war. Small British contingents had been checked and defeated, which necessitated an escalation of force. In 1900, these enlarged formations swept the Afrikaner conventional forces from the field, but, although their capitals were captured, resistance continued. Guerrilla units, the commandos, ranged across the veldt, attacking isolated posts and the railways. The British responded with their own innovations, taking civilians and resources from the countryside and concentrating them in camps alongside the railways, constructing chains of blockhouses to protect their lines of communication (each containing a platoon of soldiers), and conducting 'drives' of extended lines of men to comb out sectioned areas. There was severe criticism about these 'methods of barbarism' at home in Britain, not least when several thousand Afrikaner civilians died of infections in their internment camps. There was even admiration for the defiant bands of commandos who, against the odds, conducted a hit-and-run campaign. Some became notorious household names, including Botha, de Wet and Smuts. It was this war, and the manner of its conduct, that Lawrence would have grown up with. He was an impressionable 12 years old in 1900.

The South African War and the many colonial conflicts that preceded it meant professional military officers were conscious of the fundamental elements of war and the trade-offs they imposed. There was familiarity with the demands of campaigning in 'small wars', and one of the most cited British authorities of the period was Charles Edward Callwell. In his manual of 1896, Callwell had warned that: 'Guerrilla warfare is what the regular armies always have most to dread, and when this is directed by a leader with a genius for war, an effective campaign becomes well-nigh impossible. The guerrilla has ever been a thorn in the side of the organised force.'[45]

In response, Callwell urged his readership to act with resolution, and early, to target 'whatever they [the insurgents] prize most, and the destruction or deprivation of which will probably bring the war most rapidly to a conclusion'.[46] The secret was not only to rely on 'vigorous leadership and the rapid movement of columns from place to place' but to develop 'an elaborate strategical organization'.[47] This consisted of sectioning territory, the establishment of secure posts with proper supply, methodical clearances, and then highly mobile pursuits of fleeting guerrilla bands, striking them before they could 'withdraw and disband'.[48] The objective was to make the counter-insurgents' presence felt everywhere.[49] The flying column was especially important, because 'the more mobile it is the more suddenly it can deliver its strokes'; for 'the essence of combatting guerrilla warfare,' Callwell added, 'is to hit unexpectedly and hard'.[50] Carrying off civilians' flocks, crops and supplies could also induce guerrillas to show themselves, or, in a draconian fashion, impound the population's resources until they agreed to surrender their weapons and turn in the ringleaders. Critical to the success of locating guerrilla groups, however, was an espionage network 'drawn from the more intelligent members of the community who may side with the regular forces'.[51]

The strategy of conventional war, like small colonial wars, required a thorough understanding of the constituent elements. The political objective of a campaign tended to imply the defeat of the enemy army in order to seize their capital. This would yield 'not only the seat of government and the legislature, but also the centre of communications and the main emporium of the nation's commerce', thus imposing 'a complete dislocation of the executive system, ... the collapse of trade, and ... financial ruin'.[52] The means and ways to achieve these objectives meant the thorough arrangement of weapons, logistics and manpower, the 'reach' of an armed force, through shipping or transport; and the mobilization of resources, both financially and through key minerals. Strategic planning also required assessment of the actors, the capacity of the government, the people and the military to wage war, and the justice of the cause in terms of international laws, norms and principles.

War itself imposed severe demands and the British had been influenced strongly by the liberal tradition of the nineteenth century, which held war to be an aberration and a detrimental interruption to the free circulation of trade. On the other hand, that same tradition had lauded wars of principle against tyrannies, be that dictators or the inhuman practices of slavery. Lawrence read that war generated that dynamic tension between the elements of what Clausewitz had deemed 'the remarkable trinity' of governments, their militaries and the population, but also of passion, reason and chance events.[53] War also imposed paradoxes for strategists: cost versus benefits; rational decisions versus human emotion; the limits of resources imposed as culminating points versus point of concentration; line or face versus depth; the latent threat of deterrence versus the actual use, and thus expenditure, of force; limited war versus all-out total war; leadership and specialism versus a common struggle for all; opportunism versus deliberate planning; or the asymmetry of forces, strategies and efforts versus the dynamic of interaction, which can defeat plans and exhaust the more powerful, especially where the guerrilla uses the enemy's strength against him. Lawrence believed these trade-offs would ebb and flow, depending on the context.

Wars in the early twentieth century exposed the difficulty of how to identify or capitalize on the opportunities presented by battles, which, hitherto, seemed to be the best way to achieve one's military and political objectives. As conflicts became dominated by weapons of greater range, so troops became more dispersed. This made it more difficult to communicate with distributed units, especially when the chief forms of communication at the beginning of the twentieth century were limited to human couriers, signal flags, heliograph, vulnerable telephone or telegraph, and cumbersome radio sets. Military engagements had spread over much greater areas, and into depth, while railways and motorized transport meant that a successful attack could be sealed off, and any advantages in manoeuvre lost before they could be exploited.

Military professionals were also uncertain how to cultivate exceptional leadership. They admired selected commanders of the past, and sought to emulate them, nurturing their genius through training in endurance and character. Most officers believed that the study of military history might reveal the processes of war, as principles, tactics, or other successful techniques.[54] This search for insight made certain works very popular, but, in the early twentieth century, the increasing popularity for 'nations in arms' of mass citizen armies created its own anxieties. The question was whether men from industrialized and increasingly urban backgrounds would have the will to endure the conditions of campaigning and the costs of war. Modern weaponry had increased the chances of death and injury, and military theorists contemplated victory through annihilation by firepower. Manoeuvre could get the forces to the right place and at the right time to confer an advantage on the battlefield, but if the adversary possessed a force similar to one's own, it was down to the fighting spirit, the willpower of the men, to make the difference.[55] In the early twentieth century, Europeans contemplated the 'racial fitness' of their own nations to endure this modern form of war. Most contemporaries believed that long wars imposed too great a burden on their nations, and therefore the objective was to seek a rapid and comprehensive victory. The result was that the theory of war was reduced to the use of force to acquire a position of political advantage through decisive battle, in the shortest possible time, but without much consideration of the immediate cost.

Most viewed guerrilla warfare as mere harassment, unable to turn the tide of a major war, and not much more than lawless violence. It exhausted armies but implied little chance of success, and was therefore denigrated. But Clausewitz identified the essence of guerrilla warfare in the following terms:

> By its very nature, ... scattered resistance will not lend itself to major actions, closely compressed in time and space. Its effect is like that of the process of evaporation: it depends on how much surface is exposed. The greater the surface and the area of contact between it and the enemy forces, the thinner the latter have to be spread, the greater the effect of the general uprising. Like smouldering embers, it consumes the basic foundations of the enemy forces.[56]

Clausewitz also noted that there were specific and limited conditions under which a general national uprising could succeed. He wrote:

> The war must be fought in the interior of the country; it must not be decided by a single stroke; the theatre of operations must be fairly large; the national character must be suited to that type of war; [and] the country must be rough and inaccessible, because of mountains or forests, marshes or the local methods of cultivation.[57]

He offered a prescient insight by suggesting that success would depend on the insurrection occurring within the framework of a war conducted by regular troops, as part of an 'all-encompassing plan'. The commander, he argued, could best support the insurgents by detaching 'small units of the regular army'. Their role was to encourage resistance by their presence, since locals would otherwise lack the confidence to take up arms.[58] Lawrence's campaign would adhere closely to this Clausewitzian conception.

To some extent, Clausewitz betrayed a common, if unstated, concern amongst regular officers that armed citizens might get out of control and perhaps turn the violence against their own government. Baron Antoine de Jomini also observed the difficulty, and the undesirability, of mobilizing populations in a 'National War', but, unlike Clausewitz, he did not see it necessarily as a last resort. There could be strategic advantage in generating a vast guerrilla war, and the difficulties that Napoleon faced in trying to contain the Spaniards after 1808 provided striking evidence of its effectiveness in tying down regular forces needed elsewhere.

In 1900, many anticipated the shape of a future war relatively accurately, especially the employment of mass armies and the extensive use of modern artillery. Military professionals were aware of the influential ideas of Jan Bloch, who had forecast a rising casualty toll and a vast stalemate caused by extensive earth fortifications and entrenchments.[59] Bloch had in mind the closing stages of the American Civil War around Petersburg in 1865 or siege warfare in the Russo-Turkish War of 1877, and contemporaries were aware of a similar situation that had developed around Port Arthur in the Russo-Japanese War of 1904–5: soldiers were dug into the ground for their survival, and assaults across the open between the lines had resulted in catastrophic losses. But few reached the judgement that Bloch did, that war, as it had been understood hitherto as a combination of firepower and adroit manoeuvre, 'was now impossible'.[60] He envisaged trench stalemate, strategic impasse, and consequently revolutionary unrest that would tear down the European empires.[61]

The solution, on which most military professionals agreed, as noted above, lay in the willpower, the motivation, and the enduring morale of the citizen armies they would field. In the South African War and the Russo-Japanese War, which had featured trench systems, barbed wire, machine guns, and heavy artillery, military officers pointed out to Bloch and his adherents that the scale of geography and the formidable defences had been overcome by manoeuvre, offensive action, and the disciplined resilience of British and Japanese troops.[62] Far from producing stalemate, defences that Bloch had described as insurmountable had been traditional, temporary affairs and the victorious side had been the one that kept attacking.[63]

Bloch was not the only one imagining catastrophic, insurrectionary wars to come. H. G. Wells wrote *The War in the Air* in 1907, not long after the first powered flight of the Wright brothers, and his work was serialized in the *Pall Mall Magazine* in 1908. It captured the popular themes of the day: a fascination with the new air technology, the prospects of fluid wars of manoeuvre, inter-continental conflicts, war with Germany, an invasion by Asia, and a widespread fear of the devastation of civilization.[64] Wells advocated an embrace of the new scientific and technological revolutions underway, while warning that it would need radically new forms of human organization and dedicated, professional and technocratic individuals to pioneer it.[65] Thus a desire for progressive liberalism, looking forward to an enlightened and free world-state, was entwined with darker ideas that the ill-educated masses needed leadership. In considering future war, Wells foresaw a strategic stalemate and international collapse in an industrialized conflagration, the impasse being broken only by massed air power.[66]

The paradox of confident prediction was that it was fear that was driving the European powers into war. Fear of rivals, of the destruction of their nation or empire, or fear of the revolutionary potential of millions of disgruntled and impoverished workers: these were the factors that drove so much of the decision-making of the 1910s. Fear had generated the alliance blocs that confronted each other in continental Europe, and there was an ominous sense in Britain that Germany was attempting to undermine, subvert, and replace its influence around the globe, through its commerce, its aggressive naval construction programme, and through ambiguous agencies that appeared throughout the world.[67] German engineers, commercial traders, missionaries, archaeologists and many other professions came under suspicion. These were not entirely exaggerated concerns: the German Zimmermann Plan of 1914, named after the Kaiser's Under-Secretary for Foreign Affairs, was a blueprint to raise a pan-Islamic jihad across the Middle East that had been in gestation before the war broke out.[68] Soon after, the German embassy in Constantinople had established an intelligence and propaganda team to generate jihadism across the Middle East, Africa and Asia.[69]

At the outbreak of war in 1914, aged 26, Lawrence was despatched to Cairo to join what would become the Arab Bureau.[70] This intelligence organization was tasked with collecting as much information as possible on the Ottoman Army in the Middle East.[71] The first two years of the conflict were therefore spent in deskwork, but the material he handled gave him a perspective on the direction of the war in the Middle East. He also learned that Emir Hussein of the Hashemites, Grand Sharif of Mecca and Medina, had approached the British for protection against the repression of the Ottoman Empire and its new militant Turkish leadership. Hussein intended to preserve control of the holiest cities in the Hejaz, but, then, to extend his dominion over all of Arabia to subordinate his rivals such as Ibn Saud and Ibn Rashid. In the short term, he had to survive, as the Ottomans meant to purge him and his family. It was this Hashemite uprising that changed Lawrence's fortunes.[72] In June 1916, when the revolt broke out, Mecca was captured by the rebels, but almost immediately the rising foundered. Medina remained firmly in Ottoman hands and the rebels were forced to make ineffectual demonstrations in its environs. From the north, Ottoman reinforcements were expected, and their superiority in armaments, manpower strength and air power seemed to indicate that it was only a matter of time before the Arabs were crushed.

Lawrence accompanied an official British visit to the Hejaz to assess the situation, and in just ten days he visited all of Hussein's sons and travelled into the interior. He met Feisal, who had already gained some military experience before the war in inter-clan conflicts, and Lawrence volunteered to act as a liaison officer to Feisal's command.

From that point on, Lawrence started to determine his own fortunes.[73]

2

Depth not Face

The Making of an Insurgency

The war imposed considerable strain on the Arabian population. The Ottoman authorities requisitioned livestock, goods and manpower.[1] There was an increasingly severe attitude towards any form of dissent. But the immediate issue that affected the majority of the six million who lived across the region was rising prices.[2] Coupled with a new authoritarianism from Istanbul, Arab resentment increased considerably. Nevertheless, few made any show of resistance until 1916. The Ottoman Empire was able to wield sufficient power to overawe the population, and its possession of modern armaments, railways and financial controls gave it an overwhelming advantage. Moreover, the Sultan could still command authority: he was the Caliph (Khalif) of the Muslim world, and despite the draconian Turkification policies of the governing Committee of Union and Progress (CUP), it was not easy to disobey the authority of such a figure.[3] As a result, thousands of Arab men were conscripted into the Ottoman Army, subjected to strict discipline, and driven to the fighting fronts, without any sign, yet, of mutiny or disobedience.[4]

Sharif Hussein exemplified the complexity of allegiance. His heritage, a descendant of the Prophet through the Qureshi line, gave him prestige in the eyes of the majority of Arabs in the Hejaz. This influence made him a potential threat to the Ottoman regime. Before the war, Hussein had been detained in Istanbul until the old Caliph, Sultan Abdül Hamid II, conferred on him the title of Emir of the holiest cities of Mecca and Medina in the Hejaz in order to prevent the CUP from appointing their own candidate. In 1909 the Sultan was overthrown and succeeded by Mehmed V, and the CUP's relationship with Hussein worsened. The revolutionary and dictatorial triumvirate of the pashas, Enver, Talaat and Djemal, was eager to assert political control over the Hejaz and extend the rail links there, largely to be able to deploy troops more rapidly in the region if required, although the justification they gave was to facilitate the Hajj.

Hussein opposed the notion of a penetrating railway, ostensibly to protect the incomes of camel drovers who carried the pilgrims to the Holy Places, but his motives were revealed in a secret pre-war meeting, in the spring of 1914, between his son, Abdullah, and the Consul-General of Egypt, Lord Kitchener, with his British Secretary in Cairo, Ronald Storrs.[5] Hussein and his sons, while eager to resist Istanbul, by force if necessary, needed British support. Kitchener had refused, knowing that the policy of the British government at that time was to preserve the Ottoman Empire against its European rivals. Kitchener was right to argue that Britain had no interest in intervening in what was an internal matter for the Ottoman Empire. Nevertheless, the presence of German engineers in the construction of the Hejaz railway was a subject of interest.

In late 1914, the Ottomans' CUP finally declared itself in favour of the Central Powers of Germany and Austria-Hungary, and launched a naval attack on the Russian coast. Of immediate concern to Britain was the two-fold threat to their own interests.[6] The first was the potential for the Ottoman Army to interdict the Suez Canal, perhaps by the distribution of mines with which to attack vital shipping. The second was the Sultan's call to arms, the declaration of a jihad against the British authorities, for all those Muslims living within the British Empire. Since more Muslims dwelt in the British Empire than any other polity, this threat could not be ignored.[7]

Storrs and Kitchener therefore advocated restarting the negotiations with Hussein, asking the Sharif to dismiss any Ottoman fatwa against the Entente as illegitimate.[8] Concurrently, the Ottomans were looking for the Sharif's endorsement for their declaration of holy war. Understandably, Hussein hesitated. Then he gave his personal backing to the Ottoman cause, but refused a public declaration on the grounds that it would invite aggression by the Entente powers against Muslims.

He argued that, if the British Royal Navy imposed a blockade on the Red Sea, then the peoples of the Hejaz, who were dependent on imports of food, would be moved to rebellion. The disappointing response prompted the government in Istanbul to claim the Sharif had approved of the call to jihad anyway, but, privately, the Ottoman authorities now sought ways to neutralize the Sharif and his Hashemite family.

Meanwhile, Hussein reopened secret negotiations with the British. Storrs offered an alliance with the Sharif if he would promise to support the British war effort. In return, Kitchener, as newly appointed Secretary of State for War, was prepared to offer independence to the Arabs of the Hejaz. He endorsed a united, spiritual Caliphate, rather than a political entity, on the grounds that Britain could not determine the fate of the Arabs in their entirety.[9] The British would not favour one Arab leader of uncertain allegiances over their existing and long-standing partners, most of whom were rivals of the Hashemites. Imam Yahya of Sanaa in the Yemen was neutral, while his rival to the north, Idrissi of Sabayyeh, in the Asir, tended to favour Britain. Ibn Saud of Riyadh, who dominated the Nejd, was neutral but was inclined to support the British cause, and his contribution was to fight his chief antagonist, Ibn Rashid of Hail, who was staunchly pro-Ottoman.[10]

The neatness of these alignments was complicated by the deep-seated distrust and periodic warfare between Ibn Saud and the Hashemites, and between the Imam and Idrissi. Sayyid Mohammed al-Idrissi, a leader of African descent, had carved out his own sheikhdom in south-west Arabia having been inspired by stories of the Senussi Revolt in Libya, but the ebb and flow of conflict left the boundaries of his dominion ill-defined. Nevertheless, his opposition to the Ottomans proved valuable in drawing in troops that would otherwise have attacked the British colonial port at Aden. By contrast, the Imam of Sanaa tended to supply the local Ottoman forces, partly through fear of losing his position, but he avoided any agreement with either the Ottomans or the British to prevent too close an association with one belligerent.[11]

Hussein too delayed his response to the British overtures, knowing that he could not guarantee that many Arabs would follow him. Before the war he had been inspired by the relative success of Idrissi to the south in driving back the Ottomans, and similar unrest in Yemen. Yet, he was fearful that the Ottoman forces in the region were strong enough to crush any premature uprising. The Idrissi, for example, had been contained by two Ottoman infantry divisions.[12] Although Hussein had been brought up amongst the tribes of the Hejaz, he had also been held at the Ottoman court between 1892 and 1908, effectively as a hostage, and learned of the ruthlessness of the imperial government. He therefore developed the art of appearing loyal, while exercising self-interest. His first preference was for his own independent government, but he was hardly a natural ally of the British to achieve this. As a slave-owning and religious leader, he was deeply opposed to modernization and ruled Mecca and Medina in an authoritarian manner. Rules for public conduct were strict. Prisoners were enslaved or had body parts amputated, in accordance with traditional Sharia law. When challenged by the CUP, he claimed with sincerity that he only believed in the law and authority of God, as he interpreted it.

Paradoxically, he opposed Ibn Saud, despite their shared austere philosophy of governance. What had incensed Hussein was the Wahabi conquest of the Holy Places in the 1810s, when they had destroyed the shrines as forms of idolatry and condemned all pilgrims. The Wahabis had only been defeated after seven years of fighting and Hussein was more anxious about their resurgence of power than he was of Ottoman authority.[13]

To the British, Hussein's ambitions were initially unclear. It was only later, once the British had begun to drive the Ottomans out of the region, that Hussein began to demand the role as leader of the entirety of Arabia, and, perhaps, of the whole Muslim world.[14] Far from being a proto-nationalist struggle for the sake of Arabism, this was a bid for dynastic security and a chance to create a genuine Caliphate under his own leadership. The war was opening up the opportunity to fulfil a long-cherished ideal, but Hussein was naturally cautious, harbouring a deficit of trust.

In February 1915, he suddenly discovered Ottoman plans to have him arrested and possibly executed. There was also news of Ottoman military reinforcements heading into the Hejaz, forces that he believed would be used to suppress any unrest.[15] He immediately sent his son Feisal to gather intelligence in Damascus and Istanbul about the strength and readiness of the Syrians and other Arab factions to unite behind him. Meeting the conspirators, Feisal discovered that the nationalists were concerned that, if the Ottomans were defeated, the French would make a bid to take over Syria.[16] Yet they were reassured by news of the secret talks between Abdullah and Kitchener that seemed to suggest the British favoured independent Arab states under British protection.

The subsequent Syrian nationalist plan was enshrined as the Damascus Protocol and envisaged an Arab empire encompassing Syria, Mesopotamia and Arabia, but excluding the British port of Aden.[17] They wanted an alliance with Britain, for military and naval protection, and accepted the principle of economic preference for the British Empire. In June 1915, these plans and the Ottoman demands were considered by Hussein and his sons, before being presented as terms for cooperation with the British at Cairo. In the exchange of letters with the British, the Hashemites claimed to represent 'the whole of the Arab nation'.[18]

The British reaction was to dismiss the Hashemite claim since there was no Arab 'nation', although there was much sympathy for the idea of an independent Arab state.[19] They agreed that the first stage to the realization of that initiative was a revolt which might have the added benefit of tying down thousands of Ottoman troops. The Ottoman garrison had consisted of four infantry divisions, two in Yemen, and one each in Asir and Hejaz. The addition of another mobile brigade was imminent, and more Ottoman troops were expected. But the hope was that, with Allied operations underway in Gallipoli, their enemies would not have sufficient forces to act against Hussein. Nevertheless, the pressure was on to get the Arabs to commit to a rising before the Ottomans could swamp the region and deter the revolt altogether.

Sir Henry McMahon, the British High Commissioner in Egypt, therefore reiterated his support for an Arab revolution, while refusing to give any backing to a final territorial settlement, which, he perceived, would change as the war progressed.[20] Hussein tried to press the British on the basis that Arab defectors and deserters at Gallipoli confirmed his claim that he was the most eligible leader and that dozens of Arab personnel in Ottoman service were ready to mutiny for the national cause.[21] The claims were certainly exaggerated.[22] McMahon stated, understandably, that Britain's allies and partners in the Gulf, namely the rulers of Kuwait, Oman, the Arabian coast, the Trucial States, Qatar and Bahrain, were to remain under British supervision due to long-standing treaties. Given the costs of military operations in Mesopotamia, he also asserted that 'special administrative arrangements' would have to prevail in the districts of Basra and Baghdad. Following instructions from London, and mindful of the deep divisions amongst Arabs any exclusive Hashemite claim would cause, McMahon insisted that the British would have to remain in control of Mesopotamia to prevent 'foreign aggression'. As events turned out, the British were right: the Hashemites were not strong enough to rule Arabia against their rivals in the region and a premature commitment to Hussein would have cost the support of the other Arab leaders.[23]

Hussein now bargained hard. He maintained that, if the British delayed, the Arabs might conclude they were better off remaining with the Ottomans.[24] General Maxwell, who had replaced Kitchener in Egypt, urged that a decision be taken sooner rather than later, but the government in London was overwhelmed with the demands of the war in Europe, delegating temporary responsibility to McMahon, while delays in translation and travel by intermediaries generated further tension. Hussein added to the pressure by demanding material support in the shape of thousands of rifles, millions of rounds of ammunition, and gold, for, he claimed, the multitudes of his supporters.[25]

There was a further complication, much criticized later by Lawrence, concerning France. Britain had been compelled to acknowledge French aspirations for control of Syria in March 1915 in the Sykes-Picot Agreement. This secret wartime pact between the British and French governments to allocate defined spheres of influence across the Middle East, once the Ottoman Empire had been defeated, was not initially disclosed to Hussein. It was, in essence, a scheme to deconflict British, French and Russian interests during a period of military occupation after the fighting but before a final peace settlement determined the border. By its terms, France was to control southern Turkey, Syria, the northern Levant and part of northern Iraq; Britain was to administer the *vilayets* (provinces) of Palestine, Jordan and Iraq; for its part Russia would acquire Istanbul and Armenia.[26] The exact boundaries were not determined and the agreement was a contingency arrangement designed to coordinate war aims, but it was later regarded as a conspiratorial document and seen as evidence of betrayal by Arab nationalists.[27] They argued, subsequently, that Britain and France were insincere about an independent national homeland for the Arabs.

The chief concern was that commitments to France conflicted with British assurances, offered by Sir Henry McMahon, to Hussein. These had suggested that Damascus and most of Syria would come under

Arab jurisdiction. The British government envisaged a far greater degree of autonomy and sovereignty in their provinces than the French, even to the extent of granting the Jews a homeland of their own within an autonomous region of Palestine, as they made clear in 1917. They saw no contradiction in these arrangements, as 'federation' plans had succeeded in Canada and South Africa where there were also communal differences. Despite Lawrence's later accusations that the Allies had ignored, or betrayed, their wartime commitments to the Arabs, and concealed the truth, the British and French discussed the arrangements with Hussein in 1917.[28] The British expected that the territorial control exercised by France would be, like their own, temporary. The French colonial lobby, the Comité d'Asie, had other ideas.

In fact, the Sykes-Picot Agreement was never implemented. The real changes occurred after the war as the Allies had always intended. Territorial boundaries were settled, new Allies' interests had to be accommodated, and antagonized communities without experience of state governance had to have support against more powerful rivals. Moreover, the United States insisted on the idea of national self-determination as its guiding philosophy to the post-war dispensation, and Britain and France agreed in a Declaration, in November 1918, to the establishment of 'national governments and administrations'.[29] They insisted that this declaration superseded the Sykes-Picot Agreement, and, while the new League of Nations was to be the supervisory body, the occupied territories would be administered by Britain and France as mandates on behalf of the Arabs, until such time as full independence could be established. Lawrence refused to accept there could be any justification for delaying the inevitable and argued for immediate self-government.[30] The fact was that Arabia was simply not considered to be important to any of the contemporary imperial powers, despite the value later attached to it in the second half of the twentieth century. In this period, the brutal truth is that the deserts were regarded as worthless and the Arab peoples as barely productive. The view of the Arab form of government was far from complimentary.

All this lay in the future. In March 1916, the McMahon–Hussein correspondence concluded with the agreement that the Arabs would join the British against the Ottomans. At the same time, the Ottomans repeated their own demands to Hussein that the Hejaz and Sinai should provide tribal militias to resist the Allies.

Then the mood changed dramatically; the Ottomans' discovery of Syrian nationalist plans for an insurrection, supported by the French and British, led to a severe crackdown. Djemal Pasha's reprisals had the effect of breaking the Syrian nationalist movement, which left the Hashemites devoid of allies in this critical province. Feisal was aware of the repression and tried to persuade the Ottoman authorities to release some of the nationalist leaders, but Enver and Djemal made a tour through Syria to examine for themselves the security situation, and to find ways to raise auxiliary 'mujahideen' units of Arab volunteers without using the Hashemites as intermediaries. Hussein intervened, insisting that he could find the manpower if the Ottomans would grant autonomy for the Hejaz. Enver countered with the warning that the Sharif was in no position to make such claims, and, while threatening to imprison Feisal, he argued that, in wartime, Hussein was legally obliged to furnish the forces the Ottomans required.[31] The suppression continued and Hussein's position was becoming ever more precarious. It was clear that, despite his title, he was 'expendable'.

Feisal escaped from the capital to the Hejaz, but, anticipating unrest, the Ottomans now took the precaution of reinforcing their garrison of Mecca and Medina under the command of General Hamid Fakhreddin 'Fakhri' Pasha, a reliable officer unlikely to brook Arab truculence.[32] Fakhri Pasha intended to impose martial law and ensure the Hejaz Arabs were kept under the same conditions as the Syrians. The Ottomans knew the Arabs were divided along clan lines and undisciplined in military matters, so, although Fakhri possessed only a relatively small garrison, some 9,000 strong, his presence was expected to deter any thought of revolt.

Thus, fearing an imminent purge, and with more Ottoman troops en route to the Hejaz, the Hashemites' opportunity to resist successfully was slipping away. Yet, at this precise moment, the stability of the entire region was starting to break down. The war had severed the lucrative flow of pilgrims and cut off the grain supply from Egypt, which caused a catastrophic rise in prices.[33] The Harb clans, who had threatened to fight the arrival of the Hejaz railway before the war, until they had been confronted with eight battalions of Ottoman troops, were now at boiling point. On the other hand, many Arab leaders were utterly divided, unsure whether to try to pursue a gradual path of change or whether to risk all and fight the Ottomans.

On 10 June 1916, Hussein launched the revolt, and, after some confused fighting, most of Mecca was overrun.[34] What is clear is, at the outset, the numbers joining the revolt were relatively small. Ali, a son of Hussein, could muster only 1,500 men at Medina and with this tiny force he could only hope to delay the Ottoman troops while his father contrived to seize Mecca.

With the exception of Lawrence, the intelligence officers in Cairo did not think the revolt would survive.[35] Sir Reginald Wingate, a man sympathetic to the Arab cause, actually thought the Meccan revolutionaries were a 'rabble' who resembled the dervishes he had fought in the late 1890s.[36] David Hogarth wrote that the uprising had occurred with inadequate preparation:

[it was] in ignorance of modern warfare, ... with little idea of the obligations which its success would impose on the Sherifial family. In both the organisation of the tribal forces and the provision of armaments, far too much has been left to the last moment and to luck. If the Arabs succeed, it will be by their overwhelming numbers and by the isolation of the Turkish garrisons.[37]

Details began to emerge of what had taken place at Mecca. Although the Ottoman force had numbered only 1,500, divided into three locations, only one of these was overwhelmed on the first day of street fighting. The other two used artillery and machine gun fire to halt the Arab attacks. The result was stalemate for three days, and the Ottomans could not be dislodged until the British supplied Egyptian light guns to assist the attack. Meanwhile, at Medina, Ali's forces had attempted to seize a railway junction at Muhit but were driven off by a significant sortie. Fakhri then pursued the Arabs with two brigades, driving the rebels southwards and establishing strongpoints along his main communications routes. At Taif, south-west of Mecca, Abdullah's initial attempt to take this town also ended in failure. Entrenched infantry, machine guns and field artillery could not be overwhelmed with tribal forces when they had lost the element of surprise. Abdullah turned to psychological warfare, lighting campfires across nearby hillsides and drumming from various points to simulate a much larger force, but the ruse failed.[38]

The Arabs were also repulsed at Jeddah, where an attack by 4,000 Harb fighters was defeated by Ottoman machine gun and artillery fire.

A Royal Navy officer, who witnessed the Harb in action, described their tactics: 'They were simply advancing in a mass, quite openly, some of them firing their rifles in the air: The Turks ... waited and then poured a withering fire into their ranks.'[39] The Royal Navy and Indian Marine bombarded the port to offer some support, and used seaplanes to drop bombs at the most significant points, including their water supply, which compelled the garrison to surrender. The ports of Yanbo and Rabegh were taken in a similar way.

The Arab fighters lacked the heavy weapons necessary to capture towns and rail junctions or to hold defended positions. If they could not control routes, the Arabs could not prevent the arrival of Ottoman reinforcements. Early assessments therefore suggested that the revolt was likely to fail unless they could secure arms, especially artillery, supplies and munitions from the British urgently.[40] Ever resourceful, the Royal Navy provided 3,000 rifles, money, and much-needed food within a few days, but no one could be sure if it was enough.

LAWRENCE'S EARLY ASSESSMENTS OF REVOLUTIONARY WAR

Lawrence arrived in Arabia, at Jeddah, in October 1916 alongside Ronald Storrs to make observations. He was soon acquainted with the situation and he itemized the problems facing the revolt: the ability of the Ottomans to use the railway to reinforce and supply their garrison at Medina; the enemy's mobile columns which had driven Feisal off from Medina; the weaknesses of the Arab fighters in machine guns and artillery; the ambivalent loyalties of the Harb who were likely to join the Ottomans if they advanced into their territory; and the likelihood that Mecca would fall, and Hussein with it.[41]

Abdullah's solution was to call for a brigade of Muslim troops to be held in readiness at Suez to defend Rabegh, should it be threatened. Lawrence believed that there were no available Muslim units, that shipping was too precious to hold in perpetual readiness, and that the Royal Navy could defend Rabegh from offshore in any case.[42] Abdullah noted sourly that, since the check to the navy in the Dardanelles, the 'old legend of the British navy and its omnipotence' was irrelevant. He imagined that a nucleus of Arab regular troops being trained in Egypt would be joined by more former Ottoman prisoners of war in due course, so a British Indian brigade was a temporary measure before the Arabs had sufficient strength to converge on Medina and take the city by themselves. Lawrence countered these ideas with a demand to see for himself the situation at Rabegh, and the positions facing Feisal in the hills astride the route to Medina. In his first foray into the interior, Lawrence noted that a single British brigade would be insufficient to hold the 20-mile front that was needed just to deny the watering places, vital to the campaign.[43] Moreover, it would not be able to guarantee the allegiance of the tribes on the flanks.

From a strategic point of view, the British authorities were on the horns of a dilemma. The Ottomans would certainly march on Mecca, and they could take one of two routes to get there. The overland route was difficult, and badly supplied with water. The coastal route, via Rabegh, was far easier and replete with wells. The British therefore debated at length whether to deploy British troops to protect the vulnerable port of Rabegh and the considerable supplies they had landed there. They were eager not to offend the religious sensitivities of the Arabs so close to the holiest sites of Islam, but, at the same time, it seemed likely that the revolt might fail altogether if the small Arab contingent there could not be supplied or reinforced with regular troops.

Sir Archibald Murray, who commanded the garrison in Egypt and Sinai, was reluctant to divert limited manpower resources from the defence of Suez and the vital shipping that was needed elsewhere, including in support of Aden. Sir William Robertson, the Chief of the Imperial General Staff, agreed. But Sir Reginald Wingate was in favour of sending a brigade and Sir Henry McMahon, who was just as eager to sustain the revolt, concurred. Offering compromise, Colonel Cyril Wilson, the officer in command at Jeddah, proposed that Hussein might invite British forces to Rabegh, relieving the British government of the responsibility, but Hussein refused to call on these reinforcements.[44] It was hinted there was a risk that offended local opinion might actually neutralize support for the Hashemite cause. On the other hand, not sending a brigade could mean the loss of prestige amongst Muslim imperial subjects.

Lawrence produced the solution: sending a small contingent of military advisors to assist the Arab rebels. These men could also manage the heavier weapons, munitions and equipment the fighters needed. This had the advantage of minimizing manpower demands while producing the most effective way of sustaining the revolt.[45] It was, in today's military parlance, a 'light footprint'.

The British seizure of the ports of Jeddah, Yanbo and Rabegh, along the Red Sea coast, transformed the operational situation. While the guns of the Royal Navy protected the approaches, some 600 Egyptian troops and guns, deployed for shore defence, were landed alongside a battalion of 700 Arab regulars (mainly Iraqis who had become prisoners of war of the British but agreed to serve now against the Ottomans). As Lawrence had anticipated, British officers coordinated the new operations and their complex logistics.[46] Sir Reginald Wingate, with experience as the Governor of the Sudan, was appointed to command all operations in the Hejaz, while Jeddah continued to operate as a forward base under the command of Colonel Cyril Wilson, the former Governor of the Red Sea province of the Sudan. Colonel Pierce Joyce assumed control of Rabegh that December.[47] Colonel Stewart Newcombe, a Royal Engineer, was designated to act as the permanent liaison officer to Feisal, but delays in his departure meant that Lawrence was sent instead.[48]

When he did arrive, Newcombe took a keen interest in the Hejaz railway as the most operationally important feature of the region, and planned to disrupt all its traffic with a series of raids. While Lawrence was probably better suited to liaison work, Newcombe was closer to the classic mould of what today would be regarded as the Special Forces operator: an intrepid, daring and courageous officer conducting clandestine and hazardous missions deep behind enemy lines.

French officers under the command of the enterprising Colonel Edouard Brémond had also joined the campaign, to ensure that French interests were upheld. Their offer to 'escort' pilgrims using Muslim North African troops from the French colonies was dismissed by the British as little more than a front to conceal French colonial ambitions. It reinforced the negative impression that had been formed over the Sykes-Picot negotiations.[49] Yet the small French contingent provided much-needed professional military support to the Arabs, especially around Mecca. Brémond made various overtures to Hussein and Abdullah, while the Muslim officers of French North African regiments, Colonel Cadi and Captaine Ould Raho, worked alongside Arab raiding parties.[50] Captaine Rosario Pisani, a French officer attached to what became the Arab Northern Army, was one of the most successful raiders of all.

Lawrence had his own suspicions about the entire French mission that accompanied the Arab Revolt. He suspected that the French always intended to sabotage any Arab attempt to reach Syria, so as to make their post-war negotiating position stronger. In Cairo, there was a concern that the French might wish to take command of the Arab forces themselves, under the leadership of Colonel Brémond.

It is difficult to know exactly when Lawrence realized that the political, rather than military, dimensions were the most important to the outcome of the Arab uprising. After the war, he famously noted that one could not 'make war on rebellion', and in the 1920s he claimed that the revolt would have been more effective as a form of 'general strike'. How much of this thinking was present at the early stages of the campaign is hard to ascertain. It has been claimed: 'Lawrence understood the Arab Revolt not as a military campaign in the sense of a usual war but as a national movement, which he successfully pursued with the aid of a strategy of guerrilla warfare.'[51] If so, this would explain why he saw the military aspects as less important than the political achievement of seizing Syria along with the Hejaz, and why he was so upset by the terms of the Sykes-Picot Agreement. The problem with this assessment is that it takes post-war, Locarno-era thinking, and places it in the early stages of the war, when no one could have known the outcome of the war, its duration, or the ideological forces it would unleash.

When writing *Seven Pillars*, once he had had an opportunity to reflect, Lawrence noted that there may have been a very different kind of opportunity, from a psychological point of view, in the immediate aftermath of the outbreak of the revolt. Djemal Pasha, one of the Ottoman triumvirate, was known to be a devout Muslim, and his correspondence with Hussein indicated his desire to heal the rift the revolt represented. Reconciliation was out of the question when Syrian nationalists had been killed on his orders, but Lawrence thought, perhaps too optimistically, this might have been a chance to divide the enemy. He thought Djemal's letters were 'illuminating':

Feisal sent them to Mecca and Egypt, hoping that they would read into them what we did: but the points were taken literally, and we received injunction to reply that the sword was now our judge. This was magnificent; but in war so rich a diathetical opportunity could not be missed. True, that accommodation with Jemal was not possible. He had lopped the tall heads of Syria, and we should deny our friends' blood if we admitted him to our peace: but by indicating this subtly in our reply we might widen the national-clerical rift in Turkey.[52]

What Lawrence was exhibiting was an acute awareness of the political nature of a guerrilla war. The alignments of various communities, factions and leaders were important in the revolt, and would have been critical, regardless of whether Lawrence could conceive of a truly national movement, just in the execution of the immediate military operations.

The more pressing consideration though was the looming counter-offensive by the Ottomans. A brigade of 3,500 men, equipped with field artillery and two machine gun companies, had arrived in Medina, and Fakhri now possessed sufficient numbers, over 13,000 men, to sweep the Arabs from the field. The first Arab attempts to delay this offensive had failed, since cutting railway lines by removing rails was a minor inconvenience to an army that had had plenty of experience of this disruption. Even before the war, the Ottomans had had railway repair teams, specialist rolling stock, and all the materials necessary to manage the problem.[53]

For the Hejazis the situation appeared to be critical when, in an ignominious skirmish in December 1916, the Ottomans dispersed Feisal's 8,000-strong force with artillery and machine gun fire and an adroit manoeuvre. Lawrence related the affair which, he concluded, was not merely a question of Ottoman organizational flair or technological superiority. The patrols of the Arab leader Sidi Zeid had neglected to secure a key road to Khalis, parallel to the Arab lines, and Ottoman troops had used this unguarded route to penetrate 6 miles to the rear of Feisal's force via a wadi near Kheif. The news of this manoeuvre completely unhinged the Arab positions, and the army fled, hoping to secure their families and possessions before the Ottomans got to them first. The Ottomans then took all the abandoned posts formerly held by the Arabs. Feisal tried to rally his men at Nakhl Mubarak and engaged in a long-range shooting match. Exhausted by the fighting and still unnerved by the previous flight, the left wing, held by the Juheina, abandoned the firing line, which caused the sudden termination of the action.[54] Feisal believed there had been treachery, but, as Lawrence later discovered, the Juheina had simply given up fighting to rest.[55] The resulting chaotic withdrawal meant that Feisal had to retreat and regroup at Yanbo on the coast.

This was the context for Lawrence's observations that the Arab irregulars could neither hold defended positions nor conduct sustained assaults. It was a critical moment in his appreciation of how to orchestrate guerrilla warfare in order to overcome the obvious shortcomings of untrained, badly disciplined fighters who were unused to fighting in large formations.

Lawrence reported that 'the hill men struck me as good material for guerrilla warfare. They are hard and fit, very active, independent, cheerful snipers.'[56] On irregular Arab tactics, Lawrence wrote: 'The tribal armies are aggregations of snipers only ... they are not to be relied upon for attack in mass. [But] they are extremely mobile, and will climb or run a great distance to be in a safe place for a shot – preferably at not more than 300 yards range.' He also wrote of his concerns:

The Arabs have a living terror of the unknown. This includes at present aeroplanes and artillery ... They are not afraid of bullets, or of being killed – it is just the manner of death by artillery they cannot stand. ... their moral confidence is probably as easily restored, as it is easily shaken ... At present they only fight at night, so that the Turkish guns shall be blind.[57]

Lawrence deduced that,

The value of the tribes is defensive only, and their real sphere is guerrilla warfare. They are intelligent, and very lively, almost reckless, but too individualistic to endure commands, or fight in line, or help each other. It would, I think be impossible to make an organised force out of them. Their initiative, great knowledge of the country, and mobility, make them formidable in the hills ... they would dynamite a railway, plunder a caravan, [and] steal camels, better than anyone.

He summed up their vulnerabilities, and believed they would be defeated only if their funds were exhausted, their homelands occupied, if they attempted a pitched battle, or, crucially, if their leaders lost prestige.[58]

Lawrence contrasted the Ottoman strength, concluding that, in defensive positions, a company of Ottoman regulars could defeat an Arab army, but not in a guerrilla conflict, where the Arab fighters could disperse. Put simply: 'A difference in character between the Turkish and Arab armies is that the more you disperse the former, the weaker they become, and the more you distribute the latter, the stronger they become.'[59]

At Yanbo, Lawrence was struck by how far the hasty defensive positions that were created resembled those he had encountered in his historical studies, and how much the fortifications, and the presence of the Royal Navy's warships, restored confidence. He wrote:

> The Arabs, delighted to count up the quantity of vessels in the harbour, were prepared to contribute their part to the night's entertainment. They gave us good hope there would be no further panic: but to reassure them fully they needed some sort of rampart to defend, mediaeval fashion: it was no good digging trenches, partly because the ground was coral rock, and, besides, they had no experience of trenches and might not have manned them confidently. So we took the crumbling, salt-riddled wall of the place, doubled it with a second, packed earth between the two, and raised them till our sixteenth century bastions were rifle-proof at least, and probably proof against the Turkish mountain guns. Outside the bastions we put barbed wire, festooned between cisterns on the rain catchments beyond the walls. We dug in machine gun nests in the best angles, and manned them with Feisal's regular gunners. The Egyptians, like everyone else given a place in the scheme, were gratifyingly happy.[60]

Fortunately for the Arab defenders at Yanbo, the Ottomans were forced to consolidate their gains, and established a temporary defensive line in the hills, halfway between Medina and Rabegh. Prior to their final advance, it was necessary for the Ottomans to haul their supplies forward, and to conduct a thorough reconnaissance. Lawrence noted that the Ottomans were burdened with a large number of sick personnel, and their animals lacked fodder, which impeded their mobility. Arab raiding, even by those not connected with the cause, may have inflicted as many as 20 men killed that January, but the effect was more psychological than physical. The Ottomans found themselves in a 'ubiquitously hostile country'.[61] Lawrence concluded:

> Raids might occur at any point from ten miles seaward of Medina itself for the next seventy miles through the hills. They illustrated the obstacles in the way of the new Turkish Army with its half-Germanized complexity of equipment, when, from a distant railhead with no made roads, it tried to advance through extremely rugged and hostile country. The administrative developments of scientific war had clogged its mobility and destroyed its dash; and troubles grew in geometrical rather than arithmetical progression for each new mile its commanding officers put between themselves and Medina, their ill-found, insecure and inconvenient base.[62]

Air attacks launched from either the Royal Navy's ships or ashore, and naval gunfire, deterred an anticipated full-scale Ottoman assault on Yanbo. Even a night attack was ruled out as naval searchlights, playing across the desert approaches, created an eerie threat to the Ottoman patrols.[63] Fakhri turned instead towards Rabegh, but was again subjected to air attack, and while he could defeat the parties of Arab fighters sent against him, he could not stop their raids on his supply lines back to Medina. Lawrence believed the failure to make their attack meant, at that moment, 'the Turks lost their war'.[64]

3

Extending the Flank
The Manoeuvre to Wejh

Stumbling over rocky crags, in the dark without being detected, within rifle range of the enemy, requires courage and a degree of luck. After riding for hours over uncertain ground, Lawrence sought to test his Arab partners, and to inoculate them to the risks of close combat, but characteristically he was keen to test himself too:

> To exercise my own hand in the raiding genre I took a test party of thirty-five Mahamid with me from Nakhl Mubarak, on the second day of 1917, to the old blockhouse-well of my first journey from Rabegh to Yanbo. When dark came we dismounted, and left our camels with ten men to guard them against possible Turkish patrols. The rest of us climbed up Dhifran: a painful climb, for the hills were of knife-sharp strata turned on edge and running in oblique lines from crest to foot.[1]

Lawrence was describing an early raid near Nakhl Mubarak. Getting close to the enemy, stealthily, across broken terrain at night, was a challenge in itself. When dawn broke, the Ottomans were in fact closer than Lawrence's men had realized:

> The head of Dhifran was cold and misty, and time dragged till dawn. We disposed ourselves in crevices of the rock, and at last saw the tips of bell-tents three hundred yards away beneath us to the right,

behind a spur. We could not get a full view, so contented ourselves with putting bullets through their tops. A crowd of Turks turned out and leaped like stags into their trenches. They were very fast targets, and probably suffered little. In return they opened rapid fire in every direction, and made a terrific row; as if signalling the Hamra force to turn out in their help. As the enemy were already more than ten to one, the reinforcements might have prevented our retreat: so we crawled gently back till we could rush down into the first valley, where we fell over two scared Turks, unbuttoned, at their morning exercise.[2]

Raiding of this nature, at this early stage of the revolt, had little appreciable material, or, as Lawrence would put it, 'algebraic' effect. Yet it was a useful way for Lawrence to increase the confidence of his Arab partners. He had observed that small successes improved morale and created a desire for others to emulate them. It was also a practice that suited the temperament of untrained fighters who had a feel for the terrain, and which could exploit the weaknesses of the Ottoman forces.

The Ottoman regime was determined to recover the lost territory, crush the insurgency, and de-legitimize Hussein. Their first move was to install a new Grand Sharif, Ali Haider, in Medina. The next stage was to secure all the major towns and ports before despatching mobile columns to hunt down the individual recalcitrant factions. To supply their forces in the field, it was essential to keep open the Hejaz railway link to the north.[3] This strategic line not only connected the Arabian domains to the Ottoman capital, but it was also the lateral line of communication that could move reserves to threaten the flank or rear of any British army that attempted to push into Palestine from its new forward position in Sinai.

The Ottomans were active in their recruitment of Arabs, making use of local dependence on the Ottoman infrastructure and offering financial incentives. The cutting off of various goods from Egypt increased Arab dependence on Ottoman resources, and the Harb, who had seemed initially to be aligned to the Sharifians, were eager not offend the Ottomans on the Rabegh route lest their palm groves, on which their local economy rested, were destroyed. The southern Harb were more definitely in league with the Ottomans and news reached Feisal's forces that his men would be attacked in the rear if he advanced northwards.[4] Lawrence noted that, in the panic caused by the Ottoman approach, the 'spy system was breaking down: the Harb, having lost their wits ... were bringing in wild and contradictory reports from one side and another about the strength of the Turks and their movement and intention'.[5] Where the Arabs had seemingly enjoyed an advantage in human intelligence, this was evaporating in the face of imminent defeat.

With at least some Arabs compliant, Fakhri's force of 5,000 resumed its advance on Rabegh.[6] The situation caused considerable anxiety and a decision was made to establish a landing strip on the beach and to embark or destroy surplus stores if the Ottomans reached within striking distance. Lawrence's assessment was that the port could not be held as no prepared defences existed and a single Ottoman battalion with artillery support would capture it.[7] The port was saved, in Lawrence's view, by the relatively slow approach of the Ottoman brigade.[8] It took a further two weeks before Fakhri was ready to attack the Arab outpost at Khoreiba, in mid-January 1917. The delays were attributed to raiding and a degree of physical exhaustion induced by the terrain.

Within the Ottoman Army, the revolt produced disquiet, but no mass defection of Arab personnel. Some Turkish officers criticized their Arab comrades and refused to associate with them, but, despite the promises made by the nationalists to the British in 1914–15, most Arab personnel in the Ottoman Army remained steadfast in their service to the Sultan. Some, no doubt, hoped for greater concessions in the future by demonstrating their loyalty, but for the majority, subject to military discipline and fighting against foreigners and rebels, the choice was more straightforward.[9] Arab soldiers' accounts of their service in this war are rare, but Laila Parsons has traced the career of one, Fawzi al-Qawuqji, an Ottoman officer who fought in Mesopotamia and Palestine.[10] His loyalty to the Ottoman Army was unshaken despite increasing Turkish distrust, his arrest, and the concurrent executions of Arab nationalists. When captured by the Australians, he escaped and preferred to rejoin the Ottoman Army rather than defect to the Sharifian forces, regarding 'Lawrence's Arabs' as just another colonial unit fielded by the British.[11]

Djemal Pasha, the Ottoman Governor of Syria, engaged in psychological pressure too, and he exploited the prejudices, loyalties, religious affinity, clan divisions, and the authority of the Caliph to draw the Arabs away from the revolt. It is striking that many Arabs who remained loyal within the Ottoman Army regarded the Sharifians as a 'snuffbox army'.[12] It could be contemptuously rationalized as an unrepresentative, wild, and ineffective uprising, induced by British gold.[13]

For the soldiers of the Ottoman Army, the common experience was not some distant political promise of 'liberation', but the extreme conditions of campaigning and the obvious lethal hazards of the conflict, with death through combat or disease.[14] If there was demoralization amongst Arab troops in the Ottoman Army, they shared that characteristic not only with the Anatolian *Mehmetciks* but also with those in the ranks of the Sharifian cause. British intelligence revealed that Arab fighters in the winter of 1916–17 were hungry and downcast, while the Egyptian gunners sent to their aid were equally disenchanted, believing the 'Arab Revolt' was a lost cause.[15]

The strengths and weaknesses of the irregular Arab forces were a constant theme in Lawrence's calculations and were reflected in the British verdicts on the revolt. The Agayl, who made up the majority of fighters, believed themselves to be inherent warriors, but British assessments of their fighting styles categorized them as unsuitable for anything other than raiding. Without modern weapons or training, they could not be used to assault defended positions. Heavy weapons would also compromise their mobility, which was their chief defence until the Ottomans increased the number of aircraft operating against them.

There were other weaknesses. Arab irregulars who joined the revolt were forced to abandon their livelihoods in commerce, pastoralism or agriculture, and often refused to operate far from their homelands. They had to be paid, usually in gold, to serve on a continuous basis. This represented a considerable drain on resources. Moreover, feuding and indiscipline were perpetual problems.[16] While it is true that Feisal managed to suppress some of the excesses, the independence and rivalry that Lawrence celebrated so warmly was often detrimental.

Lawrence admitted:

Their acquisitive recklessness made them keen on booty, and whetted them to tear up railways, plunder caravans, and steal camels; but they were too free-minded to endure command or fight in a team. A man who could fight well by himself generally made a bad soldier, and these champions seemed to me to be no material for our drilling; but if we strengthened them by light automatic guns of the Lewis type, to be handled by themselves, they might be capable of holding their hills and serving as an efficient screen behind which we could build up, perhaps at Rabegh, an Arab regular mobile column, capable of meeting a Turkish force (distracted by guerrilla warfare) on terms, and of defeating it piecemeal.[17]

The solution, in fact, was to create a trained, regular Arab army. The best material for this came from former Ottoman troops who had been taken prisoner after the failed Senussi Revolt in Libya, in Mesopotamia, or in Sinai. Lawrence described them as 'heavy unwarlike Syrian and Mesopotamian townsfolk' who would 'eventually finish the war by striking, while the tribesmen skirmished about, and hindered and distracted the Turks by the pin prick raids'.[18] Lawrence therefore confessed that irregulars could not, by themselves, win a war. They simply lacked the technology and the application to take and hold territory, or effect a decisive victory, on which the outcome of a conflict depended.[19] While he romanticized and idealized the drifting irregular fighter, he was under no illusion about their limitations.

The command of the Arab regulars fell to Major 'Aziz Bey' Ali Al-Masri, with the title of the Minister of War and acting Commander in Chief of the Sharifian Army. Al-Masri had been prominent within the Tripolitanian War against the Italians in 1911, but he had sought refuge in Egypt in 1913 and lived in fear of the wrath of the secret intelligence service of the Committee of Union and Progress, the feared Teşkilât-ı Mahsusa.[20] A second former Ottoman officer, Jafar Pasha el-Askeri, who had also served with the Senussi against Britain in the fighting in Egypt's Western Desert, joined the Sharifian cause and proved to be an experienced and reliable leader. One of the determining factors in the decision of these and other Ottoman soldiers to change sides was the news of the draconian repression conducted by Djemal Pasha in Syria, and the better prospects of military service with the Arabs rather than languishing in a prisoner of war camp. Dressed in British uniforms, issued regular pay and rations, and armed with modern weapons, the numbers of regular Arab troops available soon grew to 2,000. Later in the campaign, because of stiffening Ottoman resistance, the regular contingents of the Arab Northern Army were equipped with supporting aircraft, armoured cars and anti-aircraft guns, while their strength was augmented with contingents of the British Imperial Yeomanry and units of the Indian Army.

For the time being, the bulk of the Sharifian forces were still irregulars, the largest proportion of whom were dismounted but with a significant portion of mounted men. Lawrence calculated that, in late 1916, Feisal could 'retain' up to 8,000 men, with up to 15,000 in support, but not all of these took the field at the same time. Men would spend some time with the force, then return home, often sending another as a substitute. 'This', reported Lawrence, 'is inevitable in tribal warfare.'[21]

Lawrence was not alone in considering the relative value of guerrillas. Other revolutionary writers of the period commented on the need for regular forces, and training, to turn a campaign of harassment into a decisive one. Leon Trotsky condemned the critics who claimed that guerrilla warfare was banditry, explaining that:

> While war, generally speaking, has as its aim the overthrow of the enemy, small-scale war ('guerrilla') has the task of causing difficulties to the enemy and doing him damage. From the angle of the organising of operations, small-scale war is characterised by a large degree of independence of the separate units. [It] by no means always signifies the action of spontaneously-arisen unarmed or poorly armed detachments. Guerrilla warfare can be a method of operation for thoroughly well-formed mobile units which, for all the autonomy they enjoy, are strictly subordinate to an operational headquarters.[22]

Trotsky noted that, once his enemies, the White forces, could no longer rely on external support, they ended their guerrilla warfare and turned to mass armies. He reflected that, in the early days of the Bolshevik uprising, their enemies were too disorganized to resist, and so a devolved, somewhat amateur approach by his own side, akin to guerrilla operations, could thrive. However, once their enemies became organized, it was necessary for the Bolsheviks to create their own regular force. He concluded: 'If we conceive guerrilla warfare as a method of light, swift manoeuvring and sharp thrusts, it is clear that the rebel detachments, through their very primitiveness and the extreme inexperience of their fighters and commanders, were least of all suitable for genuine guerrilla operations.' In other words, success depended on professionalizing an armed force in both conventional as well as guerrilla war. Lawrence learned this same lesson through his hard-won experience in the war.

THE STRATEGIC CONTEXT: BRITISH PLANS AND SINAI OPERATIONS

The Arabian strategy emerged more clearly after the initial crisis of the autumn of 1916 had passed. With irregular 'means', and with a limited number of 'ways', the Arab 'ends' were to liberate the Hejaz by defeating the Ottoman forces. To gain legitimacy as the true leaders of the Muslim world, which was perhaps Hussein's real ambition, it was vital to secure Medina as they had done Mecca, and, concurrently, they had to keep open the sea ports on the coast through which came all their essential supplies. At the same time, if the Ottoman line of communication and reinforcement, the Hejaz railway, could be cut, there was a chance they could prevent large Ottoman formations from concentrating against them, and perhaps starve the garrison of Medina into submission. Despite Hussein's plans, his son Feisal had another agenda: aware that he was unlikely to gain any significant position in the post-war dispensation in the Hejaz, Feisal looked to Greater Syria as a potential source of future power. It was this factor which drew the forces under his command northwards.

The British 'ends' were more limited. General Sir Archibald Murray, the military commander and political authority in Egypt, believed the Arab Revolt was capable only of drawing a portion of Ottoman forces into the strategically insignificant Hejaz, and away from the more important theatre of operations in Sinai. Murray therefore practised an economy of effort in supporting the Hashemites, and he was certainly not prepared to divide his forces and take on a secondary theatre, especially given his experience of having to suppress the Senussi on Egypt's western borders at the same time as fighting the Ottomans and their Bedouin allies in Sinai. There was also a Jihadist insurrection in the Sudan, linked to Ottoman intrigues, to suppress. Robertson, as Chief of the Imperial General Staff (CIGS), was even more trenchant: 'My sole object is to win the war', he said, 'and we shall not do that in the Hijaz or in the Sudan.'[23]

The British concerns were, from a military point of view, that there would be yet more demands for troops in this theatre when manpower was in short supply on every front.[24] Shipping shortages were especially acute. What was even more worrying was that many Indian Muslims condemned the revolt and its British backing, arguing that it was not legitimate to fight the Caliph as leader of the Islamic world. Anxious signals were conveyed from the Government of India to Sir Henry McMahon that the revolt was proving counter-productive.

The Arab Bureau added to the many demands on Murray, and their reports of the extension of the Ottoman railways in Palestine suggested that more offensive operations could be expected across Sinai. An Ottoman line extended from Jerusalem to Lydda, and, in 1915, it was pushed on to Beersheba. It was a relatively short distance to their base at El Arish, on the fringe of the Sinai, from which they could mount attacks on the Canal. By early 1916, there were just four Territorial Infantry Divisions left to garrison Egypt and protect the Canal against this threat.

The Ottomans were making fresh attempts to raid and mine the waterway and its approaches. Eight mines were recovered from the Red Sea on 9 March 1915 at a time when much of the naval force was being stripped out for the Dardanelles operations. On 22 March, a Gurkha patrol discovered part of a brigade-strength Ottoman force entrenching some 10 miles east of the Canal. A flying column was assembled, and, during a wild storm that night, they surprised the Ottoman force and routed it, with a loss of just three men. In late April, more mining attempts were made and a second Ottoman force was intercepted, with another discovered and intercepted in May. These raids underscored the importance of a defence in depth, extending out into the Sinai, since to remain on the defensive, along the line of the Canal, compelled the defenders to be stretched out, constantly subjected to attacks where the enemy retained the initiative.

The defence of the Suez Canal was the regional strategic priority. Throughout the Gallipoli campaign, and subsequently for the Allied expeditionary force in Salonika, Egypt had demonstrated its strategic importance as a conduit for manpower and supplies for the British Imperial war effort. Domestically, Egypt provided foodstuffs and cotton, exporting such vast quantities that the country became dependent on maize and wheat imports from India to sustain its own population.[25] The scheme of defence that was developed in mid-1915 therefore envisaged not a linear defence of the Canal, but a series of overlapping lines some

8–10 miles to the east, into Sinai. It was thought a light railway should be constructed to Qatiya in order to dominate the water supplies that existed there, and thus deprive any attacking force a crucial resource. As Secretary of State for War, Herbert Kitchener applied his background in engineering to the problem, detailing the great quantities of wire, telegraphic equipment, Egyptian labourers, water pumping facilities, transport, aircraft, aerodrome facilities, heavy guns and reserves that would be required.

The termination of the Gallipoli campaign in January 1916 had released Ottoman divisions for operations elsewhere, particularly in Mesopotamia, where a British offensive had been checked that spring, and in the Caucasus. When Bulgaria joined the war on the side of the Central Powers, it was possible for Germany to provide additional and much-needed munitions to their Ottoman allies. There was every expectation that, with an uplift of manpower, supplies and armaments, Suez would be under an ever-increasing threat. In early 1916, intelligence reports suggested that another major attack could be expected on Egypt.

Murray explained to the CIGS that Egypt should be defended by a forward position to prevent the Sinai being used as a springboard for attacks on the Canal, and he suggested advancing across the Sinai Peninsula to the town of El Arish.[26] While there were concerns that perhaps 100,000 (some said as many as 250,000) Ottoman troops might be massed against British positions at the eastern end of the Sinai, Murray was confident the threat could be contained.[27] The key was to take advantage of the opportunity presented and not wait until the Ottomans could bring as many as six divisions across the Sinai. With a light railway and a water pipeline it would be perfectly possible to sustain a British division, accompanied by three mobile cavalry brigades. With two further divisions on the Canal, Murray believed he could reduce the burdens in a war that was consuming every available resource.[28]

Lawrence was immensely critical of Murray's ponderous approach, especially in the 'slow and solid' construction of the logistics system. But, in contrast to the desert raiders, a conventional army required such methodical backing. Furthermore, conventional armies could take and hold ground in ways that Lawrence's forces could not. Robertson, with responsibility for the overall prioritization of the British military effort, was utterly insistent that the focus of all available resources should be against the German Army in France, and, while supportive of Murray's situation in defending Suez, he concluded that the Sinai, and especially the Hejaz operations, were a long way down in the order of precedence.[29]

Lawrence expressed his frustration with flippant praise of the Ottomans' raiding of the Suez Canal, and the apparent impotence of the garrison along it. He wrote:

> Turkey, if she is wise, will raid it from time to time, and annoy the garrison there, which is huge, and lumbersome, and creaks so loudly in the joints that you hear them eight hours before they move. So it's quite easy to run down and chuck a bomb at it, and run away without being caught.[30]

Lawrence didn't appreciate the strategic aspects of the equation. The numbers of the garrison were irrelevant. Being able to control and use the Canal was the point and the British intended to remain in possession of Suez as an avenue of supply. Lawrence was nevertheless more accurate in realizing the psychological element of the raids. Remaining on the defensive squandered initiative and left Murray anxious about the threat. The solution was to drive the Ottomans back into the inhospitable interior of Sinai, to deny them space and access to the waterway. Yet, once again, the issue was one of ruthless prioritization of material effort. Murray had already had to commit valuable resources, including shipping, to prevent the fall of the Red Sea ports to the Ottomans. Yanbo and Rabegh had been held with British forces.[31] He was now reluctant to do more.

The Ottoman Fourth Army calculated that, having been delayed in their plans by the need to defend Gallipoli in 1915, they wanted now to act quickly to disrupt the forward moves of Murray or they would be deprived permanently of a base for operations against the Canal. So, for all the criticisms, Murray's manoeuvres were made in the nick of time.[32]

To check Murray's advance, the Ottomans launched a brigade-sized raid against the British. They attacked the 5th Mounted Brigade at Qatiya, and overwhelmed the defenders, but their subsequent attacks were less successful.

Djemal wanted another more determined effort, not just to check Murray's forces in Sinai, but to reduce British prestige and cause wavering Arabs to abandon the nascent uprising. This second Ottoman assault was thus far greater in scale, conducted by the 3rd (Anatolian) Infantry Division and the German Pasha I Group, with a greater complement of machine guns and artillery units than ordinary formations possessed. Traversing the desert with wheeled guns, in the full heat of July and August, the Ottoman formation attempted another surprise attack on the British cavalry outposts at Romani. Despite losing air superiority to German aircraft, Murray's mounted and air patrols were able to obtain sufficient warning of the Ottoman approach. Around Romani's defences, some 14,000 men were therefore assembled, and the Ottoman attack was launched without the odds it required to ensure success.

Murray also anticipated the Ottomans' plan and sought to devise a scheme of manoeuvre that would take advantage of the situation. If the Ottomans chose to dig in and hold a defensive position, he would swing an amphibious force to El Arish and cut their line of communication. If they chose to attack, they would surely avoid an assault on his main defences at Romani, and instead focus of the area south of the highest ground at Katib Gannit, a vast dune in a range of sand uplands. Murray deliberately deployed a skeleton line at this point, hoping to draw the Ottomans into a prepared defence zone, and then use his cavalry and mounted infantry to take the attackers in the flank.

As expected, on 4 August 1916, the Ottomans made their assault, and the Australians, who held the ridge at the centre of the attack, put up a determined resistance. Once the Ottoman offensive seemed to have reached its limit, and they were fully committed, Murray unleashed his mounted forces. A charge by the Gloucester Hussars and Worcester Yeomanry carried them up to the summit ridge, where they were able to fire on the Ottoman batteries below. A weak Ottoman counter-attack fell apart and the Ottoman troops, without water, their position now hopeless, started to surrender. British infantry regiments began to move into the fight from the main position at Romani too, pinning the remaining Ottomans in the salient they had created by the initial attacks. The following day, 5 August 1916, the Ottomans were in retreat pursued relentlessly by both mounted and infantry units. The Ottoman defeat became a rout, and some 1,500 were killed and

4,000 taken prisoner. Far from being 'ponderous', Murray had opened the way to El Arish and ended at a stroke the Ottoman and German threat to Suez.

EXTENDING THE FLANK: THE STORMING OF WEJH

The breakthrough to the impasse between the Ottomans' threat to Rabegh and Yanbo, and the Arabs' impunity on the coast and the interior, was the manoeuvre towards Wejh, the last Ottoman-controlled port in the Hejaz. Feisal is credited in the British *Official History* with the decision, which had been advocated as early as October 1916, but Lawrence certainly had a hand in it. The decision was not an easy one, despite its first appearances. In its favour, a move north, along the coast, would, in effect, threaten the Ottomans' right flank if they attempted to advance on Rabegh and thence on to Mecca. By extending this move north almost continuously, Fakhri would be forced to either fortify his lines of communication, thus committing more men to a static defence, or risk raids against his vulnerable supply lines.[33] On the other hand, if the Arab forces left their main base at Yanbo, it could easily be lost to an Ottoman attack and with it a substantial volume of their supplies and munitions. Moreover, if intercepted en route to the north, the Arab irregulars would be dispersed. A further setback, on the scale of the retreat from Nekhl Mubarak, might even mark the demise of the revolt. Lawrence knew there was a substantial risk of an Ottoman counter-offensive.[34]

The concept of relentlessly extending the enemy's flank, and the risk that the enemy would strike at one's centre during such a manoeuvre was not original, and Lawrence would have derived the idea from his study of military history. The advantage is that it can absorb the enemy's reserve without actually fighting, drawing the adversary into an increasingly vulnerable line without depth, whereupon a strike can be made at almost any point, or, better still, at multiple points, to off balance the enemy and conceal the main attack. The manoeuvre comes with its own risks, however. Extending the enemy's front requires one to extend one's own, or to disperse forces. As Napoleon demonstrated at Austerlitz in 1805, if one is trying to extend the front, it can be exposed to a counter-offensive.[35] Lawrence's purpose was not to conclude a decisive final phase, but to weaken the Ottomans so they had no reserves left to make a counter-attack at all. If the Ottomans did bring in fresh reserves from other fronts, this at least ensured they were not available to contest a more decisive British operation elsewhere. Nevertheless, for the moment, these calculations were Lawrence's. The view at the time was still to take all of the Hejaz in order to consolidate the revolt.

Colonel Brémond met with Lawrence at Rabegh and challenged the British–Arab view that there should be a concerted assault to capture Medina, which was then still the prevailing expectation. Not only did Brémond think the Arab forces incapable of taking the city, which was true, but he was also reluctant to empower a rebellious force which might, in due course, act against Allied interests. His intention was to see British and French expeditionary forces landed at Rabegh, where they could not only take over the fighting, but also render the Arab Revolt a subordinate affair. An Allied military victory, he reasoned, would be a far more efficient way of subsequently demanding that the Ottomans relinquish Mecca and Medina, and hand them over to Hussein.[36] When Lawrence disclosed his encouragement to Feisal to take Wejh, and leave Yanbo temporarily exposed, Brémond considered it a move akin to 'suicide'.[37]

Lawrence later claimed that he had decided to leave Medina intact, since, as he put it, 'The Turk was harmless there.' He reasoned that, to 'keep his railway working, but only just, with the maximum of loss and discomfort', the Ottoman garrison would be unable to concentrate forces against mobile Arab forces. Instead, they would be locked into a defensive posture. The claim that Lawrence had decided not to take Medina, but left it as a burden on the Ottomans, has been seen as a post-war invention. It first appeared in the 1920s, in 'The Evolution of a Revolt'.[38] The purpose behind the move to Wejh, according to his actual wartime despatches, was to facilitate the siege of Medina, and to avoid the loss of Mecca. No mention was made of increasing the Ottoman burden through periodic railway raids.[39] In May 1917, taking Medina was still the focus.[40] The pressure exerted on the city, however, was not enough to take it or force it to be evacuated, and the claim that the Arabs could contain the garrison there by simply attacking the railways has been disputed.[41]

During the war, Lawrence was in agreement that Medina *should* be taken. He wrote, not of maintaining a squeeze on the garrison's line of communication, but that 'the fall of Medina is now merely a question of when the Arabs would like to put an end to the affair'.[42] The claim is further complicated because this confident assertion was at odds with his general view that the Arab irregular fighters were incapable of taking defended Ottoman positions, and certainly not one as strongly held as the city of Medina.[43]

The *Official History* doubted the claim that there was an attempt to allow the Hejaz railway to function, to 'frighten the enemy so seriously as to induce him to evacuate Medina' on the basis that the idea that 'in 1917 they ever acted upon that principle is improbable; at least it is not put forward in any contemporary appreciation'.[44] The *Official History*'s authors generously concluded there must have been a 'principle of necessity' that governed the actions of the Arab advisors. We might conclude that the logistical pressure on Medina was a consequence of more active railway raiding, rather than a conscious pre-meditated strategy.[45]

While Lawrence debated with Brémond, the Ottomans switched their attention from Yanbo towards a better objective, namely the destruction of the Arab forces in the field. Ali had launched an offensive, having heard of the threat to Yanbo and the defeat of his brother Zeid. His objective was to take on the Ottoman forces at Wadi Safra with his army of 7,000 men, hoping, in Lawrence's estimation, to draw them away from the port. With coordinated action by Feisal, there seemed a chance to inflict serious losses on the Ottomans who would be caught between them. But Feisal still needed time to rally his men who had been shaken by their previous encounter with Ottoman guns. Ali would not wait. But when he ordered the Juheina forward they refused, until Feisal rode into their camp to make a personal appeal for cooperation.

Although the two Arab leaders could command a degree of loyalty, the affair showed the allegiance of the clans was not guaranteed. Many of Ali's men refused to participate any further on the suspicion of betrayal by some of the tribes, notably the Subh. The result was that the whole of Ali's force fell back to Rabegh, with growing disorder along the way. Eventually the entire plan collapsed without ever closing with their enemy. Fortunately, the Royal Navy and the British air flight were still present at Rabegh, providing a rallying point for Ali's forces.

Under these conditions, Lawrence and Colonel Wilson pushed forward the plan of taking Wejh. Conferring on the deck of HMS

Dufferin, Feisal was nevertheless unconvinced. Rabegh could only be defended if the Royal Navy provided the necessary fire support. That was given. To the possibility of further offensives by the Ottomans, it was again to the navy and its air power that Feisal looked.[46] On the question of the allegiance of the tribes, Feisal believed he had to remain in close proximity of the clans that had gathered around Yanbo, and he would therefore delegate any moves northwards to his subordinates. As Lawrence noted ruefully, the plans being formulated were not now about 'securing a convincing siege of Medina, as of preventing the Turkish capture of Mecca'.[47]

To improve the chances of success of the move against Wejh, Lawrence appealed to Colonel Wilson and asked that Abdullah, operating near Medina, should deploy astride the railway at Wadi Ais, 70 miles from the Ottoman-held city, to create a diversion. Lawrence calculated that Fakhri would need to clear the line before making any further move and this would give Feisal's men more time to make the 200-mile march northwards along the coast. Abdullah needed persuading about this scheme, which appeared to abandon the investment of Medina, but the cooperation of the brothers prevailed; Abdullah complied. Feisal therefore remained at Yanbo to act as the unifying element for local clans, some of whom might otherwise desert the revolutionary cause, while the main body was assembled to march up the coast. A core of 1,200 Agayl, supported by other clans and factions, numbering in total 7,000, therefore began a hazardous journey. If intercepted, they would be scattered, and the morale of the Arab cause would probably be broken entirely. Equally, the two ports currently held, Rabegh and Yanbo, were now entirely dependent on the seapower of the Royal Navy and the reconnaissance of the British air wing.

Lawrence could see a virtue in his Arab force when 'there was no fighting in the bill'.[48] His calculation was that the Ottomans were still concentrating their forces for an attack on Rabegh and would probably not hear of the move, or at least not believe any reports of it. It would take them some days to redeploy in any case. He hoped to take Wejh by surprise. Lawrence also reasoned that by encouraging the Harb to conduct concurrent raids against the Ottoman lines of communications, they would become more self-sufficient and less dependent on the enemy. Lawrence added to the deception by organizing his own raid on the Ottoman soldiers at Nakhl Mubarak.[49] Plans were also laid to bring

Sidi Abdulla, the sheikh of Henakiyeh, into action against the Medina railway, via the Juheina hills.

For logistics during the march, the Royal Navy was again instrumental. Some 20 tons of water were pre-positioned during a night landing at Sherm Habban to replace a destroyed water point nearby. The sole advantage of the Arab force in transport was their greater economy in the use of camels. As the *Official History* notes, the 360 camels required by the Egyptian artillery detachment were reduced to just 80 when the guns and ammunition were placed in the hands of the Arab drivers.[50] Lawrence had mixed feelings about these guns. Although he acknowledged that the presence of 5-inch howitzers caused rejoicing, he still felt that artillery could do harm by limiting mobility, their primary asset. But he confessed that, 'if we did not give them guns they would quit'.[51] The primary value was psychological: Arab confidence was restored by having guns on their side, for it was their noise, rather than their effectiveness, that mattered in action. Lawrence noted that the prospects of being dismembered had a part to play in the Arab fighters' concern: 'they were not afraid of bullets, not indeed overmuch of dying: just the manner of death by shellfire was unendurable'.[52]

The march was just part of the plan: while Feisal's men made a landward attack on the port, the Royal Navy would bombard and land 600 regular Arab troops just to the north of the harbour in a pincer movement. To assist in the assault, 500 Harb and Juheina clansmen were embarked. With the 50 guns of six ships, and two seaplanes, it was thought there would be sufficient firepower to suppress the Ottoman resistance. Lawrence hoped that, by making it evident that the Ottoman garrison was cut off from escape by some 8,000 tribesmen on the landward side, they would choose to surrender rather than resist. Everything was set for the convergence of forces from land and sea to occur on 23 January 1917. Lawrence was so optimistic that he talked of an advance all the way to Damascus, which caused some concern at his judgement, not least amongst his British comrades. Lawrence, who admitted his mistake, was reported to his superiors as 'militarily incompetent and politically absurd'.[53]

The amphibious assault, under Major Charles Vickery, went in as planned on the morning of 23 January, supported by the fire of HMS *Hardinge*, HMS *Fox* and HMS *Espiegle*, but it was clear from the outset that Feisal's Arab irregulars were not in the vicinity. As a result, Vickery's small force was outnumbered by the 800-strong Ottoman garrison of the 129th Infantry and 500 Agayl horsemen in Ottoman service.[54] Street fighting went on all day, and the Ottomans still possessed part of the town at dusk. By dawn the next day, most of the Ottoman survivors had slipped away under cover of darkness, although a small detachment, about 200, continued to hold the mosque until they were persuaded to surrender.[55] Noticeably, the Agayl horsemen in Ottoman service had melted away at the start of the action.

Feisal and the Arab irregulars did not appear until the 25th, two full days after the planned landings. The strategic objective was achieved, but it was necessary to attribute the significance of the Wejh offensive to the *existence* of a united Arab force, rather than its operational effectiveness. For all the picturesque descriptions Lawrence could muster, he himself was forced to confess: 'Delay, confusion, hunger and thirst marred this expedition.'[56] Intercommunication between the tribes was hindered 'because no one could read or write'. The guides had no unit of measurement beyond a half day or increments that man could travel on a camel to certain landmarks, and even these were inaccurate. Lawrence could reflect that there was achievement in marching the whole of Feisal's force for 200 miles, but the ending, arriving in Wejh after the fighting and dying had been done by others, was a bitter experience.[57]

There were other successes to report. A notorious Turkish officer, Eshref Bey, who was closely aligned to the CUP, was captured in a supply column that had been ambushed by Abdullah's men at Wadi Ais near the settlement of Kheibar. Not only had the hasty attack yielded a great quantity of camels for transport, but also a haul of £20,000.[58] The march to Wejh had also attracted large numbers of Billi tribesmen, local sheikhs and some 'of the sweepings of the Wadi Yanbo', but also the allegiance of Sharif Nasir, the brother of the Emir of Medina and a respected Shia Muslim figure.

Nevertheless, there had been significant divisions amongst the Arabs as they had advanced on Wejh. Feisal narrowly averted a skirmish between Juheina fighters who wanted to seize local camels, the property of the local Billi.[59] When the Arab forces arrived in Wejh, they found a degree of destruction but they promptly sacked the town: 'they robbed the shops, broke open doors, searched every room, smashed chests and cupboards, tore down all fixed fittings, and slit every mattress and pillow for hidden treasure'.[60] The incensed townsfolk started stealing the stores that were landed for the Arab fighters and their British escorts, which led to Maulud, one of Feisal's lieutenants, being made a draconian governor. His summary punishments suppressed any further thefts.

Lawrence imbued this less-than-exemplary performance with a gloss it hardly deserved. He felt that Vickery's assault had been 'justified, in cold blood' as it gave the Arab movement control of Wejh, which, in turn, reduced the threat to Rabegh. Lawrence also claimed to have learned the first rules of Bedouin warfare.[61] The usual justification, made by Lawrence himself, was that the Ottomans were now forced to withdraw to protect the flank of their lines of communications from Medina. It appeared to be the 'strategic turning point of the Arab Revolt', particularly as it encouraged more men to join the rising.[62] Yet this appraisal deserves a more critical evaluation. In fact, at this point, the chief reason for Fakhri to consider consolidating his position at Medina was his supply problem, not the loss of a Red Sea port. The creation of the 5,000-strong Ottoman 2nd Composite Force at Tebuk, some 300 miles north of Medina, and the 1st Composite Force at Ma'an (initially 2,000 in number but which grew to 7,000) indicated that it was the railway which was considered the strategic priority in this theatre.[63] The taking of Wejh had made the Ottoman lines of communication more vulnerable, but they were held strongly.

RAILWAY RAIDS

Each week, raids on the Hejaz railway were conducted by British, French, Indian, Moroccan and Arab teams, and the Ottomans resorted to local clearance sweeps from their blockhouses, supported by lightweight artillery and machine guns. The attacks put a strain on Fakhri's ability to remain mobile in the Hejaz.

Amongst the more prominent of the raiders was Lieutenant (later Major) Herbert Garland of the Egyptian Army. He exuded a cavalier confidence in this form of warfare, and it was this state of mind that his 50 armed retainers appreciated. In one example, on 12 February 1917, he and his Arab comrades made a march of eight days by camel to within 120 miles of Medina. Expecting Ottoman trains to run only by day, to enhance their security, Garland's men found the rail line and started to lay charges in the darkness on a bridge just south of the station at Tuweira. Garland himself set additional charges some yards further south, to increase the chances of a successful detonation. It was at that point that the sound of an approaching train took them by surprise. The train paused briefly at the Tuweira station, so hopes were raised that there might be time to complete their preparations, but then it set off again, leaving barely minutes to lay a reduced explosive charge.[64] With the train just 200 yards away, Garland completed the fuse and dashed away, and the resulting explosion occurred almost instantaneously. The engine crashed off its embankment, and, with Ottoman troops disgorging from the station, the second charge was fired on the bridge, which isolated the wreck.[65]

Garland's missions, orchestrated by Colonel Newcombe, were part of a campaign known as Operation *Hedgehog*, and a number of British officers were involved. Lawrence described Garland in the following terms:

[he was] an enquirer in physics, and had years of practical experience of explosives ... he had his own devices for mining trains and felling telegraphs and cutting metals; and his knowledge of Arabic and freedom from the theories of the ordinary sapper school enabled him to reach the art of demolition to unlettered Beduin in a quick and ready way.[66]

Garland was eager to avoid the great risk that he and the raiding teams could be detected, and he designed a contact-detonator fashioned from the trigger mechanism of a Martini-Henry rifle. This new detonator saved precious time on the target and offered the opportunity to destroy trains as well as the rails. The device, known collectively as the Garland mine, was popular with the raiders. Their effectiveness was to act as a spur to Lawrence to emulate them in 1917.

The other source of friction for Fakhri was the effort made by Ali's men, particularly the Harb clans, who were also busy attacking the Ottoman lines of communications and who brought in a daily convoy of captured camels, rifles, deserters or prisoners.[67] The bulk of Ali's command actually consisted of 3,000 Arab infantry, of whom two thirds were regulars led by Aziz al-Masri; 900 men of the Camel Corps; 300 Egyptian troops; and 23 guns of various calibres. These forces were assisted by a flight of four British aircraft under Major A. J. Ross.[68] While Feisal's and Zeid's attempts to check the Ottoman advance on Rabegh had been routed at Safra and Hamra, and their interim position at Nekhl Mubarak had been abandoned, it was the presence of Ali and the air wing that deterred a final assault on Rabegh. Fakhri had chosen to bypass Yanbo and had continued to within just 30 miles of Rabegh. Here he would have faced Ali's forces and their British naval and air support, with an extended and vulnerable line of communication of 100 miles back to Medina.

Rather than Lawrence's move to another distant port changing his mind, Fakhri was reluctant to risk the main strength of his force when the other Arab force, under Abdullah, had deployed in an arc around Medina, aiming to cut off any supply routes across the desert from the north, east and south. With just 4,000 men, three machine guns and ten mountain guns, Abdullah lacked the forces needed to capture the city, even with a concerted envelopment in conjunction with Ali and Feisal, but Fakhri could not ignore these contingents.[69] The result was stalemate, but it was sufficient to convince Fakhri to reconsider his strategy. The priority for the Ottoman commander was to hold Medina, and, even if he couldn't come to grips with the Arab fighters, he could at least keep them pinned to the coast or at arm's length in the desert.

Meanwhile, the strategic priority for Murray was to ensure Fakhri was prevented from moving a significant proportion of his 12,000-strong Ottoman Army northwards against the British flank as the Egyptian Expeditionary Force (EEF) arrived on the edge of southern Palestine. Arab raids in the Hejaz, it was hoped, would prevent Ottoman redeployment.[70] Murray's systematic approach in the Sinai campaign had so far paid off. In December 1916, he had extended the railway and water pipeline as far as El Arish, accumulated his stores, constructed large canvas tanks filled with water pumped or carried by rail from Egypt, built up a vast herd of baggage camels (all duly treated for disease before being issued to their respective units), stockpiled his munitions, and deployed his acclimatized brigades. At Madgdhaba, an Ottoman garrison was surrounded and 1,300 were captured by the rapid movements of General Sir Harry Chauvel's Australian and New Zealand Mounted Division and their supporting artillery. Chauvel's men, and the Imperial Camel Corps, supported by British artillery, then captured Rafa on 9 January 1917. The taking of the settlement, again by envelopment, swept the coastal road of Ottoman forces and produced another batch of prisoners.

Confidence was therefore growing in the EEF. Advanced patrols were leaving the desert behind and entering cultivated grasslands, orchards and a landscape of villages and towns. The new British Prime Minister, David Lloyd George, was struck by the progress of the EEF, emerging, like some Biblical host, from the desert into the Promised Land. Eager to pour new energy into the war effort, and to inspire the British people, he began to entertain plans where the EEF would not just hold the approaches to Suez, but drive on to Jerusalem.

The first War Cabinet of 1917 discussed the possibility of despatching troops to Rabegh to support the Arab rebels in the Hejaz against an Ottoman counter-offensive to facilitate a Palestine campaign. The War Cabinet debated whether Murray could now despatch a brigade to assist, but the CIGS advised that such a force was too small to make a difference. Lord Curzon, the former Viceroy, and Sir Austin Chamberlain, the Secretary of State for India, insisted that the Arab cause, which was at a vulnerable early stage, must not be extinguished. Nonetheless, the Arab Revolt had yet to show much promise, and so the Cabinet turned back to more pressing concerns in Europe.[71]

Murray had reached the same verdict. If the move to Wejh was to have any lasting operational effect, particularly in convincing the Ottomans to terminate their offensive against Rabegh and Mecca to protect their railway, then they had to be persuaded that a potent threat existed. That meant that more serious raids would have to be conducted against the vulnerable Hejaz line. But from a strategic perspective, the raids were no more than harassment. Murray believed the Arab forces should use their combined strength to attack Fakhri's columns as they fell back on Medina, but although Feisal was willing, he was now too distant to conduct such an operation. Murray's concern was that the Arab railway raiders really did not threaten Ottoman control of Medina, and, while there might be a localized and temporary loss of control of parts of the railway, the Ottomans possessed sufficient force to retake and repair any section, often within a few hours.[72] They could remain in the Hejaz, continue to supply their detachments as far south as Yemen, and maintain contact with the armies in Palestine. More was needed.

The step change in insurgent effectiveness against the railways was the result of British officers leading the attacks, teaching the rudimentary business of making effective detonations, and selecting the most suitable men from amongst the Arab forces for these hazardous operations. According to the *Official History*, 'damage was now done with frequency and on a scale such as to interrupt seriously the Turkish communications'.[73] The most audacious raids targeted trains, bent long sections of track, and demolished bridges. At Al 'Ula, a strong raiding force, augmented by Egyptian and Indian troops and supported by aircraft, severed the Hejaz line for three days. This was the low-cost, high-impact warfare that Lawrence had recommended.[74]

Nevertheless, faced with more significant threats of his own in Sinai, Murray may not have appreciated the challenges still facing the Arab insurgents or their British and French embedded advisors. The difficulties of railway raiding were manifold. Assaulting groups had to travel considerable distances without support and without being detected by mobile Ottoman patrols. The limitations of water and rations meant there was precious little time for reconnaissance on the target, and charges against rails had to be laid at night to avoid being intercepted. Ottoman troops would patrol the tracks at dawn to look for signs of ground disturbance, so the explosives had to be dug in, camouflaged, and command wires concealed. In the time taken to put the charges in, a watchful guard was needed, and this required significant discipline. The size of the raiding force had to be limited to avoid detection, but this left it vulnerable if they were caught.

The Arab forces were in need of considerable volumes of arms, mules, supplies and money, the latter to compete with Ottoman inducements and to keep the fighters in the field.[75] There was extensive debate over the value of mountain artillery. Lawrence still maintained there was no use for pack guns in a mobile war, even in the hill country, because of their relative ineffectiveness. But the Arab forces found themselves outranged by Ottoman guns, usually by 3,000 yards, and they demanded the means to retaliate. It was for this reason that Lawrence later adopted field artillery, armoured cars and self-propelled Talbot guns.

At this moment, for Lawrence, there was little time to consider further the requirements and shortcomings of the ordnance, for his task now was to encourage more Hejaz Arabs to join the revolt, and to coordinate the movements of the three Arab armies against Medina. The first call was to Abdullah, and an appeal for him to completely block the line to the city. This was a grave request, for it was clear that the Ottomans would make serious efforts to clear their lines. Abdullah took the message 'coolly', but there was little opportunity to discuss the matter further, as Lawrence had succumbed to a fever and was incapacitated for ten days.[76]

In that period, Lawrence reconsidered the strategic situation. The enforced inactivity allowed Lawrence the chance to take stock, and to consider 'the equation between my book-reading and my movements'.[77] Looking back at his studies, he believed Clausewitz to be the intellectual superior, for his arguments were so logical as to be the most persuasive, but the deduction of that logic led inexorably to the simple 'attack' philosophy of Ferdinand Foch, whom he condemned.[78] These reflections Lawrence made after the war, since, at that time, Foch had yet to emerge as the generalissimo of the Allied armies in France. Lawrence was, in fact, rejecting the standard text about 'the destruction of the armed forces of the enemy – [through] battle', the classic Clausewitzian concept.[79] He cited another axiom, with some bitterness, that 'Victory could only be purchased by blood', believing the Arabs would not pay such a blood price. He turned therefore to Conrad von der Goltz, the German Field Marshal who had assisted the Ottomans in Mesopotamia, and his proposition that annihilation of the enemy was less likely than 'breaking his courage'.

Lawrence found himself criticizing the call for armies of mass which would wage war until the other side could no longer mount any resistance. To him, this required the virtual extermination of the enemy, a 'murder war', akin to the European wars of religion.[80] He hoped instead to find a way to drive the Ottomans out of Arabia without recourse to the full fury of blood-letting. Lawrence returned to the fundamental elements: strategy was the structure of war; tactics, its arrangements; the sentiment of the population was the business of psychology; and the purpose of the commander was to be the architect of the whole. But Lawrence rejected the ascending perspective, with a strategic aim at the top, and the descending elements of tactics, and the relative unimportance of the psychology and lives, at the base. He was formulating an entirely different approach: one that would better suit his desert war.

4

Seizing the 'Kingfisher Moment'
The Learning Curve of Resistance

In one profound paragraph, Lawrence captured the need for intense study and hard experience:

> Nine-tenths of tactics were certain enough to be teachable in schools; but the irrational tenth was like the kingfisher flashing across the pool, and in it lay the test of generals. It could be ensured only by instinct (sharpened by thought practising the stroke) until at the crisis it came naturally, a reflex.[1]

Lawrence developed a conception of warfare that emphasized, through both his studies of military history and practical experience in the desert fighting of the First World War, the pre-eminence of psychology in war. Intuition, practised by thinking through situations, applied not just to battlefield opportunism but to the handling of men in war. He argued that since war is fought in the minds of men, it should be given sufficient weight, in correspondence with material and logistical factors, in operational design. In fighting alongside local forces, Lawrence insisted this psychological aspect was critical. Combining technologically advanced units with local troops was a preference in modern Western tactics and operations in the early twenty-first century, but Lawrence's writings require careful interpretation since the context shaped his thinking profoundly.

As military historians know, it is morale, above all else, that most determines performance in combat.[2] As Ardant du Picq once remarked: 'Man is the fundamental instrument in battle ... Nothing can be prescribed ... without knowledge of the fundamental instrument, man, and his state of mind, his morale, at the instant of combat.'[3] Breaking the enemy's will to resist by inflicting casualties is the goal of the Clausewitzian conception of war, but it is extremely difficult to achieve. The degradation of will, and the general accumulated fears and anxieties, can, over time, create the same effect.[4] Material degradation can also have an impact on the willingness of combatants to sustain operations, although the relationship is far from mechanistic.

In modern war, the dispersal required to survive the effects of certain weapon systems and avoid surveillance, the devolved nature of command, and the consequent 'empty battlefield' have increased a sense of isolation and therefore significant stress for belligerents. Historical figures nevertheless promulgated a number of approaches to mitigate these effects, and, while advocates of modern and future war emphasize the decisive role of new technologies, we should not neglect the fundamental fact that war is about human resilience, morale and the desire to win. As Field Marshal Archibald Wavell once noted: 'The final deciding factor of all engagements, battles and wars is the morale of the opposing forces. Better weapons, better food, and superiority in numbers will influence morale, but it is the sheer determination to win, by whomever or whatever inspired, that counts in the end.'[5]

Lawrence emphasized the mental aspects of warfare, using the physical landscape to his advantage, and built that into a psychological equivalent. Above all, he sought to preserve the lives of his Arab fighters, knowing that if they were to suffer significant losses, their confidence would desert them and the entire revolt could fail. His objective was to incrementally increase the sureness of the insurgents, while simultaneously eroding the enemy's.

Lawrence was not constrained by the training of a professional soldier, and enjoyed more intellectual freedom as a scholar. He was, in his own words, 'as much in command of the campaign as I pleased'.[6] His reservoir of knowledge was historical, but through this, and his subsequent practical experience, he developed a peculiar understanding of how to emphasize the psychological factor in war. Of this revelation, he later wrote: 'Napoleon, in his pregnant valuation of the Mamelukes in terms of French soldiers, first gave me the idea: Ardant du Picq widened its application.'[7] Du Picq had stressed the importance of overcoming fear in battle and managing the emotions of the troops, and he had also cited Napoleon: 'Two Mamelukes held three Frenchmen; but one hundred cavalry did not fear the same number of Mamelukes; three hundred vanquished the same number; one thousand French beat fifteen hundred Mamelukes: such was the influence of tactics, order and manoeuvre.'[8] In other words, discipline, cohesion and morale were a winning combination.

Lawrence recognized that the traditional military emphasis was on concentrating maximum force against the strongest element of the enemy, to bring about a decisive battle and complete operations in the shortest time, in order to avoid exhaustion of limited resources. He stood this idea on its head. He minimized the 'algebraic' aspects of physical force, numbers and equipment, in favour of pressure on the 'bionomic' necessities (food, water, rest) of the enemy and greater stress on the 'diathetic' or 'hecastic' elements, that is, the cognitive and psychological.

The conventional approach to war was primarily about the 'algebra' of materiel and mass:

> The algebraical element looked to me a pure science, subject to mathematical law, inhuman. It dealt with known variables, fixed conditions, space and time, inorganic things like hills and climates and railways, with mankind in typemasses too great for individual variety, with all artificial aids and the extensions given our faculties by mechanical invention. It was essentially formulable.[9]

Space and time were part of this calculus, as Lawrence intended to make his Arab partners elusive by using the depth of the desert, and, ultimately, to make the Ottoman soldier afraid of his environment. The alienating experience of the desert created a deterrent for the Ottoman *Mehmetciks* in their own territory.

At Wadi Ais, Lawrence had time to ponder his understanding of war. Rejecting his 'pompous, professorial beginning', he 'took refuge in Arabia['s context]'.[10] He was struggling to articulate his ideas, reflecting, in his complex syntax, the agonies of trying to find a solution:

> [The] crisis [of war] seemed to be the breaking point, life and death, or less finally, wear and tear. The war-philosophers had properly made an art of it, and had elevated one item, 'effusion of blood', to the height of an essential, which became humanity in battle, an act touching every side of our corporal being, and very warm.[11]

Rejecting the emphasis on blood-letting, he sought the alternative in the human spirit or willpower. His conclusion was that the most variable and incalculable element of war was the human, who, subjected to all the pressures of combat, forced a commander to create a reserve. This force could be thrown in to an attack at the critical moment or shore up a wavering force with reinforcements. For Lawrence, observing the growing enthusiasm of the Arab forces, and where professional soldiers might struggle under the desert conditions of Arabia, there was an opportunity in this human frailty. He wrote:

> I was getting through my subject. The algebraical factor had been translated into terms of Arabia, and fitted like a glove. It promised victory. The biological factor had dictated to us a development of the tactical line most in accord with the genius of our tribesmen. There remained the psychological element to build up into an apt shape. I went to Xenophon and stole, to name it, his word diathetics, which had been the art of Cyrus before he struck.[12]

Lawrence articulated the traditional importance of morale, even where it was affected by new technologies such as aircraft and modern artillery. Despite all of Lawrence's setbacks, he did not lose sight of this critical and intensely human element.

Lawrence believed war was not entirely a random and chaotic activity, for there were systems, or principles, which could be applied. He admitted the importance of a grounding in military theory when he was so inexperienced and had not the 'intuition' of veteran officers.[13] While making use of a great variety of classical, medieval and modern texts on war, Lawrence believed there were common linear 'steps' and a necessary sequential approach to strategy and operations. He wrote:

> Of course, I had read the usual books (too many books), Clausewitz and Jomini, Mahan and Foch, had played at Napoleon's campaigns, worked at Hannibal's tactics, and the wars of Belisarius, like any other man at Oxford; but I had never thought myself into the mind of a real commander compelled to fight a campaign of his own.[14]

He told the British strategic theorist Basil Liddell Hart:

> [I] read some French study of Napoleon's Italian Campaign, and then browsed the despatches, a series of about 25 volumes. These interested me in his text-books, and so they got me to [Pierre Joseph] Bourcet, Guibert and Saxe, in that order. Then I read the manual of arms of the 18th century.[15]

But this study was not a passive absorption of narratives and archives: it was active. He recreated the stages of a campaign, spatially and sequentially, to better understand them:

> I made a series of maps of, and visited, Rocroi, Crecy, Agincourt, Malplaquet, Sedan and other Franco-German war places whose names I forget. But my interests were mainly mediaeval, and in pursuit of them I ... went elaborately into siege-manoeuvres ... [Yet] I also tried to get an idea of the bigger movements, and saw Valmy and its neighbourhood, and tried to refight the whole of Marlborough's wars.[16]

This was intelligent analysis of events and a genuine desire to grasp how military leaders had come to their decisions.[17] His method, 'to refight', by considering the calculations of historical figures, represented a deep study of men's thinking and behaviour, the hard 'brain-work', which he articulated to Basil Liddell Hart after the war.

He argued that one 'could follow the direction of Saxe and reach victory without battle, by pressing our advantages mathematical and psychological'.[18] The reference is interesting given the emphasis he was to place on manoeuvre, that is, the mobility of the Arabs and his 'war of detachment', which would avoid having to confront the main strength of his enemies. Saxe had suggested that multiple small engagements would eventually dissipate an enemy's strength.[19] In Lawrence's day, eighteenth-century warfare was less popular than the nineteenth-century Napoleonic style, which combined manoeuvre with decisive effect. It was widely held that a slow war of attrition or exhaustion was simply undesirable for advanced nations, as the costs on the economy or the people would be too great. The orthodoxy was to seek a decisive conflict.

Rather simplistically, this form of decisive, 'annihilationist' warfare was attributed to nineteenth-century thinkers like Clausewitz and Jomini, but the dichotomy of attritional or annihilationist warfare was actually a false one. Clausewitz condemned those who tried to suggest that war could be mechanistic and devoid of passion or that one could ignore the state of morale.[20] He had written:

> it would be an obvious fallacy to imagine war between civilised peoples as resulting merely from a rational act on the part of their governments and to conceive of war as gradually ridding itself of passion, ... [as if] comparative figures of their strength would be enough. That would be a kind of war by algebra.[21]

For all his criticism, Lawrence was closer to Clausewitz than he would care to admit.

In his references to his Oxford years, Lawrence acknowledged that he read 'Napoleon, Clausewitz, Rudolf von Caemmerer,[22] Moltke [the elder],[23] Conrad von der Goltz', and, as Lawrence put it, 'the recent Frenchmen ... [including du] Picq'.[24]

The 'recent Frenchmen' was a reference to the 'rediscovery' of Napoleonic ideas which led to an outpouring of writings that became available in English in the early 1900s.[25] The French officer corps espoused ideas that privileged a dedicated professional force, not a citizen army. But industrialization necessitated mass armies and the incorporation of reluctant *citoyens* into the ranks. Their views therefore coincided with a desire, popular amongst intellectuals, for a revivification of French culture and spirit. The growing scale and modernization of the German Army made it imperative that the solution to this threat was both ideological and material.[26]

For a scholar of war such as Lawrence, the upsurge in French literature was clearly instructive. In the pre-war years France adopted a similar model for its army as the German one, with higher formations of divisions and corps, a staff corps system, and a new arrangement of professional military education, including the *école supérieure de guerre*. Alongside the outpouring of books advocating more manpower through conscription, and national mobilization, came works on strategy. General Jules-Lewis Lewal, chief of the historical-statistical bureau, argued that war consisted of two parts: on the one hand it was concerned with speculation, or chance events, and the morale of the forces; on the other it was a product of reasoned principles.[27] General Victor Derrécagaix, deputy of the French war school, offered similar interpretations, and, like other officers, he and Lewal began to emphasize the need for *la volonté* (willpower).

Throughout the late nineteenth century, the French Army had tended to explain German military victory against them as the result of superior organization, guided by the institution of the Prussian staff. They saw von Moltke as the engineer of this scientific, bureaucratic, machine. Nevertheless, a new generation of officers, the 'recent Frenchmen', saw German success through their use of Napoleonic ideas, such as the search for a decisive battle and pursuit, or the need to mobilize society, the economy and the political system to wage war.[28] The solution, the French officers believed, was to rediscover Napoleonic techniques and generate a new intensity in war, with a much more aggressive and offensive strategic posture. At the same time, Lawrence would have read of the French disdain for the German, especially Clausewitzian interpretation of Napoleonic warfare, which, it was argued, was too simplistic. Clausewitz, they maintained, had reduced Napoleon to direct, focussed strikes, with manoeuvre subordinated to bringing the enemy to battle.[29]

After the war, Lawrence would make critical references to Foch, who had emerged in 1918 as the commander of the Allied armies on the Western Front. Foch had taught at the French war school and published *Des principles de la guerre* in 1903, which was an amalgam of the work of his contemporaries. What Lawrence objected to was the scale, and apparently simplistic approach to war, he claimed Foch represented. To those who advocated the idea that firepower would favour the defence, Foch and his colleagues at the *école de guerre* maintained that rapid-firing weapons would favour the attack: they could 'shoot in' their own forces with covering fire. They claimed that the conviction to close with the enemy would be the decisive factor.[30] Basil Liddell Hart, who wrote a biography of Foch, believed his quality was in his convictions, his energy and his persuasiveness.[31] Like Lawrence, Foch had argued, before the war, that a loss of willpower would result in a physical disaster, so this moral element was, by far, the most important.

Even before the war, the ideas of the *école* were being challenged by some senior French officers in light of the conflicts in South Africa and Manchuria.[32] General François de Négrier, for example, noted that the German reaction to this development was to plan to extend the frontages of their army, to be more dispersed and to seek to extend the flanks of the fighting. Others argued that seeking the tactical defence while maintaining a strategic offence was the best solution.[33] The authors of the *école de guerre* responded that heavier guns might be needed to overcome enemy defences, but that inflicting a severe blow on the adversary was essential. The staff of the school had maintained that the offensive spirit had to be upheld and they argued that critics like Négrier were in danger of demoralizing the junior officer corps. It was for this reason that Ardant du Picq's ideas of the 1860s on the morale of the troops were cited so prominently. The deeper anxiety was that any emphasis on defensiveness, through entrenchments or an over-reliance on firepower, would result either in an eighteenth-century staid, sterile approach to strategy, or a reluctance to engage the enemy decisively, leading to a repeat of the defeat of 1870–71.[34]

Lawrence, like many military scholars of the period, also found du Picq appealing because he did not espouse a purely offensive, or defensive, or even defensive-offensive (counter-attack) philosophy: he concentrated solely on the willingness or reluctance of men, in the extreme crisis of close combat, to fight, to endure, to go forward or retreat. Some French officers were concluding that infantrymen would have to make use of ground for cover, make night attacks, adopt an extended formation, or depend on artillery for support, but all could agree that unless the soldier was willing to risk himself, no elaborate operations could be contemplated. Regardless how one might make the approach, Picq and his followers had come to the conclusion that, in the final moments of proximity to the enemy, the 'close quarter battle', the strong impulse to attack, resolutely, mattered most.[35]

Away from the contemporary debates, Lawrence said that he preferred more ancient and medieval subjects such as 'Hannibal, Belisarius, Mohammed and the Crusades'. He confessed that, at that stage, 'My interests were only in pure theory and I looked everywhere for the metaphysical side, the philosophy of war, about which I thought a little for some years.' He was interested in individual soldiers, and 'single combats', which would suggest it was the individual psychology of war which captured his imagination.[36]

The reference to 'metaphysical' in the context of war was a contemporary concern. From the 1890s and especially in the 1910s, intellectuals and military scholars were attracted to critiques of human science and the new discipline of psychology. In France, the leading light was Henri Bergson, an advocate of *élan vital*, a dynamic and creative force in evolution, while his contemporary Georges Sorel argued that violence had a particularly powerful role to play in making history.[37] Lawrence became aware of ideas of willpower, courageous individual agency, and the transformative effect of violence through his historical studies but also through his extensive reading of Thomas Hardy, D. H. Lawrence, Thomas Carlyle, Samuel Taylor Coleridge, Lord Byron and William Blake. He acknowledged this in his correspondence and publications.

The battlefield was, however, Lawrence's most important teacher. He admitted that 'the practice of war which followed on my book study seemed to clarify my sight, and I thought I could see war whole'.[38] But it had not been a straightforward tutorial. When the Ottomans had begun their offensive from Medina to recapture Mecca, they had had to approach a line of hills some 50 miles from their start point, and beyond this for a stretch of 70 miles was a coastal plain that ran towards Rabegh. Lawrence described the defensive plan:

> Our military advisers had told us that Rabegh was the key of Mecca…
> Its defence was therefore of the main importance… They thought that
> Bedouin tribesmen would never be of any value in a fixed position,
> and that therefore an Arab regular force must be formed and trained
> as soon as possible to undertake this duty.[39]

Lawrence believed irregular fighters positioned in the hills and provided with plenty of cover would be impossible to dislodge:

> A personal reconnaissance of the Arab positions, here and in the hills where Feisal was, caused me to modify the views of the experts a little. Feisal had some thousands of men, all armed with rifles, rather casual, distrustful fellows, but very active and cheerful. They were posted in hills and defiles of such natural strength that it seemed to me very improbable that the Turks could force them, just by their superior numbers... Accordingly, I reported that the tribesmen (if strengthened by light machine guns, and regular officers as advisors) should be able to hold up the Turks indefinitely, while the Arab regular force was being created. As was almost inevitable in view of the general course of military thinking since Napoleon, we all looked only to the regulars to win the war.[40]

Lawrence then admitted, in light of events, that only appreciating the numbers of men and their apparent strength, he had come to the wrong judgement:

> The Turks suddenly put my appreciation to the test by beginning their advance on Mecca. They broke through my impregnable hills in 24 hours, and came forward from them towards Rabegh slowly. So they proved to us the second theorem of irregular war – namely, that irregular troops are as unable to defend a point or line as they are to attack it.[41]

Lawrence made his deductions from this incident which were to change his entire view of the conflict in the region: 'In the emergency it occurred to me that perhaps the virtue of irregulars lay in depth, not in face, and that it had been the threat of attack by them upon the Turkish northern flank which had made the enemy hesitate for so long.'[42]

The physical landscape had, therefore, at this point been a factor that Lawrence had over-estimated, but he had not lost sight of the relative value of distance, depth, and the proximity of support from the sea. As noted earlier, Lawrence had advised that the Arab irregulars move the base of their operations to Wejh and he believed this manoeuvre forced the Ottomans to pull back all the way to Medina lest their flank was threatened.[43] The 'threat' of Arab irregular attack was to be used to create an ever-extending flank against the Ottomans, but it was psychological rather than physical. Lawrence reasoned that if the Turkish commanders felt that their lines of communication, which ran from Medina to Syria, were under threat, they would be compelled to post larger and larger numbers of men to protect them. If the Arabs could remain concealed, and strike at points along these lines, then he believed he could fix the Ottomans and absorb their greater mass in inert defence. Ultimately, Lawrence wanted to exploit the elusive nature of the guerrilla, concealed in the depth of the desert, making periodic raids. They could only be tracked down by painstaking intelligence, and that made counter-insurgency 'messy and slow, like eating soup with a knife'.[44]

In his initial meeting with Feisal, Lawrence admitted he had been unable to convince the Emir to adopt guerrilla tactics. Feisal wanted to lead large-scale formations, ostensibly because they would attract more supporters and increase cohesion. Lawrence knew such groupings would be no match for the Ottomans.[45] Lawrence therefore reversed the dictum that victory depended on 'the destruction of the organised forces of the enemy'. He disparaged the arguments of the conventional war theorists.[46] He wrote:

> and as I thought about it, it dawned on me that we had won the Hejaz war. We were in occupation of 99% of the Hejaz… This part of the war was over, so why bother about Medina? … The Turks sat in it on the defensive, immobile, eating mules, the transport animals which were to have moved them to Mecca, but for which there were no pastures in their now restricted lines.[47]

Lawrence tended to minimize the significance and agency of his enemy. There was a strong, sometimes vitriolic criticism of the Ottomans which did not offer much appreciation of their decisions, except as bad ones. Lawrence argued that the guerrilla strategy had compelled the Ottomans to stay on the defensive in the Hejaz, without mentioning the fact that authorities in Istanbul regarded the region as a low priority. The Arabs did not constitute a serious threat, compared with the presence of large British Imperial regular forces. Fundamentally, the greater threat for the Ottomans lay in the form of the EEF that pushed across Sinai to Gaza.

Moreover, the Ottomans did not retain a garrison in Medina without purpose. The very existence of the Ottoman garrison there was sufficient to deter any further movement the British might consider into Palestine and it could act against a British thrust from their foothold at Aden. Equally, the British forces in Mesopotamia were of greater concern than the Hashemite uprising. The Ottomans maintained their Sixth Army on the Tigris to prevent any further British advances towards Baghdad, and they detached elements of this force to assert control in Persia.[48]

Lawrence's observations on the psychological effect of guerrilla operations are far more reliable. Lawrence claimed that the unfavourable military situation he had observed compelled him to reconsider the relative importance of material and psychological factors. He wrote: 'In each [tactics and strategy] I found the same elements, one algebraic, one biological, a third psychological. The first seemed a pure science, subject to the laws of mathematics, without humanity.'[49] From the algebraic perspective, Lawrence calculated that the Ottomans could not defend the 140,000 square miles of Arabia, particularly if the Arab forces were: 'a thing invulnerable, intangible, without front or back, drifting about like a gas'. He surmised this about armies:

[They are] like plants, immobile as a whole, firm rooted, nourished through long stems to the head. We [the Arab forces] might be a vapour, blowing where we listed. Our kingdoms lay in each man's mind, and as we wanted nothing material to live on, so perhaps we offered nothing material to the killing.[50]

Lawrence was saying, in effect, that as long as a population was compliant and a revolutionary force was free to manoeuvre and remain concealed, appearing as ephemeral as a vapour, it could retain the initiative.[51] The ability to strike at any point would act constantly on the mind of the enemy, but would not trouble the insurgent, who could choose the time and place of his brief exposure to risk.

This risk element was important. Lawrence believed the Arabs 'would not endure casualties'.[52] To him, the loss of an individual not only left a hole in the thin ranks of his guerrilla force, but it also extended 'rings of sorrow' through the population.[53] While they were prepared to fight for territory, he felt they were also fighting for freedom, 'a pleasure only to be tasted by a man alive'.[54] He was therefore critical of the notion of 'absolute war', advocated by Clausewitz or Foch, and argued that there were other forms, dynastic, expulsive and commercial, which achieved the goal of winning without necessarily a great deal of fighting, in the manner of de Saxe, 'to reach victory without battle, by pressing our advantages mathematical and psychological'.[55]

The 'ways' of minimizing casualties, while still achieving the psychological effect, were to remain concealed until the moment of attack, which itself would be 'directed not against men, but against his materials'.[56] This became the 'unconscious habit of never engaging the enemy at all' and thus not giving the Ottoman troops any targets. The prerequisite was excellent intelligence, and judgement – whether to make a strike, or wait until better opportunities arose.[57] In the guerrilla phase of his campaign, in 1917 and early 1918, this was largely true, although he was engaged in some minor actions, and then, in late 1918, his Arab partners were involved in much more sustained conventional fighting.

Lawrence had argued, against the caricatured Clausewitzian notion that destruction of the enemy was the primary purpose, that winning over the minds of the belligerents and the neutrals was 'more than half the battle', and that while guerrillas had 'many humiliating material limits', they had no 'moral impossibilities'.[58] Twentieth-century scholars of guerrilla warfare noted that the goal of the early to mid-term stages of any campaign is to generate a sense of insecurity, which convinces the population that the government is unable to protect it.[59] Lawrence may have already derived this from his reading of military history. Clausewitz himself had urged Prussian popular insurrection against Napoleon's occupation and had noted that attacks on lines of communication, raids on supply depots and even attacks on isolated detachments, by Spanish guerrillas, had been effective.[60] Despite Lawrence's criticism, Clausewitz had acknowledged that there were 'many ways to the aim and not every case is tied to the overthrow of the opponent', and he included the acquisition of new allies or changes in political events as offering a 'much shorter way to the aim than the destruction of the hostile armed forces'.[61] For Clausewitz, intellectual and psychological factors were critical, including the spirit of the troops and the mental capacity of the commander: these views were, in fact, close to Lawrence's own.[62]

The second element, closely related to the influence of psychology, was biological, or 'bionomics' as Lawrence called it.[63] Soldiers must eat, rest and drink, and for Lawrence the Ottomans' materiel was scarce and precious: consequently, his objective was to destroy not the army, but its material support. This included railway lines and bridges, supplies, sources of water, or their weapons to inflict 'wear and tear' on the enemy. The biological needs of an army, when affected, could reinforce the psychological effects, which Lawrence believed took precedence. He noted that generals kept a reserve because, for all their algebraic power, armies consisted of humans, and that the '"felt" element in troops', which could not be expressed in figures, compelled a general to remain alert to the fleeting, 'kingfisher', opportunities and threats posed by the irrational behaviour of men in war.[64]

In guerrilla warfare, remaining elusive was essential. Where, in conventional war, Lawrence noted, 'both forces [are] striving to keep in touch to avoid tactical surprise', by contrast, he noted, 'our war [was] a war of detachment: we were to contain the enemy by the silent threats of a vast unknown desert, not disclosing ourselves to the moment of attack'.[65] He wanted the Ottoman soldiers to fear not only the Arab raiders but also the desert itself. By deterring them from entering the desert, he would ensure mobility for the Arab forces. The Ottoman soldier had to endure the heat, hunger and oppressive silence of the wastes before him, peering endlessly into the shimmering haze or blank night, remaining constantly vigilant, and aware of the ever-present possibility of attack.

Lawrence aimed to reinforce constantly this psychological element, believing the mental preparation of his fighters was vital. Lawrence asserted:

> we had to arrange their minds in order of battle, just as carefully and as formally as other officers arrange their bodies; and not only our own men's minds, though them first; the minds of the enemy, so far as we could reach them; and thirdly, the mind of the nation supporting us behind the firing line, and the mind of a hostile nation waiting the verdict, and the neutrals looking on.[66]

Preparing the mind of 'the crowd' was solely to get it to the point 'where it becomes fit for action', and spoke of the cultivation of 'what in them profits the intention', that is, in other words, exploiting the latent beliefs that already existed.[67]

But action also had a part to play. As the campaign evolved, so the balance between risk and the need for tangible and material success increased. Lawrence wrote that General Allenby, Murray's successor as commander in Egypt and Palestine, had ordered the Arabs to move against Deraa, but there were insufficient forces available in time to meet his deadline:

> His words to me were that three men and a boy with pistols in front of Deraa on September the sixteenth would fill his conception; would they better than thousands a week before or a week after. The truth was, he cared nothing for our fighting power, and did not reckon us part of his tactical strength. Our purpose, to him, was moral, psychological, diathetic; to keep the enemy command intent upon the Trans-Jordan front.

Lawrence accepted this challenge on two grounds: 'In my English capacity I shared this view, but on my Arab side both agitation and battle seemed equally important, the one to serve the joint success, the other to establish Arab self-respect, without which victory would not be wholesome.'[68] Psychological confidence and action were cyclical and self-reinforcing.

The motivation of the Arab forces occupied much of Lawrence's time as an advisor. He concluded, somewhat romantically:

> We were a self-centred army without parade or gesture, devoted to freedom, the second of man's creeds, a purpose so ravenous that it devoured all our strength, a hope so transcendent that our earlier ambitions faded in its glare. As time went by our need to fight for the ideal increased to an unquestioning possession, riding with spur and rein over our doubts.[69]

Lawrence could not avoid entirely the desire of the guerrillas to fight their enemies, even though he emphasized 'detachment' and concealment.

In a more prosaic account for his superiors, he noted the fighters lacked discipline but they operated best in small groups of three or four men where, 'in their own valleys or hills [they] would account for a dozen Turkish soldiers'. Inactivity would produce desertions, so keeping them active, 'tapping the Turks here and there', was the means to ensure cohesion and sustain the effect. Hit-and-run fighting, with fighters disappearing off into the landscape, suited the temperament of the fighters and had the added bonus of causing 'the enemy not only anxiety, but bewilderment'.[70]

Lawrence attributed the growth of Arab resistance to the unforeseen consequences of Turkish idealism and prejudices, which had stirred a sense of consciousness amongst Arabs. Yet Lawrence regarded Arab nationalism as distinct. It did not manifest itself in institutions, but in small, parish-scale sentiment. There was little sympathy amongst the Bedouin for the intellectual versions that prevailed in Syria. In his secret despatch of 26 November 1916, Lawrence was told by his men that, if Djemal Pasha had not killed all the Syrian nationalists, then it 'would have been our duty as Arabs to do the work', since they were seen as too close to Western notions of the nation state.[71] Lawrence concluded that educating the population to support the cause, being 'taught to die for the cause of freedom', was sufficient for success, for that provided the base for any fighting forces.[72]

Since the Arab fighters were all volunteers any of them could return home whenever they felt so inclined. Lawrence noted: 'Our only contract was honour.'[73] Consequently, 'we had no discipline, in the sense in which it is restrictive, submergence of individuality, the lowest common denominator of men'. Lawrence believed: 'The deeper the discipline, the lower the individual efficiency, and the more sure the performance. It is a deliberate sacrifice of capacity in order to reduce the uncertain element, the bionomic factor, in enlisted humanity.' But Lawrence's critique of discipline reflected more his personal preferences for freedom of action. He made no mention of the value of unison, synchronization, or the ability to withstand the pressures of war. Aside from a system of penalties, discipline was instilled primarily through training, a vital component for war.[74] And in disciplined armies there was always still room for individual creativity and exhibitions of courage. In stressing the simplicity and individuality of Arab fighters and making claim that 'the efficiency of each man was his personal efficiency', Lawrence elided over the shortcomings of irregular fighters.

This was especially true when it came to their material motivation. When attacking Ottoman posts, trains and settlements, including Damascus, there was a great deal of looting and sacking. In one raid, Major Young concluded, 'the Beduin irregulars who had attached themselves to the [regular] force were quite useless, reserving themselves for a dash into the post when all resistance was over, and a first dip into whatever lucky-bag might be found there'.[75] Money was much more important than Lawrence was prepared to admit in much of his published works. While confessing that there was a considerable waste, the gold expended on the Arab cause has been estimated at £4.5 million.[76]

The Arab factions were also divided by feuds and jealousies at times, despite Lawrence's emphasis on the unity of the cause, but he did his best to make a virtue of the issue to maintain effect, once again evoking the use of the landscape. He wrote:

> The distribution of the raiding parties was unorthodox. It was impossible to mix or combine tribes, since they disliked or distrusted one another. Likewise, we could not use the men of one tribe in the territory of another. In consequence, we aimed at the widest distribution of forces, in order to have the greatest number of raids on hand at once, and we added fluidity to their ordinary speed, by using one district on Monday, another on Tuesday, a third on Wednesday.[77]

Lawrence listed the advantages of the arrangement: 'This much reinforced their natural mobility. It gave us priceless advantages in pursuit, for the force renewed itself with fresh men in every new tribal area, and gave us always our pristine energy. Maximum disorder was in a real sense our equilibrium.'[78]

The Arabs had considerable agency in this conflict. Lawrence did not acknowledge that the local leadership was using him for their own ends. Sharif Hussein sought dynastic security and perhaps an opportunity to replace the Ottoman secularists in Istanbul. Hussein knew he lacked the means to fulfil his aim unless he could get the British to assist him.[79] Material factors were therefore crucial to the sustainment of the diathetic elements here too.

For the fighters, there were other calculations. Auda abu Tayi, one of the leading irregular leaders of the Howeitat, was opportunistic and wavered in what he perceived as the advantages of the conflict, material or otherwise. There was also the question of belief: Lawrence claimed that religion was not the primary factor in the fighters' motivations, in part because the Ottomans were fellow Muslims.[80] Nevertheless, he acknowledged that, for some tribes adjacent to the domains of

Ibn Saud, the creed of Wahabism was popular. The Hejazis were more circumspect, citing the Wahabis' obsession with the 'savagery of the sharia code'.[81] Lawrence regarded the designs of the ulema, Islamic religious leaders, as 'extreme fanaticism' and 'dogmatic abstraction' without humanity that fostered division amongst Arabs. Yet it was a diathetic element he could not ignore.

Lawrence did not discount entirely the role that 'algebraic' factors could play. He knew that physically demonstrating mass could create a psychological effect, overcoming some of the social divisions that plagued the Arab revolutionary cause. He wrote:

> Feisal suggested taking nearly all the Juheina [clan] to Wejh with him and adding to them enough of the Harb and Billi, Ateiba and Ageyl to give the mass a many-tribed character. We wanted this march, which would be in its way a closing act of the war in Northern Hejaz, to send a rumour through the length and breadth of Western Arabia. It was to be the biggest operation of the Arabs in their memory; dismissing those who saw it to their homes, with a sense that their world had changed indeed; so that there would be no more silly defections and jealousies of clans behind us in future, to cripple us with family politics in the middle of our fighting.[82]

More effect was achieved by raids on the Hejaz railway in 1917 than the displays of strength, not least because, all too often, the formed bodies of Arab revolutionaries were dispersed by the Ottomans. For disruption missions, the Arabs had far greater utility as they could penetrate deep into the desert with relatively little support.

Lawrence tended to downplay the importance of conventional British naval and air power which had enabled the success of the Arab insurgents. He did so for well-known political reasons: his objective was to try to show that the Arabs were capable of operating without Western support and this autonomy reinforced the claim to independence. This indicates that subsequent attempts to follow Lawrence's maxims to the letter may be erroneous: it certainly calls into question Lawrence's judgements about the impunity of the guerrilla. In the end it was the regular army, the EEF, that provided the psychological breakthrough in the autumn of 1918, without which the Arab cause would have almost certainly faltered.

Despite the attention focussed on these episodes of fighting, Lawrence later argued that his approach was not really 'war' in its classic sense, and perhaps a more purely 'revolutionary' rather than military method might have yielded greater results:

The Arabs nearly made shipwreck through this blindness of European advisers, who would not see that rebellion was not war: indeed, was more of the nature of peace – a national strike perhaps. The conjunction of Semites, an idea, and an armed prophet held illimitable possibilities; in skilled hands it would have been, not Damascus, but Constantinople which was reached in 1918.[83]

The war of detachment, the mobilization of peoples, and the emphasis on setting an example as the means to educate a population were all seized upon by subsequent revolutionary war theorists and some practitioners. One of the problems with this view is that many more civilians were hostile to the Sharifian cause than Lawrence would admit. Major Hubert Young, who provisioned the Arab regulars, related how locals had 'turned against us', particularly when raids angered the Ottoman soldiers and they threatened reprisals.[84] The majority wanted to protect family, land and property, and a proportion sided with the authorities against the Bedouin fighters.

Lawrence's fundamentals of guerrilla warfare have been copied, emulated and adapted ever since, with varying degrees of success. Interestingly, Lawrence's 'revolutionary' conception was applicable to a successful contemporary example of revolutionary strategy, namely that of the Irish insurgents in 1919–21.[85] In southern Ireland, it was the passive withdrawal of cooperation with the British authorities, rather than the campaign of violence, which did more to produce an independent state. Lawrence was right in his assessment that action by the people (in this case, Irishmen refusing to pay tax, obey British laws, or work for British companies) was a better guarantee of success. In contrast, the revolutionary campaign of violence by paramilitaries was inconclusive, such that even Michael Collins, its most successful leader, admitted it was a costly failure: the truce of 1921 was agreed at the moment the Irish revolutionaries were under the greatest pressure.[86] Reflecting a popular unease about the use of heavy-handed tactics against the Irish population, Lawrence referred to the unrest in Ireland in a letter to Colonel Newcombe, concluding 'you cannot make war upon rebellion'.[87] Revolution is not war, although revolutions can initiate wars, and Lawrence was most interested in the revolutionary political element of resistance.[88] He was critical of the professional soldiers who failed to recognize the importance of civilian leadership and political objectives, and he believed they waged war for its own sake.

Robert Asprey, a scholar of irregular operations, believed that Lawrence had been engaged in a 'separate war', which was a 'carefully defined insurrection'.[89] Another commentator on guerrilla warfare, C. A. Johnson, argued that 'he thought of only a third of war as a military, or technical problem'. Johnson identified the consequences: 'Because two-thirds of guerrilla warfare has been ignored or misinterpreted by many recent commentators, a major confusion has entered into much thinking about guerrilla struggles.'[90] To some extent, this confusion has arisen through disagreements on the relative importance of violence in achieving political objectives. But it is also perhaps as a result of Lawrence holding two similar roles: that of political advisor to the Arab leadership while, at the same time, fighting as an active participant in guerrilla operations.

THE LANDSCAPE OF THE MIND

Lawrence was acquiring experience in guiding the guerrilla campaign, and while some of his ideas were developed after the war, he had identified many of the fundamentals.[91] He knew that the Arab fighters must avoid heavy casualties, and that meant offering no target to his enemy. The aim was to reach as many Arabs as possible, to distribute the idea of the revolution, and to use raids to both encourage resistance and to seize the initiative from the Ottomans. Depth was thus both security and the means to educate the population about the cause. Lawrence recognized that raiding not only created enthusiasm, but it also hit the most vulnerable part of the Sultan's army. Progressively attacking the lines of communication could interrupt the provisions of the Ottoman troops, and, at the same time, kept them on wearying sentry duty.

Crucially, Lawrence realized that the fighters could be quickly discouraged and so enlisting the moral support of the civilian population was vital. Physical support might be provided in terms of food and manpower, but the passive alignment of the population could ensure operational security. The great vulnerability of guerrillas is the risk of betrayal, and the Ottomans could command the loyalty of certain communities, especially the settled populations who feared or despised the Bedouin of southern and central Arabia.[92]

Lawrence had advocated the importance of psychology in war, but also its limits. His admission was that the priority was to enhance the confidence and cohesion of his own Arab comrades, to 'arrange their minds'. Having any influence on the minds of the enemy depended on whether 'we could reach them', which was more difficult.[93] Both practitioners and scholars have noted the critical importance of psychological operations. Clausewitz opened On War with a description of the unnerving approach to the field of battle, Ardant du Picq sought to convey the depth of its effects, and Napoleon believed it was simply three times more importance than mass. In his famous injunction at Arcola to his wavering soldiers, Napoleon exclaimed they should not be afraid, but 'recognise that old demon Fear', and 'drive him into the enemy's ranks'.[94] Inducing fear and confusion are central components of war. They are utterly essential when the odds are asymmetrical. In inducing anxiety, Lawrence understood that one did not need a physical presence, as long as one could play on the enemy's worst imagination.

The Ottomans were no strangers to their own form of psychological operations. Reprisals against villages or nomadic camps, in the vicinity of past Arab raids, were designed to deter resistance by social pressure from survivors or relatives, but also to induce fear of its repetition. The passage of information about a single incident could also magnify the effects of terror on the minds of the population.[95] Lawrence saw that massacres did have a demoralizing effect on the Arab fighters, and, in fear, some communities attempted to avoid participation. On the other hand, some incidents, such as the destruction of civilians at Tafas in 1918, after repeated attacks by Ottoman troops, galvanized furious resistance. Once the Ottoman regime began to weaken, pent-up anger at the reprisals unleashed a wave of counter-terror by Arab fighters and civilians.

One commentator concluded that Lawrence's emphasis on the psychological factors was 'a major innovation in modern military practice' given that approaches in the later twentieth century did not differ a great deal.[96] The basis of psychological warfare, across historical eras, is not only terror or imagination, but the play on logic, fear and desire. It requires a sound understanding of the mind of an enemy, or a neutral population, making use of their prejudices and points of reference. The product of psychological operations has to be credible for it to be effective, and that requires the adversary to be given plausible options. Lawrence and his partners therefore had to sustain raiding on Ottoman outposts, and take considerable risks deep behind enemy lines, to maintain the effect.

The results of psychological operations might be to diminish the enemy's morale and willingness to fight, or their military efficiency. The difficulty with assessing the effectiveness of Lawrence's campaign is that poor rations, frequent sickness, the sapping boredom of guarding the Hejaz line in an uncomfortable climate, and the neglect, and sometimes brutality, of the officers and NCOs of the Ottoman Army were far more erosive than the imagination of Arab raids. That said, messages of Arab atrocities could sweep through garrisons. The fact was that the raiders often could not ensure the survival of their prisoners. The wounded had to be abandoned, and if marched until exhaustion, the Ottoman *Mehmetciks* could expect to be left where they fell. Repeated raids, and the frustration of being unable to get to grips with the raiders, have led to military violence against civilians in countless historical cases. The conflict in the desert in 1916–18 was no exception. Angry Ottoman soldiers, eager to exact revenge for what they regarded as betrayal by the Arabs, and hardened by war against the taboos of death, sometimes took the law into their own hands and meted out summary punishments. These served to fuel the pro-Sharifian resistance, and Lawrence reported on how Feisal and the sheikhs would recount stories against the Ottomans in this regard.

The Ottoman Empire was facing severe pressure in 1916–17. The impact of a plague of locusts on Greater Syria, coming on the back of increased demands for manpower and foodstuffs, was catastrophic. Impoverished and hungry Ottoman citizens found themselves competing with deserters, and survival was far more important than political allegiances.[97] Djemal's repression kept the population in a state of anxious compliance, although he engaged in a programme of public works to maintain some support.[98] The majority of the population, according to Turkish veterans, kept their distance from the Ottoman government, regarded the regime as an occupation, but played little part in their own 'liberation'.[99] Instead, far from a popular uprising, we might regard this period as one of unmitigated hardship and suffering for the people of the region.

This indicates that another aspect of psychological warfare could apply, one that was the diametrical alternative of provocation, namely paralysis. Desensitizing security through repeated, seemingly innocuous probes, before a major strike, was a tactic that Lawrence himself utilized. The fact is that, for the Ottoman forces, most of the time there was no Arab presence. It was more difficult to sustain a high state of alertness when tied to defensive locations. It was for this reason that the Ottoman Army compelled its soldiers to make frequent patrols, on foot up and down the rail lines, while mounted units scoured areas in depth. In the winter of 1916–17, the Ottomans believed they could remain on the defensive in the interior, especially with the Red Sea ports under the guns of the Royal Navy. They had stopped the British advance in Mesopotamia, and recaptured Kut. They had checked the Allied landings at Gallipoli.[100] Although they had lost Erzurum in eastern Anatolia, the Russians were at least held close to the Aras River and in northern Persia. The Ottomans held the Hejaz, in part, and had strong defensive positions in southern Palestine, despite the loss of Sinai. Strategically, they held the gap between the Arab forces and the British EEF, at the centre of which was the small coastal settlement of Aqaba. But that was about to change.

5

The Indirect Strategy and the Capture of Aqaba

In Lawrence's own account of the campaign in the Middle East, the strategic breakthrough was the capture of Aqaba on 6 July 1917 which he had orchestrated. In many ways it was a plan as bold as the one against Wejh in its conception, but with fewer resources and potentially less chance of success. A relatively small Arab force had circled behind the port, skirmished against the defenders and then negotiated its handover, and, following a dramatic ride in, Lawrence immediately set off to Cairo, to report the achievement in person, before any other authority claimed the credit. It has become an iconic aspect of the Lawrence 'legend', illustrating how a weak force, brilliantly and bravely led, can achieve strategically significant results. Yet herein lies the problem. The drama of the event, and Lawrence's own retelling of it, has overshadowed its military utility and many of the setbacks that followed.

The plan had arisen in part because, in the Hejaz, there was a stalemate. Despite Lawrence's belief that Feisal's grand progress to Wejh had rallied more clans to his cause, the fact was that, after the capture of that port, many southern Hejaz fighters, far from their homelands, began to leave the force. It was the dwindling of support, in relative terms, that made it imperative to secure new recruits for the Arab irregular army, and to inspire the local population through acts of resistance. Orders from Cairo in March 1917 stipulated that Lawrence was to move to Wadi Ais to encourage Abdullah to make greater efforts against Medina and the Hejaz railway.

Raiding parties set out, consisting of small groups led by British, French and Arab regular officers, including Lawrence, armed with explosives. These repeated railway attacks had so far served their purpose: the capacity of the Ottomans to launch offensives was hamstrung by a lack of supplies. Nevertheless, the Arabs could not make any progress either. The Ottomans repaired the lines and the garrison at Medina could not be dislodged. Cairo considered the possibility of striking out of Mesopotamia because so little was being achieved from the Hejaz.[1] General Sir Stanley Maude's army on the Tigris had broken through the Ottoman trench systems in Mesopotamia and recaptured Kut in the winter of 1916–17. In March, he had taken Baghdad and opened up the potential to raise new Arab forces in the Euphrates.[2]

By contrast, Fakhri Pasha seemed to be recovering the initiative. Fakhri could not take back the Red Sea ports, but, with the assistance of Ibn Rashid of Hail, he was sufficiently supplied, despite the Hejaz railway raids, to consider a new counter-offensive. In March 1917, Ottoman regulars and Ibn Rashid's Shammar tribesmen launched sweeps west of Medina, driving off the Hashemites. The Ottoman garrison city was therefore secure, the routes to their infantry division in Yemen held, and arrangements with the Arab leaders in the south were sound, such that their men could be supplied there almost indefinitely. Crucially, the Hejaz rail route, offering a north–south axis of 'interior lines' for the defence of the Near East, was also firmly in Ottoman hands. If Lawrence's conception of war had been to render the Ottomans fixed and able only to consume the means of transport (their mules and horses), then, in March 1917, this was clearly not happening in practice.

It was therefore imperative that raids against the Ottomans were stepped up. Colonels Newcombe and Joyce recognized the importance of one particular station at Al 'Ula because of its water supply, and considered that an attack here could yield more significant tactical results, and thereby encourage the Arab fighters to sustain their resistance. A plan was therefore developed to select Arab regulars, some irregular fighters, Egyptian gunners and Indian troops to sever the railway with explosives above and below the station. At the same time, Lawrence was to take a party to conduct a similar operation near Ma'an. It was a task he did not fulfil.

Lawrence instead considered taking operations much further north, not just to conduct harassing raids on railways, but to change the direction of the campaign.[3] There were several roots to this idea. The first was a change underway in the Arab Northern Army. Regular Arab contingents were increasing in numbers and efficiency, but handfuls of volunteers were also coming in from Greater Syria, northern Hejaz and the interior, including the clans of Howeitat, Shararat, Bani 'Atiya and Rwalla. Unsurprisingly, these men looked to the north, hoping that operations against the Ottomans would be conducted there. Lawrence enthused about the support they expressed for Feisal:

> The roads to Wejh swarmed with envoys and volunteers and great sheikhs riding in to swear allegiance. The contagion of their constant passage made the lukewarm Billi ever more profitable to us. Feisal swore new adherents solemnly on the Koran between his hands, 'to wait while he waited, march when he marched, to yield obedience to no Turk, to deal kindly with all who spoke Arabic (whether Bagdadi, Aleppine, Syrian, or pure-blooded) and to put independence above life, family, and goods.'[4]

Another driving force of this general conception of moving operations northwards was that in the spring of 1917, General Murray, having advanced steadily across Sinai, clearly intended to push his EEF into Palestine, the southernmost districts of Syria. As he prepared for a major offensive at Gaza, there was the possibility that the French would land an expeditionary force of their own in Beirut. While the British would hold on to Palestine and southern Arabia as temporary wartime occupations, Lawrence could be less certain of the French intentions. He felt it was imperative to take possession of these territories before the French could.

Lawrence related the arrival of a long, intercepted telegraph message, allegedly from Enver and the German advisors in Istanbul, recommending that Fakhri should evacuate Medina, moving 'the troops by route march in mass, first to Hedia, thence to El Ula, thence to Tebuk, and finally to Maan, where a fresh rail-head and entrenched position would be constituted'.[5] While aiding the Arab cause, this move, were it carried out, would stop Murray's planned offensive into Palestine in its tracks. But Fakhri had no intention of evacuating Medina.[6]

The plan to attack the Hejaz railway was now less about stopping supplies reaching the garrison, and instead about preventing the garrison from getting out. Lawrence recalled: 'I hoped we might deter them from moving by making so many small raids on this lengthy line that traffic would be seriously disorganized, and the collection of the necessary food-dumps for the army at each main stage be impracticable.'[7] The target for the more substantial severing of the line was to be conducted by Colonel Newcombe, but Lawrence would be detailed to go to Ma'an and try to disrupt the line there too. Lawrence expressed an idea of advancing raiding parties into Syria, to destroy more Ottoman railways and bridges and perhaps foment revolt in the north to further assist the Al 'Ula mission. That was certainly the assumption in Cairo. But, according to Lawrence, it was Colonel Brémond's suggestions that really prompted a more daring plan: to capture Aqaba from the rear.[8] Lawrence wrote:

> In the midst of my touching the slender stops of all these quills there came a rude surprise … [Brémond] wanted to occupy Akaba [Aqaba] with an Anglo-French force and naval help. He pointed out the importance of Akaba, the only Turkish port left in the Red Sea, the nearest to the Suez Canal, the nearest to the Hejaz Railway, on the left flank of the [EEF]; suggesting its occupation by a composite brigade, which should advance up Wadi Itm for a crushing blow at Maan. He began to enlarge on the nature of the ground.[9]

Lawrence opposed the idea of an amphibious attack:

> I told him that I knew Akaba [Aqaba] from before the war, and felt that his scheme was technically impossible. We could take the beach of the gulf; but our forces there, as unfavourably placed as on a Gallipoli beach, would be under observation and gun-fire from the coastal hills: and these granite hills, thousands of feet high, were impracticable for heavy troops: the passes through them being formidable defiles, very costly to assault or to cover. In my opinion, Akaba, whose importance was all and more than he said, would be best taken by Arab irregulars descending from the interior without naval help.[10]

In essence, Lawrence was right that the port was strongly defended from the seaward side, making the prospect of any landing like the one conducted at Wejh costly and the expansion of the beachhead even more so. Instead, with Arab forces approaching from the desert, the port could be taken, allegedly (although not in practice) opening up a new logistics route for the EEF, and, crucially, providing a base for the supply of the Arab Northern Army. Lawrence ensured that Feisal opposed the idea of an amphibious landing, then returned to Cairo, 'in which I gave my betters much good advice'.[11] He noted, 'Murray, who had growlingly earmarked Tullibardine's brigade for Akaba [Aqaba], approved me still further when I declared against that side-show.'[12]

Lawrence's objections to an amphibious attack on Aqaba stood in contrast to his view about a much larger-scale landing near Alexandretta in 1916. He had championed that idea, believing the fastest way to cut off Turkish Anatolia from Arabia was to strike at the crucial railway and road junction by landing forces in the Gulf of Iskanderun. Despite Lawrence's claims that this was his original idea, there had, in fact, been such plans at the Admiralty for years.[13] Moreover, the General Staff and the Admiralty had already considered the idea of landings at Iskanderun, comparing them with alternatives, such as sustaining the Gallipoli campaign. At a conference at Mudros, on the island of Lemnos, Kitchener met with General Sir John Maxwell (commanding the British troops in Egypt), Sir Henry McMahon, General William Birdwood (commanding the ANZACs), Sir Charles Munro (commanding the Mediterranean Expeditionary Force), and Admiral de Robeck, who controlled all naval operations.[14] On the basis of avoiding a loss of prestige and risking widespread unrest, Maxwell, McMahon and Munro were in favour of the Iskanderun landings. They had estimated the mission would require 100,000 men. Kitchener proposed that, if approved, six divisions, with a cavalry brigade, would land and hold the area around Missis. Robeck believed the naval aspect of the operation was entirely feasible. Kitchener asked the General Staff to examine the strategic plan and make their own critical judgement.

The General Staff opposed the idea. They pointed out that the nodal point of Alexandretta favoured Ottoman troop concentrations, and, if the landing force got ashore without heavy losses, it would be compelled to hold a position some 25 miles inland and defend a perimeter of 50 miles, for which it would require 160,000 men. With experience of the loss of lives through disease and casualties at Gallipoli, the General Staff estimated the force would lose 20 per cent a month in the first three months of acclimatization, with some 15 per cent a month thereafter. There were also objections about the balance of forces and the weight of effort. The General Staff felt that to have three simultaneous operations underway in the Eastern Mediterranean risked 'a dangerous dispersion of military and naval force'.[15] Moreover, the expenditure of effort held out no prospect of weakening Germany in the main theatre in Europe. The planners felt that an 'eventual withdrawal would be difficult, perhaps impossible'. There was no sense that the Iskanderun landings would be a springboard to further operations. They were being considered in light of the Gallipoli campaign, with an inevitable stalemate.

Crucially, the General Staff argued that they had rejected the plan on the basis of strategic thinking: 'The scheme offended against a fundamental principle of strategy: to retain the power of concentrating strength for a great offensive in a decisive theatre of war.'[16] The Admiralty also returned a similar verdict, citing concern about protecting another sea route, some 400 miles long. Kitchener appreciated the U-boat threat to sea lines of communication, but also the strain it would place on munitions supply, which was limited. But the strategic context was crucial. The objections were really part of a wider debate about whether to focus all efforts on Germany in Europe, or whether to 'knock away the props' of Germany by striking against its weaker partners, including the Ottomans.

The Intelligence Section in Cairo, which had included Lawrence, estimated that a landing, if it achieved surprise, would be opposed by no more than 5,000 men, and it would take the Ottomans a week to assemble a division there. As the British force on Gallipoli was evacuated, more men would be available to the British effort in Iskanderun. No mention was made of the corresponding release of Ottoman divisions from Gallipoli, which would completely neutralize this advantage.

After careful consideration, Munro concluded that the plan was still possible.[17] In January 1916, the intelligence team at Cairo maintained that a defeat of Ottoman forces at Alexandretta would ignite a general Arab revolt in Syria.[18] But the chief objections came from the French. Colonel the Vicomte de la Panouse, the Military Attaché in London, noted that any operations at Alexandretta would have to consider French economic interests and its political position. Panouse pointed out:

> French public opinion could not be indifferent to any operations attempted in a country which it considers as destined to form a part of the future Syrian state ... and, should such action be taken, the greater part of the task should be entrusted to French troops and French generals commanding them.[19]

The British Prime Minister, Herbert Henry Asquith, informed Kitchener on 19 November that, since France was not in a position to mount any operations to the Ayas Bay, the plan had to be abandoned. There would be no *coup de main* into Syria. Lawrence confessed he was 'as sick as might be' about the French objections, concluding that, 'so far as Syria is concerned, it is France, not Turkey, that is the enemy'.[20]

The episode reveals some inconsistencies in Lawrence's conception of naval and land power in war, but also his growing awareness of the political direction, and its deflection, of strategy.

WAR IS POLITICS

It is well known that Lawrence used the cooperation of Feisal to achieve greater political and strategic results. For his part, Feisal knew that he was dependent on the British, and they would not easily dismiss French claims to the Levant, a point that had been reiterated from the outset to Hussein. Feisal also knew that this dependence on Allied money, munitions and air support meant cooperation with Britain was essential to avoid destruction at the hands of the Ottomans. Auda abu Tayi, of the Howeitat, probably did more than Lawrence to push the idea of taking Aqaba, but together they devised an operation that would put Feisal in a much stronger position politically.

The Sykes-Picot Agreement was not yet public, although Lawrence had disclosed the arrangements to Feisal sometime in 1916. For all Lawrence's protestations, the secret agreement was not, as so many claim, a design for the colonial carve-up of the Middle East.[21] As noted earlier, the two diplomats had sketched out vague spheres of influence, one for Britain and one for France, in case there was a sudden conclusion to the war, and, in May 1916, after consulting with their Russian allies, who also claimed a sphere of their own, the agreement constituted little more than zones of military occupation for the immediate post-war period. It was not a long-term design, as that would be left to the negotiations once the war was over. At best, it would enable British, French and Russian occupation zones to be deconflicted.

While the agreement has subsequently been attributed with enormous significance, primarily as evidence of an Anglo-French colonial conspiracy to subordinate the Arabs, it was never implemented and did not fully represent the actual British government plan of

Arab independence or autonomy. The de Bunsen Committee of 1915 had considered all the options for the future of the Middle East, including whether the region should remain under Ottoman rule.[22] The conclusion it reached was that Britain would continue to protect its existing Arab partners and allies, such as Kuwait, the Sultanate of Muscat (Oman), the Idrissis, the Trucial States, the sheikhs of southern Arabia (today, Yemen), and their colonial station at Aden. The region of Arabia would become independent, including the Hejaz. Mesopotamia and Palestine would be autonomous under British protection until such time as their economic and political viability could be guaranteed, although the British Government of India hoped it would be able to develop the economic potential of Mesopotamia for food production and commercial growth. Syria would be a French protectorate, but with its own government, and the British intended for the French to limit their occupation to the coast, leaving the interior, including Damascus, in Arab hands.[23]

Lawrence, as far as we know, was not aware of this official government plan, only the vague Sykes-Picot Agreement. After the war, like many others, Lawrence used the Sykes-Picot Agreement to 'prove' there had been a scheme to prevent full Arab independence, but, in many ways, this was a way of explaining the failure to unite Arabs as a single polity under the Hashemites.

Lawrence knew that the British government intended to grant independence to the Arabs of the Arabian Peninsula. His concern was always that the best lands, including Syria, would be given to France, and the French, in his view, had no intention of granting independence. This perspective he had derived from Colonel Brémond himself:

> Bremond did not tell me (but I knew) that he wanted the landing at Akaba [Aqaba] to head off the Arab movement, by getting a mixed force in front of them (as at Rabegh), so that they might be confined to Arabia, and compelled to waste their efforts against Medina. The Arabs still feared that the Sherif's alliance with us was based on a secret agreement to sell them at the end, and such a Christian invasion would have confirmed these fears and destroyed their cooperation.[24]

Informing Feisal and Hussein was designed to motivate them to follow Lawrence's own strategic plans. So, it is here that Lawrence's personal interests combined with his sense of duty, and the desire to fulfil policy. It must have been galling to Lawrence that the lands for which he and the Arabs were fighting were simply to be handed to the French once the war was over. His mission was to persuade the Arab forces to move out of the Hejaz, to push north and present the Allied leaders with a fait accompli. In short, he was trying to change policy by changing facts on the ground, and the Arab Northern Army was the 'means' to fulfil this objective.

Lawrence did much to popularize criticism of Sykes-Picot, claiming it was part of 'a lie' to the Arabs about their independence. He wrote afterwards:

> The Cabinet raised the Arabs to fight for us by definite promises of self-government afterwards. Arabs believe in persons, not in institutions. They saw in me a free agent of the British Government, and demanded from me an endorsement of its written promises. So I had to join the conspiracy, and, for what my word was worth, assured the men of their reward. In our two years' partnership under fire they grew accustomed to believing me and to think my Government, like myself, sincere. In this hope they performed some fine things, but, of course, instead of being proud of what we did together, I was bitterly ashamed.[25]

His conduct and his intelligence reports at the time do not always reinforce this neat, post-war narrative that he felt the British government was deliberately misleading the Arab leaders. Lawrence certainly had his own agenda.[26] In March 1915, after the proposed landing at Alexandretta was abandoned because of French objections, and long before the Arab Revolt, Lawrence had written to David Hogarth that, with Arab forces, the British could 'rush right up to Damascus, & biff the French out of all hope of Syria'.[27]

After the war, Lawrence reinforced the sense of shame about the Allies' plans and his part in carrying them out. But there was a wartime dimension to this too. In pushing on to Aqaba, he may have been looking for the means to redeem his failure to reach Wejh on time in January 1917, which had caused such disquiet amongst his British colleagues. Aqaba was the solution that would 'prove' the Arabs had to be taken seriously.

Another interpretation is that there was something deeper in his motivation. His growing recklessness and the cavalier attitude to his own life by mid-1917 are sometimes regarded as the manifestation of both his fear that his own government meant to betray the Arabs, promising them independence but treating them as little more than tools in the imperial enterprise, and his perceived humiliations of his early life, which he wished to expunge through some act of chivalric heroism.[28] Yet it is striking that so much of Lawrence's wartime correspondence does not support that view. Lawrence's claim that the Arabs were being betrayed comprehensively by Britain was therefore disingenuous.

There is another possibility, which has surfaced amongst biographers, that he had started to suffer what today would be understood as combat stress or traumatic stress disorder. Afflicted by dysentery in March 1917, he had confessed that it would 'crush its victims for a few hours, after which the extreme effects passed off; but it left men curiously tired, and subject for some weeks to sudden breaks of nerve'.[29] Later, in 1921, this seems to have reached a point of crisis in Lawrence's life.[30] But there was a period in the war when Lawrence himself recognized he had reached his limit. For a high-achieving, highly strung personality, this moment appeared to come in June 1917. His pocket diary has an entry that reads: 'Can't stand another day here. Will ride N and chuck it.'[31] Then he jotted (and subsequently scored out) a few lines in his notebook: 'I've decided to go off alone to Damascus, hoping to get killed on the way: for all sakes try and clear this show up before it goes further. We are calling them to fight for us on a lie, and I can't stand it.'[32] And yet, when Lawrence wrote again, and subsequently explained this part of his career that had appeared in the first draft of *Seven Pillars*, he claimed instead that he wanted to see the situation in Syria for himself, to ascertain local allegiances, and to 'learn enough to lay definite plans' because 'while I saw the liberation of Syria happening in steps, of which Akaba [Aqaba] was the indispensable first, I now saw the steps coming very close together.' This information he reasoned would allow him to coordinate the actions of the Arab revolutionaries with 'Murray in Sinai'.[33] The 1926 edition of *Seven Pillars* may be a more honest reflection, where he wrote: 'A rash adventure suited my abandoned mood.'[34] Lawrence was clearly exhausted and frustrated, not least with his Arab comrades, so the claim to want to 'chuck it' may have been insincere, theatrical and momentary.

There was also the chance that Lawrence was looking for ways to motivate his Arab partners at a time when the revolt was experiencing another lull in its fortunes. As so often, in *Seven Pillars*, he had a tendency to express this in rather dramatic and colourful ways, invoking metaphors that would appeal to his British readers. In his advance from the Hejaz northwards, he wrote: 'I felt that one more sight of Syria would put straight the strategic ideas given me by the Crusaders.'[35]

We might reasonably conclude that, at the time, Lawrence envisaged a way of revivifying the Arab resistance, by developing the revolt northwards in order to absorb yet more Ottoman resources but also to liberate Syria, the primary area of his interests. Feisal had his own agenda regarding Syria and concurred with the aspiration, despite the objections of some of the tribal leaders. Aware that he was unlikely to gain any significant position in the post-war dispensation in the Hejaz, Feisal looked to acquire a Greater Syria as a potential source of future power. It was this factor, and the coincidence of objectives with the British, which drew the forces under his command northwards.[36]

In early 1917, Aqaba was a shambles, with its battered emplacements, sections of ruined buildings and the mouldering remains of an old Mameluke fort. The Royal Navy had bombarded the port and had even sent landing parties ashore to raid it, but it had not been occupied because, tactically, the routes beyond the plain on which the settlement stood were hemmed in by mountains, and strategically, because there had been no value in holding it. Aqaba became important *after* the EEF had crossed Sinai and was in strength near Gaza, and once the Arab forces were able to operate north of the Hejaz, where they would be in a position to 'join hands'.[37] At this stage of the war, there were no ships, troops or logistics that could be spared for a deliberate operation against Aqaba.

Back at Wejh, Lawrence saw for himself the greater efforts being made to arm, equip and direct the Arab efforts against the Hejaz railway. Wilson had been summoned to help in the operation, while Egyptian troops were to be used to reinforce the Arab attack. In a meeting with Colonel Joyce, who was coordinating operations, he learned: 'many Billi, the mule-mounted infantry, and guns and machine-guns, hoped to take the fort and railway station [at Muadhdham]'. He continued: 'Newcombe meant then to move all Feisal's men forward very close to Medain Salih, and, by taking and holding a part of the line, to cut off Medina and compel its early surrender.' The emphasis on 'all of Feisal's men' was profound. Lawrence admitted that the British officers, despite their efforts, were practically doing the work themselves because of a lack of manpower.[38] Joyce believed Feisal was simply not helping because his mind was filled 'with very wide ideas' of going north.[39]

Lawrence had doubts about the planned operation. He believed that the effort should be to push the Ottomans into a prolonged defence, absorbing their manpower, rather than trying to force a decision too early. He wrote: 'Our aim was to seek the enemy's weakest material link and bear only on that till time made their whole length fail.'[40] His conclusion was to 'extend our front to its maximum, to impose on the Turks the longest possible passive defence, since that was, materially, their most costly form of war'.[41]

While time was not a limitless luxury, the Arab forces and their British advisors 'were richer than the Turks in transport, machine-guns, cars, [and] high explosive'. With these assets, Lawrence believed they could 'develop a highly mobile, highly equipped striking force of the smallest size, and use it successively at distributed points of the Turkish line, to make them strengthen their posts beyond the defensive minimum of 20 men. This would be a short cut to success.'[42]

Lawrence was critical of holding a section of the line, which would give the Ottomans a target to concentrate on and leave the flanks vulnerable. He reasoned that water was scarce and the terrain did not favour the movement of a large force, or its sustainment there. But his arguments did not convince the colonels, and all that he could get agreement on was a diversionary attack.

THE MISSION TO RECRUIT LOCAL FORCES AND SEIZE AQABA

Colonel Newcombe, accompanied by Lieutenant Hornby, assumed that Lawrence was on his way to Ma'an to conduct diversionary attacks, as he prepared for the main strike against the Hejaz railway at Al 'Ula. During the night of 6–7 July, Newcombe's party laid 500 explosive charges on the railway sleepers to the south of the station, detonating them at 0200hrs. To the north, Hornby had laid another 300 and blew his on schedule too. As the Ottomans sought to deal with the mess, they were strafed by the Royal Flying Corps on 11 July, while further night attacks were made on the line. But where was Lawrence and his diversionary attack?

The contingent that left Wejh with Lawrence was small, making it harder to detect, and allowing for more rapid movement.[43] The objective was to cross the Al Houl waterless tracts, travel over 600 miles (1,000km), and then, as Auda abu Tayi had suggested, recruit fighters from among local men en route with generous handouts of gold. The conditions, lack of water and chances of detection made this a hazardous undertaking. There was an encounter with a Shammar patrol, Arabs in Ottoman service, that led to brief skirmishing, but they slipped away. Lawrence's party crossed the Hejaz line without difficulty, despite warnings of mobile Ottoman patrols, and the Agayl blew up the rails with gelatin and gun-cotton charges, and pulled down the telegraph wires as they left the area.[44] The detonations caused the Ottoman blockhouse garrisons to open a random fire into the darkness, and that was enough to force the raiders to abandon further attacks.

Lawrence reflected on how blowing up rail lines was its own recruiting tool: 'The noise of dynamite explosions we found everywhere the *most effective* propagandist measure possible [emphasis added].'[45] It was, to use a modern expression, the propaganda of the deed. It is a reminder that war is a form of public theatre, and even clandestine operations are designed to achieve a psychological effect, either on one's partners and allies, or on the enemy.

The crossing of the Al Houl demanded considerable endurance: against the heat, lack of water and risk to the transport camels. There are several characteristics of moving through the desert that are difficult to appreciate but which can be grasped through reading Lawrence's understated descriptions.[46] The heat makes everyone silent, knocking them breathless. Even relatively gentle exertions can leave you panting, and the very fabric of your clothes seems to burn red hot on the skin. Remaining bare-headed leaves the impression of being struck on the skull with a hammer, hence the expression that the sun 'beats down'. Groups tend to move along steadily, their silence adding to the curious stillness of the air, which gives the impression of barely moving at all. Amid these conditions, Lawrence himself chose to return to find his servant who had gone missing, a feat which could easily have cost him his life.[47] Another servant, who had left the group through some accident, was later found dead and desiccated by the sun.

If the environment was not hazardous enough, a second Shammar patrol, about 20 strong, opened fire on the group one night, killing one, but they were deterred by the return fire of the picquets.[48] Three more men died of snake bites on the expedition. But the party eventually reached more hospitable ground, and water, and so was assured of its survival.

In traditional desert warfare, the key factors were the dependence on camels, access to and availability of water, and the depth of distance which offered concealment. Without all these elements, no guerrilla operation could succeed. What would change this calculus during the course of Lawrence's campaign was the intrusion of two critical elements: air surveillance and industrialized logistics. The availability of supplies, carried by motor transport, would later transform the operations altogether.[49] Yet, at this early stage, much of the movement and fighting seemed unchanged from generations of desert fighting. Historically, nomadic raiders from the interior of Arabia had engaged in commerce with settled populations nearer the coast, but they also periodically raided them, the so-called *ghazzu*. The nomads themselves lived in an almost constant state of poverty, fear, and authoritarian observance of territorial limits, personal honour, and hierarchy. Certain tribal leaders, who could command larger parties of armed retainers, might acquire the willing patronage of less wealthy men. The man who could offer camels, access to wells, metalwork for sale, and food, could also offer protection. But the tribal leaders had to demonstrate their willingness to lead, exact revenge, punish, and defend their honour. The demands of status, patronage and wealth perpetuated violence, and sustained the system. Unsurprisingly, in this campaign, while a temporary alliance under the Sharifian cause might offer some benefits, tribal leaders were suspicious of a subordination that might threaten their long-term position.

By May 1917, Lawrence and his partners had started their difficult and delicate recruitment campaign in the interior, eventually creating a force of 650 men. However, inexperience and zealousness meant that some disputed the idea of moving on Aqaba, and instead they suggested more ambitious objectives. Lawrence wrote:

In the heady atmosphere of first enthusiasm they ignored Akaba [Aqaba], and despised the plain purpose which had led us here. Nesib knew the Shaalans and the Druses. His mind enrolled them, not the Howeitat; struck at Deraa, not Maan: occupied Damascus, not Akaba. He pointed out that the Turks were all unready: that we were sure to gain our first objective, by sheer surprise: that therefore our objective should be the highest. Damascus was indicated by the finger of inevitable fate.[50]

Lawrence countered by arguing that the main Arab force under Feisal was still in Wejh, far to the south. The British Army was also entrenched in front of Gaza while the Ottomans were in strength at Aleppo as they prepared to launch their counter-offensive into Mesopotamia. Any attempt to reach Damascus would be unsupported, devoid of vital logistics, bases and communications.[51] Unable to persuade his Syrian partner, Lawrence admitted that he exploited the pride and schisms of his interlocutors, persuaded Auda to reinforce his points, and then threatened to withhold the gold that was on offer. He also pointed out that, even if they could take Damascus, they would not be able to hold it for any more than six weeks, at best. Defeat would discredit the revolt. No British force would be able to land at Beirut fast enough to rescue them.[52]

Insurgent forces are often guilty of a premature offensive against those cities which symbolize or facilitate control of a state. One might refer to the communist Vietnamese forces that briefly took Hue in January 1968, the Taliban's attempted seizure of Kunduz in 2016, or the Iraqi insurgents' overconfidence about being able to hold Fallujah in 2004. Even the classic advocate of urban guerrilla operations, Carlos Marighella, warned against trying to take and hold cities without firm control over the surrounding hinterland.[53]

In Lawrence's view, the Arabs needed Aqaba 'firstly, to extend their front, which was their tactical principle; and, secondly, to link up with the British'.[54] Taking Aqaba would convince General Murray of the Arabs' importance as a military asset, and result in an abundance of arms, supplies and equipment. The Syrian leader Nesib decided to go north to recruit his own forces and asked Lawrence to provide further funding if he was successful. Lawrence let him go, but, troubled by the idea that he too wanted to foster a pan-Arab uprising in Syria, and eager to see the mood of the populace there for himself, Lawrence also left the party bound for Aqaba and conducted a long reconnaissance deep behind Ottoman lines. The justification was: 'I undertook this long, dangerous ride, in which to see the more important of Feisal's secret friends, and to study key positions of our future campaigns: but the results were incommensurate with the risks, and the act artistically unjustifiable, like the motive.'[55] Lawrence made no mention in *Seven Pillars* of the more desperate note he had scribed, but did not send, to Cairo, and it is impossible to know what he told his Arab colleagues as the explanation for his actions.

The advance on Aqaba was almost prevented by the Ottoman Army's destruction of certain wells. With difficulty, Auda and his allies managed to extract enough to continue, but it revealed an awareness on the Ottoman side that the Arab insurgents could only use the desert with impunity if they had access to water. Furthermore, the civilian, nomadic population would only be able to support the fighters if they too could rely on the water supply. Auda was forced to consolidate, sending out a select group to purchase flour locally and to ascertain the loyalties of the population. This in itself revealed the factional nature of the Arab communities, and how these constrained the freedom of manoeuvre of the raiders.

Lawrence conceived of the next phase of the plan against Aqaba, which would involve, contrary to his theories, a direct confrontation with the Ottomans in order to secure the pass of Nagb el Shtar, near Abu el Lissan, and then to hold it, which would, again, require access to water. He wrote:

> Our idea was to advance suddenly from El Jefer, to cross the railway-line and to crown the great pass – Nagb el Shtar – down which the road dipped from the Maan plateau to the red Guweira plain. To hold this pass we should have to capture Aba el Lissan, the large spring at its head, about sixteen miles from Maan; but the garrison was small, and we hoped to overrun it with a rush. We would then be astride the road, whose posts at the end of the week should fall from hunger; though probably before that the hill tribes, hearing of our successful beginning, would join us to wipe them out.[56]

It is interesting that Lawrence assumed local clans would join the revolt, which itself depended on military success. He made no mention of his calculations if, for some reason, his partners failed to capture the pass or defeat the Ottoman garrison. He admitted:

> [The] crux of our plan was the attack on Aba el Lissan, lest the force in Maan have time to sally out, relieve it, and drive us off the head of Shtar. If, as at present, they were only a battalion, they would hardly dare move; and should they let it fall while waiting for reinforcements to arrive, Akaba [Aqaba] would surrender to us, and we should be based on the sea and have the advantageous gorge of Itm between us and the enemy.[57]

So, Lawrence appeared to believe that the Ottomans would not be mobile and would allow themselves to be fixed. A relief column, acting with mutual support, he expected to be checked because of the topography. Neither of these assumptions was necessarily correct.

Success depended on operational security. Lawrence needed the element of surprise to prevent the larger Ma'an garrison intervening. This was hardly guaranteed, as Lawrence acknowledged:

> It was never easy for us to keep our movements secret, as we lived by preaching to the local people, and the unconvinced would tell the Turks. Our long march into Wadi Sirhan was known to the enemy, and the most civilian owl could not fail to see that the only fit objective was Akaba [Aqaba]. The demolition of Bair (and Jefer, too, for we had it confirmed that the seven wells of Jefer were destroyed) showed that the Turks were to that extent on the alert.[58]

The solution was to deceive the Ottomans. In his ride to the north to ascertain the loyalties of the local populations, Lawrence had hinted that operations there, especially against the railway line near Damascus, were imminent. In other words, he hoped to convey the idea in the minds of the Ottomans that the raiders were everywhere.[59] Their elusive enemies could appear at any moment from the desert at more than a dozen points:

> We had undertaken a prolonged campaign of deception, to convince them that our objective lay nearer to Damascus. They were susceptible to pressure in that neighbourhood, for the railway from Damascus,

north to Deraa and south to Amman, was the communication, not merely of Hejaz, but of Palestine; and if we attacked it we should do double damage. So, in my long trip round the north country, I had dropped hints of our near arrival in Jebel Druse; and I had been glad to let the notorious Nesib go up there, noisily, but with small resources. Nuri Shaalan had warned the Turks for us in the same sense.

But there was more to the operation than mere rumour. Plausibility depended on material fact:

Newcombe, down near Wejh, had contrived to [deliberately] lose official papers, including a plan (in which we were advance guard) for marching from Wejh, by Jefer and the Sirhan, to Tadmor, to attack Damascus and Aleppo. The Turks took the documents very seriously, and chained up an unfortunate garrison in Tadmor till the end of the war, much to our advantage.[60]

To add to the deception, Lawrence rode with 110 fighters in a punishing schedule of six-hour bursts with one-hour intervals, day and night, to attack the line at Deraa, far to the north. Watering the camels had to be done without the knowledge of local Circassian civilians, who were well disposed towards the Ottoman authorities. At Dhuleil, Lawrence and his party avoided a guarded bridge as a target and selected Minifir, hoping that a spectacular raid would convince the Ottoman Army that the main Arab force was at Azrak. Selecting a vantage point above the line, the raiders began their observation but before nightfall a large body of Ottoman regular cavalry advanced on them. Lawrence suspected that his party had been spotted and was forced to beat a retreat to the east. The cavalry passed to the south, searching for the raiders. A new site was selected for the attack, with better observation from the summits to avoid being surprised again. Local villagers were informed of their presence this time, in the hope that they would later convey exaggerated messages of their strength.

Lawrence meanwhile laid a Garland mine at night, anticipating a train would be destroyed the next day, but there was no traffic at all. The only activity was, first, the arrival of two badly wounded Ottoman deserters. The second incident was the movement of 200 mule-borne

Ottoman infantry. Lawrence declined to ambush them because of the risk of casualties he might incur. The objective was only to create the impression of a larger force, rather than to risk battle for the sake of it. The decision angered the Arab raiders, who wanted military successes and mules as booty. One broke ranks and tried to attract the Ottomans' attention to force a skirmish, but Zaal, nominally in command of the group, prevented it. The incident showed that ambushes required a great deal of discipline, care in remaining concealed, and nerve to remain in close proximity to their enemy.

Instead of engaging in what would have been potentially a costly firefight, they laid charges the following night, blew them, and withdrew. A secondary device damaged a train the following day, and the Ottomans were forced to spend time clearing the lines in case of other hidden explosives.[61]

Handling prisoners had raised particular problems for the raiding force. Both captives died of their wounds and thirst, although they had left a note as to their location when they were abandoned by the raiders. Carrying them would have been an impossible impediment to Lawrence's movements, for the speed and mobility of the raiders was, in effect, their only security. Similarly, a Circassian who stumbled in on Lawrence's force was taken down to the railway line, stripped naked and had his feet so badly cut he would have to crawl up the line to the Ottomans, thus delaying how quickly he could inform them of the raiders' location. Desert raiders in other parts of the world had used tactics like this by tradition.

Rations were also scarce for Lawrence's fighters. At Atwi, the presence of a flock of sheep was sufficient temptation for the 100-strong force to take on a blockhouse. The Arabs carefully positioned themselves to shoot at the Ottoman garrison, and 'Zaal's men poured in their volleys, broke from the valley, and rushed forward: but the door of the northern house clanged to, and rifles began to speak from behind its steel window shutters'.[62] Once the soldiers were alerted, there was no chance of them being overrun. The Arabs therefore made off with the animals and started to loot the nearby structures. The arrival of a patrol on a trolley offered another opportunity for the raiders, and all four men aboard were shot down. The Arabs decided to set fire to the station, 'whose petrol-splashed woodwork caught freely'. The Agayl men detonated charges to destroy a culvert, the rails and the telegraph before setting off. Curiously, the explosives startled the camels and the sheep, and Lawrence admitted that he and his men wasted time trying to round up their scattered animals. Losing the camels would have been catastrophic to the raiding force, highlighting another vulnerability.

Some six Ottoman battalions were deployed to seek and destroy the Arab insurgents and ensure that the local Mutaweila tribes did not revolt.[63] Although Lawrence received news of the willingness of local clans to assist the attack on Aqaba, the Ottomans were busy recruiting their own loyalists and demanding quotas of camel-borne tribesmen by holding hostage family members of the sheikhs.[64] The Ottomans were despatching patrols of these clans to search for Lawrence's party, and the systematic destruction of wells further south, like those at Jeber and Bair, was designed to cut them off and deprive them of any ability to operate in the area. Lawrence rode with a group back to Jefer to ascertain the damage and by careful excavation they found that Ottoman explosives had capped, rather than completely destroyed the well-shafts.

While Lawrence had been on his 500-mile ride to the north, Auda and the other leaders had been involved in negotiations with the local sheikhs. The result was the combination of 500 Howeitat, 150 Rualla and Shararat, and 35 Kawakiba men. This force was too small and badly armed to take on a regular enemy who would be equipped with light artillery and machine guns. But it was also too large to conceal easily. Feeding and watering was another challenge and, at one well, Lawrence related that they drew its limited water for 24 hours. The greatest vulnerability was to air power. If German or Ottoman airmen had located them, they had no defence against air attack. This concentration of force could thus be sustained only for a short period, which made it imperative that they move quickly to their objective at Aqaba. If they were successful and took the port, they would be able to request the Royal Navy land supplies, but it was a tremendous gamble.

The next step was the attack against Fuweilah, a blockhouse which protected the head of the pass of Abu el Lissan. Lawrence wrote: 'Our attack was planned for two days before the weekly caravan which, from Maan, replenished the client garrisons. Starvation would make reduction of these distant places easier, by impressing on them how hopelessly they were cut off from their friends.'[65] But taking the post depended on being able to overwhelm it before they had a chance to warn neighbouring units.

A group was sent forward, but news came in the following day that their attack on Fuweilah had miscarried. The garrison had not been surprised, had fought determinedly from its blockhouse defences, and driven off the Arab force. Lawrence related that the Ottomans must have assumed it was a minor tribal raiding party, typical of the pre-war era, because they created a mounted patrol that would locate the nearest nomadic camp from which this raid had sprung. The Ottoman mission was punitive: they destroyed the tents and killed several of the civilians they found, even though these herders had had nothing to do with the attack on Fuweilah at all. The raiders only learned of this punitive attack after the event, but, angered by news of the wanton killing, they set off in pursuit of the perpetrators. They soon caught up with them, and immediately hurled themselves at the marching soldiers. The fighting was furious. The Ottomans tried to escape, and a running skirmish developed right back to the blockhouse. The Arab fighters, their anger roused by the whole affair, pursued the Ottomans to the very walls and they fought their way in. They took no prisoners and killed the entire garrison.

The incident raised an important and common dilemma for guerrilla forces, namely, the issue of reprisals. The support of civilians is essential for insurgents, yet the presence of insurgents is often a cause of considerable fear if violence and reprisals are likely. Insurgents may have to face the anger of local people, and make decisions about the ethics of their actions and the likely consequences for others. The issue was to reappear later in the campaign for Lawrence, but the consequences were similar – an escalation of savagery on both sides.

Lawrence makes little of the incident at Fuweilah in *Seven Pillars*, but its effects were far-reaching. Firstly, it opened the route towards Aqaba for the main body of the Arab force. Secondly, it galvanized resistance to the Ottomans in the vicinity. The Arab fighters made every effort to tell locals of what had happened, urging further acts of vengeance. But Lawrence was evidently more focussed on the military task at hand, and he designed new deception measures to cover the last stages of the advance.[66]

A small party was detached to cross the railway to the north of Ma'an and create a diversion, distracting the Ottomans from the main advance to the south-west. The diversionary group were to target the herds of sick camels that were left by the Ottomans to roam nearby pastures until they had recovered sufficiently to rejoin the logistics chain on the

Palestine front. Further attacks on the railway line were also designed to absorb Ottoman relief columns and Lawrence calculated that it would take 24 hours or more before news of this and the attack on Fuweilah reached the Ottomans and was acted upon – just enough time for the Arab force to get out of reach.

Accordingly, the railway was attacked and the small garrison of Ghadir el Haj nearby was driven off by the greater numbers the Arabs could bring to bear. Lawrence recorded how they worked quickly to destroy bridge piers and culverts, doing as much damage as possible to attract the Ottomans' attention.[67] The raiders rode on, with growing confidence in their actions. At their new camp, however, the plan began to fall apart.

The party which had overrun Fuweilah, and which therefore held the critical pass that gave access to the south-west, had been surprised to see an Ottoman column, with artillery, infantry and cavalry, marching up from Ma'an to recover the lost blockhouse. The size of this force could not be ascertained at first, but the Arab contingent had fallen back without offering resistance to avoid being trapped and annihilated. Lawrence regretted that: 'We had lost Aba el Lissan, the blockhouse, the pass, the command of the Akaba [Aqaba] road: without a shot being fired.'[68]

The Ottoman unit was, in fact, a battalion of the 178th Regiment and, having secured Fuweilah, it moved off to camp at Abu el Lissan nearby where there was water. The unit had been marching up the line on its way north, but news of the Arab attack meant that, instead of halting, they had continued in order to investigate. There was nothing they could do for the slaughtered garrison, but their strength gave rise to complacency, for the commanding officer selected a camping ground within the shaded confines of the narrow and winding valley. Auda and the main body of the Arab force marched through the evening to the site of the recent engagement, where Gasim abu Dumeik, leader of the Dhumaniyeh, was 'waiting anxiously for us, surrounded by his hard-bitten tribesmen, their grey strained faces flecked with the blood of the fighting yesterday'.[69] Although Lawrence wanted to avoid battle with the Ottoman Army, he admitted that, unless they took the pass, the entire plan was in jeopardy. Reconnaissance that night revealed their advantage over the Ottomans, possession of the high ground, and with this they thought they might inflict sufficient losses to force their adversary back down the pass.

When all were in position on the heights, the Arabs commenced a steady if limited fusillade into the Ottoman camp. This was designed to convince their enemy that only a small force opposed them, one that could be swept aside by a swift advance up the slopes. When exposed, the full weight of Arab fire would inflict casualties and compel their retreat. To prevent reinforcements coming up, the telephone and telegraph lines were cut some distance off. But, for a variety of reasons, the Ottomans did not take the bait as expected. As the sun rose, the soldiers fanned out, and began picking their way carefully into better vantage points. The Arabs found themselves engaged in a prolonged firefight in exhausting heat. The rocks on which the battle took place amplified the temperature, rifles grew too hot to handle, and water started to run out. Some fighters collapsed from heat exhaustion. The conditions were almost certainly the same for the Ottomans, trapped in a narrow defile, with little chance of getting forward or withdrawing. Lawrence must have realized that this stalemate could only favour his enemy, but in frustration, antagonized by the heat, and taunted by Auda for seeking shade, he spat out the criticism that the Arabs 'shoot a lot and hit a little'.

For Auda, a fighter of considerable experience and even greater pride, the insult was too much. As Lawrence related in *Seven Pillars*, the old man tore off his headdress and ordered his fighters to mount up.[70] For a moment it must have seemed as if Auda was about to quit the field, and perhaps the entire Sharifian cause, and when Lawrence went to join the main mounted body in the valley, he asked where Auda was, expecting to see him there. But Auda had a point to prove and his decision to launch an audacious charge turned the tide of this hitherto inconclusive action.

Lawrence recalled:

We kicked our camels furiously to the edge, to see our fifty horsemen coming down the last slope into the main valley like a run-away, at full gallop, shooting from the saddle. As we watched, two or three went down, but the rest thundered forward at marvellous speed, and the Turkish infantry, huddled together under the cliff ready to cut their desperate way out towards Maan, in the first dusk began to sway in and out, and finally broke before the rush, adding their flight to Auda's charge.

Here was a 'kingfisher moment':

> Nasir screamed at me, 'Come on', with his bloody mouth; and we
> plunged our camels madly over the hill, and down towards the
> head of the fleeing enemy. The slope was not too steep for a camel-
> gallop, but steep enough to make their pace terrific, and their course
> uncontrollable.[71]

Lawrence noted that Auda's initial attack had attracted all the attention
and the fire of the Ottomans, so the charge of his own party, on
the Ottoman flank, produced a secondary shock effect. The speed of the
camels gave very little opportunity for the Ottomans to react, and the
sudden appearance of over 400 men, an uncharacteristic tactic for Arab
forces after such a prolonged period of skirmishing, was a complete
surprise. The Ottoman troops' cohesion was thrown into chaos, and, as
they tried to pull back into cover, they were overrun.

As Lawrence reached the first soldiers, and was close enough to fire at
them with his revolver, he accidentally shot his own camel in the head
and was thrown to the ground. What Lawrence therefore missed was the
wrath of the Arab riders against the retreating Ottomans. It was striking
that over 300 were killed, while only 160 were taken prisoner. The Arabs
had been in no mood to give quarter because of the Ottoman massacre
of the Arab families, even though this particular unit had had nothing
to do with the incident. Some of the Ottoman soldiers nevertheless
did make their escape, though chased for 3 miles across open ground.
Auda reappeared with no fewer than six bullet holes in his clothing and
saddlery, and his horse had been brought down. He was satisfied that
he had proved Lawrence wrong, for the cost of only two men killed.

Lawrence tried to interrogate the Ottomans about the size and
disposition of the garrisons en route to Aqaba. He dismissed the evident
fear of the prisoners who surely believed they would all be executed.
Ignoring their pleas for mercy, Lawrence took one aside and 'was rough
to him, shocking him by new pain into a half-understanding'. Beating
the prisoner produced the confession that this battalion was far larger
than the two companies deployed at Ma'an, which was not difficult
to ascertain by other means. The Howeitat wanted to take the railway
junction and settlement there to seize booty, but they were compelled
to move on swiftly to Aqaba as their resources, gold, and rations were

exhausted.[72] Indeed, the Arabs were getting close to a 'culminating point' and still had a great deal of distance to cover. The battle had, however, created great confidence amongst the fighters. For Lawrence, Ma'an would have to wait because 'a strategic scheme was not changed to follow up a tactical success'.[73] While sending small parties to shoot at blockhouses, his priority was to 'push to the coast, and re-open sea-contact with Suez'.

After the exertions of the fighting, though, Lawrence experienced that typical post-combat inertia and sense of anticlimax. The fighters had looted the baggage, and as the night cloaked them, most wanted to rest. Auda was the one who galvanized the camp. He knew that remaining in that position meant that it increased the risks of counter-attack and failure. The Ottomans would soon realize the fate of their lost battalion and start to reinforce the area.[74] The move meant that at least 20 wounded Ottomans had to be left behind, a situation likely to bring about their death. About the same number of camels had been wounded, and it was thought that these would not last long either. The rest of the prisoners had to march, or be strapped on to the camels that could be spared.

Lawrence persuaded one of the Ottoman gendarmes to write out letters that could be delivered to the three Turkish posts that lay in front. Their commanders, at Guweira, Kethera and Hadra, were to be informed that if 'our blood was not hot we took prisoners, [and] prompt surrender would ensure their good treatment and safe delivery to Egypt'.[75] This was a way to avoid further costly actions, and demonstrated Lawrence's intuitive sense of what today would be termed 'psychological operations'.

The march to Aqaba was a hungry and slow one, and the Ottoman prisoners were therefore handed over to a local sheikh, Ibn Jad, to reduce the burden on the advance. But the wearied force still had to find a way to overcome the outposts on their route. The blockhouse at Kethera refused the offer to surrender. At nightfall, the local Arabs overwhelmed the position. As they moved on again the next day, into the Wadi Itm, Lawrence noticed that the other posts had been abandoned. His assessment was that the garrison commander had concentrated his men closer in at Aqaba, probably so as to supply them, but it may also have been a precaution, given the fate of blockhouses which did not have the mutual support of other defended posts. Local Arabs provided the crucial intelligence that the Ottoman defences were positioned to resist an attack from the sea, not the landward side:

'We heard ... that the subsidiary posts about Akaba [Aqaba] had been called in or reduced, so that only a last three hundred men barred us from the sea.'[76] The trouble was that these men were better entrenched than the locals had imagined.

There were significant disagreements about what to do next. Various ideas were posited and ruses attempted:

> We sent the Turks summonses, first by white flag, and then by Turkish prisoners, but they shot at both. This inflamed our Beduin, and while we were yet deliberating a sudden wave of them burst up on to the rocks and sent a hail of bullets spattering against the enemy.[77]

The shooting did no good, and the longer the Arabs remained stuck in their gorges, which became ovens by day, the more exhausted and dehydrated they became. Lawrence recalled their 'swollen' and throbbing heads, the hunger, and the frayed tempers. Unless they could break the impasse, the entire enterprise might have to be abandoned at the final step. So it was an added, almost unbearable strain when the third attempt to persuade the garrison to capitulate was made in an unorthodox way:

> We had a third try to communicate with the Turks, by means of a little conscript, who said that he understood how to do it. He undressed, and went down the valley in little more than boots. An hour later he proudly brought us a reply, very polite, saying that in two days, if help did not come from Maan, they would surrender.[78]

Lawrence believed the Arabs would not have the patience to wait and that a battle would end in heavy losses on his own side and a massacre of the Ottomans. A night attack, in a full moon, would be as costly as a daytime assault. So Lawrence accompanied the messenger and called for an officer to talk with. After some time, with threats that the Arabs could not be restrained much longer and the fact there was no chance of relief for the Ottomans, the officer agreed that a surrender would be effected the following day, for the daylight would reduce the chance of treachery.

However, the following morning, fresh groups of local Arabs had appeared, expecting an opportunity to shoot at the Ottomans and to loot the port. At first light, they started firing, contrary to any of Lawrence's plans. The Ottomans returned fire and it looked as though the scheme was once again in danger of collapse. The firefight was stopped when Nasir led his mounted Agayl forward and across his own front, which caused the Arabs to stop shooting. The Ottomans also ceased their firing. Lawrence seized the opportunity to re-commence the surrender negotiations.

The outposts of Aqaba were thus captured, more by negotiation rather than fighting. As the Arabs approached the port, still more volunteer fighters had come forward, which tipped the relative strengths of the two sides.[79] The Ottoman commander, realizing he was cut off without hope of relief, and now outnumbered, had no choice but to surrender, and Aqaba was taken on 6 July 1917.[80]

The importance of the action was not the manner of Aqaba's capture, despite the dramatic image of a charge in to the port in a sandstorm, but its strategic value. Taking Aqaba had the potential to reconfigure the situation in the Middle East by neutralizing the threat to the right rear of the EEF at Gaza, and offering a new base for the Allies and the Arabs with which to strike against the Hejaz railway and the open Ottoman flank. The orthodox interpretation of the campaign emphasizes this potential. The problem with this view is that events after July did not fulfil that hope at all. Indeed, the Arab Revolt was about to experience its most significant crisis.

6

Culminating Point at Aqaba

The seizure of Aqaba occurred at almost the same moment that General Sir Edmund Allenby succeeded Murray as commander of the Egyptian Expeditionary Force. According to the *Official History*, Allenby, when informed of the capture of Aqaba, 'at once realized that it would alter the conditions of the desert war'.[1] A distant and minor campaign now offered the potential to be useful as a diversion, and to link together the two operational theatres.[2] This, however, demanded coordination, and that, in turn, meant that the Arab forces would have to come under the direction of Allenby's GHQ. The Arabs would act as a screen and a harassing force, and, in return, they would be supplied centrally by the EEF as well as the Royal Navy.

The immediate problem for Lawrence at Aqaba was the hunger and exhaustion of the Arab force and their Ottoman prisoners. The town was in a poor state, much damaged by naval bombardment and looting. There was little to consume locally.[3] There was also the question of an Ottoman counter-attack.[4] Petra, the Rose City, was to be held with a strong detachment, while Auda's Howeitat would be spread in a semi-circular screen to the north. But it was not enough to secure their gains. To hold the port, Lawrence needed the support of the British armed forces. For all his faith in the Bedouin orchestrating their own independence, he knew full well that, without Arab regulars, this was an illusion. Lawrence decided that he had to report the capture in person to GHQ Cairo, to persuade the commanding general that he must now commit more resources to the Arab cause. No one else was eligible for the task, but Lawrence was much weakened by the previous weeks' rides so the gruelling crossing of Sinai required considerable effort. When he reached Suez, and having overcome the difficulties of getting a bureaucratized army and civil administration in Egypt to understand who he was, he managed to arrange for supplies to be despatched to Aqaba by ship, along with £16,000 in gold for the Arabs' reward, and the prisoners taken off the shore. The crowning achievement for Lawrence was being granted an audience with the Commander in Chief, who, he was surprised to learn, was Allenby.[5]

Murray's inability to push through the Ottoman defences at Gaza, in two serious battles, had led to his recall. Now Allenby was eager to increase the weight of firepower and manpower for his coming offensives into Palestine, but his interest was sparked by the prospects of manoeuvre, based, in part, on his own background in the cavalry, and by the excellent corps commanders in the EEF, Philip Chetwode and Harry Chauvel.[6]

Lawrence assessed his own contribution by invoking history: 'In my report, thinking of Saladin and Abu Obeida, I had stressed the strategic importance of the eastern tribes of Syria, and their proper use as a threat to the communications of Jerusalem.'[7] The interview consisted of the diminutive Lawrence laying out his conception of how the Arabs could assist in the forthcoming operations, out on Allenby's right flank: 'He did not ask many questions, nor talk much, but studied the map and listened to my unfolding of Eastern Syria and its inhabitants. At the end he put up his chin and said quite directly, "Well, I will do for you what I can."'[8] He was true to his word on that score, including the offer of 'two hundred thousand [gold] sovereigns' to fund the Arab campaign.[9]

Gilbert Clayton of the Arab Bureau dismissed Lawrence's desire to be in command at Aqaba, and appointed Colonel Joyce, with a logistics team, and armoured cars, with aircraft to follow. The Royal Navy constructed a pier (later two), with which to ensure an efficient system of supply at the port. Lawrence pushed for Rabegh, Yanbo and Wejh to be shut down in favour of Aqaba as the new base of operations. His argument was that the Medina investment was now a backwater to the far more important Palestine–Syria front. He was refused, although it was agreed that all the stores at Wejh would be shifted to Aqaba.

Lawrence claimed that he offered that Feisal would come under Allenby's command, although he had not put this idea to Feisal himself. Nor had he raised this with Wingate, who favoured the Hejaz front, not the one in Syria. This delicate negotiation was left to Clayton.[10] It was, in fact, Allenby's intention that the Arab forces come under his command and align to his overall direction. He had agreed to support the Arab force at Aqaba, realizing that it could provide a new flank against the Ottoman forces dug in at Gaza, but for that to happen, he had to be able to coordinate the movements of the forces in that theatre. Rather than Lawrence's offer, it was really Allenby's expectation in return for the support he could offer and the necessity of the campaign at that point, that determined the chain of command.

The most challenging task of persuasion on the direction of the campaign would involve Sharif Hussein. It seemed very unlikely he would give his ascent to Feisal's subordination or to the new focus on offensive operations to the north when the Hejaz remained partially in Ottoman hands. Lawrence offered to go to Jeddah to make the attempt, but he would do so through an Arab and familial voice: to increase the chances of success, Lawrence disembarked at Wejh and was flown inland, rather than taking the 100-mile trails by camel, to get Feisal to put forward the idea as his own. Overnight, Lawrence related the advantages of working with the EEF to Feisal, and the result was that the Arab Northern Army, as it was now known, was to march up to Aqaba, with the regulars under Jafar al-Askari being transferred by ship. Cyril Wilson was the model assistant, making arrangements for stores and ammunition to go with them all. Feisal wrote a persuasive letter to his father, which Lawrence would take with him to Jeddah. But, in the event, it was Colonel Cyril Wilson who was instrumental in talking Hussein around, and getting agreement on the new plans.[11]

The significance of Aqaba was not lost on the Ottomans. Recapturing the port would require the commitment of troops which were simply not available, and so the solution lay in recruiting a larger Arab force to rival those led by Feisal and Hussein. Knowing that the Arab clans were often enemies, the Ottomans offered financial incentives to various groups to abandon the Allies. In fact, inactivity at Aqaba fuelled the old tribal resentments, and there were even disagreements between Feisal and Hussein about the future of the revolt.[12] The Ottomans made air attacks against the port, hoping to disrupt any build-up of logistics, which further demoralized the Arab fighters.[13]

Ottoman recruitment was concentrated in the Jordan Valley. Circassians formed a volunteer cavalry force of two squadrons which proved valuable in mobile patrolling against the Arab raiders. Kerak, a mixed Muslim and Christian community, fielded a volunteer militia.[14] More success was achieved with the generous Ottoman funding of Howeitat, Rwalla, Billi and Bani Atiyya clansmen. With assurances of more money, generous rationing, regular artillery, and air support, the Ottomans were almost in a position to recapture Aqaba using these Arab volunteer formations. Since the Arab forces were abandoning pastoralism or agriculture, and often refused to operate far from their homelands, the fighters had to be paid, usually in gold, to serve on a continuous basis, as the British had already discovered.[15]

Here lies the enigma about the fall of Aqaba. Although heralded as the 'breakthrough' in the Arab campaign, it is striking how nothing was done for so long after the event. The delay was in part a question of logistics. Feisal took time to move his headquarters from Wejh, and supplies had to shipped to Aqaba from Egypt and from the south. There were inevitable hold-ups. But there was little appreciable progress otherwise. Lawrence, when reporting to Cairo, had sketched out a plan for Arab operations that included a renewed assault on the railways at Hemmah, across the Yarmuk River, a *coup de main* seizure of Deraa, the expulsion of Turkish posts in the Jordan Valley and the plain of Esdraelon near Acre and Tyre and finally an assault on Damascus.[16] This was, in part, Lawrence's attempt to persuade Allenby that the Arabs could be taken seriously, rather than a definite strategy. But Allenby accepted that 'The advantages offered by Arab co-operation on lines proposed by Captain Lawrence are, in my opinion, of such importance that no effort should be spared to reap full benefit therefrom.'[17]

The initiative appears to have returned to Djemal Pasha and the Ottomans at this point. Two telegrams reached Lawrence that Auda, one of his closest allies, had accepted Ottoman entreaties to defect.[18] Lawrence was alarmed as Auda had appeared to be the most committed of the Arab lieutenants. The threat was therefore potentially very serious: 'Mohammed el Dheilan was capable of double play, and Ibn Jad and his friends were still uncertain.'[19] Lawrence admitted: 'Treachery had not been taken into account when Nasir and I had built our plan for the town's defence.'[20] Lawrence returned to Aqaba, and quietly asked Auda and his comrade, Mohammed, about the correspondence with the Ottomans at Ma'an. Auda made light of it all, claiming it had been a ruse to get money out of the local Ottoman garrison, and it was a sham. Lawrence described their story as 'farcical' but listened more sympathetically to their complaints that no artillery or troops had yet come to their aid. Worse, they were genuinely angry that they had been given no specific rewards for capturing Aqaba.

Naturally, they were keen to know how they had been exposed. Lawrence related that the negotiations 'were on a slippery ledge'. He explained: 'I played on their fear by my unnecessary amusement, quoting in careless laughter, as if they were my own words, actual phrases of the letters they had exchanged.' He then added quickly that Feisal was coming up with the entire army, with artillery, armoured cars, regular troops, money and supplies. He had the ace hand, and Auda was at a disadvantage. Lawrence guessed that the offer of a substantial financial advance would be enough to keep him on the Allied side, and, if the British did not keep their word, he would return to some arrangement with the Ottomans. This pragmatism was at odds with Lawrence's portrayal of Auda as a fearless, noble and largely patriotic figure.[21] Such a description fitted with his desire to construct characters according to an Arthurian framework. Sergeant Marcel Matte of the French contingent, who met Auda at Wejh, saw him as 'sly, wily, and avaricious'.[22] The best we can say is that Auda was acting in his own interests. Lawrence suppressed the suspicion of treachery when he returned to Egypt, in case the authorities changed their mind about the Arab Revolt.[23]

Lawrence admitted, in the weeks that followed, that all his time was taken up trying to resolve disputes. The Meccans clashed with the other factions interminably.[24] These incidents, although a common occurrence throughout the campaign, indicate that the momentum of operations had been lost. The inactive fighters were restless and prone to disputes over both plans and the sharing of the spoils.

The solution to the possible fragmentation of the Arab force was to send the Hejazis away and recruit men from the Levant and the interior, and then to conduct more raiding against Ottoman lines of communication to encourage others to join the Sharifian cause. Consequently, there were more tactical successes against railways. It was clear to Lawrence the strength of the 'revolt' still lay in a strategy of guerrilla warfare.

The temporary loss of momentum made it clear that, despite assumptions about the inevitability of Lawrence's successes, victory for the Arab forces was not a foregone conclusion. Moreover, as subsequent operations at Gaza, Amman and Megiddo demonstrated, the Arab Revolt was less important than the relentless pressure exerted by the EEF. Without Allenby's army, the Ottomans would have been free to sweep away the Arab Revolt, regardless of raids on their lines of communications. In other words, the most significant factor in the seizure and retention of Aqaba was still the British armed forces and their vast algebraic resources.

Lawrence now had to consider not just the ways and means, as he had some months before at Wadi Ais, but the ends of his strategy too. He wrote that there had been insufficient thought given to the overall objectives of the desert war hitherto:

Such haphazard playing with the men and movements of which we had assumed the leadership disgraced our minds. I vowed to know henceforward, before I moved, where I was going and by what roads. At Wejh the Hejaz war was won: after Akaba [Aqaba] it was ended. Feisal's army had cleared off its Arabian liabilities and now, under General Allenby the joint Commander-in-Chief, its role was to take part in the military deliverance of Syria.[25]

So now, the Arab Revolt would be bound to the fortunes of Allenby and the EEF. The British were going to drive north, and that suited Lawrence's own purposes.[26]

The problem, as Lawrence saw it, was that the Bedouin were not interested in a lasting political settlement. He described them poetically as like the desert grass, blooming only briefly before waning into the dust. What he needed was the loyalty of the settled populations, associating the fixed nature of the peasants and their cultivated lands with the permanence of their political economy. The challenge was that the nomadic peoples of the plains and deserts were so different from the coastal populations, and that the geographical barriers of rivers and mountains created even larger obstacles to any idea of a united region. Languages, religions, rituals and more divided them all. The large urban centres had systems all of their own.[27] Lawrence was correct in his assessment that Feisal must win over the social geography if he was to succeed in gaining the allegiance of the inhabitants. The 'human terrain', as modern military personnel would style it, was now the centre of gravity of the political war.

The only points of unity which might be utilized were the common use of the Arabic language, and the sentimental attachment to the notion of a Caliphate. Lawrence admitted that even if such a polity could be constructed, it would be as alien as Turkish governance. Local autonomy would be sought again. The only reason for even considering a unifying project was the demands of the war. Lawrence calculated:

> Arab Government in Syria, though buttressed on Arabic prejudices, would be as much 'imposed' as the Turkish Government, or a foreign protectorate, or the historic Caliphate. Syria remained a vividly coloured racial and religious mosaic. Any wide attempt after unity would make a patched and parcelled thing, ungrateful to a people whose instincts ever returned towards parochial home rule. Our excuse for over-running expediency was War.[28]

Once settled on the idea of a political alliance of the Near East under Feisal's unifying leadership, Lawrence returned to the question of ways and means. He wrote that the fundamental requirement was mobility, and borrowed from axioms he had remembered from his readings, but with the startling analogy of the desert as the sea:

> In character our operations of development for the final stroke should be like naval war, in mobility, ubiquity, independence of bases and communications, ignoring of ground features, of strategic areas, of fixed directions, of fixed points. 'He who commands the sea is at great liberty, and may take as much or as little of the war as he will.' And we commanded the desert. Camel raiding parties, self-contained like ships, might cruise confidently along the enemy's cultivation-frontier, sure of an unhindered retreat into their desert-element which the Turks could not explore.[29]

The quoted line was Francis Bacon's 'Of the True Greatness of Kingdoms and Estates'. Bacon's remark was to reinforce the idea that naval battles were often decisive ends of a conflict, but also avoided the drain or risk of land power. Command of the sea conferred a degree of impunity and offered opportunities to strike on land at a time of one's choosing.[30] In this Lawrence conceived of his method:

> Discrimination of what point of the enemy organism to disarrange would come to us with war practice. Our tactics should be tip and

run: not pushes, but strokes. We should never try to improve an advantage. We should use the smallest force in the quickest time at the farthest place.[31]

The means of war, its algebra, were to be superior at the point of contact. Lawrence insisted on:

a technical superiority over the Turks in the critical department. I sent to Egypt demands for great quantities of light automatic guns, Hotchkiss or Lewis, to be used as snipers' tools. The men we trained to them were kept deliberately ignorant of the mechanism, not to waste speed in action upon efforts at repair. Ours were battles of minutes, fought at eighteen miles an hour. If a gun jammed, the gunner must throw it aside and go in with his rifle.[32]

The other tool was explosives, and, in many ways, this was a 'dynamite war', although Lawrence lamented the absence of long-range artillery, and the disadvantage of short-range guns. Laying explosives and being dependent on shoulder arms meant that, if there were skirmishes, they had to be at relatively close quarters. Lawrence's use of the term 'snipers' tools' indicates what he would have preferred to possess. The repeated accurate shooting of soldiers, by unseen snipers, has a disproportionately depressing effect on all troops. It was this precise impact that Lawrence wished to achieve.[33]

Denial of intelligence to the Ottomans was vital. The diversity of the Arab war parties 'threw the enemy intelligence off the track', since there were no fixed sizes to any of their units. Groups were assembled from their own tribal areas, and sometimes, if rarely because of feuds and suspicions, they were combined. Lawrence boasted that the fighters could deceive Ottoman intelligence because their formations were loose, whereas 'we knew them exactly; each single unit, and every man they moved', which was almost certainly an exaggeration.

Nevertheless, his claim has greater validity in one respect. He wrote:

We on the Arab front were very intimate with the enemy. Our Arab officers had been Turkish Officers, and knew every leader on the other side personally. They had suffered the same training, thought the same, took the same point of view. By practicing modes of approach upon the Arabs we could explore the Turks: understand, almost get inside, their minds. Relation between us and them was universal, for the civil population of the enemy area was wholly ours without pay or persuasion. In consequence our intelligence service was the widest, fullest and most certain imaginable.[34]

The base at Aqaba was reinforced as planned, with the regular Arab troops under Jafar al-Askari, armoured cars, Feisal's forces, and Egyptian labourers. But the build-up was matched by German and Ottoman efforts. Their Ma'an garrison was increased from a battalion to a reinforced brigade of over 6,000 men, and it possessed a cavalry regiment and mounted infantry for mobile operations. It was placed under the command of Colonel Behjet, a veteran of the fighting in Sinai. The German air force, consisting of one squadron, provided aerial reconnaissance and a ground attack capability.[35] In sum, this force was not fixed to the defence of the railway junction, but had the ability to strike across the desert and mountains. Ma'an itself was fortified with more entrenchments and festooned with barbed wire. Its approaches were covered by machine guns and mountain artillery, with fixed lines for night fighting. The railway brought down significant volumes of stores, sufficient to withstand a siege or to support the manoeuvre of its battalions into the hinterland. With Ma'an secure, they advanced towards Guweira, Auda's territory, and fortified the critical pass at Abu el Lissan with 2,000 men. A strong cavalry screen operated to the western flank, covering the routes from Wadi Musa. They had, it seemed, sealed off the road out of Aqaba.

The Arab Northern Army was lucky that there were no regular Ottoman Army operations against Aqaba itself: the Ottoman intention was rather to set off feuds and rivalries amongst Arabs that would ensure that the Sharif's cause would collapse. When the first Ottoman–Arab attack was made, the Howeitat and Bani men stood by idly, while the volunteers of Kerak drove off the Sharifian outposts and seized livestock and supplies for themselves. No further progress was made and Aqaba was not threatened, but, as intended, divisions had been sown. The Ottomans continued to court the Arabs back to their side.[36] Indeed, there was condemnation of the Arab Revolt and the connivance of the British and French in trying to establish an Arab kingdom, under Hussein, across the entire Middle East. In secret correspondence to Feisal, the

Ottomans argued that the British intended to make slaves of the Arabs, rendering Mecca and Medina mere protectorates which would be cut off from the rest of the Middle East and therefore dependent on British supplies of food, fodder and finance.[37]

Lawrence advised that the Arabs should recover the initiative with probing attacks, and these would also delay any major assault on the port itself. The first step was to draw the Ottomans into fighting within the Wadi Musa, where the terrain would favour the irregulars. The initial skirmishes confirmed this. A small detachment of Delagha tribesmen shot at and drew after them Ottoman patrols. Local people, even though rivals of the roving Delagha, were rewarded with gold for information on Ottoman movements. This ensured they did not oppose the tribesmen. Maulud, one of the most experienced Arab commanders, then moved several hundred fighters up to Petra, amidst its ruddy-coloured historic ruins. From here, small raids were organized, to seize Ottoman horses or rifles, and otherwise harry their enemy. Lawrence anticipated this would so frustrate the Ottomans, they would make an aggressive, larger offensive move in the direction of Petra. All these obscuring operations would further delay an attack on Aqaba.[38]

Greater disruption was caused by air attacks. Captain F. W. Stent led his small Royal Flying Corps flight against Ma'an, taking enormous risks to land on the desert floor, without a prepared airstrip, then:

> he ordered low flying, to make sure the aim; and profited by reaching Maan, ... dropping thirty-two bombs in and about the unprepared station. Two bombs into the barracks killed thirty-five men and wounded fifty. Eight struck the engine-shed, heavily damaging the plant and stock. A bomb in the General's kitchen finished his cook and his breakfast. Four fell on the aerodrome. Despite the shrapnel our pilots and engines returned safely to their temporary landing ground at Kuntilla above Akaba [Aqaba].[39]

Lawrence recounts how they remained in the desert, and made a second raid against the Ottoman encampment at Abu el Lissan: 'They bombed the horse lines and stampeded the animals, visited the tents and scattered the Turks. As on the day before, they flew low and were much hit, but not fatally. Long before noon they were back in Kuntilla.'[40] The low-level flying improved the accuracy of the attack, but it gave the

Ottomans the opportunity to bring their fire to bear on the flimsy, slow aircraft. Yet the pilots were undeterred:

> Stent looked over the remaining petrol and bombs, and decided they were enough for one more effort. So he gave directions to everyone to look for the battery which had troubled them in the morning. They started in the midday heat. Their loads were so heavy they could get no height, and therefore came blundering over the crest behind Aba el Lissan, and down the valley at about three hundred feet. The Turks, always somnolent at noon, were taken completely by surprise. Thirty bombs were dropped: one silenced the battery, the others killed dozens of men and animals. Then the lightened machines soared up and home to El Arish.[41]

It is difficult to appreciate now how intrepid and daring this operation had been. The risks were enormous, but they had been offset to some extent by the element of surprise.[42] The effect of these raids on Arab morale was significant, and it forced the Ottomans to adjust their relative superiority over their adversaries. More effort had to be made to 'harden' their defences at Abu el Lissan, and Ottoman air patrols had to consider the possibility of air to air combat, or the detection of surprise raids.

Despite Lawrence's upbeat account of the operations out of Aqaba, not all was going according to plan. He admitted that he had to 'hammer on against the Turks through month after month of feckless disappointment', which reveals something of the true state of conditions at the port and in the interior.[43]

The Germans and Ottomans retaliated with their own air attacks. While Lawrence was crossing the plain of Guweira, one aircraft had dropped three bombs on the Arab encampment ahead of them, without effect, but it was a stark indication that the Arab raiders could no longer guarantee their security in the desert.[44] Aircraft gave the Ottomans a crucial surveillance capability, increasing the Arabs' difficulties in remaining undetected. It was another signal that one era of warfare was giving way to another, one in which air power would end decisively the inviolability of the desert.

The Howeitat, who were supposed to form the bulk of Lawrence's raiding party, were near mutiny with jealousies over the distribution of gold and authority.[45] The smaller clans were resentful of the more numerous Howeitat. Lawrence tried to placate the factions, without success. Some southern clans threatened to abandon the whole force. Part of the problem was the inactivity of the fighters, which was breeding discontent. It was the same in Wadi Rumm, where other clan sheikhs were suspicious of the Sharif, the Abu Tayi, and the pretensions of the Howeitat.[46] Even Gasim abu Dumeik, who had led the daring attack at Abu el Lissan, was full of vitriol about the Sharifian cause. He argued that he would sooner join the Turks, a point which alarmed some of his clansmen, but reflected the deep disappointment at this stage of the campaign. Lawrence could only threaten that, if his clan withdrew, they would forfeit all future benefits. He noted that the groups were close to fighting each other.[47]

The situation was serious enough to merit Lawrence's immediate departure from a planned raid to warn Feisal and get his intervention.[48] Although he did not spell it out, this level of fragmentation could threaten the entire revolt. Without cohesion, on which any progress depended, the entire campaign was at risk of failure. He rushed back to Aqaba, acquired a trusted mediator, and set off back to the raiding party. There was some pacification of the arguments that had characterized the previous nights, but the group that embarked on the raid was still divided. Different clans refused to ride together, or take orders. The nominated leader of the raiding group commanded no authority, so Lawrence took over:

> Poor Sherif Aid's uselessness, even as nominal leader, forced me to assume the direction myself, against both principle and judgement; since the special arts of tribal raiding and the details of food-halts and pasturage, road-direction, pay, disputes, division of spoils, feuds and march order were much outside the syllabus of the Oxford School of Modern History.[49]

The more serious risk was that faced by those engaged on advisory work amongst local forces. To assume too much authority could lead to resentment and blame, and thus alienation from the mission. On the other hand, the Arab fighters were aware that the technical expertise in explosives, machine guns and mortars, the 'enablers' in modern military parlance, were vital. It is never easy to advise, to 'lead from behind', and it is always a matter of fine judgement and mutual trust. Constant consultation was the key, and Lawrence related that he rode up and down the whole time, listening and talking to each clan leader in turn, along the straggling line of march.

So, what had Lawrence learned, this far into the campaign, about the conduct of war? The challenges of maintaining cohesion amongst the tribal forces were now very evident, making it all the more important that Feisal became the unifying authority for the Arab Northern Army. The new focus of the desert campaign, and the fact that the Ottomans were not only being reinforced, but were adapting to the constant raiding, compelled further changes in the Arab force. The upgrading of the fighters, with modern firearms, machine guns and explosives, was essential, not just for their effectiveness but for their confidence. Air power was now making a greater impact on this theatre of operations, so the deployment of air assets for reconnaissance, deterring Ottoman and German flights, and attacks on ground targets was another strong imperative. Lawrence knew that the Arabs were required to coordinate their operations with the British forces in Palestine, but he believed the irregulars were unsuited to this, so Feisal's tribal army was gradually transformed into a mixed contingent of semi-trained and regular troops, supported by French artillery, British armoured cars and heavy weapons detachments. Major Young wrote: 'Gone were the picturesque days of lone-handed enterprise and dashing raids with troops of Beduin.'[50] Tribal factions were increasingly limited to short, local missions or allocated to controlling their own districts.[51]

Lawrence was now in a position to develop the lessons he had learned into a mature conception of guerrilla war. He had to blend regular, conventional military power with smaller, irregular forces. He had to combine them in a comprehensive campaign of informational and psychological operations, a phenomenon often referred to today as hybrid warfare. Nevertheless, this development was not without serious setbacks that almost cost him his life. In fact, the fighting that lay ahead threatened to defeat the entire northern extension of the Arab Revolt.

7

Railway Raids and Lawrence's Conception of Mature Guerrilla Warfare

On 28 March 1917, Lawrence accompanied a raiding party of Ateiba to attack the Hejaz railway at Abu el Naam, a mission that would coincide with the British offensive at Gaza. Crossing the desert proved relatively easy and the raiders were soon in a position close to the Hejaz line. The raid was preceded by a ruse designed to combine deception with the exhaustion of the bionomic resilience of the local Ottoman forces. At night, the Arab raiders had fired a few rounds into an Ottoman blockhouse, forcing its garrison to remain alert all night to an imagined assault which did not, in fact, materialize.[1] Having tired the defenders out in this way, Lawrence adapted the original plan of making a demonstration with a mountain gun before a full attack:

> Shakir told me that he had brought only three hundred men instead of the agreed eight or nine hundred. However, it was his war, and therefore his tune, so we hastily modified the plans. We would not take the station; we would frighten it by a frontal artillery attack, while we mined the railway to the north and south, in the hope of trapping that halted train. Accordingly we chose a party of Garland-trained dynamiters who should blow up something north of the bridge at dawn, to seal that direction; while I went off with high explosive and a machine gun with its crew to lay a mine to the south of the station, the probable direction from which the Turks would seek or send help, in their emergency.[2]

It would take an hour to lay the mines in the dark, but, anticipating the derailment of an approaching train, machine guns were placed to overlook the spot and maximize enemy casualties. The actual minelaying took four times longer than expected, and an exhausted Lawrence barely managed to return to the main body in time for the engagement to commence. Several rounds from the mountain gun plunged onto the Ottoman station, and one hit a carriage, starting a fire. The engine was rapidly uncoupled and set off, running into the mine that Lawrence and his party had laid. The damage was superficial and the Arab machine gunners, fearing they had been abandoned, had set off to rejoin the main body without orders and so missed the opportunity to attack the engine, leaving the Ottoman crews free to repair their precious locomotive. At the main position, the Arab raiders could not press the assault on an entrenched Ottoman garrison of some 300 men, while the 'smoke was too thick for us to shoot', so Lawrence broke off the action. In the affair, Lawrence noted they had taken 'thirty prisoners, a mare, two camels and some more sheep; and had killed and wounded seventy of the garrison, at a cost to ourselves of one man slightly hurt. Traffic was held up for three days of repair and investigation. So we did not wholly fail.'[3]

Lawrence, still disappointed by this raid, took a party of 40 Juheina to mount another attack on the line at Madahrij the following day. Passing through in turns oppressive heat and a torrential storm, the raiding party lost the element of surprise to a lone picquet. The group arrived on the line in the dark, laid mines for four hours, and brought up camels to create the impression that a large force had merely crossed the line, for the mud made it obvious that men had approached the rails. The ambush was set and machine guns placed overlooking the mined section, but all that passed was a simple trolley manned by five Ottoman soldiers. Fortunately, this patrol did not detect the mines, nor did a unit of 60 men who had been sent out to replace telegraph poles knocked down by the previous night's storm. At dusk, the motionless ambush party saw another clearance patrol of 11 men carefully examine the rails and sleepers. They seemed to detect something. With bated breath, Lawrence watched as the inspection team poked at the ballast and examined the site. Miraculously, they did not find the buried explosives and passed on to the south. Later a train came up, full of refugees, but it passed right over the detonator without triggering the device, which had somehow failed.[4]

The raiders, who had expected a large explosion, had rushed to firing positions, but this alerted the Turkish patrol which retired back to Madahrij, and, with the garrison now alive to the presence of the Arab insurgents, the Ottomans opened fire. Bugles were sounded to the south, indicating that the next fortified post had been informed of the threat.[5] The line of retreat was badly chosen and Lawrence now realized that the machine gun team, with a mule, would not escape any mounted Ottoman force sent to intercept them. They had to pull back through the hills, and direct the machine gun team and an escort back to Wadi Ais. The remaining Juheina then taunted the Ottoman garrisons with brief appearances and even a visit back to the railway line at nightfall, which provoked more shooting, without effect. Cloaked with darkness, Lawrence took the opportunity to recover the mine, a hazardous undertaking, and established the problem with the detonator. Risking the Ottoman preference to remain in cover and not venture into the desert after them, the raiders re-laid the device, blew up a culvert, pulled down telegraph poles and escaped.[6] Some time later, an Ottoman train with a working party ran over the mine which went off successfully.

Lawrence believed that 'mines were the best weapon yet discovered to make the regular working of their trains costly and uncertain for our ... enemy'.[7] This was indeed a prescient observation, for the mine and improvised explosive device were thereafter a critical tool in every insurgent's arsenal. The remote action of a device protected the assailants, allowed them to keep the initiative by choosing its location and timing, and maximized damage and cost on their enemy. Detection was time-consuming, often exhausting, and uncertain.[8] Lawrence concluded that, as a result, 'the Turkish garrisons suffer badly from nerves'.[9] The chief problems with the mines were that they were prone to failure, the laying of them placed the security of the insurgents at risk, and their victims might just as easily be civilians as military personnel, perhaps alienating the very population the insurgents sought to win over.

Lawrence met Lieutenant Henry Hornby, of the Royal Engineers, as he returned from one of his own raiding missions, sunburnt, his uniform ragged, but exuding that determined air of a professional soldier. Lawrence reported that the Arabs held Hornby and Colonel Newcombe in high esteem, speculating that they would virtually sleep on the rails, or try to bite through the metal if their explosives ran out. It was a touching admiration, but while estimating that 'For Turkish labour battalions they kept busy, patching culverts, relaying sleepers, jointing new rails; and gun-cotton had to come in increasing tons to Wejh to meet their appetites', Lawrence noted with envy: 'They were wonderful, but their too-great excellence discouraged our feeble teams.'[10] Lawrence was eager to have Arabs do the mining and would have preferred to have no British presence at all, which, at this stage of the campaign, would have been impossible.

Prior to the next attack on Musaw'warrah (Mudawarra), Lawrence hoped to be able to assault the station itself, but the raiders were reluctant to contemplate it. The compromise was to conduct a close reconnaissance to ascertain its defensive strength. The last source of water as they moved in was fouled by dead animals, a deliberate Ottoman ploy to render it unpotable.

The first reconnaissance to a ridgeline overlooking the station, where Ottoman sangars and trenches stood, gave them far too little information, so they descended to get closer, taking care not to alert some guard dogs. This silent reconnoitre did not yield much more. Locating the Ottoman machine gun posts proved especially difficult, as all the positions were well dug in. The stone buildings looked impervious to a mortar bomb, and the garrison was larger than the raiding group of 116 'unhappy', that is divided, men.[11] The decision was taken to bypass the station and attack the more vulnerable railway instead, and, if possible, take a train with it.

The site selected was ideal for the laying of explosive, with a concealed route for the electrical command wire. The challenge was again digging the charges in, without leaving considerable evidence of surface disturbance. Moreover, the command wire was stiff, and the twanging coils kept reappearing above the sand. This necessitated re-burying it several times which took five hours of work.[12] The other problem was that the firing point did not have line of sight to a culvert where the charges were laid, so one man had to remain 50 yards in front of it. On the other hand, some high ground overlooked the whole site, 200 yards away, providing good cover for an ambush team, the mortar and the machine gun. Crucially, there was an escape route to the rear, and a pursuing force would have to scale the cliffs, under fire, which would give the raiding party a chance to break clean. The difficulties of laying an ambush were not just in the siting of it though. Lawrence noted that the men with baggage camels insisted on sitting on the ridge top, with their animals, visible to all around. This gave away their position to an Ottoman outpost 4 miles to the south, and warning shots indicated that they had been spotted.

The Ottomans waited until dawn and sent a 40-man patrol in extended order up astride the line. Lawrence recognized the dilemma this presented. If the raiders remained concealed, it would take the Ottomans about an hour to come level with them, with the risk the charges would be discovered. Too strong a demonstration would simply bring up more Ottoman reinforcements. Instead he resolved to have a small party offer a few shots, and gradually move off in a different direction, in the hope of drawing the Ottomans after them.[13] This seemed to work, initially.

Another smaller foot patrol of nine men marched up the line, and, unaware of the presence of Lawrence's ambush, they nestled under a culvert to get out of the noonday sun, for the day was now hot. The raiders were reassured that this patrol showed no signs of rigorous investigation about their surroundings. But then, a new force appeared, in company strength of 100 men, marching in extended line from the Musaw'warrah Station: another clearance effort. Their axis was directly towards the ambush site, so the raiders started to mount up, planning to abandon the mine in place and return when the Ottomans had become complacent.

Just as they started off, a train began to approach the nearby station, offering the chance to detonate the charges after all. The raiders had to scramble back into position, the riflemen concealed behind the lip of the ridge that lay just 150 yards from the line. Lawrence relates that, with the sound of the engine labouring along the line towards them,

> An Arab stood up on high behind the guns and shouted to us what the train was doing – a necessary precaution, for if it carried troops and detrained them behind our ridge we should have to face about like a flash and retire fighting up the valley for our lives.[14]

To deter attack, the Ottomans aboard the train were shooting into likely cover, seemingly aware of the threat.[15] This suggests that the presence of the Arab party had been taken more seriously than Lawrence had hoped. He found himself in the final minutes wondering whether a large Ottoman force aboard the train would recover from the mine attack and overwhelm his smaller party.[16] But the two locomotives with their ten box cars rounded the bend as hoped, and Lawrence signalled for the charge to be blown:

> There followed a terrific roar, and the line vanished from sight behind a spouting column of black dust and smoke a hundred feet high and wide. Out of the darkness came shattering crashes and long, loud metallic clangings of ripped steel, with many lumps of iron and plate; while one entire wheel of a locomotive whirled up suddenly black out of the cloud against the sky, and sailed musically over our heads to fall slowly and heavily into the desert behind.[17]

Lawrence dashed up to the mortar and machine gun platform, while the Arab fighters opened up on the stationary wagons. The Lewis gun raked the tops, and Lawrence was able to see Ottoman soldiers falling from the fire, while a significant number jumped out of the far side to take cover behind the embankment of the rail line.[18] The Bedouin had rushed forward, perhaps prematurely, and at close range found themselves under the sustained fire of the detrained troops: '[The Ottomans] had got behind the bank, here about eleven feet high, and from cover of the wheels were firing point-blank at the Beduin twenty yards away across the sand-filled dip.' Lawrence was concerned because 'the enemy in the crescent of the curving line were secure from the machine-guns'. Two of the Arabs were shot down. However, the second round of the mortar landed right behind the embankment, inflicting casualties.[19] Realizing this bank was no longer providing any cover, the soldiers tried to run back along the line or across the open ground behind the train. The Lewis guns used the sway of traversing fire to mow down the escaping troops. In ten minutes, the ambush was over.[20]

Immediately, the Musaw'warrah company changed direction towards the railway line, while the troops who had been advancing from the south, spotting the clouds of smoke and the baggage camels running back to Lawrence's position, now stepped up their convergence on the ambush site. The ambushers were now in danger of being caught between two pincers, but instead of preparing to escape, they were busily engaged in looting the wrecked train to obtain material profits as compensation for their hardship and hazard. Lawrence estimated they had less than 30 minutes to get away.

Inspecting the smashed train, Lawrence believed the damage had proven the value of the electrical detonator over the contact mine, and to ensure that the leading engine was unusable, Lawrence set a small charge against the cylinder and blew it. The Arab fighters were euphoric but utterly focussed on the goods they could carry away, and seemingly impervious to the entreaties of the wounded and mainly sick soldiers who had been in the train. Some women, who had been able to crawl out of the wagons, were hysterical with fear and loss. Lawrence, being obviously foreign, was the subject of entreaties for mercy from survivors of the attack, as they believed the Arabs would simply murder them. A group of Austrian officers, mostly wounded, who were supposed to be artillery instructors, also asked for assistance, but fearing treachery, one had opened fire, so the Arabs had killed them. The only sensible element for Lawrence was the discovery of some Egyptian soldiers who had been taken prisoner in the south. Now released, Lawrence found these disciplined men more reliable to herd the enemy prisoners.[21]

The retirement from the ambush was chaotic. At one point, Lawrence and the two regular army sergeants accompanying him found themselves alone, with no sign of any camels, as the Arabs dispersed as fast as they could across the plain with their booty.[22] Fortunately, they were rescued, along with their guns, the exploder, and the precious wire, in a hasty and undignified manner.[23] The spare ammunition and ammonal had to be piled in a heap and a fuse set. Fortunately, the resulting detonation convinced the Ottomans that they should pause and take cover, and this gave the Arabs precious time to increase the distance between their pursuers and themselves. Lawrence later learned that one of the slaves, under his own command, had been left behind for dead. Despite returning to overlook the site of the attack, now firmly in Ottoman hands, he believed there was no chance of his survival.[24] Lawrence noted that wounded men, if too difficult to move, were killed off by fellow tribesmen to avoid torture. He wrote: 'the Turks did not take Arab prisoners. Indeed, they used to kill them horribly; so, in mercy, we were finishing those of our badly wounded who would have to be left helpless on abandoned ground.'[25]

Lawrence took another party to find baggage camels but they were shot at, the rifle fire being augmented by long-range machine gun fire. The Ottomans, sensing they had caught a small group, moved around the flanks to envelop them. The Arabs dashed away, and returned accurate fire, checking the pursuit. They repeated the tactic of withdrawing and firing from a ridge, before retreating again. Fortunately, one of the sergeants, hearing the gunfight, rode up to offer assistance, and his Lewis gun had a significant effect.[26]

The problem was that the encumbrance of prisoners and wounded, and the lack of water, compelled the party now to double back towards the nearest well at Musaw'warrah, albeit the contaminated one, and to make stealthy use of it. Lawrence noted how his force was now more of a vulnerable caravan than a raiding party. But they escaped, disappearing into the vastness of the desert via Lawrence's favourite red sandstone-vaulted Wadi Rumm, and on to Aqaba. News of their raid encouraged the restive tribesmen, and stirred a jealousy for similar boasting among them. Although it took some days to mount another raid, there was no shortage of volunteers.[27]

The raiders were again deterred by blockhouses, and minelaying as usual took hours, but Lawrence found that corralling the undisciplined, if enthusiastic, tribesmen was more trying than the task of attacking the railways. Lawrence listed the challenges as: 'In the six days' raid there came to a head, and were settled, twelve cases of assault with weapons, four camel-liftings, one marriage, two thefts, a divorce, fourteen feuds, two evil eyes, and a bewitchment.'[28]

Once again, an experimental mine proved problematic, as one train passed clean over it without setting it off, and so a more reliable electrically detonated charge was laid. Ottoman patrols swept the line repeatedly. On one occasion, a 12-man group seemed to march slowly ahead of an equally agonizingly slow train. Finally, the train drew level with the ambush:

> not until the engine was exactly over the arch did I jump up and wave my cloak. Faiz instantly pressed his handle, and the great noise and dust and blackness burst up, as at Mudow-wara [Musaw'warrah] a week before, and enveloped me where I sat, while the green-yellow sickly smoke of lyddite hung sluggishly about the wreck. The Lewis guns rattled out suddenly, three or four short bursts: there was a yell from the Arabs, and, headed by Pisani sounding the women's vibrant battle-cry, they rushed in a wild torrent for the train.[29]

As the train itself was uncoupled and began rolling away, an Ottoman colonel spotted Lawrence by the track and shot him, grazing his hip.

The ambush, however, had been successful, killing 20 soldiers and producing a crop of prisoners who now feared they would be massacred.[30] The bulk of the train was full of rations, some of which were carried off, while civilians who had been on board were ordered to march north. The Ottomans did their best to pursue, getting to within 400 yards in their counter-attack, but the Arabs were soon concealed in the hills and so escaped, once more laden with goods.[31]

Lawrence was keen that the Arabs learned the art of attacking trains and lines for themselves, and, with the help of more experienced advisors, they accounted for 17 trains.[32] He assessed: 'The loss of the engines was sore upon the Turks. Since the rolling stock was pooled for Palestine and Hejaz, our destructions not merely made the mass evacuation of Medina impossible, but began to pinch the army about Jerusalem, just as the British threat grew formidable.'[33] In meeting Allenby a second time, Lawrence articulated the argument that has become a controversy amongst historians, that 'my hope to leave the line just working, but only just, to Medina; where Fakhri's corps fed itself at less cost than if in prison at Cairo'. The logic was, as noted before, 'The surest way to limit the line without killing it was by attacking trains.' He continued, accurately, that the Arabs were not yet strong enough to seize a rail node like Ma'an, and capturing thousands of Ottoman prisoners, if Medina fell, would impose a burden on the Egyptian economy, so a slow, attritional strategy was the best. This was almost certainly Lawrence's retrospective post-war rationalization, as he sought to explain why the Arabs had been unable to drive the Ottomans out of Arabia.

Allenby was discerning. He asked Lawrence to say why, given his assessment of the Ottoman weaknesses caused by railway raids, there was a strong enemy force moving westwards into Wadi Musa, and thus potentially onto the British left flank. Lawrence replied that he intended to tie the Ottomans down there in the mountainous country, so there would be little chance of them moving as far as the British positions in Palestine.

The Ottomans had been making determined efforts to change the situation in Palestine and the Hejaz. In March, there was extensive fighting around Medina, as the garrison tried to drive off and defeat the Arab Southern Army. The following month, the pro-Ottoman Emir of Hail, Ibn Rashid, had attempted to move a large column of supplies to Medina, but was intercepted at Hanakiye, 80 miles to the north-east of the city, by Zeid.[34] Although Rashid's force escaped, they abandoned some 200 men, four mountain guns, 3,000 camels with their loads and 3,000 sheep. The loss of such crucial supplies was significant. Rashid's failure also had other consequences. He concentrated 1,000 mounted followers at Medain Salih, on the Hejaz railway, 200 miles north of Medina, which represented a threat to the small mobile raiding forces of the Sharifian cause. Nevertheless, distrust developed between him and the Ottoman command and Rashid was held under open arrest to keep the Shammar aligned with the Ottoman war effort.

With great daring, Lieutenant Colonel Newcombe and Major W. A. Davenport conducted a raid at Qalat Zumrud, between Rashid's base and the force at Medina. Described by the *Official History* as 'one of the most successful raids of the whole campaign', the raiders, consisting of Indian cavalry, French Algerians and Egyptian troops led by British officers, destroyed 3 miles of the Hejaz line in a single attack. Arab fighters provided a demonstration at Zumrud, and captured a fortified post with the station. Major Joyce made another attack to the south, destroying 2,000 rails and several culverts. It has been estimated that there were as many as 30 separate raids in this period, each inflicting various levels of damage.[35] The Ottomans were now forced to garrison the entire line with forts, blockhouses and observation posts. The stations were held by entrenched companies, while smaller defences were manned with platoons and sections.[36]

The achievement of the Arab insurgency is often attributed to this tying down of Ottoman troops, which is undeniable, but the criticism that the Ottomans had committed an error in holding a single line, giving up control of the desert, as a zone, is perhaps overstated.[37] The fact is that deserts are irrelevant in assessments of control. Insurgents and counter-insurgents must control the population, so the territorial space or transport networks are merely the means or ways to achieve that objective. This was exemplified in depictions of the conflict between the Syrian government and their insurgent enemies in the 2010s: the so-called 'spider maps' that showed areas of control as colour codes indicated that it was the routes, transport nodes, and settlements, not the desert space, that mattered most. Access to water determines what can be held and what can only be considered a transit area. Holding the desert is of no value, and Lawrence too aimed to take and hold the cities in the Near East by means of winning the most important asset of all, the allegiance of the people.

But there were more pressing issues. The Ottomans had concentrated 6,000 men at Ma'an and in September 1917 this force was joined by the Ottoman 7th Cavalry Regiment, which seemed to herald an attack. Abu el Lissan, the forward base, was already garrisoned with 2,000 men. To Lawrence, here was the anticipated counter-offensive ordered by Djemal Pasha, the Governor of Syria (a fact contrary to Basil Liddell Hart's later view that Djemal could not 'muster the nerve for the attempt').[38] With the fall of Abu el Lissan, the only way to defend the route to Aqaba was to harass the flank of any Ottoman force moving southwestwards towards the port. The avenue for this was the Wadi Araba and its branch, the Wadi Musa, that led eastwards into the mountains. Here, at the ancient city of Petra, the Arabs had established a base for their raids. The Ottomans had therefore resolved to take Petra first, thus securing their lines of communication to Abu el Lissan and beyond.

While the Royal Flying Corps conducted attacks on Ma'an and Abu el Lissan, and Lawrence carried out his raid near Musaw'warrah, Arab forces took Shobek in early October, just 20 miles north of Ma'an, thus threatening the Ottomans' supply lines for their intended attack against Petra and Aqaba. They were driven out, but only after tearing up rails of the light railway extension.

The Ottomans persisted in their offensive but were checked. Lawrence claimed:

> Jemal's great attack on Wadi Musa made no noise. Maulud presided beautifully. He opened his centre, and with the greatest of humour let in the Turks until they broke their faces against the vertical cliffs of the Arab refuge. Then, while they were still puzzled and hurt, he came down simultaneously on both flanks. They never again attacked a prepared Arab position. Their losses had been heavy, but the loss of nerve at finding us invisible and yet full of backlash cost them more than the casualties. Thanks to Maulud, Akaba [Aqaba] became quit of all concern for its own present safety.[39]

The verdict was fascinating, in part because Lowell Thomas, Lawrence's American publicist, set Lawrence himself at the heart of the action. He created the fiction that Lawrence had established a headquarters in the heights above the ruins of Petra, recruited local men by appealing to their women, and, although their lines had wavered, they had fought off three converging columns.[40]

The actual events at Wadi Musa appear in the British *Official History* and seem markedly different from the versions furnished by Lawrence or Thomas.[41] The Ottomans, in a brigade of four depleted infantry battalions, with four mountain guns and the 7th Cavalry Regiment, were held up in the defiles, and suffered some losses. The Arabs, in two strong mounted companies of 350 men and 200 irregulars, possessed two mountain guns of their own and four machine guns. The Ottomans tried to soften up the Arabs with an hour-long bombardment and a bombing attack by aircraft, before advancing into the hills. They drove in the outpost line but were attacked in the flank by a carefully positioned Arab detachment. The *Official History* recorded that the irregular 'Arab camel-men behaved badly', suggesting that they withdrew prematurely, but Maulud, who had once been a regular Ottoman cavalry officer, was able to hold Petra against the onslaught. Claims that 400 Ottomans were killed are impossible to verify.

The threat to Aqaba had not entirely passed, however. The Ottomans still possessed Abu el Lissan. The subsequent withdrawal from this position came for reasons unrelated to the events at Petra – the exceptionally bad weather, which was debilitating for a force on such an extended and vulnerable supply line. The deciding factor was Allenby's offensive at Gaza. Holding such an exposed forward position was not necessarily an advantage when the Ottomans needed mobile forces that could converge on Arab fighting groups or provoke them into battle by laying waste to their sources of supply – a traditional strategy dating back to the classical period.

In October 1917, Lawrence had anticipated that Allenby would soon break through at Gaza, seize Jerusalem, and possibly reach Haifa. This promoted the imperative to raise the Arabs in all the districts east of the Jordan, and converge on Deraa, the most significant railway junction. The dilemma was that, if they acted prematurely, they would be driven off and the Arab cause would lose the reputation for continual success on which it relied.[42] He wrote:

> I pondered for a while whether we should not call up all these adherents and tackle the Turkish communications in force. We were certain, with any management, of twelve thousand men: enough to

rush Deraa, to smash all the railway lines, even to take Damascus by surprise. Any one of these things would make the position of the Beersheba army critical: and my temptation to take our capital instantly upon the issue was very sore.[43]

The difficulty of the decision was acute, as Lawrence related:

Deraa's sudden capture, followed by a retreat, would have involved the massacre, or the ruin of all the splendid peasantry of the district. They could only rise once, and their effort on that occasion must be decisive. To call them out now was to risk the best asset Feisal held for eventual success, on the speculation that Allenby's first attack would sweep the enemy before it, and that the month of November would be rainless, favourable to a rapid advance.[44]

The possibility that the British Army would not break through at Gaza made Lawrence advise delaying the attack on Deraa. But it was also because he knew the Arab forces still could not capture a fortified Ottoman settlement. The notional 'twelve thousand' he spoke of could not be guaranteed either. Some sheikhs were promising to deliver Deraa if the word was given, but this bravado was common. The alternative was to create a significant enough diversion, so that the Ottomans committed resources in the wrong direction. This would serve Allenby's purpose but not risk the Arab forces in an engagement that they could not be certain of winning.[45]

Allenby, however, needed the railway junction at Deraa to be knocked out, so it was decided Lawrence would lead a mining raid on the railway at Yarmuk, to cut the line for up to two weeks.[46] The Yarmuk River had carved its way through a precipitous wall of hills, and the rail line had been built along the valley floor across multiple bridges, which would be vulnerable to explosives. To approach the valley undetected would require a march of 420 miles in a wide arc through the desert to the east. The objective was to sever the line by 5 November 1917, to coincide with Allenby's advance, which would cut off Ottoman reinforcements and prevent the retreat of their army intact. Lawrence would lead a hand-picked party, consisting of 50 men of the Beni Sakr and Abu Tayi, and take along specially manufactured charges that could cut the steel girders which supported the bridges.

The late addition to the team was Abd el Kader el Jezairi, a descendant of the Algerian resistance leader who had fought the French. Colonel Brémond warned Lawrence about this figure at Aqaba, but Lawrence attributed his vehemence to French prejudice. Abd el Kader offered the chance to use Algerian exiles who lived in the Yarmuk as auxiliaries for the mission, but in reality his stories of escape from the Ottomans were exaggerations. He was a Jihadist, resentful of Lawrence's status as a British Christian within the ranks of an Arab Muslim force, and he shared the values of Djemal Pasha. Lawrence attributed his disloyalty as jealousy, but it is likely he was simply working for the highest bidder.[47]

Lawrence reflected that the third element of his plan was to attack the railways elsewhere, which would have the effect of slowing down the logistics support for Ma'an, thus making offensive action against Aqaba more difficult, if not impossible. These operations had to be executed quickly, since, with the Ottomans blocking the pass from Aqaba, it would take time to reach the rail line by a circuitous route.

Allenby opened the Third Battle of Gaza at the end of October 1917. The EEF was in much better shape now than it had been in the past. It had been expanded to ten infantry divisions and four mounted divisions, with 116 heavy guns with which to pound the Ottoman defences. This force was supported by new aircraft, particularly the Bristol fighter plane, which gave the EEF a technological advantage on their front. The army was grouped into three corps. The XXI Corps of three infantry divisions, facing Gaza and its south-eastern approaches, was commanded by Lieutenant General Edward Bulfin. Opposite Beersheba, Lieutenant General Chetwode commanded XX Corps, with three infantry divisions with an attached Yeomanry division, while Lieutenant General Harry Chauvel's Desert Mounted Corps faced Beersheba's south-eastern approaches. The vital ingredient was, however, Allenby himself.[48] He insisted on visiting every part of the front, and news of his appointment produced a positive effect on the troops. His physical presence, his experience, his willingness to talk to soldiers, and his unwillingness to tolerate oversights amongst his officers had an energizing effect across the army.[49] Allenby's attitude was that, if they were to break through, there could be no half measures.

The key to the Gaza defences was the 'hinge' at Hureira and Tell esh Sheria. The fortifications in front of Gaza would only be passable if there were overwhelming artillery concentrations, and even then, it was thought that, if there was a breakthrough, the Ottoman Army would merely regroup in one of several parallel lines of defences further back. A comprehensive victory was needed.

The eastern flank extended into the desert, with too little water to support large formations like the Desert Mounted Corps. The trick was to persuade the Ottomans, with major attacks on the flanks, that Gaza was the main objective and any assault on the eastern end, at Beersheba, was the secondary objective, while the centre remained inviolate. Having drawn the Ottoman reserves to the two ends of their line, Allenby would unleash his concealed main effort at the now depleted and unsupported Ottoman centre.

There were rising expectations about the coming offensive. The War Cabinet insisted that, by the autumn, Allenby should 'strike the Turks as hard as possible'.[50] The *Official History* offered the reasoning that, 'A big victory in Palestine would tend to strengthen the confidence and staying power of the people at a season when a like success in Europe was improbable.'[51] Mindful of the public's sense of gloom at losses in an interminable war, Lloyd George wanted Allenby to capture Jerusalem 'as a Christmas present for the British nation'.[52] Of greater concern was the effect of a catalogue of setbacks suffered by the Allies. Italian and French troops had shown signs of restiveness: in the spring there had been mutinies along the Chemin des Dames. The Russian war effort was collapsing, and a Bolshevik takeover was the beginning of the end there. The implication of this failure was that Ottoman troops might be released from the Caucasus front to fight in Palestine. According to Lloyd George, Allenby was expected to defeat and then pursue the enemy 'to the limit of his resources', but Allenby's intelligence seemed to suggest that the Ottoman and German force at Aleppo, and forces drawn from Mesopotamia, could bring the available enemy army up to a strength that could match his own. Robertson, as CIGS, wrote to Allenby and cautioned: 'It will be a good thing to give the Turk in front of you a sound beating, but ... the further we go north the more Turks we shall meet; and the greater will be the strain upon our resources.'[53]

The actual Ottoman forces in Palestine consisted of the Ottoman Eighth Army, commanded by Kress von Kressenstein, made up of two corps, with a total strength of 40,000 infantry and some 1,500 cavalry. The first of these, the XXII Corps, was made up of two infantry divisions and held the entrenched positions at Gaza, while the

XX Corps, also of two infantry divisions, held the line to the east of Gaza towards Beersheba. The Seventh Army, under General Fevzi Çakmak, held the area around Beersheba. An understrength formation, the 27th Infantry Division, with a mixture of supporting regiments, was based in the town itself but this force was made up of 4,400 troops armed with 60 machine guns and 28 field guns. Von Falkenhayn, the German commander in the whole southern Palestine sector, expected the British to concentrate on Gaza and therefore he held several divisions in reserve. His strategic surprise was his Yıldırım (Lightning) and German Pascha II forces. These two elements were made up of seasoned troops and equipped with a larger than normal establishment of field artillery and machine guns. Bristling with firepower, they were to have a decisive effect on any battle.

The battle (31 October–8 November 1917) opened with a dramatic and sustained artillery bombardment on the defences of Gaza.[54] This was extended by Chetwode's XX Corps battering the defences of Beersheba. The infantry of the 60th and 74th Divisions approached this eastern flank methodically from the south-west, the troops following just 30 yards behind a curtain of explosions. Ottoman gunners laid down retaliatory fire, and progress was slow because of the resistance shown by the Ottoman infantry.[55] It was not until the evening that all their objectives were secured. During the night, the Desert Mounted Corps rode around to the east of Beersheba, and, with the Ottoman defenders focussed on the British infantry to the south-west, the British, Australian and New Zealand mounted troops launched their attack. The New Zealand Mounted Rifles fought hard to take a high point dominating the town, known as Tel es Sabe.[56] Once this was taken, and on Allenby's direction, the Australian 4th and 12th Light Horse Regiments charged through the twilight, 800 strong, into Beersheba. Under machine gun and small arms fire, the leading squadrons dismounted when they reached the Ottoman trenches and engaged in a close-quarter battle, while the rest rode into and through the defences. The arrival of the supporting infantry completed the capture of Beersheba, and the Ottomans were forced to withdraw to the north, towards the Judean Hills via the Hebron road.[57]

But this was just the first stage of the battle. The attack on Gaza itself got underway on 1 November with Bulfin's XXI Corps artillery bombarding the Ottoman trenches, before the infantry came on just behind an exploding barrage. The troops started to fight their way into the forward outposts, but, contrary to the Ottomans' expectations, the main attack had not yet come.[58] The Ottomans were committing their reserves to the battered defences of Gaza, confident that they could hold the British.[59] Gradually the manpower available in the rear at Hebron was being depleted. Now there were too few resources to stop a major attack on the centre, at the hinge of Hureira and Tell esh Sheria. On 6 November, the main attack swept in against this section, and the Ottoman line was broken open.[60] A gap 7 miles wide was created, through which Allenby's reserves now advanced. At Beersheba, the XXI Corps and Desert Mounted Corps were prevented from exploiting their initial success by Ottoman reinforcements, but to the west, Gaza was now no longer tenable, and the town was evacuated on 7 November.[61] With the centre gone, and Beersheba and Gaza lost, there was no hope for the Ottomans to stop the British on this line. They pulled back into the hills, fighting to hold every high point. As Allenby's forces approached Jerusalem, there were vigorous Ottoman counter-attacks. But despite a spirited attack south of the old city and another at Nabi Samwill, and the deteriorating weather, the Ottomans were forced to seek stronger defences in the rocky heights to the north.

THE YARMUK RAID, NOVEMBER 1917

As Allenby drove the Ottomans from their defences at Gaza, reconnaissance missions were made along potential routes into Palestine which could provide water for advancing regular troops, and, after several successful minor operations, there were high expectations of Lawrence's mission to sever the Damascus–Medina railway in the Yarmuk Valley, deep behind Ottoman lines. But there was no news of Lawrence, and air reconnaissance revealed that the bridges of Yarmuk were intact. Something had clearly gone wrong.

The 50-strong raiding party that had set out had been augmented by British and Indian personnel, whose role was to provide an overwatch of fire support while Lawrence laid the charges. Captain George Lloyd had been sent along to accompany Lawrence on the initial part of the journey and to replace him if he was killed. This was due, in part, to mounting concern about Lawrence's fitness for the task, especially his state of mind.[62] Lloyd had written to Clayton in Cairo reporting that Lawrence thought he would not be coming back from this raid.[63]

The march took the raiders in a circuitous route around Abu el Lissan, which was still held by the Ottomans, up through Wadi Rumm, and on into the interior. Mounted patrols were avoided, but Abd el Kader insisted on riding with his own party, which may have given him ample opportunity to report to the Ottomans on the progress and purpose of this raid.[64] The main body crossed the railway at Shedia without incident, cutting telegraph lines in the traverse, but a smaller group, with Abd el Kader, were spotted and attracted Ottoman fire from a blockhouse.[65]

On reaching Auda's temporary encampments, there was little enthusiasm for the Yarmuk raid, and Lawrence's hope to recruit men for the attack was dashed. Worse, scouts reported the approach of an Ottoman force consisting of cavalry and mule-mounted infantry, suggesting some breach of security.[66] Auda's 30 men joined Lawrence's force, which fanned out and took refuge in watercourses, with their Vickers and Lewis machine guns mounted on the flanks. Their position gave them a fair 800 yards of open ground which the Ottomans would have to cross to reach them. The alarm had nevertheless been false, and Abd el Kader's party emerged over the horizon instead, from the direction of the Ottoman blockhouse. Lawrence still did not make the connection to detect betrayal.

A second alarm occurred when a group of Beni Sakr, a tribal raiding party, made a sudden rush on them from three sides and opened fire. Although the incident passed off without casualties, the tribesmen insisted on riding around and through the camp, firing their rifles. Feasting appeared to reconcile the groups, and periodically Lawrence and his companions could hear the heavy artillery of Allenby's offensive far to the west. It was this sustained fire that may well have drawn the Ottomans away, despite their evident knowledge of the presence of the raiders.

Amongst the Arabs, there was some sympathy for the Turks coming under such intense and sustained firepower. The British were allies but also foreigners, while the Ottomans, although despised, were nevertheless familiar. The juxtaposition of the Indian and British personnel amongst them must have created its own peculiar tensions. Lawrence turned the situation to his account. Once again, he used the long marches to get to know the genealogy, manners, dialect and beliefs of the Beni Sakr, in preparation for operating amongst them in the future.

On the approach to Azrak, another alarm was abated when a group of Serhan tribesmen first fired on Lawrence's force, then approached with enthusiastic support for Feisal. The meeting provided detailed intelligence on the Yarmuk bridges, which, contrary to expectation, were strongly garrisoned. The area was full of troops collecting timber too, making any movement hazardous. The settled local populations detested the Beni Sakr and therefore supported the Ottoman authorities.[67] Worse, the likelihood of bad weather meant that escape routes could be cut off by swollen rivers. Movement without detection was looking more and more unlikely. However, the leading Arab figures, with Lawrence, tried to persuade the local Serahin to support the mission, and they placed Abd el Kader in command of them. The next day, as the party paused at Azrak, it seemed el Kader had disappeared in the direction of Jebel Druze to the north with all the plans of the intended raid.

Lawrence decided to make a new plan, namely to attack the bridge at Tell el Shehab, but there was still a significant risk of interception or ambush, since their location was now known to the Ottomans.[68] A force of mounted Circassians was seen searching for them, but while checking wells, 'they had missed us, to our mutual benefit, by five minutes'.[69] Crossing the railway at night, the raiders discovered at dawn that their laager was actually within range of the nearest Ottoman post. This meant remaining on the alert all day as Ottoman foot patrols passed within earshot. The day gave Lawrence the opportunity to assess the next stage of the route, which would require an 80-mile ride, the demolition, and return. His evaluation was that the Indian personnel were exhausted and would not make the distance, so he selected six men, one Vickers machine gun and a handful of Beni Sakr.[70] The explosive charges were also reorganized for speed of handling on the objective. Most of the Serahin were left behind.

Several times on the approach march, Lawrence's group was detected by civilians close to Deraa, which resulted in shooting. These incidents, the traverse of cloying ploughed ground, and the unexpected broken terrain caused further delays. Urging the party to move more quickly merely caused the riders to be strung out in the darkness. They arrived above the bridge in the Yarmuk gorge and scrambled down rain-soaked slopes. The Indian machine gun detachment was positioned to cover the tents of the guards, while Lawrence took 15 men forward to reconnoitre the final few yards to the bridge itself. Just at that moment, one man dropped a rifle and the Ottoman sentry spotted the machine gun team as it was repositioning itself.[71] His fire turned out the guard, and the Beni Sakr men, in a vulnerable position close to the rail line, opened fire to save themselves. The Ottoman soldiers dropped into their trenches and continued to fire. The Vickers machine gun, which was not in a firing position, could not get into action and was caught on a forward slope. The fighters, fearing they would be hit and be detonated by the explosives they were carrying, dropped all the charges and made off.[72]

Lawrence joined the retreating party, but the villages along their line of escape had heard the shooting, and the raiders, in fear of being attacked, opened fire on the civilians, and seized the nearest goods. This caused further commotion, and local men mounted up in pursuit. Lawrence noted that 'settlements for miles about manned their roofs and fired volleys'.[73] The party slithered its way back into the hills and relative security.

The mission had failed. The railway line was not cut, the force was scattered, and dissent was magnified by tiredness, hunger and the magnitude of the setback.[74] To compensate, and to restore the honour of those who had taken part, Lawrence reluctantly agreed to conduct an attack on the Hejaz line, although he refused to risk the exhausted Indian troops, and that meant leaving behind their medium machine gun. They were ordered off, under the command of Lieutenant Wood (who was sick), to Azrak. The remaining 60 men followed Lawrence and his companion Zaal to Minifir in the rain.

On their final approach to lay their explosives at a culvert attacked once before, they were surprised by a train. Missing this target added to their disappointment. Splashing about in the mud, they fixed their charge to a bridge, but, with insufficient electrical cable, they had to leave the wires' ends exposed and wait for the moment to rush forward to fix the exploder. Leaving the entire apparatus in place risked detection by Ottoman patrols.

As dawn broke, just as all signs of disturbance on the site had been hastily concealed, the first train appeared, but there was no time to fix the detonation device before it had rushed by. Early warning teams were therefore posted further out, in the hope of some success. The anticipated Ottoman patrols trudged by, also downcast by the rain, until finally the look-outs signalled that a train was at last approaching. The raiders took position, and Lawrence waited until the locomotive was directly over the culvert: when he sank the plunger, nothing happened. Clearly seen, Lawrence could only wave at the passing troops, hoping to be mistaken for a herder.[75]

Five hundred yards past the mine, the Ottoman train halted and an investigative party of Ottoman soldiers came to search for Lawrence, but by then he had escaped. He had removed the exploder and buried the wires in the mud as best he could, but anxious moments passed before the ambush team could be sure the charges had not been found.[76] Interestingly, if the mine had been fired, it is unlikely that Lawrence would have survived. There were dozens of troops on board the train, and his only route to safety was across over 200 yards of open ground. Without a supporting medium machine gun, there would be no chance of holding off a counter-attack.

The succession of failures, the cold, and hunger, caused significant disagreements in the raiding party. Lawrence did little to improve the mood with a sarcastic criticism of the Serahin, and he had to be rescued. He did manage to get the electrical circuit to work again, but the entire day and night was spent in a fruitless vigil for a train. None appeared. Succumbing to the miserable conditions, the raiders lit a fire, killed and ate a camel, and remained in position – a risky decision, though Ottoman patrols continued to march down the line without finding them.

Finally, on 11 November 1917, Lawrence was able to intercept a passenger-carrying train, and blew the mine as intended, but his proximity to the seat of the explosion meant he was injured and dazed by the pressure wave and debris:

> I touched off under the first driving wheel of the first locomotive, and the explosion was terrific. The ground spouted blackly into my face, and I was sent spinning, to sit up with the shirt torn to my shoulder and the blood dripping from long, ragged scratches on my left arm. Between my knees lay the exploder, crushed under a twisted sheet of sooty iron. In front of me was the scalded and smoking upper half of a man. When I peered through the dust and steam of the

explosion the whole boiler of the first engine seemed to be missing. I dully felt that it was time to get away to support; but when I moved, learnt that there was a great pain in my right foot, because of which I could only limp along, with my head swinging from the shock. Movement began to clear away this confusion, as I hobbled towards the upper valley, whence the Arabs were now shooting fast into the crowded coaches.[77]

In trying to help Lawrence, who they assumed to be wounded, seven of the Arabs were hit by Ottoman fire.[78] Lawrence had been luckier: he had a broken toe, several grazes, and flesh wounds. Recovering himself, Lawrence observed that the first trucks were smashed, and with them the horses they had been carrying. The engines were destroyed. The carriages to the rear were derailed but intact, and he estimated that there were some 400 troops on board. Also on the train was the Ottoman commander of VIII Corps, Mehmed Djemal, who was on his way to take command around Jerusalem. Lawrence's force was outnumbered and so there was little chance of capturing the train, or looting it, as the Arab forces expected. Nevertheless, one party, which had been firing from the north spur, did manage to reach the train and seize rifles and other spoils. Lawrence now regretted severely his decision not to bring the Vickers machine gun.[79]

Recovering their wounded, the Arabs' fire slackened, and the Ottomans felt emboldened to make a counter-attack against the ambush. The raiders therefore quickly reorganized and waited until the Ottomans were on an exposed slope, then fired into them, causing a number of casualties. The Ottomans consequently moved to the left and right, hoping to envelop the ambushers. Lawrence realized that, with 20 lost on his own side, the position was untenable. They made short rushes to the summit, with Lawrence in evident pain, before escaping on their camels. Their first pause was made after they had put 5 miles between themselves and their pursuers. They then had a chance to tend to the wounded, with rudimentary measures, and Lawrence paid the fighters and compensated the families of those who had been killed.

Retiring to Azrak, Lawrence made the ancient fortress his temporary base. This served the dual purpose of controlling its nearby market and ensuring that the locals, including reluctant leaders, were not dependent on the Ottomans. Fresh provisions were sought in Jebel Druze, and rations suitable for the Indian soldiers were ordered up from Aqaba, while the old fortifications were improved with machine gun and rifle platforms. One ante-chamber was converted into a mosque. This little enclave gradually became a beacon for Armenian refugees, Ottoman Army Arab deserters, and visiting sheikhs. Lawrence found that the material improvements they could offer, drawn up from Aqaba, were significant in recruitment. He wrote:

> Everybody learned that in Akaba [Aqaba] there was plenty, coming across the open sea from all the markets of the world; and so the Arab cause which was theirs by sentiment, and instinct and inclination, became theirs by interest also. Slowly our example and teaching converted them: very slowly, by our own choice, that they might be ours more surely.[80]

Lawrence also used the opportunity of bad weather in the winter for a reconnaissance of the area around Deraa, and the best approaches for any subsequent offensive. While he acknowledged that heavy rain had delayed Allenby's offensive from reaching beyond the Judean Hills, there was every expectation that the British would resume their advance in the spring. To get better acquainted with the railway junction, Lawrence assumed a disguise and hoped to slip into the town. He noted:

> We mounted the curving bank of the Palestine Railway, and from its vantage surveyed Deraa Station: but the ground was too open to admit of surprise attack. We decided to walk down the east front of the defences: so we plodded on, noting German stores, barbed wire here and there, rudiments of trenches. Turkish troops were passing incuriously between the tents and their latrines dug out on our side.[81]

The Ottoman base also possessed Albatross aircraft, idle because of the foul weather. Lawrence claimed at this point to have been briefly captured, although, if untrue, it might suggest he was trying to compensate for his operational failure.[82] He described an attempt to recruit him, then beatings, but the enigma of the incident has been debated endlessly by his biographers and critics.[83] What is clear is that Lawrence himself was sick, suffering from his injuries, disconcerted by his role as a foreign advocate of a nationalist cause, and stung by repeated setbacks or the inertia of the winter. Lawrence therefore quit the mission: 'I flung away from them in a rage, determined to go south and see if anything active could be done, in the cold weather, about the Dead Sea, which the enemy held as a trench dividing us from Palestine.'[84] His colleague, George Lloyd, noted: 'Lawrence is not well and talks rather hopelessly about the Arab future he once believed in.'[85]

On the way, Lawrence was again almost killed by a party that intended to rob him, but he bluffed his way through with faux confidence, despite the rounds fired.[86] He developed a fever, but had to travel in the dark, in foul weather, to avoid further encounters with hostile elements. Exhausted, Lawrence reached Aqaba, and soon after was ordered up to Allenby's headquarters.

Conveyed by aircraft, he reported the failure of the mission to Yarmuk, but, to Allenby, these were now past tactical details that had little bearing on a much bigger operational picture. Lawrence was authorized to accompany Clayton in the ceremonial entry into Jerusalem, an opportunity which he knew would appeal to this scholar of the Crusades. Lawrence acknowledged the event as 'the supreme moment of the war'.[87]

But from this high point, he found that the greatest challenge was yet to come.

8

Movement as the Law of Strategy
The Battle of Tafila

There were several factors that compelled Allenby to use the Arab Northern Army as a flanking formation during his proposed advance into Palestine. He had been checked temporarily in the winter of 1917 by the formidable topography of the hills north of Jerusalem. While not of great elevation, they were sufficient to favour the Ottoman defenders. Covered in boulders and rocky outcrops, the steep slopes made all movement slow, and thus exposed assaulting troops to withering fire. Today, standing on the tops close to Nablus, it is easy to see the difficulties Allenby faced. Narrow defiles and inadequate roads made manoeuvre extremely challenging. This implied that either he had to drive head-on up the Esdraelon coastal plain or seek a wider flank.

Allenby implored Lawrence and Feisal to bring the Arab forces up to the Dead Sea, creating an almost continuous front. Such a long line would make it far more difficult for the Ottomans to be certain of the axis of any breakout.[1] Accordingly, the Arab Northern Army would be marched up from Petra and Guweira, driving the Ottomans back towards Shobek and Tafila.[2] Allenby requested that, as a secondary objective, the Arabs take possession of Tafila and then attempt to halt the traffic crossing the Dead Sea, which was the means the Ottomans used for supplying their troops on its western side, threatening Beersheba and Allenby's own extended flank. Lawrence offered more, hoping to take the entire Dead Sea coast, and recommended positioning the Arab regulars, 3,000 strong, at the northern end, from where they could be supplied using Allenby's logistics chain, including an extension of the Jerusalem railway, rather than distant Aqaba. The objective set was to be on the Jordan in March, so Lawrence took much-needed leave in Cairo while others made the logistical arrangements, which, according to Lawrence, amounted to the provision of 'fifty tons a day'.[3]

Holding any position in the Dead Sea area would be challenging. On 31 October, in light of Allenby's breakthrough at Gaza, Colonel Newcombe had dashed up to the Hebron road with just 100 fighters, aiming to create a diversion in the enemy's rear until the cavalry of Allenby's force could relieve them. Attempts to rouse the local Arabs of Dhahriye to fight failed. On 1 November, they repulsed an Ottoman company sent against them, and then held on for a further two days. But then the dwindling number of fighters found themselves attacked from the north and south by six battalions of Ottoman troops accompanied by 300 German infantrymen, a total of 3,500 men.[4] In intense fighting, Newcombe's machine guns were knocked out and 20 of his command were killed. Surrounded, outnumbered, and with no sign of relief, Newcombe bowed to the inevitable and surrendered. This brilliant, if desperate diversion succeeded in causing considerable confusion, but the Ottomans held to their line across the Judean Hills.[5]

That winter, the Ottomans were still entrenched at Abu el Lissan in some strength, although railway raids necessitated the rotation of garrisons along the line, and frequent patrols. Having repulsed the Ottoman brigade at Wadi Musa, Maulud had extended his reconnaissance screen and conducted opportunistic raids on the Ottoman logistics near Ma'an. The seizure of their camels, and the death of transport animals in the winter months, caused significant problems for the Ottoman commanders, and necessitated the reduction of the Abu el Lissan garrison. Eventually, in early January 1918, the Ottomans decided to withdraw from the exposed post, and concentrated nearer the railway at Waheida (or Uheida, today's Aweeda), 6 miles from Ma'an, with their main position at Semna.

The interlude of operations gave Lawrence and Colonel Joyce the opportunity to conduct a reconnaissance by motor car, exploring the routes to Musaw'warrah on 26 December 1917. The journey was possible in part because Egyptian labourers had spent months building a road up Wadi Itm from Aqaba to Guweira (Qawirah), where a forward base now existed. From there, several vehicles were used for the reconnaissance mission, and the surface proved to be no obstacle for the

Rolls-Royce cars. Sections of soft sand were traversed with hastily laid brushwood tracks. Musaw'warrah was reached in just two days and so the decision was made to bring up armoured cars to conduct a raid to commence on 1 January 1918.[6]

The armoured car detachments in the Middle East consisted of two types of vehicle: the Rolls-Royce turreted armoured car, which mounted a Vickers belt-fed machine gun, and the Talbot, which sported two 10-pounder guns. The eight vehicles taken on the raid against Musaw'warrah made good progress, again taking just two days to reach their allotted point of attack. This was a station a few miles north of the town. Rather than using explosives against the railway, the attack made use of the Talbot guns. One vehicle opened up on the fortifications about the station, while three more operated on the flanks. The crews were impervious to the Ottomans' rifle fire, prompting Lawrence's famous remark that 'armoured car work seemed fighting de luxe'.[7] He admitted there was no intention of taking the post, since there was no provision for prisoners and they did not expect the dug-in Ottoman troops to capitulate, but the success of the raid prompted a second attack at Shahm. Here, long-range fire from the Talbot guns, at 2,000 yards, bombarded the station. Again, the raiders drew off.

Lawrence's assessment of the operation is instructive. He confessed that the mission had been to see if the armoured cars could negotiate the topography and navigate their way through a range of hills and inhospitable terrain, rather than make any difference against the Ottomans on the railway. He admitted:

> Our anxiety and forethought had been all to reach the railway through the manifold difficulties of the plains and hills. When we did reach it, we were entirely unready for action, with not a conception of what our tactics or method should be: yet we learned much from this very indecision.[8]

The armoured car attacks left the Ottomans in an extremely difficult position. The only certain means to contest them lay in artillery, but short of setting mountain guns at regular intervals, there was little to stop armoured cars overmatching isolated detachments along the railway. That said, the British raid had not taken any fortified station, so there was some confidence that entrenched and protected infantry could still hold their posts. Moreover, aircraft might be able to challenge the impunity of the armoured car detachments, if they had sufficient warning of their approach.

Lawrence could not understand why the Ottomans clung to the railway that supported Medina. He was convinced that the German staff, including General von Falkenhayn, advised the Ottomans to relinquish the city and withdraw all their troops to Syria. The Ottomans would not, apparently, let go of their claims to the Hejaz because of the threat to their legitimacy and subsequent peace negotiations. But Lawrence was also critical of the British position which, influenced by Hussein, continued to invest in operations by Ali and Mohammed to capture Medina. His frustration grew at the seemingly pointless task. When ordered to cut the line to Ma'an, Lawrence claimed that they had feigned 'a show of impotence' which the British command accepted as evidence of native inferiority. Lawrence suggested that he 'could not be bothered' to explain his purpose.[9]

Yet the fact was that Lawrence and his irregular Arab forces were not strong enough to take Ma'an. His claim that Maulud was effectively investing the town was inaccurate. The Ottomans were perfectly capable of supplying and holding this fortified position. Lawrence had set up his argument to discredit those who rivalled the claim to independence through his own Arab Northern Army and his chosen candidate for leadership, Emir Feisal. The raid by armoured cars had had nothing to do with an Arab contribution, a point which Lawrence conveniently omitted to mention. Yet the British raid was in many ways a clear metaphor for the entire campaign: it was this advanced technology, modern weapon systems, armoured vehicles and air power, along with the mass of Allenby's conventional forces, that was turning the tide in the campaign. Lawrence was reluctant to acknowledge this critical fact, except in the most opaque terms.

On the other hand, these criticisms must be tempered by the clear acknowledgement of his situation. Relatively small numbers of fighters and their British and French advisors were operating deep inside Ottoman territory, with minimal support, against significant odds. Such a hazardous position was sustained through courage and resolution, regardless of the numbers. And without the full support of the local population, many of whom still favoured the Ottomans, there were limits to what he, and his comrades, could realistically accomplish.

TACTICAL SUCCESS OR OPERATIONAL FAILURE?

Without fanfare, on 3 January 1918, some 1,000 Arab personnel, a mixture of mounted irregulars and regulars, led by Sharif Nasir and Nuri as-Sa'id respectively, reoccupied the pass at Abu el Lissan. As the *Official History* notes, they succeeded in crossing the Hejaz line to establish a base on the plain of Jefer (Jafr), to the east of Ma'an. They then moved off to conduct a raid against the outposts around Ma'an itself. On their return, they attacked the station at Jurf al Darawish.[10]

The plan, Lawrence related, was to capture the area by simultaneously attacking from different axes.[11] The small station at Jurf was entrenched, protected by a fortified hillock that mounted a single piece of artillery and two machine guns. However, the hillock was itself dominated by a ridgeline, which fell to the Arab force without a shot being fired. Nasir's mounted detachments placed cut-off groups north and south, on the railway line, and at first light, they brought into action a gun they had conveyed to the top of the ridge. Its third round detonated right on the Ottoman artillery, which prompted the Beni Sakr men to mount up and launch a charge. Nuri tried to halt the attack, since the Ottomans were still well protected by their trenches and machine guns. Unable to stop them, the regulars opened up with everything they had, lacing the Ottoman positions with suppressive fire. Fortunately, the sheer weight of fire meant the defenders could not react in time to the mounted force who were approaching rapidly. Abandoning the trenches, the garrison took refuge in the stone-built station buildings. Nuri then dashed forward with the regulars, and used the Ottoman artillery to fire point-blank at the station walls. The garrison capitulated, and some 200 Ottoman personnel were taken prisoner for the loss of two men killed. Jurf yielded a great quantity of supplies, which were distributed amongst the men, and the station was razed. The relief force, which came up by train, was fired on and withdrew back to Ma'an.

The cold and foul weather, and the inevitability of an Ottoman counter-attack, meant that Jurf could not be held, and so the raiders trekked off through the snow. This period of severe weather, which had caused so many problems for the British around Jerusalem, created considerable hardship for the Arab forces on their retreat to Jefer.[12] The high elevation of their base provided no protection against the storms and cold, which reduced morale amongst the fighters. Lawrence remarked that the Arabs 'existed in an aching misery which froze the hope out of them'.[13] Nevertheless, to maintain momentum, Sharif Abd el-Mayin was ordered to take his contingent up from Petra, through the frozen hills and woods, towards Shobek, preparing the southern axis of advance on Tafila.

Tafila was a cluster of settlements above the southern edge of the Dead Sea. The first of these was adjacent to a light railway (an extension of the Hejaz line). Once again, the Ottomans were in a position that was overlooked by a ridge that they had failed to fortify. Guns mounted on this high ground bombarded the Ottoman defences below and the station buildings caught fire. The Arab forces fell on the retreating host and were only checked by the determined resistance of a disciplined Ottoman company 'under', it was said, 'an Albanian officer'.[14] This group fought its way steadily back up the rail lines, while the rest fled. But, once again, the Arabs had overrun a badly sited position, seized its stores, and defeated a demoralized Ottoman detachment.

Nasir then made a long night march from Jefer, crossed the Hejaz railway, and continued up through the hills to appear above the main settlement of Tafila at dawn. Although he had no guns, he sent forward a message to demand the Ottoman troops there surrender or be bombarded. The ruse failed, and the soldiers sent a defiant fusillade of rifle fire up to where the Arab forces were positioned. The unusual aspect of the Ottoman situation was that the local population, the Muhaisin, were allies, with no love of the Bedouin or of Feisal's cause. There were also communities of pro-Ottoman Senussi and anti-Ottoman refugees, including the victims of Ottoman repression, the Armenians.

The situation changed, however, when Auda of the Abu Tayi made threats, which generated collective fears of a massacre. The locals therefore decided to surrender, and the entire settlement fell to Auda's and Nasir's men. The civilians nevertheless concealed their food and had sent away their flocks, hoping to keep them from the avaricious and hungry Arab fighters. The absence of supplies and the deep rivalry between the Arab groups, especially the Howeitat and Abu Tayi, created an air of tension which seemed to presage the outbreak of violence. There was further anxiety when the regulars of Jafar al-Askari failed to appear as expected. Their rations had given out and they had been forced to call a halt. Jafar and Zeid, acting as Feisal's representative, therefore appeared in the nick of time, and sent Auda's force to the rear to avoid a collision.

Zeid also distributed gold to placate the disappointed fighters.[15] It was enough to ensure some semblance of order and preparations were put in place for the next phase of the drive towards the Dead Sea.

The Arab forces were nevertheless surprised that the Ottomans set out from Kerak to recover Tafila. Lawrence assumed the cluster of settlements was of no value and therefore the counter-attack was 'the rankest folly', but he underestimated its importance to a regime facing immense logistical strain.[16] The area was a valuable one for much-needed grain and fodder.[17] Lawrence believed Tafila was of little consequence to the Arab forces because, from his perspective, the Arabs simply 'wanted to get past it' and cut the Ottoman lines of communication to Jericho, but one cannot assume what is no value to one's own side also means little to an enemy.

The Ottoman force was a composite brigade under the direction of the commander of the 48th Division of the Amman Sector, Hamid Fakhri Bey. He had pushed down to Kerak by rail some 900 infantrymen from the 151st and 152nd Regiments and the Muratteb Battalion, 100 cavalrymen, a company of gendarmes, two Austrian howitzers, and 23 machine guns. He had impressed local transport at the rail junction and marched post haste. Lawrence admitted that the Arab picquets were surprised at Wadi Hesa and fell back in the afternoon of 24 January, and by nightfall, the Ottomans were approaching the villages of Tafila.

Lawrence preferred to hold the settlements, in order to keep the local civilians aligned to the Sharifians, but Jafar Pasha and Zeid overruled him, insisting on holding the ridge that overlooked the settlements to the north. Lawrence was concerned that the slopes were too easily approached and both the eastern and western flanks were vulnerable, being in dead ground from which the position could be enveloped and rolled up. At midnight, the Arab forces started to slip away from the settlements to Wadi el-Ghuweit to the north and east, but the civilians became anxious, assuming the Ottomans would inflict reprisals for any disloyalty. The withdrawal soon took on the impression of a rout.[18] Lawrence acknowledged: 'in the blustering dark the confusion and crying through the narrow streets were terrible'.[19] Although Lawrence attempted to reassure some that the Arab fighters were going to fight, the haste meant that 'children were trampled on, and yelled, while their mothers were yelling anyhow'. The flashes of Ottoman rifle fire were visible too, and the Arab riders 'fired shot after shot into the air to encourage themselves'.[20]

Furious with the audacity of the Ottoman attack, Lawrence urged Zeid to punish his enemy. He argued that to remain on the defensive gave the Ottomans the initiative, and he contended that two Hotchkiss machine guns might be pushed forward to 'test the strength and disposition of the enemy'. At the very least, this would halt the Ottoman advance, and force them to adjust to the new threat. It would also fix them, tactically, and allow the Arabs to manoeuvre around them.

The first firefight was intense, and, with the assistance of local fighters, they forced the Ottoman cavalry screen back into the Wadi Hesa plain, to rejoin their main body. Emerging from their overnight encampment, the whole Ottoman brigade now deployed, and drove back the Arab fighters who had pursued too close. Machine gun and Howitzer fire indicated that the engagement was swaying in the Ottomans' favour. Lawrence urged Zeid to commit more men to the fight, but, sensibly, there was no rush to action. Zeid wanted to get a clearer picture of the location of the Ottoman forces and that meant waiting on the reports of his forward detachments. However, one of the Arabs' machine guns was destroyed, and the Ottomans were coming on fast.[21]

Lawrence took off, with his bodyguard, to the east, and encouraged Agayl tribesmen to deploy along a ridge that lay in front of a significant gorge, stiffened by the presence of a machine gun. This he labelled 'Reserve Ridge', believing it a fitting place from which to conduct a final stand before 'breaking clean'.[22] Going further forward, across a triangular plain some 2 miles wide, Lawrence encountered the Arabs who had conducted the initial engagement. They reported the loss of several men, and their machine gun, at the pass which marked the entrance to the triangular plain. The Ottomans were approaching from the north, with the road to Kerak as their axis.[23] To the west, the Arabs held a high ridge strongly, but the main body of the Ottoman forces was soon established on its northern spur. At the same time, another contingent had fanned out to the east, taking up a position on the northern spur of an eastern ridge. Here they set up an observation point and arranged their mountain guns. From it they could direct accurate Howitzer fire onto Zeid and Jafar's men and they dominated the plain.[24]

Lawrence gathered a small detachment of 60 men, which was right in the path of the Ottoman advance, and ordered them back to the 'Reserve Ridge' to collect more ammunition, theirs being spent.

The rearguard down in the triangular plain, under Lawrence's direction, attracted more sustained fire:

> The Turks, knowing we were there, had turned twenty machine-guns upon it. [Our position] was four feet high and fifty feet long, of bare flinty ribs, off which the bullets slapped deafeningly: while the air above so hummed or whistled with ricochets and chips that it felt like death to look over.[25]

The advance party withdrew, under fire, to the main ridgeline, which gave the defenders an elevation of 40 feet, and here they regrouped. The Ottomans, now in possession of the settlements and the pass that had been held by the Arab advance guard, also began to consolidate on their ridgeline positions. Lawrence ordered that his machine guns be fired periodically into the new Ottoman locations, but no counter-attack was to be made. A lull descended on the battlefield.

Although they had been driven off their first line of defences and bundled out of the plain, the Arab forces still controlled the deep gorge of Siez el-Zeraq and above it, running east-west, Lawrence's 'Reserve Ridge'. To take these, the Ottomans would need to either push along the ridges they occupied or advance across the open plain in front of them. It can only be assumed that Hamid Bey was pausing on the assumption that the action was over. He had, to all intents and purposes, dispersed the Arabs. Indeed, if the raiders had followed their usual practice, they would have withdrawn. But Zeid did not retreat. He repositioned some of his forces alongside Lawrence's men, who had now been joined by stragglers from other parts of the ridge. Zeid brought up more machine guns (to a total of 13), mounted infantry, some of the armed villagers and a mountain gun.

Seeing the Ottomans had stopped, Zeid sent Rasim Bey, an Arab regular officer, further out to the east, with all the available mounted troops and five machine guns to conduct an outflanking manoeuvre. To the west, local men, about 100 strong, accompanied by three machine gun teams, started to work their way along a deep wadi that ran up to the far right flank of the Ottoman line.[26] To cover these converging arcs, a small detachment was sent back into the plain with four more machine guns. Their distracting fire caught the Ottomans' attention as planned.

The initial mustering of the Arabs up on the ridge to their front had attracted more shelling and machine gun fire, and Lawrence noted:

'We reminded one another that movement was the law of strategy, and started moving.'[27] He advised that riding out to the flanks would leave the enemy line perfect for rolling up, the equivalent of fighting just one man on the extreme flank.

The Ottomans seemed to be aware of an impending counter-attack, and brought up more machine guns along the ridges overlooking the plain. Lawrence was critical of their siting, describing the ground as likely to produce showers of shrapnel flints. The Vickers gun was set at a high angle to produce a beaten zone of falling rounds on these positions. Nevertheless, while it was their flanks that were far more vulnerable, the distracting fire from the Arab centre still held the Ottomans' attention.

The armed villagers of El Eima, having closed to within 300 yards of the Ottoman right, opened fire with a volley that cut down the Ottoman machine gun teams, and then continued their fusillade, accompanied by Zeid's Hotchkiss guns.[28] The firing on this position alerted Lawrence on the Reserve Ridge, and, observing the mounted forces closing rapidly on the Ottoman left, he called for a general advance: 'Their arrival convinced us to abandon Marshal Foch and to attack from, at any rate, three sides at once.'[29] The critique of Foch was surely misplaced: it is likely the French officer would have approved of the manoeuvre.

Enveloped, the Ottoman centre tried to extract, its leading files crowding to get through the pass. The village force continued to sweep the Ottomans off the ridges, and the Arab horsemen, sensing victory, rode down everyone in their path. Armenians, alongside Lawrence, howled with vengeance, and the Ottomans were pursued across the Wadi Hesa plain or into the defiles. Lawrence did not witness the destruction that followed. By his estimation, the entire Ottoman brigade was wiped out.[30] The Ottoman commander, Hamid Bey, was killed, and the mountain guns lost, but the Turkish Official History recorded that over 400 safely recovered to Kerak, representing losses of about 100 men.[31] The British *Official History* noted that the Ottomans used their dismounted cavalry and 'checked the Arabs'.[32] Lawrence stated that they had taken 250 prisoners and only 50 fugitives reached the railway, the rest being 'shot … ignobly as they ran'.[33] His estimation was that between 20 and 30 of the Arabs had been killed, with an unspecified number wounded, representing 'one sixth of our force'. The freezing conditions, and a sudden blizzard, accounted for more of the wounded. Indeed, the worsening weather, especially the snow, forced the entire operation to a halt.

The orthodox interpretation of the battle of Tafila on 25 January 1918 is that it was an unprecedented victory for the Arabs.[34] The *Official History* concluded: 'the defence of Tafila was a brilliant feat of arms'.[35] An Ottoman brigade, numbering around 900 men, was routed and the Arabs were left in possession of the field. Yet this record of success might need a reassessment. The Ottomans soon recovered Tafila because the Arabs lacked the resources to sustain themselves, amidst worsening meteorological conditions, in such an exposed position.[36] The Arab losses Lawrence spoke of were severe, and such a small force could not expect to take casualties of this magnitude in another action. By contrast, the Ottomans could reinforce any threatened point and they still held the railway firmly. When they made their counter-offensive, they advanced from two directions, one from Jurf, the other from Qatrani, 35 miles to the north-east of Tafila. Zeid was forced to withdraw on 6 March 1918, and, according to the British *Official History*, he 'was defeated on the Shobek-Tafila road'.[37] Tafila itself was taken without fighting on 18 March. In its context, then, Tafila, while a short-term success, does not look like the achievement Lawrence claimed it was. We might speculate that there was a degree of overconfidence about the entire action. Lawrence was certainly not following the precepts of guerrilla warfare that he mapped out after the war, especially the injunction to conduct a 'war of detachment'. This pitched battle favoured the Ottomans in that it allowed them to bring to bear their heavy weapons against an otherwise elusive enemy.

The battle of Tafila had little negative impact on Ottoman morale, while the defeat of Zeid's men and the recovery of the settlements probably did much to restore their confidence. By contrast, the winter weather deepened the deterioration of Arab morale. Lawrence made no mention of the fate of the local population once they were reoccupied, and while it can be assumed the Armenians remained defiant, the allegiance of the other communities had been far more fluid. We might therefore revise the assessment of Tafila as a short-lived tactical success which presaged an operational setback. A hint of Lawrence's own disappointment appeared in *Seven Pillars*, amidst regret for the casualties, where, referring indirectly to himself, he wrote: 'A battle might be thrilling at the moment for generals, but usually their imagination played too vividly beforehand, and made the reality seem sham; so quiet and unimportant that they ranged about looking for its fancied core.'[38] The battle's 'sole profit lay, then, in its lesson to myself'.[39] He claimed to have written a Clausewitzian-style report of the action for General Headquarters in Palestine, as if it was a parody by a military amateur, but that only seems to underscore his misjudgement of the whole affair. Guerrilla forces are successful in using violence against inanimate targets and, even when in larger numbers, taking on a regular military force can only result in significant casualties. Their strength is in their being, their psychological pressure, and their political agenda, not in their military prowess. Tafila was not a victory, but a harsh lesson.

The consolation for Lawrence was that an Arab contingent, led by Abdulla al Feir, managed to raid the Dead Sea coast and destroy some small boats, although not the full complement of vessels that were supplying the Ottomans on the western side. They took the landing point by surprise and captured 60 prisoners.[40] Nevertheless, there was no further movement against the Ottomans and even the men of Kerak, waiting for the signal to join Zeid in an uprising, were disappointed when no Sharifian forces appeared. Lawrence acknowledged that, because of the weather, they would simply not reach Jericho or the northern shores of the Dead Sea.

Lawrence was compelled to return to Guweira to call for more money to be sent up, the funds having been depleted by the need to pay for wages and rewards around Tafila. The cold weather conditions imposed inactivity that not only used up the money, but increased the strain on the Arab fighters in the hills. All movement was challenging. Lawrence's own journey to Guweira was made in bleak conditions. His party he described as having 'the most dolorous expression of resigned despair ... for we were filthy and miserable'.[41]

At Guweira, Lawrence reunited with Colonel Joyce, and fresh British personnel including Lieutenant Colonel Alan Dawnay, who had brought up some armoured cars. They discussed Tafila but also the difficulty of getting the Beni Atiyeh tribal irregulars to accompany the armoured car unit to counter-attack Tafila. Lawrence attributed the problem to the difficulties of regular and irregular cooperation.[42] Later, he explained this in more detail, suggesting that irregulars would invariably hold back when regulars were present, to let them do the fighting. Cooperation was a frequent problem between the various contingents in the campaign, although the British resolved this problem more often than not by insisting on a unified command.[43] Nevertheless, when accompanying tribal leaders, such as Mohammed Ali el Beidawi, it was impossible to assert any authority.

The £30,000 of gold Lawrence had requested was delivered and he set off again to rejoin Zeid. En route, he stopped at Maulud's new position and his description of the situation illustrates the conditions which typified all the armies posted in the hills of the region that winter:

> These men of Maulud's had been camped in this place, four thousand feet above the sea, for two months without relief. They had to live in shallow dugouts on the hill-side. They had no fuel except the sparse, wet wormwood, over which they were just able to bake their necessary bread every other day. They had no clothes but khaki drill uniform of the British summer sort. They slept in their rain-sodden verminous pits on empty or half-empty flour-sacks, six or eight of them together in a knotted bunch, that enough of the worn blankets might be pooled for warmth. Rather more than half of them died or were injured by the cold and wet; yet the others maintained their watch, exchanging shots daily with the Turkish outposts, and protected only by the inclement weather from crushing counter-attack.[44]

Lawrence concluded that these Arab regulars had been vital in holding the routes to Aqaba: 'We owed much to them, and more to Maulud, whose fortitude stiffened them in their duty.'[45]

Having delivered the funds to the tribal groups loyal to Feisal and Zeid, Lawrence turned his attention to conducting reconnaissance rides for the forthcoming spring campaign season. The first objective was to scout the routes to Kerak across the Wadi Hesa to the north. The reconnoitre appeared so straightforward that Lawrence returned immediately to Zeid to urge an advance within the month, linking up with Allenby's right flank, which he estimated to be on the Jordan River. Zeid refused on the grounds that all of the gold that Lawrence had hauled through the winter snows was already spent. Worse still, those who had been paid all lived south of the Wadi Hesa, and none of them would venture further north because of long-standing feuds with the rival clans.[46]

Lawrence relayed that Feisal could depend upon 40,000 men but these were only paid if called up for active service and even they were contracted for just a month. He estimated that his allowances, paid by Britain, could have fielded only a maximum of 17,000, but this many never took the field at the same time. Petitions for extra payments had been frequent, but not always paid. In contrast, Zeid had clearly met every demand and as a result there were no funds left. Lawrence confessed that he was 'aghast' because 'this meant the complete ruin of my plans and hopes, the collapse of our effort to keep faith with Allenby'.[47]

Lawrence could not think of a solution. He wrote: 'All night I thought over what could be done, but found a blank; and when morning came could only send word to Zeid that, if he would not return the money, I must go away.' Lawrence reported to Joyce, who had come up from Guweira and who himself made an appeal to Zeid, but, without the means, Lawrence explained he would have to go 'back to Allenby to put my further employment in his hands'. Lawrence's hopes, and promises to Allenby the previous autumn, that he would get the Arabs to move northwards in parallel with the EEF and clear the area east of the Jordan had failed. He therefore set off for Beersheba, which was now the shortest route to the British Headquarters. When he arrived, Lawrence seemed to feel a strong sense of failure. In summing up his injuries and recent hardships, his verdict was that, having handed over the funds to Zeid, his plans had come to naught.[48] Worse, he criticized his 'daily posturing in alien dress, preaching in alien speech' and his misplaced faith in the idea that the Arabs would end the war by being able to defend themselves 'with paper tools'.

At the headquarters, Lawrence learned that Jericho had been captured by the EEF, but, more importantly, that the War Cabinet had decided there should be greater efforts in Palestine and Syria. Allenby had been urged, by Lloyd George's trusted colleague, Jan Smuts, the former Afrikaner guerrilla commander, to take Damascus and Aleppo. Smuts' visit, in February 1918, was to implement Joint Note 12 of the Allies' Supreme War Council, which demanded a more aggressive policy of offence, but Allenby was constrained by logistical and climatic considerations. To his credit, Smuts accepted Allenby's observations and his report to the War Cabinet confirmed the obstacles in the path of the EEF. He also echoed Allenby's insistence on a methodical advance with troops properly prepared and supported. The rhetoric of Joint Note 12 was hard to realize in practice when there was now every expectation that the thousands of German troops who were released from the Russian theatre (following the Bolshevik Revolution) would soon be unleashed on the Western Front against the British and French forces. The German High Command calculated that they had a window of opportunity of a few months where their fresh troops and greater strength in divisions would prevail over the tired Anglo-French armies, and before the Americans could arrive in larger numbers.

Although Lawrence was ready to quit, David Hogarth and Gilbert Clayton soon talked him round. Allenby requested that Lawrence guide the Arab forces to protect his right flank, as he pushed the EEF up to Damascus. Lawrence did not mention the failures he had experienced and, having pointed out that it could not be done under present conditions, he finally agreed that, with more resources, and a phased approach, it could be done.[49]

The first phase was to seize and hold Ma'an. The approach would be to take a larger contingent of Arab regulars to the north of the town, cut the Hejaz railway but hold it, forcing the Ma'an garrison to leave their defences and fight in the field. Lawrence wanted baggage camels, artillery, machine guns and some means to prevent the Ottoman forces at Amman coming south to relieve Ma'an.

The second phase would be for the EEF to secure Amman, and thus sever the Hejaz permanently while opening up the route to Damascus. But in the discussions at the Corps conference, there were some significant points. While Lawrence welcomed the opportunity to have two units of the Camel Transport Corps that could sustain 4,000 regular Imperial and Arab troops at least 80 miles in advance of their current base, and with Allenby's assurance that he intended to take and hold Es Salt with an Indian brigade, he was reluctant to commit to a joint operation. So while there was an agreement that the Arab Northern Army, augmented with British firepower, would assault, seize and hold Ma'an, there was no agreement on the role of Arab irregulars around Amman. The British commanders were eager that locally recruited men should join in Allenby's advance there, assisting with the destruction of the railway. Lawrence, concerned that any setback would ruin the prestige of the Arab cause, advocated that the British should first secure Salt and Amman. On having Arabs accompany the British, he wrote: 'I opposed this, since the later retirement to Salt would cause rumour and reaction, and it would be easier if we did not enter till this had spent itself.'[50]

This verdict suggests Lawrence had less faith in the Arab forces than perhaps is assumed. His confidence had been shaken by Zeid's ineffectual leadership, by the losses at Tafila, and by the inertia of the Arab fighters in the recent winter months. He also felt that the Arab irregulars were just not suited to working in close proximity with regular troops, or willing to press home an assault on prepared defences and then hold them against a modern army. Lawrence also advised against co-locating regular Muslim troops, such as Egyptians, alongside the Arab irregulars: 'The mixture of Egyptian troops with tribesmen was a moral weakness. If there were professional soldiers present, the Beduin would stand aside and watch them work, glad to be excused the leading part. Jealousy, superadded to inefficiency, would be the outcome.'[51]

For their part, the Arab officers under Feisal doubted the British and their intentions. Setbacks led them to question whether it was worth continuing at all; some thought they should perhaps seek a separate peace with the Ottomans.[52] The British officers also raised another practical problem: how to distinguish Arab units friendly to the campaign and those who were working for the Ottomans. Lawrence again advocated independent sectors for action, known today as AORs or 'Areas of Responsibility'.

The solution that was worked out was that the Arab regulars, enabled by the British transport and heavy weapons support, would take Ma'an simultaneously with Allenby's capture of Salt. Then, the Arab regulars would move up to be resupplied at Jericho, using the camel transport to conduct any other actions within their 80-mile operating radius.[53] Once Amman was secured by Allenby, the Arab forces would press northwards.

Lawrence was conveyed, via Cairo, to Aqaba and reported the plan to Feisal. The failure of the advance on the Dead Sea was clearly a surprise to Feisal and Lawrence's indifference to Tafila even more so. The new plan, to seize Ma'an, probably did little to assuage his concerns, given that it was to be an attack against some 6,000 Ottoman troops. If the Ottomans fell back on their fortified defences, even after a reverse, this would be a serious undertaking. Feisal's perturbed position was worsened by the news that Tafila had fallen back into Ottoman hands, which he felt would 'do his reputation harm'.[54] Lawrence tried to reassure him that the Ottoman commitment to Tafila merely reduced the size of the garrison at Ma'an, and that Allenby's offensive on Amman would draw more Ottoman forces away, but Feisal was evidently not persuaded. The most convincing aspect of Lawrence's argument was that Allenby had set aside another £300,000 and the valuable camel transport for the Arab cause.

Once again, the situation calls into question Lawrence's later assessments about how guerrilla warfare should be conducted. It is when things are going wrong that leadership is truly tested. It is easy to lead when things are going well, but when a force is checked, defeated, suffering losses, sick or in retreat, then special qualities are called for. Lawrence's response to the setback and inactivity at Tafila, and the intransigence of Zeid, was to quit. His personal courage, in making the hazardous journeys through winter conditions, sometimes alone, is not in doubt, but his response to the failure of his plan to advance to the Dead Sea was hardly dogged or imaginative: there was no fall back plan, no 'plan B', and he had no other options to offer. Moreover, the solution to the impasse was provided by Allenby, not Lawrence. Allenby's design was to escalate force, using the algebra of numbers, in transport, manpower, manoeuvre and money, or in the form of more advanced technology. Lawrence embraced this offer because he had no choice, underscoring the dependent nature of the relationship of the Arab forces. The bionomic and diathetic elements were still part of Lawrence's calculus, but took a more subordinate position in his thinking in the first months of 1918.

At this point, Lieutenant Colonel Alan Dawnay took over the new Hejaz Operations Staff to improve logistics and coordination within the Sharifian army.[55] Dawnay commanded a shipping liaison officer, an ordnance officer, supply officers and an intelligence team, giving a much-needed professional touch to the increased scale of British support. Although he did not have Arabic, his tact and thoroughness made a significant difference. Dawnay's appointment brought to an end the period Lawrence called 'the wild-man show'.[56] In essence, it represented the professionalization and coordination of Arab operations.

Dawnay would orchestrate a three-pronged manoeuvre against the Ottomans. The plan was for a wing of the Arab Northern Army, in the centre, under Jafar Pasha al-Askari, to attack the line north of Ma'an and draw out the garrison, while Joyce commanded a southern wing, consisting of the armoured cars, to cut the Hejaz railway and thus the Ottomans' lateral communications. The northern wing with Lawrence accompanying Zeid and Nasir would operate between Salt and Allenby's columns as they advanced on Amman. Lawrence was assigned to raise support amongst the local Beni Sakr clans nearby.

Things were not going to go as planned.

9

Fighting Alongside Local Forces

The plan began to unravel for unexpected reasons which had nothing to do with the enemy and everything to do with leadership. Maulud, who had defended Petra, sought to alter the plan in the centre. Dissatisfied with the idea of an attack to the north of Ma'an, he argued that they should make a determined assault on Ma'an itself and other Arab leaders supported him. Joyce tried to reason with them, but soon after fell sick with pneumonia and had to be evacuated, his health having been broken by the climate and his unceasing drive. Dawnay was his replacement and he implored them to adhere to the plan, repeating the points that Joyce had made that the Arabs lacked artillery, and their inexperienced troops would not be able to defeat entrenched Ottoman regulars.[1] Lawrence noted that Arab pride was at stake, and so, regardless of the odds, they would not accept any British advice.

It was, no doubt, at this point, that Lawrence's injunctions on how to work with local forces came to the fore. In *Seven Pillars*, he noted that he had to march in step with the desires of the Arabs, even though the British really were 'all-powerful, with the money, the supplies and now the transport, in our hands'.[2] He recorded that they had to 'go slow with the self-governing democracy, the Arab Northern Army, in which service was as voluntary as enlistment'. In essence, Lawrence was warning that, if offended, these fighters would just abandon the Arab cause altogether, leaving him in exactly the same situation as had occurred at Tafila: deprived of any willing manpower, and therefore simply unable to execute the mission.

Lawrence praised the informal organization and dispersal of local fighters, for it was their amorphous structure that made them far harder to detect: 'Our largest resources, the Beduin on whom our war must be built, were unused to formal operations, but had assets of mobility, toughness, self-assurance, knowledge of the country, intelligent courage. With them dispersal was strength.'[3] The elusive nature of Arab irregulars added a psychological burden to the enemy: in the minds of Ottoman soldiers, the Arab raiders were invisible, unknown and ambiguous. Their threat was continuous and ever-present, even when they were not, in reality, present at all.

Lawrence claimed that regular soldiers were 'made a caste by great rewards in pay, dress, and privilege: or being cut off from life by contempt'.[4] He was critical of Egyptian soldiers who 'belonged to their service without check of public opinion'.[5] He thought the British Army had put a stop to discipline-through-physical-pain by 'civil decency', but its systems of pack drill, fatigues and field punishments meant he regarded his own army as no better than the Turkish 'Oriental system'. In order to draw a clear distinction with the Arab fighters, Lawrence argued that his men could not be punished, ignoring the sanctions meted out to two of his bodyguard in the winter of 1917–18 and the execution of a fighter for murder. He argued that the imminence of active service made them 'like the Army of Italy' under Napoleon, ready to fulfil their duty to defeat the enemy. He described them as 'pilgrims, intent always to the little farther'.[6]

He continued that they had no discipline, in the restrictive sense. His personal resentment of discipline, drawn from his own background, suggested that its purpose 'was to render the unit the unit, the man a type; in order that their effort might be calculable ... the deeper the discipline, the lower was the individual excellence; also more sure the performance'.[7] For Lawrence, discipline was the means by which outcomes could be measurable and the uncertain bionomic, human factors reduced to a negligible degree. Lawrence instead praised the individuality of his Arab irregular fighters, claiming 'the efficiency of our forces was the personal efficiency of the single man'. This verdict should not be unexpected from an individual who did not find it easy to work in teams, nor perhaps saw any virtue in them. All his life he had tended to work alone.

The argument culminated for Lawrence in the idea that the nervous energy he could summon for irregular fighters suited the short-term crises of guerrilla warfare, whereas the sustained violence of conventional war demanded a more enduring form of resilience that armies created through the regimentation of men in discipline. This verdict was summed up in Lawrence's typical literary style:

> For with war a subtle change happened to the soldier. Discipline was modified, supported, even swallowed by an eagerness of the man to fight. This eagerness it was which brought victory in the moral sense, and often in the physical sense, of the combat. War was made up of crises of intense effort. For psychological reasons commanders wished for the least duration of this maximum effort: not because the men would not try to give it – usually they would go on till they dropped – but because each such effort weakened their remaining force. Eagerness of the kind was nervous, and, when present in high power, it tore apart flesh and spirit. To rouse the excitement of war for the creation of a military spirit in peacetime would be dangerous, like the too-early doping of an athlete. Consequently discipline, with its concomitant 'smartness' (a suspect word implying superficial restraint and pain) was invented to take its place.[8]

The paradox is that the obstruction to the British plan was being made not by irregular fighters, but by the trained regular officers of the Arab Northern Army – the men who understood, appreciated and practised discipline, and had shown the stoicism that Lawrence had praised in the frozen foxholes of the previous winter (at a time when the irregular fighters had sought shelter or melted away). They were now the ones insisting on a more direct operation, in part to prove their worth.

Lawrence's claim that 'in our articulated war, the sum yielded by single men would at least equal the product of a compound system of the same strength' was simply not borne out by the facts on the ground. The irregulars had repeatedly failed to produce the 'value-added' in their operations. The product of the hundreds of men participating in the railway raids was far less than that achieved by disciplined companies of the Imperial or Arab Northern Army in taking and holding key positions. Team efforts had, contrary to Lawrence's judgement, consistently achieved better results.

The individual qualities Lawrence expected of the fighters, however, resonate far more strongly with those who, throughout history, have engaged in irregular warfare, usually deep behind enemy lines. He called for 'special initiative, endurance, enthusiasm' and regarded irregular war as 'far more intellectual than a bayonet charge'.[9] The 'moral strain of isolated fighting' Lawrence described was an experience that would be recognizable amongst Special Operations Executive, MI6 and OSS operators in the Second World War, and amongst CIA or Special Operations Forces personnel in missions after 1945.

'Moral strain' and 'cohesion' are two sides of the same phenomenon, namely morale. Morale itself is considered to be a form of willpower, which is reinforced and sustained by cohesion in groups, although it can just as easily describe an individual's singular determination. Cohesion is a rather intangible concept, but suggests a bond generated from shared hardships, the result of repeated training, and the common identity of locality, language, nationality, clan or regiment. It is a 'glue' consisting of honour, standards and 'in-group culture', often based on a common experience. The product of cohesion is an increased willingness to take risks, endure casualties, and persevere through extreme trials, yet remain committed to a particular mission or group. After the First World War, Lord Charles Moran, who had served as a Medical Officer with the Royal Fusiliers on the Western Front and wrote an account of anxiety entitled *The Anatomy of Courage*, made an arresting analogy on morale, suggesting it was a form of an account.[10] Repeated stress, such as combat, would deplete this account, and would eventually break the individual, unless there was some restorative system, which could take the form of periodic rotations and relief, the comradeship of personnel in cohesive groups, welfare measures, or empathetic and inspirational leadership.[11]

In war, there are various depleting elements on morale. Armies in retreat, poorly led, suffering debilitating sickness, facing setbacks, and then deprived of information are the most at risk. Troops making progress, wisely led, healthy and fit, equipped with superior systems, and fully informed will exhibit the highest morale. All generalizations have their exceptions, but the progress of the Arab forces, if not Lawrence himself, was in line with these patterns, even where Lawrence tried to claim exceptionalism. Lawrence's contribution, like those of Joyce, Hornby, and others, was to give the Arabs successes through raids, building their confidence in the process.[12] Seizing Aqaba and conducting successful tactical actions at Petra and Tafila reinforced the improving cohesion and morale of the Arab Northern Army. Having endured the winter hardships together, there were further enhancements to the cohesion of the Arab regulars. Their call to assault Ma'an, contrary to their British partners, was thus understandable. It was the product of a process of growing cohesiveness and increasing determination.

Lawrence was eager to preserve the idea of a successful Arab revolt, to enhance its prestige, and build popular backing for it. He says relatively little in his accounts of direct talks with the people that might persuade them to fight, as this he left to the local sheikhs. There are scattered references to persuading some of these local leaders to support the Arab cause, and one or two of them are given more extensive coverage, such as Auda and Nasir. The consistency, however, is his view that there must be clear legitimacy in the leadership of the insurgency. This he embodies not in Hussein, whom he regarded as too suspicious and truculent, but in Feisal:

> Such people demanded a war-cry and banner from outside to combine them, and a stranger to lead them, one whose supremacy should be based on an idea: illogical, undeniable, discriminant: which instinct might accept and reason find no rational basis to reject or approve. For this army of Feisal's the conceit was that an Emir of Mecca, a descendant of the prophet, a Sherif, was an otherworldly dignitary whom sons of Adam might reverence without shame. This was the binding assumption of the Arab movement; it was this which gave it an effective, if imbecile unanimity.[13]

Handling local forces required particular attributes, but the technical aspects of the demolition operations against the Hejaz railway raised the perennial problem of training (which took time and education) and skills (which demanded repeated rehearsal). Newcombe and Hornby, short of time, took upon themselves the technical tasks, leaving their Arab partners as 'close protection' teams. They drove themselves hard, wearing out their camels and exhausting their limited supplies in repeated missions. 'Newcombe is like fire', their Arab allies used to complain; 'He burns friend and enemy.' Lawrence noted they admired 'his amazing energy with nervous shrinking lest they should be his next friendly victims'.[14]

Lawrence provides further insight into the management of local forces, including the importance of empathy and understanding:

> If they suspected that we wanted to drive them either they were mulish or they went away. If we comprehended them, and gave time and trouble to make things tempting to them, then they would go to great pains for our pleasure. Whether the results achieved were worth the effort, no man could tell. Englishmen, accustomed to greater returns, would not, and, indeed, could not, have spent the time, thought and tact lavished every day by sheikhs and emirs for such meagre ends.[15]

He observed their customs closely. Lawrence also related the courtesies of greetings, or presentation of gifts, in the form of clothes, camels, horses and weapons. Lawrence provided a list to guide other liaison officers, known as the '27 Articles'.[16]

An effective fighting force depends not only on its motivation, training, or the proficiency in its arms and equipment, but also on its selection. Not all men were suitable for the demands of war, although the harsh environmental conditions faced by the Bedouin made them hardy and more tolerant of tough campaigning. Moreover, long-standing feuds seemed to inure them to the possibility of combat, injury and death. Auda abu Tayi was an indication that the best local fighters, with a criminal background, were also the hardest to handle or direct, unless it suited their interests:

> His patience in action was extreme: and he received and ignored advice, criticism, or abuse, with a smile as constant as it was very charming. If he got angry his face worked uncontrollably, and he burst into a fit of shaking passion, only to be assuaged after he had killed: at such times he was a wild beast, and men escaped his presence.[17]

Lawrence eventually acquired a bodyguard of outcasts about 90 strong. He appealed to the strongest single men, usually those with a reputation for misconduct. British officers referred to them as cut-throats, and Lawrence admitted they were prone to violence.[18] They were disciplined for misdemeanours by El-Zaagi, a Sharifian lieutenant whom Lawrence trusted. But they were volunteers, without contract, who could leave his service at any time. It seems only one chose to do so, since this role carried a degree of prestige. The terms and conditions of service were tough. Lawrence insisted that every man had to be prepared to ride long distances, day and night, at short notice. He paid them the same wage as regular camel-borne troops, but gave them the animals, so the wage was effectively a degree higher than that of their peers. Lawrence insisted on having the very strongest and fastest riding camels that could be obtained.

Half of the bodyguard consisted of Agayl tribesmen; the other half were a mix of clans and communities, which, through feuding, ensured that betrayal was less likely. The mixed nature of the force meant that, regardless of the district, when despatched as individual spies, they attracted little attention. The purpose of the bodyguard was thus two-fold: to gather intelligence from sources which Lawrence himself would otherwise compromise, and to prevent his betrayal by Arabs who might be tempted by the Ottoman bounty that had been offered for his capture.

If the Arab forces were to exploit the closer proximity of the Egyptian Expeditionary Force, and operate against the Ottomans with any degree of effectiveness, then they needed to be better trained, armed, and equipped. The most significant fire support came in the form of a flight of 14 Squadron of the Royal Flying Corps (RFC) and later, after the capture of Aqaba, by X Flight. This air support had provided crucial reconnaissance of routes and Ottoman positions. X flight had helped contest Abu el Lissan, encouraged a defensive mindset in the garrison at Ma'an, and compelled the Ottomans to increase their air cover with German squadrons.[19] By the time of Lawrence's advance towards Syria, the RFC were routinely supporting his ground moves. In the final operations, Lawrence also got the support of 1 Squadron, Australian Flying Corps. The British regular army and RFC also provided the armoured cars, motorized tenders and Talbot self-propelled guns which added much-needed firepower to the Arab units and conducted their own raids against the Hejaz railway. Armoured cars played an important role in the more sustained operations against Ottoman forces around Amman, Deraa and Ma'an.

The key point here is that, despite the romantic image of Lawrence's Bedouin fighters conducting repeated raids on railways, his campaign was turning into a combined arms operation, involving armoured cars, cavalry, regular infantry and air power. For all the qualities of lightly armed camel-borne irregular fighters, this new arrangement was a far more effective combination.

THE POLITICS OF MOTIVATION

Keeping the Arabs in the war on the Allied side was not straightforward. Arab leaders were divided amongst themselves at a local level, but also in regional groupings, and pre-war intra-Arab conflicts continued during the conflict, and after. Any post-war settlement was likely to be complex. Across the wider Middle East, there were other communities to consider too – the Assyrians, the Druze, the Kurds, the Armenians, Jews, Christian Arabs, the urbane Lebanese, the pastoral Mesopotamians and a number of other minorities. Some still felt a strong sense of identity in Ottomanism; others were now deterred by Turkish nationalism or the violent reputation of the Bedouin, and sought a new dispensation. The more educated and Westernized looked to emulate the statehood and national identity of shared communities with a common language; but the majority looked to their heritage, culture, religious and ethnic differences, or simply sought to survive the soaring prices, waves of disease, the looting armies, and the violent banditry of opportunists.

From Cairo, Commander Hogarth reassured Sharif Hussein in January 1918 that the British were committed to enabling the Arabs the 'opportunity once again of forming a nation in the world' and that there was no question of replacing Ottoman subjugation with British colonial rule. In light of the British government's announcement, through the Balfour Declaration, Hogarth also explained that Jewish opinion had to be considered as they too sought a homeland in the Near East. The British were naturally careful to assure the Arab leaders that 'it being clearly understood that nothing shall be done which may prejudice the civil and religious rights of existing non-Jewish communities in Palestine'.[20] The British government was motivated by a desire to encourage the Anglo-American Jews to support the war effort, as the United States joined the Allies, because Jewish opinion was anti-Tsarist and therefore not well disposed towards the Entente. The motive was also to find suitable partners in the Palestine region who could temper more strident French demands for a 'Greater Syria'.[21]

Hussein and Feisal showed relatively little interest in the indigenous and Arabic-speaking Jewish population, while with the 'colonial Jews' or Zionists there was mutual indifference. The Foreign Office reiterated Hogarth's points and denounced the Ottoman attempt to sow discord in the Middle East, reaffirming the British government's willingness to liberate the Arabs.

Initially, Sir Mark Sykes was more anxious that the Arabs might seek to establish their own control and try to prevent fulfilment of the agreement he had made with Picot, namely to hand over Syria to France. In assessing the priorities of this war, the British government needed to work with the French in Europe, and create sufficient concession in the Middle East to maintain that relationship, while working to preserve, as far as possible, Britain's own interests in the region, including maintaining its reputation for consistent support to the Muslim world. It would require some compromises to ensure this balance.

Lawrence wrote that he had only learned of the full details of the Sykes-Picot Agreement at a meeting with Sykes on 7 May 1917, but his dismay was that the Arabs were not going to be granted full independence immediately, only autonomy. The meeting had evidently been stormy.[22] Sykes believed immediate independence would lead to 'poverty and chaos', suggesting that a transition and British protection were essential.[23] He believed it would take ten years before the Arabs could form a nation. Lawrence, who had his own misgivings about Arab unity, claimed the Arabs had legitimacy to govern because they were fighting for their independence. Lawrence probably hoped to get the best arrangement he could for the Arabs, and he opposed the French control of Damascus and Syria, but that did not mean he opposed the British project of trying to obtain federated, autonomous regions for the Arabs entirely: he merely saw this as a temporary stage to full independence. This was, in fact, in line with the British government's policy, detailed in 1915–16. Only later did Lawrence claim he had consistently resisted his own government.

Gilbert Clayton, the head of the Arab Bureau in Cairo, had refused to send an angry letter from Lawrence to Sykes the previous summer, on the basis that the Sykes-Picot Agreement, 'never a very workable instrument', was 'now almost a lifeless monument'.[24] Allenby's advance through Palestine was changing the facts on the ground. Although a small French detachment still accompanied the Sharifian Arabs, the

French were aware they were dependent on Britain's willingness to honour the Sykes-Picot talks and the temporary plan they had sketched out. Sykes, becoming conscious that the French colonial lobby had more ambitious, permanent designs on Syria, now repudiated the former agreement with Picot, arguing that he hoped to realize the idea of Arab autonomy and persuade the French of the case.[25] By 1918, he believed the agreement that bore his name was 'dead and gone, and the sooner scrapped the better'.[26] It had, after all, been a temporary measure, and Britain had consistently favoured independent and autonomous states for its Arab partners.

When the Bolsheviks seized power in Russia in the autumn of 1917, they were eager to discredit the imperialist powers, and they published all the Tsarist 'secret treaties' in November that year. These were reproduced by the world's press, including the Sykes-Picot Agreement.[27] There were accusations of betrayal, because McMahon's correspondence, showing favour to an Arab state under the Hashemites, appeared to contradict 'territorial awards' to Britain and France. Djemal Pasha, the Ottoman Governor of Syria, used the information to communicate with Feisal, offering an amnesty for all the Arabs in revolt against the Ottoman Empire.

Colonel Joyce and Lawrence (promoted Major with a CB in recognition of the taking of Aqaba and his missions deep into Syria behind enemy lines) reassured Feisal at his headquarters that the Ottomans had distorted 'either from ignorance or malice' the original intent of the Sykes-Picot Agreement, deliberately omitting, for example, the British commitment to obtain the 'consent of native populations and safeguarding their interests'. Far from his later claims that he thought the British were misleading the Arabs, Lawrence was, at that time, already showing his disappointment at the failure of a united Arab cause. In early 1918, he was concerned about its cohesion and the chance that the Ottomans, with their German partners, might still build an anti-Sharifian movement amongst the Arabs.[28]

General Allenby was supportive insofar as he had any powers to influence events. He was categorical in refusing to allow the French sole jurisdiction over Jerusalem in December 1917. When he assumed command, the Arab capture of Aqaba in July 1917 had demonstrated to him the military value of Arab forces operating behind or on the flanks of Ottoman regular formations, and he did his best to find the resources, aircraft, troops and camel transport that they needed. Nevertheless, Allenby's priority was to defeat the Ottomans so that an agreement could be worked out by the diplomats after the war.

Diplomatic relations between Hussein and the British were already strained by the Sharif's claim to be the 'King of Arab Lands'. His ambitions were impossible for the British to support in their entirety because to do so would mean abandoning long-standing allies, such as the Emir of Kuwait, the sheikhs of the Trucial States, Ibn Saud of Riyadh, or the sheikhs of southern Arabia. London and Cairo also knew that Hussein's fortunes were dependent on British military success, and so they signalled their conditional support for his territorial claims by referring to Hussein as 'King of the Hejaz'. Hussein grew more suspicious of his partners, and more antagonistic towards his Arab rivals.

Inter-Arab conflict was a serious concern, even within the ranks of the Sharifian forces. Abdullah's irregulars threatened their own Arab regular army officers, largely because of the latter's former Ottoman service. In one operation, advised by Major W. A. Davenport, at Bowat station north of Medina, the Bedouin were incensed that Arab artillery officers were reluctant to attack, and would 'draw their knives ... and make suggestive gestures across their throats'.[29] In the subsequent assault, some of the regular infantry officers went to ground and refused to go into action with the rank and file, and the attack collapsed.

Tensions between Hussein's Hashemites and the forces of Abdul Aziz Ibn Saud were increasing too.[30] Harry St John Bridger ('Jack') Philby, of the Indian Civil Service, was recruited from Cambridge and deployed to southern Arabia in November 1917 to act as liaison officer to Ibn Saud. His mentors were Sir Percy Cox and Gertrude Bell, but what they had not foreseen was Philby's developing personal agenda. Like Lawrence, Philby favoured his own protégé as the king of Arabia, and, in another similar vein, Philby travelled extensively to accompany his Arab partner and show that his was the candidate most worthy of support.[31] He made the crossing of the desert from Riyadh to Jeddah, ostensibly to mend relations between the two Arab rivals, but, in fact, as a way to demonstrate that Ibn Saud commanded the loyalty of the Bedouin of the interior.

The matter was brought to a head by the oasis dispute at Kharma, 60 miles east of Taif. The local population were followers of Wahabism, but they had been on operations with Hussein's forces near Medina until a disagreement broke out between their sheikh and Abdullah. When they were threatened with punishment by the Hashemites, they retreated back to Kharma and claimed the protection of Ibn Saud. The Hashemites were undeterred and launched a mounted attack, only to be driven off by the local Kharmite Wahabis.[32] Had it not been for Ibn Saud's preoccupation with the threat posed by Rashid and the Shammar around Hail, the Saud-Hussein conflict resulting from this incident could have become serious and disrupted all operations around Medina. For the time being, it was Lawrence's opinion, that the Hashemites were the dynasty most likely to form a unifying government over the Arabs, that held sway; but Philby was to win the argument after the war.

At this point, in mid-March 1918, Lawrence prepared to execute the three-pronged Arab campaign against the Hejaz railway to prevent its use against the EEF, in coordination with Allenby's assault on Amman. For Lawrence, it seemed to herald the beginning of the end of operations south of Damascus.

It was to prove a tragically premature assessment. He called it: 'the ruin of high hope'.[33]

By, With and Through

Integrating Local Forces in Allenby's Campaign

As the main axes of Arab attacks extended eastwards in March 1918, Lawrence led the contingent that would link up with Allenby. His men paused at Atatir, waiting for the signal to cross to Themed, in the heartland of the Beni Sakr, thus providing a presence that would prevent the Ottomans advancing into the area on Allenby's flank, Lawrence pondering that 'we ought to link up with the British comfortably without firing a shot'.[1]

Allenby knew that the value of the Arab irregulars was in their ability to cause disruption and facilitate deception. While the main Arab force commenced the siege of Ma'an, Lawrence's smaller contingent was located within 50 miles of Amman, giving the impression of another forward move there.

Then suddenly news arrived that Amman had fallen, but, as they started on the final leg of their deception mission, further reports came in that the British were falling back. Another messenger carried the story that Salt had also been evacuated. A fourth messenger confirmed that Amman still lay in Ottoman hands, but Lawrence was not satisfied and sent one of his own bodyguard to check the situation. Contingency plans were worked out in the interval, but it was not until that night that Lawrence's follower returned with the news that 'Jemal Pasha was now in Salt, victorious, hanging those local Arabs who had welcomed the English' and 'The Turks were still chasing Allenby far down the Jordan Valley.'[2] The turn of phrase is a combination of Lawrence's own style and his desire to convey the elaborations of his messenger. Allenby was not chased 'far down the Jordan Valley', but his operation against Amman was checked.

The effect on British, and, by extension, Lawrence's own prestige, was detrimental. Lawrence appeared to regret having promised the deliverance of Amman. He wrote: 'That we should so fall down before the Arabs was deplorable ... they had never trusted us to do the great things which I foretold.'[3] There was no choice but to withdraw his force, especially the Indian troops that accompanied them. On the return, they attacked a small eight-man Ottoman patrol on the Hejaz line, although without coordination, resulting in one seriously wounded fighter; his servant, Farraj. The casualty delayed the party, only 16 strong, when a force of 50 dismounted Ottoman infantry appeared, supported by more aboard a motorized trolley. Leaving the wounded in the hands of the Ottomans invited an atrocity, and it was customary for the Arabs to either remove their wounded or finish them off. It therefore fell to Lawrence to administer the *coup de grâce*. To prevent disputes arising as to who would inherit the fallen fighter's camel, Lawrence shot the animal too.[4] To avert Ottoman reprisals, prisoners that had been taken in other raids were released.[5]

What had happened to the EEF's plan? Allenby had been instructed to resume his offensive in February 1918 but he knew he could not progress north into Syria until he had neutralized the 20,000 Ottoman troops on his eastern flank. His first manoeuvre, to take Jericho, was successful, with the town falling to Allied troops on 21 February. Allenby next seized the hills above Wadi Auja, which put Jericho and its line of communication beyond the reach of Ottoman artillery.

As Allenby's columns advanced on Amman in March 1918, heavy rains made all movement arduous and prevented the deployment of field artillery. Nevertheless, at Es Salt, en route to Amman, they found the Ottoman garrison had fled and the locals were celebrating their liberation.[6]

General Liman von Sanders, now the commander of the Yıldırım Group, had called in his more exposed posts, including Es Salt, in order to concentrate his forces around the perimeter of Amman. He knew that the city represented the last rail link with the garrison in Medina, and therefore was a vital junction for the entire campaign theatre.[7] He called for further reinforcements from the north and despatched Ottoman cavalry to threaten the British lines of communication astride the Jordan River. Meanwhile, Allenby's force, still struggling through the rain and mud, was forced to transfer its arms, equipment and baggage to camels and mules because of the difficulty in moving wheeled transport. Conditions continued to deteriorate. Men and animals died of exposure on the wind-swept slopes of the valley. Consequently, the British force that arrived in front of Amman was exhausted before the fighting had even begun.[8] A single EEF brigade, armed only with the ammunition and guns they could carry, launched four days of assaults against strong positions. The 2,000 city defenders were dug in, armed with 70 machine guns and supported by field artillery whose fire could saturate the approaches. Further Ottoman reinforcements arrived during the fighting. Yet Liman von Sanders was so concerned about the mounting casualties and wavering resolve of the defenders that he ordered their positions to be held regardless of the cost.[9] The British and Imperial forces could not, however, sustain the assault indefinitely. On 30 March 1918, they commenced their withdrawal, accompanied by large numbers of refugees from Es Salt who feared Ottoman retribution.[10]

The *Official History* explained the cause of failure clearly. The weather conditions which had imposed delays and prevented the movement of heavy artillery meant that the British troops did not have sufficient fire support to take such a well-defended position.[11] Armoured cars could not be brought beyond Es Salt, which limited manoeuvre and prevented any encirclement of the city. As a result, it recorded dryly, 'the main objects of the raid had not been achieved'.[12]

OPERATIONS AGAINST MA'AN

Lawrence caught up with the main body of the Arab Northern Army shortly after it had taken Jebel Semna, a feature some 3,000 feet high that overlooks Ma'an. The Ottoman guns were soon shelling the heights, but with little effect. Lawrence was able to report to the Arab officers that there was also fighting about Jerdun, where the second Arab thrust had been due to take place.[13] By mid-afternoon, parties of prisoners and captured machine guns were arriving from the north, and there were reports that a vast quantity of track had been torn up. The third strike had been to the south, led by Nuri, and he rejoined the main body later the same day, with the news that he had attacked Ghadir el Haj station,

T. E. Lawrence; adorned as a Prince of Arabia, but, in essence, a military advisor who wanted to reward those who fought alongside Britain. (James A. Cannavino Library, Archives & Special Collections, Marist College, Marist Special Collections, B&W glass plate 1262.48)

Mecca, the first city to be liberated by the Arab revolutionaries and the seat of power of the Hashemites. (Library of Congress LC-DIG-matpc-04661)

Yanbo, the site of the critical moment of the revolt in 1916: its loss would have marked the end of the uprising had the Royal Navy not intervened. (© IWM Q 59408)

Wejh, the port seized by British and Arab forces as part of a strategy of 'extending the enemy's flank'. (© IWM Q 58992)

The Hejaz railway, the vulnerable Ottoman line of communication from Anatolia to Medina. (Library of Congress LC-DIG-matpc-09357)

Raids on railway lines proved ineffectual, leading to attacks on locomotives and trains. (© IWM Q 58704)

The Egyptian Expeditionary Force (EEF), including men of the New Zealand Mounted Rifles Brigade (the Australia and New Zealand Mounted Division), which fought from Suez, through Sinai, to Syria. (© IWM Q 12692)

The declaration of jihad in Medina in 1914: an event as significant strategically as the Ottoman offensives against Suez. (Library of Congress LC-DIG-matpc-10475)

At Gaza, where the clearing of Ottoman forces from Sinai opened up the possibility of an offensive through Palestine, Suffolk Yeomanry bivouac on the Gaza–Beersheba line in 1917. (© IWM Q 12856)

Above • Sharifian forces at Aqaba: the strategic breakthrough for the reputation of the Arab forces, if not quite in a physical sense. (Marist Special Collections, B&W glass plate 1262.15)

Inset • Colonel Newcombe, commanding officer of the disruption campaign known as Operation *Hedgehog*. (© IWM Q 58806)

Arab regulars: stiffening Ottoman resistance demanded higher calibre forces.
(© IWM Q 12301)

Hybrid war: Talbots and a Rolls-Royce armoured car in support of Arab irregulars.
(Marist Special Collections, B&W glass plate 1264.2)

Hybrid war: air power, such as the Bristol Fighter, gave critical support to the Arabs.
(© IWM Q 63798)

Feisal, the commander of the Arab Northern Army, and subsequently HM the King of Iraq.
(Marist Special Collections, B&W glass plate 1263.6)

Auda abu Tayi flanked by his brothers. (Marist Special Collections, B&W glass plate 1332.34)

The Grand Sharif of Mecca, Hussein, 'King of the Hedjaz', who aspired to lead the entire Arab world. (© IWM Q 59888)

Turkish troops on the Nablus Road, Jerusalem, trying to stem the advancing tide of British Imperial forces. (Library of Congress LG-DIG-matpc-06378)

Abdullah ibn Hussein, later HM the King of Trans-Jordan, and Ali ibn Hussein with Motlog el Himrieh at Amman. (© IWM Q 60166)

Field Marshal Sir Edmund Allenby, who saw the strategic value of the Arab forces, but insisted on their operational subordination to ensure a synchronized campaign. (© IWM Q 82969)

The country east of Aqaba: ideal for concealing guerrilla forces. (Library of Congress LC-DIG-matpc-15967)

Above left • Sharif Nasir and Jafar al-Askari at Shobek, north of Wadi Musa. (© IWM Q 59559)

Above right • Sir Ronald Henry Amherst Storrs as the Military Governor of Jerusalem, welcoming a mufti during the Nebi Musa pilgrimage in Jerusalem, 26 April 1918. (© IWM Q 12794)

This aerial photograph over the Jordan shows a Bedouin encampment dotted on the banks, illustrating their vulnerability to air attack. (Library of Congress LC-DIG-matpc-15837)

The Yarmuk Valley: scene of the ill-fated raid of November 1917.
(Library of Congress LC-DIG-matpc-17036)

Crossing the Jordan Valley: twice the EEF was repulsed at Amman after its arduous march across
this landscape, which hampered cooperation with local forces.
(Library of Congress LC-DIG-matpc-22084)

Left • Azrak: Lawrence's medieval base in the desert. His room for planning the 'war of detachment' was above the gate. (Library of Congress LC-DIG-matpc-06440)

Below • The Imperial Camel Corps on the march to Musaw'warrah. (© IWM Q 105536)

Ottoman troops repairing the track at Ma'an after one of the Arab raids.
(© IWM Q 60116)

Captain (later Major) Herbert Garland,
antecedent of the Special Forces officer.
(© IWM Q 59338)

T. E. Lawrence, David Hogarth and Colonel
Alan Dawnay in conference in 1918.
(National Portrait Gallery x19908)

Megiddo, September 1918: Turkish transport and prisoners, desperate for water, near Mejdel.
(© IWM Q 12974)

Allenby arrives in Damascus to establish the military occupation, with delegated authority to Feisal. (© IWM Q 12390)

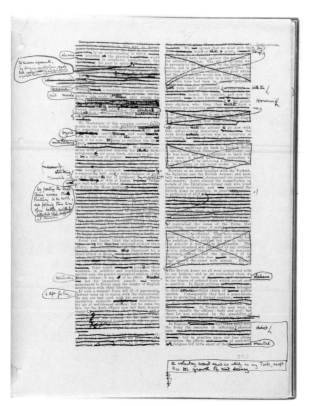

The Seven Pillars of Wisdom, from the Lawrence Exhibition, Magdalen College, Oxford.

War is politics: the Arab delegation at Paris.
(Marist Special Collections, B&W glass plate 1265.26)

Above left • Winston Churchill at the Cairo Conference, 1920, with Lawrence and Prince Abdullah. (Library of Congress: Matson LC-USZ62-65460; LC-DIG-matpc-20843)

Above right • Basil Liddell Hart (right), the strategic writer who built on Lawrence's ideas. (LHCMA, 9/13/17)

The legacy of the Arab forces: the Trans-Jordan Frontier Force at Petra.
(Library of Congress LC-DIG-matpc-13490)

Sir Colin McVean Gubbins, the architect of
Special Operations Executive, who drew on
some of Lawrence's thinking. (Photograph by
Walter Stoneman, 1944: National Portrait
Gallery x75742)

Scholar of guerrilla war: T. E. Lawrence
portrait by Harry Chase, September 1919,
while at All Souls College, Oxford. (Marist
Special Collections, B&W glass plate 1262.44)

destroying five bridges and a thousand rails in the process. Temporarily, Ma'an was cut off from both directions.[14]

When Lawrence rejoined Feisal, he learned more about the setback at Amman, but also that Dawnay was now poised with the armoured car detachments at Guweira, ready to attack Musaw'warrah. Yet the council of war in Feisal's tent was not without its difficulties.[15] Nuri complained about the level of support he got from the Abu Tayi clans, which incensed Auda, and Lawrence's intervention made it worse. The next day, however, the same Abu Tayi tribesmen attacked outposts on the eastern side of Ma'an, and a position was taken that yielded 20 prisoners. There seemed to be no question of calling off the assault on the town and its railway station, even though its purpose, to support Allenby's offensive against Amman, was now redundant.

The Arab Northern Army achieved some success in storming Ma'an railway junction on 16–17 April, over-running sheds that led into the station itself. Critically, the advance stalled when the French artillery under Captain Pisani ran out of ammunition. As they paused, the Arab forces were subjected to retaliatory fire, and, without guns in support, they were driven off. The advance and the withdrawal had been made under machine gun fire, resulting in casualties that deterred another attempt.[16] Lawrence tried to portray the event as evidence the Arabs 'were good enough without British stiffening', a fair claim, but one that could not disguise a tactical failure.[17] Supporters of Lawrence tend to attribute the setback to the shortage of French munitions, or even French treachery, but the rather more prosaic and accurate explanation can be found on dozens of First World War battlefields: defending forces, if properly protected and resourced in their entrenchments, held a significant advantage over assaulting troops out in the open.[18]

On 18 April, Jafar drew off his attacking force and consolidated on the Jebel Semna. He invited the Ma'an garrison commander to surrender, but the Ottoman officer replied that he would defend his post, as ordered, to the last cartridge. He could check the Arab forces and await reinforcements from Amman with some confidence, despite the damage to the railway. In due course, as expected, the Ottomans retook Jerdun, and brought a caravan of pack animals carrying food and ammunition into Ma'an. There were no subsequent Arab efforts to take the station or the nearby town and the Ottomans' relief force of 3,000 men forced the Arabs back to their start lines. From an Ottoman perspective, the defence of Amman and

Ma'an were successful and connected actions. They had held off attacks at two significant nodal points, maintaining their defences in the region.

They must also have been encouraged by the news from Europe. At the end of March 1918, the Germans had launched a large-scale offensive on the Western Front, and, by April, this offensive was driving the British and French armies back. Russia was already out of the war, and concluded terms of surrender at Brest-Litovsk favourable to Germany. The Allied cause was at a low ebb.

Lawrence decided that, with the Ma'an operation thwarted, he would accompany the armoured car attack led by Dawnay, offering to act as the liaison officer between the Arab irregulars and Egyptian personnel. To some extent, Lawrence parodied the regulars' detailed planning and coordination, but the attack was conducted with the synchronization that Dawnay had expected. This was a combined arms operation, where the armoured cars and Talbot guns provided mutual support, their fire protected the Arab irregulars in a dismounted assault, and a strafing attack by aircraft at Tell Shahm covered the final advance on two axes.[19] As planned, the Ottoman outpost was overrun before dawn, forcing them to surrender. Bridges on the Hejaz line were destroyed with a hundredweight of gun-cotton soon after. Also as planned, four armoured cars trained their machine guns on a nearby hilltop sangar known as Rock Post, and the Arab assault carried it without difficulty.

Lawrence and Hornby then took 2 tons of gun-cotton down the line, detonating culverts and rails at intervals. The falling debris landed amongst the armoured car teams, but without mishap: 'One twenty-pound flint clanged plumb on a turret-head and made a harmless dint.'[20] In the subsequent attack on another sangar, South Post, the Arab irregulars did not make their advance by stages, each covering the other as planned, but galloped right up and into the position. The Ottoman garrison made a token resistance, then capitulated. The assault teams therefore turned their attention to the station at Tell Shahm. Peake led the attack from the north, with reluctant Egyptians who were 'not fierce for honour', while aircraft bombed the Ottoman trenches. The armoured cars drove steadily inwards, firing as they went. The Ottoman troops again had no answer to this combined arms manoeuvre and waved white flags of surrender to avoid annihilation.

Lawrence noted that there was then a scramble for loot, in which 'everybody smashed and profited', with a haul of food, arms and ammunition.[21] The only shock was the chance detonation of a trip-wire mine by a stray camel, which 'caused a panic'. The indiscipline worsened when the Egyptians were ordered to guard a storehouse, but the Arab irregulars, in their frenzy to acquire as many goods as possible, opened fire on the guards.[22] The collision was only averted by allowing a further spree of expropriation, but the crush of thieves was so great that the walls of the store 'burst'. The whole affair had almost ended with a 'Green on Blue', the military term for local forces killing their foreign advisors.[23] The following morning, the Arab forces, who had acquired a great deal of materiel, had disappeared. Only a handful remained, leaving Dawnay with a dilemma about further operations. The Arabs would have made an ideal formation for reconnaissance of the next Ottoman position along the line at Ramleh. The situation revealed yet another significant weakness of the irregulars. Without the regular troops, and the technological advantage of British aircraft and armoured cars, the station would probably not have been taken. No assault would have been made in any case without some material benefit. The unedifying motive of the Arab raiding party in this case was not the high-sounding cause of national liberation, but avarice.

It fell to the armoured cars to conduct their own reconnaissance, and two vehicles were sent, one covering the other in bounds. The station they found deserted, but wired up with explosives. A dismounted close reconnaissance revealed stores of supplies. This gives some indication of the Ottoman approach to the defence of the Hejaz line at this stage of the war. It seems that this minor halt could be held without troops, using the deterrent effect of booby-traps. More significant stations, such as Tell Shahm, had their own garrisons and entrenchments, and, from these, patrols could be launched to clear the line to the north and south.

Lawrence relates that there was no hope of continuing beyond Ramleh because, without Arab numbers, the small British contingent could not defeat the larger garrison at Musaw'warrah. He recorded that the Egyptian troops were 'too little warlike', a reference to their growing reluctance to risk their lives.[24] A reconnaissance in force came within line of sight of the station and its defences, but accurate fire from four Ottoman guns at a range of 7,000 yards was sufficient to threaten the armoured car formation. Lawrence's party therefore returned to Ramleh and set about further demolitions. Bridges and rails were blown, and to the south, Feisal had sent Mohammed el Dheilan to carry out similar destruction. Lawrence deduced that 'the active defence of Medina ended with this operation'. This was only partially true. An *active* defence suggests that Fakhri Pasha's division could operate from the defences of the city, and by cutting him off it did indeed deprive the Ottomans of the vital logistics and transport needed for sweeps out of Medina. On the other hand, Medina remained in Ottoman hands up to and beyond the end of the war.

THE SECOND OFFENSIVE AGAINST AMMAN

After the armoured car and railway raids, Lawrence returned, with Dawnay, to Allenby's headquarters where he learned of the plans for a second offensive towards Amman. There was immediate concern because the operation was based on the opportunity apparently offered by the Beni Sakr to furnish 20,000 tribesmen. The leader making the offer was Fahad, in conjunction with Marzuq al Takheimi, and Lawrence suspected that it was unlikely that these men could raise more than 400 men.[25] However, Allenby's headquarters staff knew they would be unable to secure the route to Amman with their own forces because divisions were being withdrawn for service in France. The replacement of British with Indian troops from the Mesopotamia campaign was not complete yet either, so the offer by the Arabs had been accepted more readily.[26] Lawrence's narrative gives the impression that the decision to go for Amman again was entirely founded on the assurances of the Beni Sakr, but that is somewhat misleading. There was pressure on Allenby to maintain an offensive posture for strategic reasons. Lord Curzon told the War Cabinet that the focus of the Central Powers was swinging 'toward the east'. Allenby was ordered to resume an offensive so as to absorb the Ottoman Empire's Yıldırım reserves and prevent their use in other theatres, such as the Balkans.

The Ottoman possession of Amman was still a threat to any further movement northwards into Syria. After the first assault on Amman, the Ottomans had been directed by Liman von Sanders to probe the defences north of Jerusalem and to try to recapture the bridgeheads over the Jordan, but, despite heavy shelling, they did not succeed. Nevertheless, the Ottoman manoeuvre was a reminder that any advance towards Damascus would either require a significant force to be held on the Jordan, which would not achieve the government's intentions, or an offensive to contain the Ottoman divisions in Amman. Allenby therefore chose the second course of action, hoping it would fulfil several wider strategic imperatives.

Allenby's second operation against Amman involved the use of mounted forces to cut the routes into the city.[27] General Sir Harry Chauvel, commanding the Desert Mounted Corps, was concerned that one of these proposed cut-off contingents was to consist of the recently recruited Beni Sakr, whose loyalty was uncertain. The suspicions proved correct for the clans did not appear, and almost certainly passed on details of the assault plan to Liman von Sanders' headquarters.[28] The result was that the German and Ottoman defenders were able to intercept the advancing British mounted forces. Reinforcements had to be sent to extract units which were in danger of being encircled. By the beginning of May 1918, the second Amman raid had failed.[29] Yet, despite the operational setback, Allenby had succeeded in persuading Liman von Sanders to deploy more men in and around Amman, leaving the front north of Jerusalem with fewer reserves.

From Lawrence's perspective, the operation ruined any chances of Feisal working with the Beni Sakr because relations between the British Headquarters and those clans were compromised.[30] Lawrence noted they were 'cautious and very wealthy' which made them far less likely to seek cooperation with any outsiders.

The other implication of the failure of the second Amman operation was that there were no resources available for an offensive that summer, which handed the initiative temporarily back to the Ottomans. Lawrence feared that 'the Turks might now have leisure to sweep us off Aba el Lissan, back to Akaba [Aqaba]'.[31] It was tempting to blame Allenby for the situation, but Lawrence weighed up the relative value of the stronger, conventional partner:

> He was threatening the enemy by a vast bridge-head across Jordan, as if he were about to cross a third time. So he would keep Amman tender. To strengthen us on our plateau he offered what technical equipment we needed. We took the opportunity to ask for repeated air-raids on the Hejaz Railway. General Salmond was called in, and proved as generous, in word and deed, as the Commander-in-Chief.[32]

Allenby thus provided not only material support but also the presence that tied down the Ottoman forces and prevented the counter-offensive that Lawrence had feared. If the Arab Revolt had occurred outside of the context of the Great War and the enormous commitment of British Imperial forces to the Middle East, it seems highly likely that the Arabs would have been subjected to the full might of the Ottoman military apparatus and defeated inside a year.

Lawrence also noted, almost in passing, the very significant observation that it was the Royal Air Force, retitled from its army association as the Royal Flying Corps, that kept up the pressure on the rail and logistical hubs of the Ottoman Army. He admitted: 'Much of the inactivity of the enemy in our lean season was due to the disorganisation of their railway by bombing.'[33] In other words, a vital element in preventing the Ottomans from exploiting the situation or being able to use their initiative, was the interdiction of their most 'critical vulnerabilities', as they are known in operational doctrine; in this case, communications, transport and supply.

And transport was the issue that Lawrence seized upon opportunistically when he learned that the Imperial Camel Brigade was to be broken up for manpower. The camels had been allocated to the various Indian divisions, but Lawrence persuaded Allenby that, by giving them to the Arab forces, he could 'put a thousand men into Deraa any day you please'.[34] The offer was appealing to the Commander in Chief because Deraa was the critical junction that linked the rail lines, and the logistics, of the Ottomans north of Jerusalem, along the axis to Amman, and back towards the heartland of the Sultan's domains.

However, Deraa was deep behind Ottoman lines, and represented an exaggerated ambition. Even if it could be taken 'any day', an assaulting force would be subjected to focussed counter-attacks from every point of the compass. The Ottomans would never allow such a key nodal point to be wrested away without intense resistance. To hold such an exposed position, without considerable support, was simply impossible. And to gesture theatrically that it could be done by a 'thousand men' merely exposed the full measure of its absurdity. When Lawrence wrote, 'the Arabs could now win their war when and where they liked', he probably believed it, but such a colourful statement does not stand up to military analysis.[35]

News that so many camels would be made available certainly impressed Feisal and the sheikhs in his camp at Abu el Lissan.[36] It restored faith in Lawrence and in the British cause, doing much to repair the loss of prestige incurred by the two setbacks before Amman.[37]

Joyce was encouraged too, but remained sanguine. The camels would have to be moved and seasoned on fewer rations, while operations were sustained against Ma'an and the Hejaz railway. To increase loads and speeds of the existing camel supply system, which was in the hands of the Egyptians under British command, Lawrence prematurely offered to have the Arabs take over the entire operation. The proposal was accepted immediately, which threw things into chaos. There was an urgent need to recruit camel drivers, but the additional burden of supply and logistics at Aqaba, in the hands of British officers, increased exponentially. There were sudden shortages in everything that had been provided by the scientific arrangements of the British-Egyptian authorities: stores, saddles, clerks, drugs and veterinary staff.

Fortunately, there were tactical successes to encourage the overstrained forces. Jerdun was taken, the third time, and then relinquished again. Zeid continued to conduct raids around Uheida. The armoured car squadron had intercepted an Ottoman column that had advanced from Ma'an and defeated it.

Nevertheless, the Ottomans had a sizeable force at Amman and there were evident preparations to lift the Arab siege of Ma'an, if it can be called that, by despatching reinforcements. The delays to that action were caused by Royal Air Force bombing raids. To add to the effect, Lawrence and his partners believed they could make further interdictions of the Hejaz railway, and buy more time. Preventing the relief of Ma'an, in turn, delayed any Ottoman offensive that would clear the Arabs from Abu el Lissan and thus Aqaba. Jafar al-Askari suggested using poison gas to defeat the Ottoman defenders, but Joyce rejected the idea.[38] The agreed plan involved feints by Nasir's mounted Arabs and a more determined attack by the Egyptian Camel Corps, under Major Peake and Lieutenant Hornby.

The first attack, against Hesa station, went as planned. Nasir's parties cut the line north and south, while Peake used mountain artillery to bombard the Ottoman defences. The final rush, by the Arab irregulars, secured the position. Peake and Hornby then set about the destruction of the entire complex, along with 14 miles of railway. This would deny a forward base for any actions from a northerly direction, thereby reducing the number of avenues the Ottomans could take in any counter-offensive.

Nevertheless, Lawrence noted that Nasir's forces had been subjected to effective air bombardment by German or Ottoman aircraft. They hid themselves under cliffs to reduce the likelihood of attack, not least because one party, while watering their animals, had been killed by a single well-directed bomb. The Ottomans also sought out the Arab forces in their forward locations on the ground, especially around Wadi Hesa. One column, consisting of camel and horse mounted troops, advanced on Faraifra. Nasir had 600 irregulars under his command, and while pinning these Ottomans with machine gun fire, he sent 100 Abu Tayi forward to within 100 yards of the settlement and ordered them to seize or kill all the Ottoman camels and horses they could. The Ottomans responded with air attacks, and Lawrence had a narrow escape as a stick of bombs straddled his observation point. Some of his escort were killed.[39]

There was also greater risk through Ottoman recruitment. Having hosted Lawrence for dinner, Fawaz, a sheikh of the Faiz section of the Beni Sakr (and seemingly a prominent figure in the Damascene nationalist movement) at Ziza, then sent for Ottoman assistance while Lawrence and the others were sleeping. Nawaf, the brother of the head of the Beni Sakr, warned Lawrence of the treachery. The party prepared to sell their lives dearly, but Lawrence had no wish to be caught in a hand-to-hand struggle, and he slipped away. Soon after, the turncoat Fawaz was killed.

Undeterred, Lawrence returned to the planning of the summer's operations. This would still prioritize delaying tactics to thwart an Ottoman counter-offensive, but include preparations for a return to the offensive. Lawrence evidently hoped to use Arab forces for this, rather than call upon Allenby (whom, he knew, was temporarily held up by the need to transfer British troops to France and bring in Indian Army formations). In an attempt to reinforce faith in Britain, and himself, Lawrence laid out the plan as he saw it to Feisal:

> It would be yet a third month before they [the Ottomans] attacked us in Aba el Lissan. By then our new camels should be fit for use in an offensive of our own. I suggested that we ask his father, King Hussein, to transfer to Akaba [Aqaba] the regular units at present with Ali and Abdulla. Their reinforcement would raise us to ten thousand strong, in uniformed men. We would divide them into three parts. The immobile would constitute a retaining force to hold Maan quiet. A thousand, on our new camels, would attack the Deraa-Damascus sector. The balance would form a second expedition, of two or three thousand infantry, to move into the Beni Sakhr country and connect with Allenby at Jericho.

The logic for Lawrence was to assist the primary operations by the EEF:

> The long-distance mounted raid, by taking Deraa or Damascus, would
> compel the Turks to withdraw from Palestine one division, or even
> two, to restore their communications. By so weakening the enemy,
> we would give Allenby the power to advance his line, at any rate to
> Nablus. The fall of Nablus would cut the lateral communication which
> made the Turks strong in Moab; and they would be compelled to fall
> back on Amman, yielding us quiet possession of the Jordan bottom.[40]

The plan depended on the release of more Arab troops, particularly
trained regulars, rather than the mobile irregular groups that Lawrence
had previously championed. It was predicated on the idea of fixing the
Ottomans at Ma'an, a deep raid to Deraa to draw Ottomans into a
defence of that area, and linking up with Allenby with some 2,000
men to assist in pushing the Ottomans out of the Jordan Valley and
the mountains of Moab. These planning assumptions were overly
optimistic. It would depend on Ali and Abdulla being willing and able
to release the troops they had around Medina and get them up to Ma'an
in time to participate in the operations. It imagined that the Deraa
operation could succeed by using surprise, against a prepared Ottoman
garrison that enjoyed air support and therefore enhanced reconnaissance
capabilities. It also assumed that 2,000 Arab regulars could achieve, in
the Beni Sakr country, what a larger and better-armed force of British
and Imperial troops had been unable to do in the spring.

In *Seven Pillars*, Lawrence blamed the intransigence of Hussein,
but he was saved from his dangerous and ill-considered thinking by
the new Chief of Staff, Brigadier General Sir William Bartholomew,
who explained that Allenby's own offensive plans for September only
required the Arabs to take a single force of 2,000, borne by camels, to
Deraa, to coincide with a much larger attack by the entire Egyptian
Expeditionary Force.[41]

The campaign in the Near East was about to take a significant turn.

11

Towards Armageddon
Operations Against Deraa

Liman von Sanders had different strategic priorities than Allenby. He intended to keep the Yıldırım force, his operational reserve, in situ in Syria, to delay the EEF and where possible prevent the despatch of Allied reinforcements to Europe, where events had begun to turn against the German Army. As a result, the Ottoman and German troops had to occupy a 60-mile-long line that was harder to hold than at Gaza, the strong defensive system that had kept the EEF in check for months. Worse, they had to do so with only 15 per cent of the numbers ordinarily deployed for zoned defence. The Ottoman positions, just north of Jerusalem and extending out to the coast, would depend now on the tactical effects that could be achieved by infantrymen, machine gunners and artillerymen dug in along that line. Behind the forward defensive zone, an area that spread into depth so as to absorb Allied artillery fire, there were, in theory, units that could be brought forward rapidly, to retake the strongpoints from exhausted and depleted Allied attackers. The strongpoints, carefully selected, were designed not to hold lines, as had been the case hitherto in this war, but to sweep areas with fire. Continuous trench systems were not necessary, and an outpost line had only to detect an enemy advance and inflict as many casualties as possible, while artillery fire was ranged in to break up and destroy an assault.

What Liman von Sanders was aware of, but Allenby could not see, was the deterioration taking place amongst the ranks of the Ottoman

Army. Supply shortages were increasing the levels of sickness and affecting the soldiers' morale.[1] Diseases such as cholera, typhus, and the appearance of other infections affected the Yıldırım force. Although Turks later blamed Arab soldiers for the subsequent breakdown of morale and the inability to hold the line above Jerusalem, it is clear that, after four years of war, there was a widespread sense of exhaustion across the Ottoman Army.[2] British military intelligence reports noted that the numbers surrendering were on the rise and, significantly, these were drawn from the entire spectrum of Ottoman ethnicities.[3] From an operational perspective, Ottoman battalions were reduced in strength to somewhere between 150 and 200 men. The troops were tired, demoralized and, faced with Allenby's more numerous and motivated force, they saw little chance of survival.

Another factor lay in favour of the British, and that was that an attacking force retains the initiative. It can choose where and when to strike, and a defender will remain uncertain as to which attacks are feints, or probes, and which are the main thrusts. Allenby went to great lengths to conceal the direction of his long-awaited offensive on the Ottoman lines. Lawrence described deception as 'a main point of strategy'.[4] Some 15,000 wooden and canvas horses were built and dummy camps erected around Jericho to persuade intrusive reconnaissance pilots that the EEF intended to attack from the Jordan Valley towards Amman. Lawrence wrote that Allenby 'hoped to make such demonstrations as should persuade the Turks of a concentration there in progress. The two raids to Salt had fixed the Turks' eyes exclusively beyond [the] Jordan.'[5] EEF units were moved at night, and camouflaged by day. Air patrols did their best to deny access over Allenby's formations. Bridges were built across the Jordan to give the impression of an impending thrust, and false wireless traffic was generated to support the idea of preparations. Captured guns were fired periodically at Ottoman positions as if there was a plan to soften up the defences.

The challenge was to prevent the Ottomans simply withdrawing their coastal defences a few miles, where Allenby intended the main weight of his attack to fall. If they pulled back soon after an attack had commenced, it would mean the concentration of British firepower would fall into empty space, and a concession of a small amount of territory would waste the Allied resources while preserving the Ottoman manpower.[6] The attack therefore had to fix the Ottomans in place, as they had at Gaza the previous year. Or it had to hold them long enough that a mounted force could drive deep into the Ottoman rear, enveloping and isolating pockets of resistance, preventing them from establishing a new line.[7]

The Arab forces had a part to play in the deception. They could make it appear that they were the auxiliary support to an attack on Amman. They could also assist in getting forces to drive into depth once the main attack had begun; but before this could be prepared, Lawrence and Dawnay first had to stabilize their front. The Ottomans had driven the Arab forces of Nasir out of Wadi Hesa in July and it looked as if they would be able to push forces as far as Abu el Lissan by August. Lawrence confessed: 'Unless we could delay the Turks another fortnight, their threat might cripple us.'[8]

Dawnay requested the assistance of the remaining unit of the Imperial Camel Corps, led by Major Robert Buxton.[9] The plan was for them to conduct a long-distance raid, giving the Arabs a precious respite, while adding to the impression the British intended some wide flanking manoeuvre against the apparent 'main objective' of Amman. Lawrence summed up the planning:

> That Buxton should march from the Canal to Akaba [Aqaba]; thence, by Rum, to carry Mudowwara [Musaw'warrah] by night attack; thence by Bair, to destroy the bridge and tunnel near Amman; and back to Palestine on August the thirtieth. Their activity would give us a peaceful month, in which our two thousand new camels could learn to graze, while carrying the extra dumps of forage and food which Buxton's force would expect.[10]

Joyce and Young disagreed with Lawrence, based on calculations they had themselves made about the available logistics and the distances to be covered with the forces available.[11] They believed that to take the bulk of the Arab forces north, on the offensive, would not be achieved before November, while the raid by the Imperial Camel Corps would consume resources needed for the main effort. As Lawrence noted: 'They had figured out the food, ammunition, forage, and transport for two thousand men of all ranks, from Aba el Lissan to Deraa. They had taken into consideration all our resources and worked out schedules by which dumps would be completed and the attack begun.'[12]

But Lawrence raised several objections. The first was that operations in November would not align with Allenby's scheme of manoeuvre and, further, would suffer from worsening weather. He disputed their calculations too. He gave Dawnay:

> my estimate that our two thousand camels, in a single journey, without advanced depots or supplementary supply columns, would suffice five hundred regular mounted infantry, the battery of French quick-firing '.65' mountain guns, proportionate machine-guns, two armoured cars, sappers, camel-scouts, and two aeroplanes until we had fulfilled our mission.[13]

Lawrence gained the approval of the General Headquarters in his arguments, much to the irritation of Joyce and Young.[14] Joyce felt that the Arabs would not fight as well if the Imperial Camel Corps arrived alongside them, a point Lawrence himself had made. He felt Lawrence's calculations were wrong and condemned the logistical plan to attack Deraa as 'impossible'.[15]

Lawrence argued that the Camel Corps contingent would operate in areas where Arab forces were not present, and the ambiguity of their strength and location would be amplified by rumours in Ottoman minds, and compel them to protect their railway against what might be perceived as a mobile brigade. This carried some weight as an idea, but it was based on the assumption that locals would be unaware of the presence of the British force and that the Ottomans would remain ill-informed. There was no reference to Ottoman and German air reconnaissance which would ruin the deception at a stroke.

To Young's objections, Lawrence made little headway, but insisted that, in previous operations, Arab irregulars had covered vast distances with relatively little in terms of fodder and food. Lawrence assumed the force, just 500 strong, could live off the land and forage could be obtained easily after an abundant season.[16] Lawrence continued to strip out the alleged needs of the Arab forces: 'I went on to cut down his petrol, cars, ammunition, and everything else to the exact point, without margin, which would meet what we planned.' Young was still unconvinced for mathematical reasons: 'In riposte he became aggressively regular. I prosed forth on my hoary theorem that we lived by our raggedness and beat the Turk by our uncertainty. Young's scheme was faulty, because [it was] precise.'

Lawrence then outlined the plan against Deraa:

> We would march a camel column of one thousand men to Azrak where their concentration must be complete on September the thirteenth. On the sixteenth we would envelop Deraa, and cut its railways. Two days later we would fall back east of the Hejaz Railway and wait events with Allenby. As reserve against accident we would purchase barley in Jebel Druse, and store it at Azrak.[17]

Lawrence got his way, largely because of the sponsorship of GHQ and the Commander in Chief, and because coordination of effort was prized over the detailed, meticulous planning that would be required for conventional operations by regular troops. Lawrence only had to make a demonstration, to appear at the precise moment, with 'three men and a boy with pistols' if necessary, as Allenby had put it, to achieve the mission.[18] Lawrence was also eager to restore the confidence of the Arab forces at a time when inertia might again threaten their cohesion and commitment, as it had after Aqaba and in the winter of 1917. He needed momentum. Part of that confidence-building appeared in the distribution of British medals, while Nuri Pasha selected 400 men for the Deraa expedition, a process that led to much eagerness amongst the fighters who wanted to be considered the most worthy. Lawrence nevertheless confessed that the relationship between British and Arab personnel was beginning to break down. He referred to them as 'family rifts' that were 'inevitable', and blamed his own high-handedness of demands in contrast to Joyce's emphasis on teamwork.[19] Lawrence admitted his overconfidence had a purpose, to galvanize a mission rather than having no operations at all, since, once things were underway, he could fulfil his 'preference for botching it somehow' as opposed to doing 'a thing perfectly'. These sentiments, expressing the value of improvisation, had their merits, but such a spirit is always a trade-off against a well-planned, rehearsed and supported mission.

The priority in the execution of the plans was to ensure the allegiance of the clans as far north as Feisal currently possessed influence, and to warn them of their role in the coming offensive. Second, there were preparations to be made in terms of positioning supplies, in the reconnoitring of landing grounds for air operations, and in planning and checking routes in the roadless spaces of Arabia for the armoured cars.

Lawrence then turned his attention to the Imperial Camel Corps raid. He took Feisal into his confidence, then briefed the Imperial Camel Corps officers on what today would be termed 'cultural awareness', urging them to use every power to avert friction with the Howeitat through whose lands they would have to traverse. Lawrence led them up from Aqaba, through Wadi Itm, thence to Wadi Rumm. He was filled with praise of the way the British troops worked with the local Arabs at the wells, and especially the diplomacy of the officers, many of whom spoke Arabic. Lawrence then returned to Aqaba to collect his bodyguard, all 60 of them, and marched to Guweira. Almost immediately, Feisal urged him to take an aircraft to join him at Jefer, where he would brief Nuri Shalaan.

Meanwhile, Major Buxton and the two companies of the Imperial Camel Corps reached the vicinity of Musaw'warrah Station before dawn on 8 August 1918. Some 315 men in total, they had neither the usual ratio of strength to overwhelm prepared defences, nor artillery support: they were dependent on the element of surprise. At dawn, they stormed the station entrenchments, sweeping the parapets with Lewis guns while bombing parties cleared the positions at close quarters. Lawrence related the action in detail:

Before midnight white tapes were laid as guides to the zero point. The opening had been timed for a quarter to four but the way proved difficult to find, so that daylight was almost upon them before things began against the southern redoubt. After a number of bombs had burst in and about it, the men rushed up and took it easily – to find that [another bombing party] had achieved their end a moment before. These alarms roused the middle redoubt, but only for defeat. Its men surrendered twenty minutes later. The northern redoubt, which had a gun, seemed better-hearted and splashed its shot freely into the station yard, and at our troops. Buxton, under cover of the southern redoubt, directed the fire of Brodie's guns which, with their usual deliberate accuracy, sent in shell after shell.[20]

In the fighting, Buxton's men took two guns and 120 prisoners, for the loss of 17 casualties. Later in the afternoon, a final Ottoman bastion, to the north of the station, was bombed by the Royal Air Force and surrendered.[21] Lawrence produced a slightly different second-hand account.[22] Regardless of the discrepancy, Buxton could not have known the auspicious nature of the date of his assault. On the Western Front, the defeat of German forces was underway and the Kaiser had been informed that this, 8 August, was 'the black day of the German Army'. The tide of the war was turning.

To exploit the operational success of the taking of Musaw'warrah, which had so long defied Arab raiders, Buxton turned his attention to the Hejaz line further north, hoping to blow the bridge nearest Amman. The raid at Musaw'warrah had been a significant gamble, but had achieved its object, and must have created dilemmas for Ottoman and German planning staff in Amman and Damascus. It therefore seemed worth the risk to mount a second operation.

At the same time, Lawrence met with Feisal as arranged at Jefer, where many tribal leaders had gathered. Lawrence explained the British position, while Feisal offered a more nationalistic agenda: 'Many times in such councils had Feisal won over and set aflame new tribes, many times had the work fallen to me; but never until to-day had we been actively together in one company, reinforcing and relaying one another, from our opposite poles.'[23] The technique was interesting, and Feisal put forward his appeal with long pauses to allow for an imagination to savour the ideas, but also to convey gravitas, for wise men are known to speak at a measured pace and in low tones. Lawrence praised Feisal's technique, conveying the impression of a stature that was not always the case in reality: 'He went on to conjure up for them the trammelled enemy on the eternal defensive, whose best end was to have done no more than the necessary. While we abstinents swam calmly and coolly in the friendly silence of the desert, till pleased to come ashore.'[24]

Despite his praise, several British officers attached to the Arab forces, comparing them unfavourably to regular troops, were quick to condemn them. Major Garland complained to Colonel Wilson that the British were received with resentment and Nasir treated him and his comrades as little better than slaves. Like many of his countrymen, he concluded that only flattery seemed to satisfy Arab pride. Getting them to follow directions or exercise normal military control was out of the question, he lamented.[25] Major Vickery was even more scathing, believing that the Arab irregulars were not suited for fighting, only for plundering.[26]

Sensing his critics' suggestions that the Arab leaders were motivated, not by nationalism, but by gold, Lawrence claimed that this reward was not mentioned: 'The money was a confirmation; mortar, not building stone. To have bought men would have put our movement on the base of interest; whereas our followers must be ready to go all the way without other mixture in their motives than human frailty.'[27] But here we only have Lawrence's word for it, and given Lawrence's previous comments about the failure to sustain operations beyond the winter of 1917 at Wadi Hesa, it seems inconceivable that there was no question of reward and cost. Lawrence claimed, 'we did refuse to let our abundant and famous gold bring over those not spiritually convinced'.

Lawrence was prepared to admit, however, that motivating men in groups, by appealing to emotion, was far more effective than appeals to a rational individual. He noted: 'With man-instinctive, anything believed by two or three had a miraculous sanction to which individual ease and life might honestly be sacrificed. To man-rational, wars of nationality were as much a cheat as religious wars, and nothing was worth fighting for.'[28] This rousing of the clans to fight left Lawrence, the representative of a modern world, feeling uncomfortable, and raised questions about the Machiavellian demagoguery at work, as he asked: 'did not the being believed by many make for a distorted righteousness?' He did not answer his own question with any clarity. War requires leaders to make clear-cut, sometimes ruthless decisions about the individuals they have guided, led and trained. Some aspects of leadership are a form of theatre, as the Greeks understood very well. John Keegan, the military historian, referred to the 'mask of command', acknowledging that leadership in the crisis of war is a combination of acting a part, while genuinely fulfilling its self-sacrificial requirements, for under stress or not, soldiers will not follow a fake.[29]

Allenby had urged Feisal not to make any rash movements towards Deraa and Damascus, but to move in concert with the British advance on his left. This was to prevent the defeat of the Arabs, for, if they got too far ahead on the flank marches, and the British offensive was held up, they would be exposed to the full weight of a retaliatory counter-offensive by the Ottomans, which would do irreparable damage to their cause and deprive Allenby of a valuable partner. Lawrence, as before, confessed to have spoken rashly and argued that the Arabs should rush Damascus, since, even if they lost it, it was better to have had the honour of taking it. Dawnay had cautioned against such sentiments. Lawrence was allowing his political ambitions to get ahead of sound military judgement: coordination and cohesion were essential against the Ottoman forces in the Near East. To advance piecemeal invited defeat.

Perhaps more astonishing was Feisal's comment that 'if the British were not able to carry their share of the attack, he would save his own people by making a separate peace with Turkey'.[30] Lawrence admitted that Feisal was still communicating with Djemal, and by extension the Ottoman authorities, although most commentators have been prepared to suggest this was only for a position of advantage in any peace settlement. The majority posit there was no sincerity to the idea of reconciliation with the Ottomans, as too much blood had been spilt for that, and conclude that negotiations were a useful way to gauge the adversary's responses, and the commitment of one's partners. Nevertheless, on 10 June 1918, Feisal had written to Djemal that 'Syria's relationship to the Ottoman Empire should be like that of Prussia, Austria, and Hungary' and Lawrence confided that Feisal was 'selling us [out]'.[31]

The Ottomans had continued to make entreaties to the Hashemite leaders. They had offered autonomy for the Hejaz in any post-war settlement, then Syria too, and finally even Mesopotamia. Hussein was to be granted his own monarchy, to match the British offer. Some of these concessions were Djemal's initiative, based on the concept of Islamic unity, although he was aware that Turkish nationalists increasingly regarded Arabia as a liability. Granting the Arabs autonomy retained them as grateful partners, but freed the Turks from the costs of occupation and reconstruction. The Ottomans reinforced their arguments by claims that the British and French intended to colonize the Arab territories. Djemal cited the much-publicized Sykes-Picot Agreement, the lie of 'conspiracy' being released by the Bolsheviks as a mechanism to discredit all imperialists.

Lawrence mocked the arrangements as 'an old style division of Turkey' where, in an apparently confused bureaucratic manner, 'the British finally countered document A to the Sharif, B to their Allies, C to the Arab Committee, [and] document D to Lord Rothschild'.[32] Lawrence's conduct in the peace settlement process of 1919–20 did not indicate this same level of sarcasm, as we shall see, so we may conclude that he grew dissatisfied some time after the war. Where he was consistent was in his determination not to allow French domination of Syria. Lawrence later claimed that, during the war, the British government promised the Arabs that they could keep what they conquered, and this had encouraged the Arabs to continue fighting, and ensured that Lawrence sought to reach Damascus ahead of the EEF to claim the city 'by right of conquest'. But in the short term, Feisal received Djemal's envoy, Emir Mohammed Said, and proposed that in return for peace between the Arabs and the Turks, the Ottoman Army should immediately evacuate Amman. Needless to say, this proposal, which was quite insincere, was rejected. Lawrence deliberately withheld news of these negotiations from his superiors in Cairo or Allenby's headquarters, fearing the Arabs would be rejected as partners. His justification was that the British government had not kept him informed of their own talks, although some 'friends' had, and he was anxious that London might try to make peace with the Ottomans at the expense of the Arabs.

Lawrence's attempt to act as his own diplomat, without reference to his government, the officers of the intelligence bureau in Cairo, or Allenby's staff, was evidence of his poor judgement, and, regrettably, a degree of arrogance. Lawrence was disappointed by the apparent contradictory assurances given to each of Britain's allies, although the degree of 'contradiction' has been exaggerated by many authorities since.[33] It was of course understandable that he would want to ensure that his Arab partners were granted their aspirations, particularly as they had fought for their cause of independence, but to formulate his own policies at the grass roots, without sight of the issues at the national or international level, risked jeopardizing any agreement at all. Lawrence had not seen the government's de Bunsen Committee report, he had not been involved in talks with the French, and he had not witnessed the significant loss of life of British forces in both Mesopotamia and Palestine, which added a moral imperative to the British government's sense of ownership of any settlement.

In contrast to the huge commitment Britain was making in terms of manpower, munitions, aircraft, shipping, gold, and in the lives they had sacrificed in Sinai, Kut, Gaza, the Judean Hills and a dozen other battlefields, the Arab commitment, and their losses, were very slight indeed. The British provided the heavy weapons, supplies, money, air cover and manpower that enabled the Arab Northern Army to advance from Aqaba to Aleppo. Without Britain, the Sharifian army would not have been able to achieve its ends and would have languished in the Hejaz, if it had survived at all. Lawrence's sarcasm towards his own countrymen's efforts was therefore misplaced and badly misjudged. His redeeming attribute was that he knew it, and devoted an entire chapter of his memoir to self-criticism.[34]

All the arguments and disagreements about the role of the Arab forces, their integration with the British Army, and the final political dispensation, were not going to be realized until Lawrence could reconfigure the 'means' at his disposal. In the development of his ideas, he came to appreciate that the new technologies of air power and armoured vehicles necessitated a different approach to warfare, one that was now to provide a significant breakthrough in his campaign and his ideas on war.

12

Hybrid Warfare
Air and Mobile Operations

Chance events and the friction of war had the power to change the plans that Lawrence and his partners made, but more definite factors, such as stiffening Ottoman resistance, had necessitated the support of armoured cars and air power. By the middle of 1918, the Arab forces had become dependent on these means. Nevertheless, they were still forced to abort raids because of the strength or mobility of the Ottoman Army and air force. It was an indication that Lawrence's enemy was adapting and developing better counter-measures.

Adaptation had become the hallmark of Lawrence's operations. Preparations continued for the coming Allied offensive in Palestine, and he conducted a long-range reconnaissance with a Rolls-Royce armoured car, examining the routes that would be needed for subsequent columns of vehicles. He was also interested in alternative bases for operations, where there were sources of water and grazing; 'shallow systems running into Sirhan, by Amman'. Revealing his constant recalibration, Lawrence admitted: 'if evil came to us at Azrak, our next refuge should be Amman, if accessible to cars'. As all commanders would recognize, 'Such battalions of "ifs" skirmished about every new plan continually.'[1]

Azrak was selected as the best site for a temporary base (previously there had been too little water and grazing for it to be a viable summer post) and a landing strip. From this forward position, it would be possible to launch air attacks into Amman and beyond. The only blemish on this reconnaissance occurred on the return, when it was discovered that camel drivers and refugees had stolen stores arranged for Buxton's column, the Arab troops, and the armoured cars which were bound for the north. A reduced force therefore made the advance, and Buxton demonstrated his skills in rearranging the manner in which his forces moved, the carriage of loads that best suited the animals, and the loose dispersal of groups which meant it was easier to cross obstacles and broken terrain without loss of speed. Lawrence noted: 'Our Imperial Camel Corps had become rapid, elastic, enduring, silent; ... Each march saw them more workmanlike, more at home on the animals, tougher, leaner, faster ... and the easy mixing of officers and men made their atmosphere delightful.'[2]

Despite the success of the march, which brought them closer to their objective of the railway and bridges near Amman, they were spotted by a German or Ottoman aircraft.[3] Lawrence despatched a scouting party 'into the villages below us, to get news, and warn the people to keep within doors'.[4] But they returned with the unwelcome intelligence that Ottoman Mounted Infantry were nearby, and any encounter with them would blow the element of surprise completely. As Lawrence put it: 'They returned to say that chance was fighting against us.'

This discovery meant another revision of the plan, as Lawrence explained:

> The camel corps were to dismount nearly a mile from the bridge ... and advance on foot. The noise of their assault, not to speak of the firing of three tons of gun-cotton against the bridge-piers, would wake up the district. The Turkish patrols in the villages might stumble on our camel-park – a disaster for us – or, at least, would hamper us in the broken ground, as we retired. Buxton's men could not scatter like a swarm of birds, after the bridge explosion, to find their own way back to the Muaggar [the forward base]. In any night-fighting some would be cut off and lost. We should have to wait for them, possibly losing more in the business. The whole cost might be fifty men, and I put the worth of the bridge at less than five.[5]

Herein lay the classic commanders' dilemma: to rationalize the cost-benefit equation of an operation. Lawrence believed the purpose of the mission was to 'frighten' the Ottomans, and to distract their attention, or put another way, the purpose was to have a cognitive and psychological effect, for which the material destruction of a bridge was less important.

The fact that more hostile aircraft appeared, searching for the column, made it clear that the Ottomans would be alert, prepared, and therefore better able to resist them.

The Imperial Camel Corps had ridden to within 15 miles of their final objective, but with the element of surprise lost, Buxton withdrew, with his command intact, back to Bayir and then Beersheba. The *Official History* records that they had covered 700 miles in just 44 days, but mention must also be made that this Lilliputian regular force was operating without air support deep behind enemy lines where some 10,000 Ottoman troops were distributed.[6]

It looked as if the mission had failed to achieve the 'disturbance' to the Ottoman mind that Lawrence intended. The aircraft that had flown over them may have ascertained their strength, but they would have concluded that this was another Arab raiding party rather than a large British force. So Lawrence adopted a psychological tactic:

To gain what we could, I sent Saleh and the other chiefs down to spruce their people with tall rumours of our numbers, and our coming as the reconnaissance of Feisal's army, to carry Amman by assault in the new moon. This was the story the Turks feared to learn: the operation they imagined: the stroke they dreaded. They pushed cavalry cautiously into Muaggar, and found confirmation of the wild tales of the villagers, for the hill-top was littered with empty meat tins, and the valley slopes cut up by the deep tracks of enormous cars. Very many tracks there were! This alarm checked them, and, at a bloodless price for us, kept them hovering a week.[7]

Like all psychological and deception operations, the information had to be credible. The fact that British and Arab forces were present, and the Ottomans knew that an offensive against Amman had been attempted before, made this report plausible.[8] Certainly the locals' stories could not be discounted entirely, and the Ottomans took the wise precaution of despatching fast moving, mounted reconnaissance parties and aircraft to search for the British-Arab forces.

On return to Abu el Lissan and Feisal's camp, Lawrence learned that the Sharif, Hussein, had promoted Jafar al-Askari to the rank of general, which undermined Feisal's authority.[9] Jafar offered to resign, Feisal sought clarification from Hussein, and was duly criticized for insubordination. Hussein went further, when Feisal resigned as commander of the Arab Northern Army, and appointed Zeid. Zeid refused to accept the appointment. The imbroglio imposed a delay on all operations and created a great deal of uncertainty about the future of the revolt.[10] Lawrence feared the delay, at a critical point, could mean they would not be able to support Allenby. The Arab cause itself might start to unravel. Lawrence recorded: 'Nuri might take suspicion of my change [of plan] and fail at the tryst [of coordinating with the other Arab forces]; and without the Rualla half our efficiency and importance at Deraa on September the sixteenth would disappear.'[11]

Worse, there were signs of division and 'a mutiny of the troops'. Lawrence stated: 'They had heard false rumours about the [leadership] crisis. Particularly, the gunners misunderstood, and one afternoon fell out with their officers, and rushed off to turn the guns on their tents.'[12] Fortunately, all the breech blocks were taken out of the guns, and Lawrence helped the officers placate the disgruntled troops. He also arranged for Feisal to make an appearance, because they were convinced he had resigned and deserted his men. The Arab fighters were not all convinced, but a deal was made that they would march up to Azrak, as planned, and await the good faith of Feisal. If he did not deliver, they would be free to return home and abandon the revolt. The rank and file were also told, more bluntly, that the continuation of rations and pay would depend on their remaining with the movement. Lawrence was doing his best to keep to the timetable set by Allenby, but at this stage the Arab revolutionary cause was hanging by a thread. A defeat at this point would probably break the whole movement.

Lawrence understood the political aspect of his strategy too. He wrote:

We could put in the attack on Deraa, which was what Allenby expected from us; but the capture of Damascus – which was what I expected from the Arabs, the reason why I had joined with them in the field, taken ten thousand pains, and spent my wit and strength – that depended on Feisal's being present with us in the fighting line, undistracted by military duties, but ready to take over and exploit the political value of what our bodies conquered for him.[13]

The Arab fighters needed to have their leaders at the front, and, while Lawrence rationalized this as fulfilling political aspirations, there was no escaping the fact that this was a necessary condition to preserve the cohesion of the revolt. Lawrence noted that Hussein did not 'apologise', but that was immaterial: it was Lawrence's intention to have the British government and Allenby protect and promote Feisal as their protégé and partner in the future division of the Levant. He still hoped to avoid 'scission' but Arab divisions were the reality, even between the Hashemite leaders, and certainly between the factions, clans and sections of the population. In the end, Lawrence resorted to manipulating the text and translations of the correspondence between Feisal and Hussein that had to be transmitted via Cairo and Aqaba. It is likely, if Lawrence's testimony of the conversation is correct, that Feisal knew what Lawrence was doing, referring gratefully to a 'restoration of honour … for all of us'. The leadership crisis had been averted, for the time being.[14]

Speeding in a Rolls-Royce past columns of baggage camels and troops, with the prospect of an offensive operation ahead, with armoured cars, machine gun teams, artillery detachments, mounted infantry and air support, Lawrence was warned that the Ottomans had commenced a counter-offensive, southwards from Wadi Hesa:

> At Bair we heard from the alarmed Beni Sakhr that the Turks, on the preceding day, had launched suddenly westward from Hesa into Tafileh. Mifleh thought I was mad, or most untimely merry, when I laughed outright at the news which four days sooner would have held up the Azrak expedition: but, now we were started, the enemy might take Aba el Lissan, Guweira, Akaba [Aqaba] itself – and welcome! Our formidable talk of advance by Amman had pulled their leg nearly out of socket, and the innocents were out to counter our feint. Each man they sent south was a man, or rather ten men, lost.[15]

In other words, Lawrence was delighted that the Ottomans were committing troops which otherwise would defend the area and hold up the advance. He was correct about the timing. An Ottoman offensive just a few days before, when the Arabs were in confusion and the preparations for their attack on Deraa were incomplete, would have caused such delay that it could have jeopardized the operation. The Ottomans were looking to consolidate their defensive perimeter and disrupt any attack towards Amman, but Wadi Hesa was an important area when the resources, not least food supply, were so critical for the Ottoman Army.

Conditions in the Ottoman Army were deteriorating rapidly from mid-1918. There were insufficient rations, more sickness, and the first signs that cohesion was failing: some soldiers deserted, but most went rearwards to find and steal supplies.[16] The situation had become so bad that General Liman von Sanders gave up all hope of offensive, or even counter-offensive, operations. The best he could hope for were defensive actions that held up the Allies until an armistice could be considered, and then, if he could hold on to Ottoman territory, the peace settlement would still decide in Germany's and the Ottomans' favour.[17]

Lawrence and his party, including two aircraft held in readiness, based themselves at Azrak, waiting for the date to strike. They had the confidence of allegiant tribes in the surrounding area, and Lawrence freely contemplated that coming mission, as well as the options and consequences: 'These plans were a feint against Amman and a real cutting of the Deraa railways: further than this we hardly went, for it was ever my habit, while studying alternatives, to keep the stages in solution.'[18]

Lawrence related how the subsequent operation was 'the most perfect in English history' because it was an application of brain rather than force. This reference was to the privileging of deception measures.[19] Lawrence reiterated his part in that plan:

> the feint was accomplished. We had sent our 'horsemen of St. George', gold sovereigns, by the thousand to the Beni Shakr, purchasing all the barley on their threshing floors: begging them not to mention it, but we would require it for our animals and for our British allies, in a fortnight. Dhiab of Tafileh – that jerky, incomplete hobbledehoy – gossiped the news instantly through to Kerak [the Ottoman garrison].[20]

Meanwhile, Captain Hornby had been organizing his own forces around Jericho, ostensibly for a defence if the Azrak–Deraa operation miscarried, or for an offensive if the opportunity arose. But here the recent Ottoman advance had jeopardized this design:

> [Hornby's] plan was to move about the nineteenth, when he heard that Allenby was started; his hope being to tie on to Jericho, so that if we failed by Deraa our force could return and reinforce his movement: which would then be, not a feint, but the old second

string to our bow. However, the Turks knocked this rather crooked by their advance to Tafileh, and Hornby had to defend Shobek against them.[21]

This was proof that, despite all the problems the Ottomans faced, they were not entirely 'fixed' and they were showing remarkable resilience.

Having considered a feint against the Hejaz line to the north of Deraa to prevent reinforcements coming in from Amman, which was a task that would be allocated to a Gurkha detachment, Lawrence now contemplated three options against Deraa itself:

> [The] main purpose was to cut the railways in the Hauran and keep them cut for at least a week; and there seemed to be three ways of doing it. The first was to march north of Deraa to the Damascus railway, as on my ride with Tallal in the winter, cut it; and then cross to the Yarmuk railway. The second was to march south of Deraa to the Yarmuk, as with Ali ibn el Hussein in November, 1917. The third was to rush straight at Deraa town.[22]

The final option depended on the ability of the Royal Air Force to conduct a significant bombardment. Lawrence wrote: 'The third scheme could be undertaken only if the Air Force would promise so heavy a daylight bombing of Deraa station that the effect would be tantamount to artillery bombardment, enabling us to risk an assault against it with our few men.'[23] Since neither the RAF officers not Dawnay could guarantee that, because of the need to bring up and assemble aircraft within striking range for this task, the three options were to be held 'equal in our judgement' until one week before the attack date. When that time came, it was evident that there would be only sufficient aircraft for an air demonstration, and this would merely be used to cover the movement of the Arab force as it skirted around Deraa to attack, and close permanently, the Hejaz railway.

Lawrence's supporters point out that the offensive against Deraa was only an option for the Arabs, since Allenby's army could not yet reach it.[24] On the other hand, only Allenby could break the three Ottoman armies in Palestine and Syria. Lawrence and the Arabs could cut off the Ottomans' supplies, for a while, but the actual decisive victory could be achieved solely by the regular army, and by the penetration in depth by Allenby's cavalry brigades and the air force. So this stage of the campaign does reinforce Lawrence's view on the conduct of guerrilla warfare, but it is not a full explanation of the outcome of the operations.

Lawrence certainly now appreciated the growing importance of air power. He realized that air bombardment would substitute for a mobile artillery barrage, but it required 'weight' to be effective. His ideas foregrounded what was later to be called 'hybrid warfare', where Western air strikes would be used in support of local irregular forces in Afghanistan in 2001, in northern Iraq in 2003, and again in Libya in 2011. Aircraft provided the devastating firepower, while mobile ground forces moved fluidly towards the key objectives, using their local knowledge of the terrain and population to locate and defeat an enemy otherwise indistinguishable from the civilian population. In 1918, Lawrence recognized the value of this combination, although, as noted before, he appears to have dismissed the importance of enemy air surveillance, which neutralized the impunity of insurgents in the expanse of the desert.

As the date of the offensive neared, Lawrence observed the arrival of the various Arab factions, the Druzes and local peasants, the armoured car squadrons, Gurkhas, Egyptian Camel Corps, engineers, Indian troops, gunners, and the British officers. Joyce was effectively in command of the advisory role and the British units, while Feisal marched in at the head of the Arab regulars to command all the local forces. Lawrence himself confessed to a state of exhaustion, with his nerves gone, but his role was now more subordinate in operations, logistics and advisory work, and the release from responsibility, as so often happens, cut that taut sense of purpose.

The preliminary raid set off as planned, with the Gurkhas supported by armoured cars and Camel Corps riflemen, and guided by local Rualla. Lawrence wrote:

> they went off to cut the railway by Ifdein. The scheme was for Scott-Higgins [and the Gurkhas] to rush a blockhouse after dark with his nimble Indians ... Peake [and the Camel Corps] was then to demolish until dawn. The cars would cover their retreat eastward in the morning, over the plain, upon which we, the main body, would be marching north from Azrak for Umtaiye, a great pit of rain-water fifteen miles below Deraa, and our advanced base.[25]

The advance continued, on schedule, to make the demonstrations around Deraa on 16 September as planned. Nevertheless, the initial plan at first miscarried. The main body was some 1,300 strong with another 1,000 distributed further to the west, and Lawrence emphasized the need for the sheikhs to exercise control over the Bedouin, lest it alarm the local settled populations. These populations, perhaps through fear of Ottoman reprisals, rather than panic at the appearance of the Bedouin, actually prevented Scott-Higgins' and Peake's attack.[26] The raiders had been forced back 'because of trouble with Arab encampments in the neighbourhood of [t]his proposed demolition'.[27]

Lawrence's solution was to set off by camel himself, with a contingent of Agayl, to blow the line with gun-cotton. They reached the railway quickly, in time to witness the aerial combat between a Bristol fighter and a German aircraft. The German plane went down, but the Bristol was too badly damaged to be retained, and Lawrence noted bitterly that the air support they needed for subsequent operations was reduced to a single, outdated plane.[28] Yet the raiders continued, conducted a reconnaissance of an unguarded section of line at dusk, and resolved to return the following morning to carry out a much larger demolition of two bridges, supported by armoured cars, thus fulfilling the original plan.

As preparations were underway, the power of a surprise air attack became evident. Lawrence wrote of its impact:

> About two in the afternoon, as we drove towards the railway, we had the great sight of a swarm of our bombing planes droning steadily up towards Deraa on their first raid. The place had hitherto been carefully reserved from air attack; so the damage among the unaccustomed, unprotected, unarmed garrison was heavy. The morale of the men suffered as much as the railway traffic: and till our onslaught from the north forced them to see us, all their efforts went into digging bomb-proof shelters.[29]

Lawrence had planned that two armoured cars would cover his charge-laying against the bridges, but he was surprised to see that the section of Ottoman troops in the nearest blockhouse had jumped out of their entrenchments at the first sight of the cars and 'rifles in hand, advanced upon us in open order: moved either by panic, by misunderstanding, or by an inhuman unmixed courage'.[30] There was no contest: the Ottoman soldiers came under machine gun fire from the impervious cars, suffered casualties, and, without hope of survival or retreat, capitulated.

After setting and blowing the charges, the withdrawal was less successful. As Ottoman reinforcements closed in, one of the armoured cars was grounded and suffered serious damage. It lay stuck, just 300 yards from the railway line, and therefore exposed to enemy fire. Joyce rushed back to assist, just as the driver organized an emergency repair. It was a desperate innovation, but the broken vehicle was nursed along at a walking pace with the British officers, Lawrence, the Arab guides, and the Ottoman prisoners accompanying it on foot.

Lawrence reflected on the importance of the raid. Deraa was temporarily cut off from the north, and therefore the advance could continue with its garrison contained. 'This', wrote Lawrence, 'was the side of quickest reinforcement for Deraa, and its death made our rear safe.' There was a secondary benefit, in that it protected Zeid's forces at Abu el Lissan: 'for the Turks massed in Tafileh would hold up that attack till their communications were again open'.[31]

Lawrence rejoined the main body by the following morning, 17 September, despite terrain that was unsuited to armoured cars, to witness the dash of Rualla horseman onto the Hejaz line, further to the north of Deraa. Their arrival was at first unopposed, so few precautions were taken, but the nearest Ottoman post could not resist the opportunity to fire into the stationary mass of mounted men, and the Rualla were soon dispersed. A second hasty attack was orchestrated, and one man was killed before the post was taken. This left the entire line free to be torn up.

Lawrence recalled his satisfaction at the sudden change in the operational situation, which had strategic significance: 'So the southern ten miles of the Damascus line was freely ours by nine in the morning. It was the only railway to Palestine and Hejaz and I could hardly realize our fortune; hardly believe that our word to Allenby was fulfilled so simply and so soon.'[32] Surveying the distant horizon, he added:

> northward to Damascus, the Turkish base, their only link with Constantinople and Germany, now cut off: southward to Amman and Maan and Medina, all cut off: westward to Liman von Sandars [sic] isolated in Nazareth: to Nablus: to the Jordan Valley. To-day was September the seventeenth, the promised day, forty-eight hours

before Allenby would throw forward his full power. In forty-eight hours the Turks might decide to change their dispositions to meet our new danger; but they could not change them before Allenby struck.[33]

The immediate concern was to start demolition work before the Ottomans could react. Already in Deraa there were signs of preparations for a counter-attack. Lawrence admitted that the first signs were 'disturbing' because eight or nine aircraft were being dragged from hangars. Since the Arab forces had no air defence capability, and they would have no cover in such an exposed location, they would not stand a large-scale assault from the air. The Ottomans were clearly making preparations though for a combined operation: infantry were being assembled and a train was under steam. Guns were already firing a screen of shells towards the Arabs to cover these preparations. The other Ottoman positions, to the north and west, had not yet reacted, but they could not rule out the possibility that these too would become the axes of subsequent counter-attacks.

As Peake detonated the first of 600 Tulip mines, a device designed to warp rails and metal sleepers, the first Ottoman reconnaissance aircraft appeared overhead. Soon after, the entire air wing of Deraa made their attacks:

> three two-seaters, and four scouts and an old yellow-bellied Albatross got up in quick succession, and circled over us, dropping bombs, or diving at us with machine-gun fire. Nuri put his Hotchkiss gunners in the rock cracks, and rattled back at them. Pisani cocked up his four mountain guns, and let fly some optimistic shrapnel. This disturbed the enemy, who circled off, and came back much higher.[34]

The Arab forces dispersed to reduce the likelihood of being targeted. Despite the aerial bombardment, and the strafing, the demolition continued methodically, possibly because the airmen were more concerned with the concentrations of mounted men and armoured cars. Without a ground attack, it was unlikely the progress of the demolitions could be halted.

Joyce explained to the other officers, including Lawrence, that it was for this reason they could not set off to attack the Yarmuk section of the railway. An alerted Ottoman garrison would be too strong to overcome without the entire Arab Northern Army, but to move such a large group would invite severe casualties through air attack, and leave the current demolition exposed to an Ottoman counter-attack on the ground. In fact, although the Sharifian forces did not know it, the Ottoman commanders received utterly confusing intelligence: 'one of these reports said that Sharif Feisal was advancing on Deraa with a force of eighteen thousand men, while another contradicted this and said there was no cause for alarm, as Feisal was three hundred miles away.'[35]

One option was to contemplate taking a smaller party to conduct a more limited attack on the Yarmuk section, but the situation called for the bulk of the force to remain where it was, for now. At that point, Hugh Junor, the pilot of the outdated B.E. 12 that had been left at Azrak, suddenly made an appearance, and attacked the more numerous Ottoman aircraft. This was an extremely courageous act, and it worked. Junor sped away to the west, across the rail line, and drew the Ottoman aircraft after him.[36]

Nuri seized the opportunity to gather a few hundred of the dispersed Arab regular infantry, the mountain guns led by the French officer Pisani, and as many of the local Hauran militia as could be found, to set off towards the Ottoman position at Mezerib, concealed by thicker, cultivated vegetation. The main body remained in place, hoping to protect the demolitions still underway. Nuri's objective was to reach the Palestine branch of the railway, to destroy the line there, although the odds against such a small force were growing now that the element of surprise had been lost.

After 30 minutes, Junor reappeared overhead, still pursued, and Lawrence, anticipating that he would soon need to land if he was to have any hope of survival, organized the hasty clearance of a landing site alongside the railway line. Junor, still under fire, out of petrol, and in an extremely hazardous situation, managed to land, although the wind caught his flimsy craft and flicked it over at the last second.[37] Miraculously unhurt, Junor coolly detached the Lewis gun and Vickers machine gun from the fuselage, retrieved his remaining ammunition, and hopped into the Ford car that had sped over to rescue him. All the while, the Ottoman aircraft continued to strafe the ground around them. One of the Ottoman planes then dropped a bomb close by, but the entire party withdrew unscathed. Astonishingly, this remarkable man then asked for another task within five minutes of the incident.

He was given one of the Ford cars and he drove off, blew a section of the railway himself, and only stopped when he came under Ottoman fire again. He withdrew, reluctantly, without injury.

Lawrence now decided to join the party making towards Mezerib, hoping to increase its chances of success, while Joyce formed a rearguard, with the Gurkhas, armoured cars, and a few hundred Arab irregulars. As they set off across the open plain, they were pursued by the Ottoman aircraft. Lawrence stated:

> An aeroplane crawled over us, dropping bombs: one, two, three, misses: the fourth into our midst. Two of my men went down. Their camels, in bleeding masses, struggled on the ground. The men had not a scratch, and leaped up behind two of their friends. Another machine floated past us, its engine cut off. Two more bombs, and a shock which spun my camel round, and knocked me half out of the saddle with a burning numbness in my right elbow.[38]

When he had the opportunity to examine his arm, he discovered his wound was superficial, but it had been close. Subjected to machine gun fire, Lawrence's bodyguard spread out, in the hope of lessening the number of casualties. Fanning out in this way gave the bodyguard the chance to appear across a wider area, and as they moved through the villages and fields, they inspired more local Arab men to join them.[39] Within hours, Lawrence's men were accompanied by a large number of followers. Lawrence recalled: 'The field-paths were full of these fellows, pouring out afoot from every village to help us.'[40] At Mezerib itself, Lawrence caught up with the contingent that had set out earlier, and, despite reports from locals that the Ottoman garrison was a strong one, the Arab forces closed in on it, expecting it to capitulate:

> We passed the stream, and walked together up the far bank knee-deep in weeds till we saw the Turkish station three hundred yards in front. We might capture this before attacking the great bridge below Tell el Shehab. Tallal advanced carelessly. Turks showed themselves to right and left. 'It's all right,' said he, 'I know the stationmaster': but when we were two hundred yards away, twenty rifles fired a shocking volley at us. We dropped unhurt into the weeds (nearly all of them thistles), and crawled gingerly back, Tallal swearing.[41]

Some of the Arab forces assembled for an assault, but Lawrence deterred them, for fear that a machine gun would wipe them out. There was a hasty consultation. They concluded that 'a delay at Mezerib might lose us the bridge, a greater objective'. Lawrence counselled that they could rely on the demolition already carried out by Peake, and that, by the end of the week, Allenby would have transformed the situation, so there was little point in taking undue risk. The result was that, in a few minutes, Pisani brought up his mountain guns and fired them, at close range, into the station. The machine guns also fired streams into the buildings. After a pause, it was Nuri who walked forward alone to demand the surrender of the 40 Ottoman soldiers who had held the place. The victory was followed by a 'frenzy' of plundering, in which the station, sidings and rolling stock were stripped of everything, largely by the locals. Lawrence and his men cut the telegraph lines, and detonated mines on the railway's points.[42] A small locomotive appeared and withdrew, uncertain of the strength of the Arab force, and a reconnaissance aircraft circled overhead. By nightfall, the Arab raiders had set the station and wagons ablaze, and the fiery beacon drew in dozens of curious local men from the entire district.

Lawrence attempted to glean intelligence from the multitude, although their stories varied so much it was a challenge to sift the factual from the fanciful. Lawrence related the difficulty, despite the importance of the task:

> Visitors were our eyes, and had to be welcomed. My business was to see every one with news, and let him talk himself out to me, afterwards arranging and combining the truth of these points into a complete picture in my mind. Complete, because it gave me certainty of judgement: but it was not conscious nor logical, for my informants were so many that they informed me to distraction, and my single mind bent under all its claims.[43]

There was great enthusiasm surrounding the events, and high expectations that Deraa must fall that night. Lawrence and Nuri tried to explain, to the hundreds now assembling, that this was not their purpose. Lawrence knew that even a relatively slow counter-offensive by the Ottomans would come in sufficient strength to drive them out of Deraa, even if it could be captured, and that would produce disillusionment amongst the Hauran population.[44] They had to wait until Allenby's offensive got underway, to draw the Ottoman reinforcements away. More importantly, the task of the Arab Northern Army was to occupy the attention of the Ottoman forces and add to the impression that they were part of a larger manoeuvre against Amman. It was precisely Lawrence's task to distract the Ottoman reserves, but this was a point that he could not explain to his immediate audience in a way they would understand.

So, the next objective was not Deraa, but the bridge at Tell el Shehab. A local lad offered details of the garrison and explained that he could bring the commander to Lawrence to make terms of surrender.[45] Astonishingly, the Armenian-Ottoman officer appeared soon after and agreed to facilitate the capture of his own post, against the Ottoman-Turkish subalterns and NCOs. The plan was for the officer to have a team of Arabs slip into his apartments, whereupon he would call in his subordinates in turn, where they could be taken prisoner. A cordon of gunmen would surround the post, to burst in if the plan went awry. Explosives were prepared to make an immediate demolition on the line. The assaulting force was briefed in the dark, and set out through defiles along irrigation ditches, which, Lawrence noted with trepidation, were exposed to ambush if the Ottoman turncoat was unfaithful after all. They crept close to the railway, only to discover a train in the valley below them.

Waiting in the dark to ascertain the reason for the unusual alertness of the garrison, Lawrence was suddenly approached out of the gloom by the lad who had created the scheme. He brought unwelcome news: the unexpected arrival of a train packed with German and Ottoman troops from Afuleh rendered their bold mission impossible. These reinforcements were destined for Deraa, and their task would be to reopen the line that Lawrence and his partners had just destroyed. The Armenian officer had been arrested for being absent from his post, and the entire force, alert to the possibility of raiders, was not only alert and well armed with machine guns, but active in their patrolling. Lawrence's men lay silent just 100 yards in front of them, and the chances of discovery were increasing every minute.

Lawrence explained his reasoning, founded on a sense of the value of guerrilla or hybrid operations, in his quick discussion with Nuri about what they should do, and the risk-calculus of his decision:

Nuri Said offered to take the place by main force. We had bombs enough, and pistol flares; numbers and preparedness would be on our side. It was a fair chance: but I was at the game of reckoning the value of the objective in terms of life, and as usual finding it too dear. Of course, most things done in war were too dear, and we should have followed good example by going in and going through with it. But I was secretly and disclaimedly proud of the planning of our campaigns: so I told Nuri that I voted against it. We had today twice cut the Damascus-Palestine railway; and the bringing here of the Afuleh garrison was a third benefit to Allenby. Our bond had been most heavily honoured.[46]

The raiders therefore slipped quietly away, and resisted the temptation to provoke the garrison with a parting shot that would generate confusion.[47] Discretion won out, and the entire force disappeared into the night to regroup, while one small party moved further down the line to detonate two small devices: insufficient to do much harm, but enough to occupy the attention of the German and Ottoman troops and therefore cover the departure of the Arab raiders.

An analysis of the campaign at this point indicates that the Ottomans were being distracted by Lawrence's raids. The local defenders were reacting to the cutting of the railway, but these appeared to be another set of nuisance attacks rather than a full offensive. The movement of German and Ottoman troops from Afuleh was a lateral move, west to east, rather than a north–south one, and that contingent was small, so it seems clear that the Ottomans did not believe the Arab attacks constituted as grave a threat to necessitate a larger deployment. On the other hand, time was running out for the Ottoman armies in Palestine, as the opening of Allenby's massive offensive was imminent. Lawrence could afford to take some risks, although he was eager not to squander the lives of Arab personnel.

As Lawrence planned to move to the south of Deraa, to cut the line there, he made recommendations that the main body should concentrate at Umtaiye because it offered the opportunity to move on any axis to exploit whatever opportunities arose next.[48] Lawrence recorded his thinking: 'for [Umtaiye], with its abundant water, splendid pasture, and equi-distance from Deraa and Jebel Druse and the Rualla Desert, seemed an ideal place in which we might rally and wait news of Allenby's fortune'. He continued: 'By holding Umtaiye we as good as cut off the Turkish fourth army of beyond Jordan … from Damascus: and were in place quickly to renew our main-line demolitions, whenever the enemy had nearly set them right.'[49] In fact, the position was to prove precarious.[50]

Withdrawing from Mezerib, Lawrence sent home the hundreds of villagers, which had the effect of confusing the aerial reconnaissance sent up to find them. He wrote: 'Turkish aeroplanes were humming overhead, looking for us, so we sent our peasants back ... for their villages. Consequently, the airmen reported that we were very numerous, possibly eight or nine thousand strong, and that our centrifugal movements seemed to be directed towards every direction at once.'[51] This presence of the local population, seemingly part of the insurgency, was to have profound consequences later.

Lawrence had soon reached a position above Nisib with mounted infantry and the French mountain guns. With his gunners protected by the undulations of the ground, a deliberate fire was opened against the nearby Ottoman railway station, some 2,000 yards away. In due course, the station and yards had been struck repeatedly. A group of Arab machine gunners worked their way forward under this covering fire, and then raked the entrenchments, but the Ottomans were in no mood to give in. They returned accurate fire. Neither side inflicted any losses. But Lawrence explained that his plan was merely to keep the Ottoman garrison pinned down, while a more determined assault was prepared against a redoubt that protected a large bridge outside the station and its nearby village. This attack began with two guns directing their fire on the redoubt while machine guns opened up on the village. Somehow, and Lawrence does not make it clear how, the villagers pleaded for the fire against their village to cease. Communicating amidst the battle underway is hard to conceive but Lawrence claimed the locals ejected the handful of Ottoman riflemen, leaving the redoubt's garrison to be the target of the full weight of French and Arab gunfire.

It appears that all four artillery pieces and some 24 machine guns were directed against the redoubt, but it still took some time to suppress the fire coming from within. The garrison survivors dashed to the rear, using the cover of an embankment to escape towards the larger force at the station. Lawrence's men also used the cover of the ground to get close under the parapets of the redoubt. But the risk of exposure was too high. The Ottoman fire had been intense enough to deter any final rush. Lawrence decided to investigate with his closest companions, and together they berated their fellows for not getting forward. In the last dash, they found the redoubt had indeed been abandoned.

They laid charges while the mass of camels, troops and guns crossed the line to the east. After an hour, the column was clear and the charges detonated. The explosion was vast, enough to blow down pillars five feet thick. Amidst the billowing black cloud, there was some alarm that Lawrence had been killed, and then further anxiety that a company of mounted infantry had been lost, but the blast gave them direction, and Lawrence emerged unscathed. The whole force therefore moved away into the night for the security of the desert.

That security was not afforded to the local population, and Lawrence's camp was soon overrun by local men asking whether the Arab raiders were intending to flee, to leave the civilian population at the mercy of the Ottomans. Many feared the reprisals that had been meted out at Es Salt. Lawrence and Nuri decided to visit the nearby settlement of Taiyibe that night, because the passage of the armoured cars there had caused considerable alarm and the villagers were planning to appeal to the Ottomans for support. Lawrence, eager to show that local allegiances were more certain, later claimed they only wished to appeal for clemency, but it seems more likely they were willing to offer information to the Ottomans.[52] They made no moves to do so while Nuri and Lawrence remained, but their silence later convinced the Ottomans that they must be in league with the raiders: consequently, Taiyibe was shelled the following day. As Joyce rode through it some time after, he was fired at by the locals, now suspicious of all outsiders.

Ottoman shelling was subsequently directed against the Arab encampment, the gunfire coming from an armoured train with an aircraft acting as a spotter. The shells pitched into the dispersed camping area, killing only camels, but they forced the Arabs to shift to a safer location. The Ottoman spotter aircraft landed through some technical problem, and was soon after joined by two more aircraft, which encouraged Joyce and the other officers to contemplate a sudden armoured car attack on them. Two cars were to be used, with volunteers selected for the mission. After a 5-mile drive, they got close to the landing site. When closing to 1,200 yards, they were suddenly stopped by a great hidden ravine, and, despite motoring at speed to get around it, the pilots were alerted and set off, ignoring the armoured cars' long-range machine gun fire that produced spurts of dust close by. The third enemy aircraft refused to start, and the two-man crew were forced to take cover as the cars ripped belts of machine gun fire into it.

The two escaped aircraft were not so easily despatched. Lawrence related their counter-attack, which came close to destroying the cars:

> The two escaped machines had had time to go to Deraa, and return, feeling spiteful. One was not clever and dropped his four bombs from a height, missing us widely. The other swooped low, placing one bomb each time with the utmost care. We crept on defencelessly, slowly, among the stones, feeling like sardines in a doomed tin, as the bombs fell closer. One sent a shower of small stuff through the driving slit of the car, but only cut our knuckles. One tore off a front tyre and nearly lurched the car over.[53]

The cars returned to the forward base at Umtaiye. But, while it provided a brief resting point, it was inadequate for local defence. Lawrence reflected on the relative value and vulnerability of the place:

> Strategically, our business was to hold on to Umtaiye, which gave us command at will of Deraa's three railways ... Yet tactically Umtaiye was a dangerous place. An inferior force composed exclusively of regulars, without a guerrilla screen, could not safely hold it: yet to that we should shortly be reduced, if our air helplessness continued patent.[54]

It was the relative weakness in air power that was proving to be the greatest risk to their survival. The Ottomans and Germans had at least nine aircraft available for surveillance and ground attack. Crucially, the prospect of repeated bombing threatened to deter the Arab irregulars from sustaining the campaign.[55] The forward base was just 12 short miles from the Ottoman air base, and it lay in open desert. Its location was obvious because it was the only viable water supply for the large numbers of camels and horses the Arab Northern Army depended on. This mass of animals and men made a tempting target. Lawrence noted that the Ottoman bombardments so far 'had been enough to disquiet the irregulars who were our eyes and ears. Soon they would break up and go home, and our usefulness be ended'.[56]

Lawrence therefore resolved to go to Allenby's headquarters and request air support, but in the meantime, while the forward base had to be prepared to stay on the move, the initiative could be regained by attacking more points on the Hejaz line, south of Deraa. This would distract the defenders, deter Ottoman advances towards the main body and keep the Arab fighters busy. The problem Lawrence encountered was that there was considerable disquiet amongst his own bodyguard. The men feared retribution and punishment because of their reluctance to fight at close quarters at Nisib. The Imperial regulars were also at their limit. Lawrence therefore suggested sending the Egyptians and Gurkhas to Aqaba, but using them to attack the railway en route.[57] To augment their firepower on the first leg of that mission, an armoured car would go with them.

The raid was, in Lawrence's own words, 'a muddle', because Lawrence got lost and emerged not in support of Peake's men, but in front of the Ottoman post at Mafrak. Turning back, he eventually located the Egyptian and Gurkha force as it blew 30 mines on the line. Lawrence could not identify a group of horsemen that rushed by his vehicle, but took advantage of the Ottomans being illuminated on the railway to fire streams of green tracer rounds at them. The Ottoman soldiers took cover and returned fire, piercing the car's petrol tank. After an emergency repair, Lawrence set off to find Peake's group, but there was no sign of them, so he had to wait until dawn to get another chance. In the light of the morning, they reunited, and, somewhat chastised, they headed to Azrak.

Here they reported to Feisal, discussing options. Then Joyce arrived with his own threefold plan to protect Zeid at Abu el Lissan, support Jafar at Ma'an, and then join Hornby to galvanize the Beni Sakr to advance again. Soon after, more news came: Allenby's offensive had begun, scoring significant victories from the outset. To clarify the way forward, Lawrence immediately flew to Palestine, to report directly to Allenby himself.

The overall plan was explained to him, and Allenby was insistent upon a coordinated effort, combining each of the corps' continuing attacks with the Arab forces on the right flank. There was no question of Lawrence being permitted to make his dash for Damascus, because his role was to keep the pressure on lest the Ottoman formations recover and regroup. If they did, they would simply establish a new defensive line some way to the north. Preventing their recovery held out the possibility of shattering the Ottoman resistance once and for all. Lawrence pleaded his case for air support, conscious that, on Allenby's front: 'It was the R.A.F., which had converted the Turkish retreat into rout, which had abolished their telephone and telegraph connections, had blocked their lorry columns, scattered their infantry units.'[58] But to reach the Arab forces rapidly with aircraft and all their associated logistics seemed impossible, until it was proposed that two fighters would be escorted by a Handley Page bomber and another aircraft, carrying fuel and spares.

Landing grounds were prepared at Urn el Surab, as the Arab forces had been bombed out of Umtaiye, losing some regular troops and gunners to those Ottoman bombardments. Small parties slipped back to Umtaiye to collect water, but the new dispersed camp was relatively safe by comparison. The arrival of British fighter aircraft, and news of Allenby's successes, lifted Arab morale. There were their own stories to tell, of raids and ambushes, but the overall sense of momentum was being restored.

It was not long before this was put to the test. An alarm was sounded, and the newly arrived pilots were scrambled. Lawrence reported:

> There were one enemy two-seater and three scouts... after five minutes of sharp machine-gun rattle, the German [aircraft] dived suddenly towards the railway line. As it flashed behind the low ridge, there broke out a pennon of smoke, and from its falling place a soft, dark cloud. An 'Ah!' came from the Arabs about us.[59]

Not more than 30 minutes later, another German aircraft appeared, and, after a chase for several miles, it too was shot down.[60] Lawrence agreed to fly back to Azrak, the changed situation meaning that he could recover Peake's Egyptians and Gurkhas, and then return by car to welcome in the giant Handley Page. He noted how the distances shrank and time was reduced acutely for the airmen, compared with the hard labour of movements on foot or by camel. He collected Feisal at Azrak and then sped north once more, ordering any scattered units to concentrate at Umtaiye again, and to prepare for the final offensive. By the time Lawrence reached the main body of the Arab force, the Handley Page bomber had arrived. The scale of the machine impressed everyone, and generated a sense of awe amongst the Arab irregulars that their partners, the British, could command such technology. Unloading its stores, the giant aircraft was used to make a bombing run against Deraa and Mafrak, the effects of which are hard to discern.[61] Encouraged by the sense that the Ottomans could be taken on more directly, Feisal now had 4,000 committed men about him, of which a quarter were regulars. To test the new combination, with armoured cars and guns to protect them, an attack was made on the Turkish repair parties on the railway line. With ample fire support, the Rualla excelled, and the British demolition parties destroyed all that had been put right by the Ottomans.[62]

Lawrence conducted his own armoured car raid against the line near Mafrak, but the German unit they had encountered in the previous aborted raid was still in the area, and the intensity of the machine gun fire that met them on their approach was a surprise. To attack the line, Lawrence decided to use the armoured protection of the vehicle to get right up under the arch of a vulnerable bridge, but the car was subjected to constant fire. A number of 'aimless shells' searched for the vehicle too, perhaps from a trench mortar. Lawrence had to abandon the attempt since 'about fifty yards from the bank, with enough machine-gun bullets for a week's fighting rattling off our armour, ... someone from behind the line bowled a hand grenade at us'.[63] The risk of detonation of the gun-cotton aboard was considerable and the car had to beat a retreat.

The incident reveals that the Germans and Ottomans were adapting effectively to the threat of air attack and assaults by armoured cars. They had not only 'hardened' their defences around the stations with bomb shelters, entrenchments and blockhouses, but also created a more mobile defence of quick reaction forces with their own air support. The increasing number of surveillance aircraft was also striking. Lawrence's decision to resume his attack at night indicated that these defences were making daylight operations too hazardous, and darkness conferred a crucial tactical advantage. In fact, he did not get the opportunity and the task of attacking Mazrak was left to the Handley Page bomber. Its hundred-pound explosives caused severe damage and the Ottoman defensive system was unable to prevent it. Indeed, the fact that the fires burned all night was the first indication that the Ottoman Army was beginning to fail.

Rumours were now brought in to the forward base at Umtaiye that 'the [Ottoman] Fourth Army was streaming up from Amman in a loose mob'.[64] The Beni Hassan, who were cutting off stragglers and weak detachments, compared them to 'gipsies on the march'.[65] Here was, as Lawrence would style it, another 'Kingfisher moment', to be seized quickly. He counselled the Arab leaders:

> Our new endeavour should be to force the quick evacuation of Deraa, in order to prevent the Turks there reforming the fugitives into a rearguard. ... I proposed that we march north, past Tell Arar, and

over the railway at dawn to-morrow, into Sheikh Saad village. It lay in familiar country with abundant water, perfect observation, and a secure retreat west or north, or even south-west, if we were directly attacked. It cut off Deraa from Damascus; and Mezerib also.[66]

Major Young was not the only one to think the plan was 'unsound'.[67] He calculated that just 600 Arab regulars, six guns, and ten machine guns could not hope to hold off the divisional strength of Ottoman forces that might move in their direction, particularly if they were caught on the line of march. He explained Lawrence's attitude, like that of the Arab officers, to be 'intoxicated with General Allenby's and our own success' so it was 'not easy to form a cool judgement'.[68]

The Arab forces would leave the armoured cars and Lawrence ordered the aircraft to return to Palestine, since he believed he did not need them. This was an odd judgement. Admittedly, the nature of the terrain made it difficult to use armoured cars on the route to Sheikh Saad, but to relinquish the aircraft which could have played a crucial role in the pursuit seemed unsound. The conclusion must be that Lawrence had been loaned the air support for a brief period and now that the Ottoman Fourth Army was showing signs of rupture, these air assets would be needed by Allenby against remaining resistance on the main front.

The emphasis of the coming days was going to be on penetration deep behind the Ottomans' lines. But, this time, the Arab forces would encounter a broken army, and find themselves emerging from the shadows to fight the final battle.

The Deep Battle

Megiddo and the Final Phase of Guerrilla Operations

General Allenby intended to break out of the Judean Hills and the plain of Esdraelon in September 1918. The plan for the battle of Megiddo, as it would come to be known, was to utilize an elaborate deception plan to conceal the main point of attack, then to concentrate devastating artillery fire on the closest Ottoman lines, but then, having broken through on a narrow front near the coast, to use mounted units and air power to penetrate, rapidly, into depth. The objective was to move fast, to unhinge the defenders and overwhelm them before they had the ability to regroup. The Arab forces were to provide one of the most critical elements of the deception plan, but, if possible, they were to attack the transport infrastructure deep in the rear, preventing reinforcements from moving into Allenby's primary area of operations.

This was not intended, in fact, to be the classic 'phase 3' of guerrilla warfare, a phrase from Maoist doctrine used to describe the transition from hit-and-run clandestine raiding into a conventional attack that could seize political power. The battle of Megiddo did, however, create the conditions where something approximating this phenomenon was the consequence. The Arab Northern Army, despite its title, in fact numbered just 4,000 men, three quarters of which were irregulars, some of whom were mounted men although most were on foot. Once the offensive got underway, the Arab Northern Army was initially in a precarious position. As various Ottoman formations tried to escape Allenby's onslaught, by moving north-east, away from the axis of the main advance, it placed them on the same path as the much smaller Arab force.

The weakness of Lawrence's situation was exposed within minutes of the departure of the aircraft on which he had depended for support. Lawrence recalled: 'We, watching their line of flight, noticed a great cloud of dust added to the slow smoke from ruined Mafrak. One machine turned back and dropped a scribble that a large body of hostile cavalry were heading out from the railway towards us.'[1] The Arab force was not in a 'trim' condition to fight against a large mobile formation, being strung out on the march. So, 'we wavered whether to run or stand', until Lawrence advised a retreat, dispersing units to escape the hostile body that was bearing down on them.[2]

Fortunately, the armoured cars had spotted the enemy force, and, as the Rualla horsemen prepared to create a delaying action, it emerged that the Ottomans were in fact fugitives. Some reached the Arabs and pleaded for water, but the majority, out on the plain, were making for Deraa. The sight of the Arab horsemen produced memories of their previous attacks, and there was something of a panic. Guns and wagons were abandoned, and the mass of retreating men and horses started to run.

Without support, it seemed impossible to take on such a large force, however weak it appeared. The Arabs moved off, and considered the most prudent course to follow: a 'halt gave some people time to review the proceedings, and new questions arose as to the wisdom of crossing the railway again, to put ourselves in the dangerous position of Sheikh Saad, astride the retreat of the main Turkish forces'.[3] Some believed they had fulfilled their bargain with Allenby, and could now withdraw 20 miles to the east, leaving Deraa and its demoralized troops to fester. Lawrence disagreed, and his reasoning was to remain active, not only to maintain support for Allenby's operations, but to secure a better position for the Arabs after the war. This meant taking Damascus, and, in the short term, contesting Sheikh Saad and Deraa. As he wrote:

Evidently, by thrusting behind Deraa into Sheikh Saad we put more pressure on the Turks than any British unit was in place to put. It would forbid the Turks fighting again this side of Damascus; for which gain our few lives would be cheap payment. Damascus meant the end of this war in the East, and, I believed, the end of the general war, too; because the Central Powers being inter-dependent, the breaking of their weakest link – Turkey – would swing the whole cluster loose. Therefore, for every sensible reason, strategical, tactical, political, even moral, we were going on.[4]

But not all agreed. Sabin, an officer of the Arab Northern Army, argued that the risks were too great for such a small force and 'stressed the military aspect: our fulfilled purpose and the danger of the Hejaz Railway'. He laid out the factors: '[It was] too late to cross to-night. Tomorrow it would be madness to attempt the operation. The line would be guarded from end to end by tens of thousands of Turks pouring out of Deraa. If they let us over we would only be in still greater danger.'[5]

But Lawrence's arguments won and, the following day, the entire Arab Northern Army, swelled by locals who joined it en route, covered a front 2 miles wide. The Ottomans had, contrary to all expectations, repaired the railway, and three trains passed northwards, but the Arabs ran fluidly over the line and blew up the tracks once more. Independent raiding was also encouraged: 'we went to Nuri Shaalan, Auda, and Talal, and asked what local effort each would undertake. Talal, the energetic, would attack Ezraa, the big grain depot to the north: Auda was for Khirbet el Ghazala, the corresponding station southward: Nuri would sweep his men down the main road, towards Deraa, on chance of Turkish parties.'[6]

This independence of effort was vital because of the many feuds and disagreements that still plagued the Arab cause. Lawrence recalled, on entering Sheikh Saad: 'in our ranks we had hundreds of deadly enemies, their feuds barely suspended by Feisal's peace. The strain of keeping them in play, and employing their hot-heads in separate spheres, balancing opportunity and service that our direction might be esteemed as above jealousy – all that was evil enough.'[7]

The raids were a success. Abd el Kader had been found and his contingent driven off; railway trucks were seized; and German and Turkish prisoners taken. A British aircraft dropped a message that there were greater successes to report: Bulgaria had surrendered. Lawrence confessed the news was met with indifference, because he and others did not realize its significance beyond signalling that the war was coming to an end. The capitulation of Bulgaria effectively severed the railways by which Germany was supplying, and propping up, the Ottoman Empire.

Its vital lifeline had been cut, and the meagre resources remaining would soon be exhausted.

There were still tactical alarms. As Lawrence and his comrades took to the high ground to plan their next move, they discovered a small column of machine gunners (allegedly a mixture of German, Austrian and Ottomans). They were ambushed: 'The officers showed fight and were instantly killed. The men threw down their arms, and in five minutes had been searched and robbed.'[8] Other groups were spotted out on the ground before them, all parties trying to make use of the night to escape the British onslaught behind them.[9] The Howeitat either cut them down or made them prisoners for local villagers. The majority were unarmed and exhausted.

The next day, more news came in of Ottoman units taking to villages to fortify themselves, or perhaps escape destruction, and a detachment was sent out to round them up. But, more significantly:

A man cantered in, to inform Tallal [one of the sheikhs] that the Germans had set fire to aeroplanes and storehouses, and stood ready to evacuate the town. A British plane dropped word that [General] Barrow's troops were near Remtha, and that two Turkish columns, one of four thousand, one of two thousand, were retiring towards us from Deraa and Mezerib respectively.[10]

Lawrence was encouraged, and calculated that only a moderate effort was required, for the occupation of Sheikh Saad was sufficient to deny the Ottomans a defensive position. He reasoned that guerrilla tactics would keep a sword at their back:

It seemed to me that these six thousand men were all that remained of the Fourth Army, from Deraa, and of the Seventh Army, which had been disputing Barrow's advance. With their destruction would end our purpose here. Yet, till we knew, we must retain Sheikh Saad. So the larger column, the four thousand, we would let pass, only fastening to them Khalid and his Rualla, with some northern peasantry, to harry their flanks and rear.[11]

The other Ottoman column was set on the trajectory towards the village of Tafas, and Tallal begged that some action be taken to divert its course. Lawrence, knowing that the Arab units were worn out, agreed to take his bodyguard out to occupy a ridge outside the village, and to conduct a 'retiring action' that would delay the Ottoman troops until some 500 Arab regulars and Pisani's guns could be marched up. In fact, Lawrence arrived too late to prevent a mounted regiment of Ottomans from gaining the village. He noted that shots rang out within it, and palls of smoke were rising, suggesting some reprisals were underway. Those who escaped told of atrocities.[12]

Lawrence had his men open a long-range fire on the Ottoman column as it emerged from the settlement – it was a mixed force of cavalry, infantry, machine gun teams and field guns, all protecting a baggage column in the centre. It was the field artillery that responded to Lawrence's desultory, harassing fire. Then, Pisani came up, and with the accompaniment of the Hotchkiss machine guns, they commenced firing into the Ottoman rearguard. Lawrence and his companions entered the deserted village to find it full of dead civilians, some of whom had been butchered.[13] They were all moved to anger by the scene, and Lawrence issued the command: 'The best of you brings me the most Turkish dead.'[14] The killing of the Ottoman wounded and stragglers began almost immediately. Lawrence recalled: '[We started] shooting down those who had fallen out by the roadside and came imploring our pity. One wounded Turk, half naked, not able to stand, sat and wept to us. ... the Zaagi, with curses, ... whipped three bullets from his automatic through the man's bare chest.'[15] Tallal launched his own personal charge at the retreating column and was killed, so Auda took command and manoeuvred his men, and the local peasantry who had come up, in such a way as to divide the Ottomans into three distinct groups.

As Lawrence related, the most stubborn resistance was offered by a party of Germans, Austrians, and Ottoman officers, who were equipped with machine guns and cars. This group drove off repeated assaults by the Arabs.[16] The faster escaping columns were less cohesive and were consequently pursued into separate sections, and cut down, piece by piece, until virtually wiped out. Lawrence had ordered no prisoners should be taken, but the instruction made no difference to the Arab fighters, all of whom were looking for revenge. The peasants acquired the weapons, horses, mules and baggage of the Ottoman retreat, but Lawrence recalled there was a blood lust abroad that was more important to the Arab veterans than material possessions: 'In a madness born of the horror of Tafas we killed and killed, even blowing in the heads of the fallen and of the animals; as though their death and running blood could slake our agony.'[17]

Yet the German and Austrian party had been taken alive, and an estimated 200 prisoners were now lined up. Lawrence claimed that he was initially willing to spare them, as witnesses to the atrocity perhaps, but one of the Arab fighters had been bayoneted in the final close-quarter fighting, and left, pinned to the ground, probably moments before they had surrendered. The fear and contempt for the Arabs as fighters, and the involvement of the civilians in the insurgency, especially the peasant fighters who had recently joined and who had been responsible for killing wounded Ottoman soldiers, were certainly the driving forces for revenge against German-Austrian and Ottoman troops. Lawrence overlooked the consequences of this people's war. He was personally enraged by the nature of the killings, and the impaling of a comrade.[18] The order was thus given to kill all the prisoners, and, realizing what was about to happen, they stoically 'said nothing in the moments before we opened fire'.[19] Lawrence did not describe the shooting down of these men, but added a comment that seemed to indicate it had taken time, for he wrote: 'At last their heap ceased moving.'

By nightfall, the pursuit was still underway, but now on a wider front. Lawrence wrote:

> Every field and valley had its Turks stumbling blindly northward. Our men were clinging on. The fall of night had made them bolder, and they were now closing with the enemy. Each village, as the fight rolled to it, took up the work; and the black, icy wind was wild with rifle-fire, shoutings, volleys from the Turks, and the rush of gallops, as small parties of either side crashed frantically together.[20]

The Ottoman forces were in retreat and were being pursued by a variety of groups. From Lawrence's description there appeared to be no central direction, but a series of skirmishes as groups encountered each other in the darkness. The Ottoman soldiers seemed to be utterly exhausted, and, despite the danger, some fell to the ground to rest. They 'had lost order and coherence, and were drifting through the blast in lorn packets, ready to shoot and run at every contact with us or with each other'.[21] Lawrence admitted that, in this moving battle, some of the

Arab fighters were 'uncertain', a reference to their caution at attacking so many Ottomans and their own fatigue after days of continuous operations.

The only solid units were the Germans, whose discipline held firm, despite the odds against them.[22] Lawrence famously offered his admiration for this cohesion, a striking contrast to his earlier dismissal of the value of discipline:

> Here, for the first time, I grew proud of the enemy who had killed my brothers. They were two thousand miles from home, without hope and without guides, in conditions mad enough to break the bravest nerves. Yet their sections held together, in firm rank, sheering through the wrack of Turk and Arab like armoured ships, high-faced and silent. When attacked they halted, took position, fired to order. There was no haste, no crying, no hesitation.[23]

Lawrence was eager to leave the harrying of this defeated Ottoman force, believing there would be a more significant rearguard, undoubtedly still cohesive, to tackle. If the British forces could not keep up their own pursuit, the Ottomans might regroup and consolidate a line of defences. Lawrence was calculating that the whole Ottoman force needed to be kept on its exhausting retreat, and broken up, along its entire length.

There were opportunities opening up. There were rumours that Deraa had been abandoned. If true, it offered a chance to put a force across this vital junction, which would drive the Ottomans into different streams and deprive them of critical resources. Lawrence rallied the Rualla fighters, and they rode on to Deraa, skirmishing with separated Ottoman detachments on the way. When they arrived at the town, on 26 September, the Arabs did not pause, 'taking the station at a gallop, jumping trenches and blotting out the scanty Turkish elements which still tried to resist'. The Rualla and the locals plundered the place, 'finding booty in the fiercely burning storehouses whose flaming roofs imperilled their lives'.[24]

Lawrence then went back to Sheikh Saad where there was some confusion: passing Ottoman detachments were attacked, and there were episodic rumours of counter-attacks; many of the sheikhs were out with their men hunting for Ottoman stragglers and booty, but the distribution of the spoils had re-awakened clan jealousies. Clearly there were violent incidents, and Lawrence acknowledged that the British officers and the Arab leaders were struggling to maintain the peace. In the early hours, Lawrence set out again, passing the Arab mounted infantry heading towards Deraa. Reaching the station, Lawrence found Nasir establishing an administration. Lawrence assisted but 'in an hour of talk I built up publicly a programme of what the situation would demand of them' to hold the town, which left the Arabs in shock. The main concern was that, if the British, advancing from the west, did not reach them, the Ottomans might wrest it back from them.

In fact, the British forces under General Barrow had arrived and were in the process of enveloping Deraa to assault it. Lawrence had to explain that the forces in front of the British and Indian troops were their Arab allies, although there was a near miss when British aircraft mistook one Arab mounted contingent for Ottoman horsemen.[25] The incident indicated that liaison between the Arab and British forces was crucial. Barrow had been ordered to take control of Deraa, so Lawrence's insistence that the Arabs were already doing that came, according to Lawrence, as an unwelcome statement.[26] Barrow denied there was any disagreement.[27] Both were evidently tired and eager to fulfil their own designs, but much flexibility and goodwill are always required when regular troops find themselves operating alongside local, irregular forces and their advisors.[28] One has the superiority in weapons, logistics and strength; the other all the hard-won local knowledge and experience of being there. It was hard for both Lawrence and Barrow to appreciate their respective positions, and there was too little time to explain. Lawrence insisted that he had to set the tone, from the start, that the Arabs governed in Deraa. But it was Barrow's willingness to respect the Arab wishes that went a long way in everyone's estimation of future Anglo-Arab relations.[29] The only aspect Barrow could not tolerate were the atrocities against the Turkish wounded.[30]

Meanwhile, the daylight heralded the spectacle of hundreds of prisoners being brought in. Lawrence recalled: 'everywhere we were taking men and guns. Our prisoners could be counted in thousands.'[31] Barrow was eager to press on and plans were made that his troops would advance towards Damascus, having reported their position to Chauvel. Lawrence was asked to continue the support to the right flank of Allenby's army. Nasir and the Rualla, however, were already engaged in their constant harassing attacks on the rear of the Ottoman

Fourth Army, as it continued to struggle northwards. Further to the west, Allenby's mounted forces were tearing apart the other Ottoman divisions and riding deep into their rear. The added factor was the role of the Royal Air Force, which was doing significant damage. Had aircraft been available to Lawrence's Arab partners at this stage, the magnitude of their results would have been just as significant.[32]

Lawrence drove up towards Damascus by car, but rejoined the camel-mounted forces that were parallel with Barrow's leading units, and overtook the British, intending to reach the Syrian city first. But Lawrence was also acting as a scout, keeping observation on the retreating Ottomans. He was privately critical of the more cautious advance of Barrow, and he could not appreciate that, after weeks of fighting over the Judean Hills, these men were unwilling to be counter-attacked on the line of march, which had been the tactic of their enemy hitherto.[33] Ahead, Lawrence found that the sheikhs, including Nasir and Auda, were actively engaging the rear of the Ottoman column, which, far from being 4,000 as previously estimated, was nearer 7,000 in number. One detachment, of 2,000 men, was cohesive enough to periodically halt, fire its mountain guns, and withdraw in sections. This suggests that the Ottoman Army, while beaten, was not incapable of resistance, although Liman von Sanders was simply unable to stop their retreat.[34] There was a chance that some defence of Damascus might yet be organized, and, to take the city, Lawrence would still need the British and their guns, aircraft, and greater numbers.

The Rualla had moved around the flanks of the Ottoman column, and Auda offered to establish an ambush on a ridge ahead of the retreating troops, which would be enough 'to delay only for an hour' until Barrow's forces could catch up. Lawrence rushed back to the leading detachment of Indian cavalry, but was frustrated when, deploying, it was caught in Ottoman gunfire, and retired. Higher authority was sought out, and both horse artillery and British Yeomanry were rushed forward as it grew dark. The united charge of Arab and British mounted men drove the startled Ottomans back, off the road, and up into the face of Auda's ambush. The combined effect of British artillery, the twilight charge and the unexpected rapid fire across the ridge to the front, broke what cohesion was left in the Fourth Army.

The finale was the ride to Damascus, but a night march was ruled out because of the remaining Ottoman troops who, through desperation, would resist. Word was sent to Damascus that preparations should be made to form a local government, but the city leaders, and the former Ottoman commander, had used their initiative and 'the Arab flag was on the Town Hall before sunset as the last echelons of Germans and Turks defiled past'.[35] The Germans destroyed their stores and surplus ammunition to prevent them falling into Allied hands, and this made an ominous backdrop to the entry into the city.[36] The first meeting of the various Arab leaders was marred by arguments, fighting and old disagreements. Witnesses reported that the 'Algerians', including Abd el Kader, had remained loyal to the Ottomans to the last moment, then declared their allegiance to Feisal and claimed to be in command of the city. The multitude of disagreements boded ill for any sense of pan-Arab government.

Lawrence was compelled to conduct a coup, to install Shukri Pasha Ayubi as acting Military Governor, with the assistance of the Bedouin.[37] He installed a rudimentary administration, empowered with emergency measures. The impatient work was hampered by the levels of infection, damage, lack of food and general insecurity, but Lawrence was in a hurry to establish an authority before the British, or the French, assumed control. In fact, from a legal point of view, Damascus was an occupied enemy territory and the responsibility of the British, under Allenby, just as Jerusalem had been in December 1917. In his haste to set up an independent 'state', he left himself exposed. General Chauvel had offered to assist, but Lawrence had refused because accepting British help would destroy at a stroke any claim to legitimacy, independence or competence in Arab governance. So while he worked, Abd el Kader and his followers attempted a counter-coup, rousing the Druzes with offers of plunder from the Maronites and denouncing the Bedu followers of Lawrence as 'creatures' under Christian control. El Kader's narrative was based on the iconography of Sunni extremism, but the Druze rioters, who had taken to the streets at night, were more interested in material possessions.[38]

In the morning, Nuri placed machine guns to cover the city centre, while Lawrence and the other leaders drove the rioters and conspirators from the northern suburbs into the centre with gunfire. Bursts of machine gun fire then dispersed the riot, and el Kader's putsch was broken up.[39] The fighting ended when Chauvel marched his men through the city centre. There were only a handful of casualties, but

Lawrence was irritated by the press corps who exaggerated the fighting. It was a very modern problem – that an urban skirmish, in the presence of the media, was sensationalized and distorted from its context, with far-reaching consequences.

In time, the administration started to function, but the tasks before it were overwhelming, and few had stopped to consider the Ottoman wounded and sick, slowly dying through neglect in nearby barracks and hospitals. A lack of all fundamental resources made this and other tasks like it almost impossible without external assistance.[40] In many ways, it was probably dawning on Lawrence that to refuse support was becoming a greater risk to the security and operation of the city, and, by extension, the region. Lawrence was disappointed that the Arab forces had also seized Beirut: 'I had warned them, when they took Damascus, to leave Lebanon for sop to the French and take Tripoli instead; since as a port it outweighed Beyrout, and England would have played the honest broker for it on their behalf in the Peace Settlement.'[41]

Allenby's arrival transformed the situation completely. Lawrence recalled:

> In ten words he gave his approval to my having impertinently imposed Arab Governments, here and at Deraa, upon the chaos of victory. He confirmed the appointment of Ah' Riza Rikabi as his Military Governor, under the orders of Feisal, his Army Commander, and regulated the Arab sphere and Chauvel's. He agreed to take over my hospital and the working of the railway. In ten minutes all the maddening difficulties had slipped away.[42]

Sir Harry Chauvel was unimpressed by Lawrence's account of how the administration in Damascus was established and how Lawrence's version of affairs was accepted by the *Official History*.[43] The fact was the Australians had held the city, and the Arab contingents arrived some time later with the 4th Indian Cavalry. For Chauvel, much of the chaos had simply been avoidable.

But now the endings came quickly. In order to impress upon Feisal the significance of the forthcoming French administration, Allenby had summoned the Arab leader for a meeting ahead of the planned 'triumphal entry' to the city. Quite unexpectedly, Lawrence claimed he had not known about the forthcoming French military control of Syria and Lebanon, which was untrue, and he refused to work with a French liaison officer. It was for this reason that Lawrence offered to resign, and Allenby, incensed, accepted immediately.[44] Soon after, the Ottoman government collapsed and the new authorities in Istanbul agreed to an armistice at Mudros, bringing the world war in this theatre to an end.

The Arab forces, a mixed force of regulars and irregular fighters, had emerged from a guerrilla campaign into mobile conventional warfare. Their pursuit and exploitation of the retreating Ottoman Fourth Army had added to Allenby's military victory, but no contemporaries were under any illusion that the Arab forces could have achieved success on their own. Lawrence could be forgiven for his desire to amplify their achievement, not least because Feisal's command had come so far, endured air attacks and stiffened Ottoman resistance, and yet remained cohesive. It was appropriate that Allenby gave the Arab forces the opportunity to celebrate their contribution to the campaign by a formal entry into Damascus. Yet the arrival at Damascus was, in many ways, not the end of the struggle: it was the beginning. The problem of establishing a political authority, post-revolution, is always difficult. There are high expectations. Casualties add moral pressure to the desire to see a fitting reward for the army that has done the fighting. But, without a common enemy, all the divisions amongst the Arabs were suddenly exposed.

Although departing, Lawrence's interest in the Arab cause was by no means over; neither were his observations on war, nor the challenges of making peace. In fact, these were only now beginning to emerge, and Lawrence would soon find himself engaged in an entirely different, political struggle just as demanding as his wartime endeavours.

14

Lawrence on Strategy and Politics

At the Paris Peace Conference, Lawrence hoped to achieve his strategic ends by 'other means'. Throughout the war, each of the belligerents had set out to achieve the best military outcomes and the largest territorial acquisitions in order to improve their positions at the peace table. The priority was to decide on the future of Germany, and then the rest of Europe. The Middle East and the Ottoman Empire were considered as secondary matters, alongside the German colonies of Africa, East Asia and the Pacific.

Lawrence attended Paris as a member of the British delegation, acting on behalf of the Foreign Office as the advisor to Feisal. His instructions were to ensure that the Arabs cooperated with British interests, that is, to come to an agreement with the French.[1] That was easier said than done. The French refused to recognize Feisal as an official delegate at all, until Lawrence and the British authorities managed to rush a letter from Emir Hussein which gave Feisal powers of *pleins pouvirs* to act as the spokesman of the Arabs of the Hejaz and Levant.

Lawrence put forward a map of how he imagined the northern Middle East, which gave the interior to the Arabs, but also the Syrian coast, under Feisal.[2] French territorial control was to be limited to Lebanon and the Armenians were to be awarded the area around Alexandretta. Zeid was to be given eastern Syria, protected by Britain, and British jurisdiction would include Mesopotamia and, perhaps, northern Iraq, under Abdullah. Palestine he accepted as an international zone, but the area from Gaza eastwards to the southern Dead Sea and down to Aqaba was to be British. Southern Arabia, we may assume, he envisaged as remaining in Arab hands, save Aden, the British port.

Lawrence was confident his views would be accepted.[3] Several contemporaries used their conversations with Lawrence as a form of endorsement, indicating the authority he carried on Arab affairs. The British War Cabinet contemplated how Lawrence should be rewarded and honoured.[4] But they rejected his map and proposals all the same.

The ending of the war, where the insurgents were to achieve their objectives through negotiations alongside the world's major states, is not representative of insurgents' experience, or, indeed, most proxy forces, in the period after 1918. In essence, for all the difficulties in working with the French over Syria, Lawrence and the Hashemites were negotiating as allies of the victors.[5] Guerrilla forces normally find their first difficulty is gaining any legitimacy. Most governments will seek to discredit armed insurgents, denying them any legal status and regarding them as criminals. Their tactics, necessary for survival against stronger adversaries, delegitimizes them and even makes it difficult for their state sponsors to argue for legal recognition. Had the Ottomans and the Central Powers won the war, the Arabs would certainly have been denied any recognition and would have had to be subject to intense repression.

The political scientist Barbara Walter notes that this question of legitimacy is a serious obstacle when committing to peace. She demonstrates that the first step, entering into talks, is the most hazardous. Even if insurgents can reach this first stage, it is clear that, while negotiations are conditions-based, there are inevitable changes in the process of negotiation as it proceeds, none of which carry any guarantees for the weaker side. Amongst Walter's many insights is the idea that both insurgents and their opponents will change their objectives during talks, adjusting to what is possible, where opportunities might exist, and where even the most strongly held ideological positions may need to be adjusted.[6] Continuing military operations while in talks is also a tactic that has benefits at the negotiating table, to 'up the ante'. For many insurgents, talks are merely a ruse to buy time when under military pressure.

Contrast Lawrence's situation with that of two contemporary insurgencies, the Irish and the Bolsheviks. Between 1919 and 1921, the Irish had no international representation, no international military allies, and lacked the means to overcome the British or fight them to exhaustion, as the Arabs had done against the Ottomans. In Russia, in the fighting of 1918–22, the Bolsheviks were isolated internationally, confronted by foreign interventions, and barely held on in the midst of a civil war and complete economic collapse.

In one respect, though, there was a parallel. As the talks were underway in Paris, Ibn Saud took the opportunity to attack his Hashemite rivals and make a bid for control of the Hejaz. Saud was angered by the pretensions of Hussein, not least the claim to be 'King of Arabia', and irritated by the Hashemite edicts in Mecca. There had already been skirmishing between the Saudis and the Hashemites, but, in May 1919, Ibn Saud despatched 10,000 cavalry and 4,000 well-armed dismounted men to inflict a decisive defeat on Hussein. The situation revealed the difficulty for Britain in arming and financing two rival factions over the war years. The Foreign Office had backed the Hashemites, while the Government of India had funded the Saudis. Without a common enemy, the conflict between the Arabs had increased in likelihood, and the negotiations in Paris were not keeping pace with events on the ground.

Abdullah tried to halt the Saudi offensive but was defeated and his army routed. As they streamed westwards, the Foreign Office was forced to issue an ultimatum to Ibn Saud. If he did not withdraw, the Royal Air Force would be sent to interdict his army. The India Office too urged Ibn Saud to withdraw. Lawrence was nevertheless perplexed. He had assured the Foreign Office that if Saud threatened the Hejaz, the Hashemites would be able to deal with it.[7] The fact that the Hashemites had suffered such a comprehensive defeat undermined not only his own credibility, but his claims about the Hashemite capability to govern Syria.

It was the Americans who provided a new opportunity for the Hashemites to achieve their objectives, when, thanks to President Woodrow Wilson's insistence, there was to be a commission of enquiry into local allegiances which would help fulfil the principle of self-determination. The British offered Sir Henry McMahon and David Hogarth to accompany the American officials, Dr Henry King and Mr Charles R. Crane, to the region, but the French refused to send any delegates. After two months of delay, imposed deliberately by the Quai D'Orsay, the British gave up. The Americans went ahead on their own and returned with the recommendation that there should be mandates, care-taker administrations, for a limited period, for Syria, Palestine and

Iraq. King and Crane recommended an American mandate for Syria, Britain in Iraq, but none for the French. They also recommended that the Zionists should abandon any idea of a 'commonwealth' within Palestine, as the British had suggested in 1917.[8] All sides, including the American administration, ignored these findings and continued to negotiate on their own terms.

The interlude had given Lawrence an opportunity to start work on his memoir, *Seven Pillars of Wisdom*, but that work was influenced strongly by the frustration he felt at the failure to fulfil what he considered to be the essentials for the Arabs who had fought for their cause. Much of the commentary about 'betrayal' was not therefore his sentiment during the war, but belongs to his feelings in 1919–20. The idea that he wanted full Arab independence, much broadcast by his supporters, is only part of the story. This was the eventual aspiration, but his concern was typical of his generation and the same as the position of the British government. He believed the Arabs needed British assistance in organization, finance, and military protection, in the short term, before becoming independent partners in the long term.

Where there was disagreement and concern at the Foreign Office was with regard to Lawrence's attitude towards the French. The intransigence by the French authorities could not be overcome if Lawrence continued to dig his heels in. A note was sent to Balfour, in Paris, from the Foreign Office, that Lawrence's continued presence was 'likely to cause us serious embarrassment with the French'.[9] The British delegation in Paris argued that Lawrence was still the best hope of keeping Feisal and achieving a settlement 'without bloodshed'.[10]

The hard fact was that Britain wanted a firm alliance with France in 1919 for future European security arrangements, and that meant cooperation with them over their stated interests in the Middle East. France was determined to govern Syria, regarding it as an essential base to balance Britain's dominance in the Eastern Mediterranean. They regarded it as the only suitable compensation for long-standing humiliations over Suez, Egypt and the Sudan, where Britain had thwarted French interests for 40 years. The problem for Britain was that its model of governance was so different from that of France. While the British sought local intermediaries to govern, under British protection, for some mutual economic advantage, the French insisted on a political, linguistic and military subordination. Lawrence urged the British model, claiming:

'If the French are wise and neglect the Arabs for about twelve months, they will then be implored by them to help them.' He continued: 'If they are impatient now, they will only unite the Arabs against them.'[11]

Lawrence nevertheless had fallen foul of the Foreign Office and was withdrawn from the peace conference. It made no difference, as Feisal had already resolved not to accept any French proposal, from the British or directly from the French, about the future of Syria. Feisal left Paris to consult the Syrians, while Lawrence took to the press. His letter to *The Times* on 11 September 1919 argued there had been no inconsistencies in British government assurances, namely, that Syria would be an independent Arab territory. Lawrence insisted that the Arab opinion must be considered.[12] The Foreign Office were displeased that Lawrence made reference to official records and his description of himself as 'independent', when he had been acting as a civil servant. But the fundamental issue was still that Lawrence could not accept the compromises the British government felt it had to make to retain the French relationship, a theme that was plaguing other aspects of Britain's foreign policy at the time, especially when the new League of Nations was dependent on their close cooperation.[13]

In Syria, France refused to acknowledge any independence for Syrians. This, and the announcement of the establishment of mandates, ratified at the San Remo Conference in April 1920, caused widespread local anger. Small groups of Syrians started attacking symbols of French authority, and violence escalated. The French Army used the opportunity to issue an ultimatum against the Arab leaders in Damascus and marched on the city. Lord Curzon, the Foreign Secretary, urged Feisal to accept the French demands to avoid a conflict, and he did, but the Syrian nationalists did not. A small detachment at Maysalun mustered to take on the French Army, but were defeated. Feisal was unceremoniously deported.

It was just as Lawrence was at his lowest ebb in terms of personal confidence, afflicted by a sense of guilt and culpability for the failure to achieve imminent Arab independence, that his name was associated with success and public popularity. Lowell Thomas's illustrated lectures and film show of Allenby and Lawrence in the war was not only an instant success in Britain, but became an international sensation. Lawrence, making an incognito visit to one of the showings, was surprised to be converted into 'a matinee idol'. The newspapers amplified the appeal of the performances, and Lawrence made the apotheosis from military advisor to legend, a feature that his untimely death served to increase. As audiences thrilled to scenes and stories of desert adventure, Lawrence himself was despondent, walking the streets of London in the early hours, eating little, agonizing over *Seven Pillars*, line by line. When summoned by the King, George V, for a decoration, he refused the award on the grounds that he had failed to achieve what he felt was owed to the Arabs for their efforts in the war.

OPPOSITION TO THE IRAQ REVOLT OF 1920 AND THE CAIRO CONFERENCE

During the negotiations in Paris, Lawrence came to believe the centre of gravity in Middle Eastern affairs was shifting towards Mesopotamia.[14] In a period before the discovery of oil reserves in Saudi Arabia, he assessed that Iraq would be the most dynamic of the Arab regions. Syria, by contrast, he thought too agrarian. That said, he did not think Basra would be as important as the Government of India thought it might, and, perhaps in an effort to persuade Europeans about the greater relative importance of the Levant, he emphasized the 'Mediterranean' focus of all the Semite peoples. He hoped particularly for Arab and Zionist cooperation, not least because he believed that Jewish energy, industry and finance would fuel the economic 'take-off' of the Near East and thus the entire region. The survival of the British Empire, he reasoned, needed the cooperation of local people for its governance and security. Like most of his generation, he imagined dominion status, and equality within the empire, of all the colonies.[15]

The military occupation of Mesopotamia had continued after the war, and it was administered as an enemy territory until the establishment of British civil government under Sir Arnold Wilson, with the close support of Gertrude Bell.[16] The arrangement frustrated those Arabs who had hoped for independence, and the announcement of the conclusions of the San Remo Conference, which made the new state of Iraq one of the mandate territories, sparked mass demonstrations. Many Iraqis feared that, despite wartime assurances of liberation, the British intended to turn the country into a colony. Protests were led by prominent religious figures and often orchestrated by tribal elders or former Ottoman Army officers. Their protests were emboldened when it became evident that British troops were being withdrawn and demobilized.

The proportion of British officers in the Iraq garrison was also lower than usual, since many were tasked with assisting in the civil administration. Although under the direction of the Indian Civil Service (ICS), there were too few to run a normal bureaucracy, so there was a dependence on individual political officers, either ICS men or army officers, to act as governors, protected by small contingents of British and Indian troops. Naturally this penny-packeting of military power, while offering a physical presence, was unsound if there was any significant unrest. There had already been trouble. The Kurds had resisted British administration in 1919, while concerns that the Turks might try to retake Mosul meant that garrisons in the north were ordered not to relinquish territory and had to remain spread out. The result was that Lieutenant General Aylmer Haldane, who took command in March 1920, inherited a force that was largely 'fixed' and that would find abandoning any part of the country difficult, lest it be interpreted as weakness.[17]

After protests at Deir-es Zor, Sir Arnold Wilson established meetings with prominent sheikhs in order to explain the purpose of the mandate form of government and to reassure them about Britain's intentions. While some Iraqi leaders were guaranteed their autonomous status by the British, others were still suspicious. Wilson believed the fractured nature of Iraqi society, with sectarian divisions between Sunnis and Shias, a collection of minorities, and a sizeable but independently minded Kurdish population, meant that British rule would probably be required for years. His main concern was that social divisions might be exploited by the Turks, the Bolsheviks or radical Islamists, and the idea of local antagonism did not seem, in relative terms, a great threat.

In fact, the inspiration for violence came from an unexpected quarter. The Sharifian Arabs threatened to invade Iraq from Syria and encouraged the tribes of the north to kill all the British personnel they could find. Despite the daily patrolling of aircraft and armoured cars to the border at Tel Afar, on the night of 3 June 1920, Iraqi gendarmes mutinied and killed their British commanding officer. Tribesmen of the Shammar clan, loyal to the pro-Ottoman Ibn Rashid, then joined in and killed the remaining British officers, sacked the town and ambushed a British patrol. In Mosul, Iraqi Christians were attacked and murdered.

The British response was swift and comprehensive. The tribesmen were defeated outside Mosul, and they fled across the border back into

Syria. Tel Afar was retaken and demolished, and its population relocated deeper into Iraq.

A second wave of violence burst along the Euphrates, and, by July, most settlements were in tumult. Again, the British recovered the situation. At Hillah, Iraqi dissident leaders were arrested. The RAF flew sorties against rebellious villages, interdicting armed groups. The unrest thus began to dampen, and the rebellion appeared to have been suppressed successfully.

But more serious fighting was to follow. At Rumaitha, there was another outbreak, and the small British garrison there was besieged. A relief column came under fire and was beaten back. Crucially, in an ironic parallel with Lawrence's campaign, the railway between Basra and Baghdad was cut, and other means of communication were destroyed, including telegraph, telephone and river craft. At Samawah, a British detachment managed to get through to reinforce a small garrison, but soon after the railway link was broken and a relieving troop train was attacked: the Indian troops aboard were wiped out.

While defences south of Baghdad were reinforced, and troops belatedly concentrated, Brigadier General Frank Coningham, who commanded 51st Brigade, was ordered to relieve Rumaitha. As he advanced, he secured the railway line as his main line of communication with a series of blockhouses at 2-mile intervals, each held by a half company of around 40 men. The construction of these sandbagged bases nevertheless consumed much-needed manpower, just as the Ottomans had found only two years before. The topography also imposed delays, as deep ravines and broken rail tracks had to be traversed. Raiding during the advance was sporadic, but on 19 July a few miles north of Rumaitha, Coningham encountered a series of entrenchments held by about 5,000 Iraqis. Clearly directed by former Ottoman officers, the defences incorporated dried canals as communication and fire trenches, and the whole system was concealed with vegetation. Villages were incorporated into the fortifications too, acting as miniature fortresses and high points for observation.

Coningham launched three successive assaults, and each time his brigade was forced back. At dawn on 20 July he tried again, this time with a detachment of Lewis gunners from 1/10th Gurkhas assaulting on one flank: they poured enfilade fire into the Iraqi defences. The entire defensive system then collapsed and Rumaitha was quickly relieved.

At this point, the British government came under severe criticism for the whole policy of occupation and suppression. Lawrence's intervention was significant. Thanks to Lowell Thomas, Lawrence was now a household name. Consequently, his letter to *The Times* had an even greater impact. He had written, with the letterhead of All Souls College, Oxford: 'The Arabs rebelled against the Turks during the war not because the Turk Government was notably bad, but because they wanted independence. They did not risk their lives in battle to change masters, to become British subjects or French citizens, but to win a show of their own.'[18] But he was disingenuous and inaccurate when he wrote: 'Mesopotamia ... never fought the Turks, and only fought perfunctorily against us. Accordingly, we had to set up a wartime administration there. We had no choice; but that was two years ago, and we have not yet changed to peace conditions. Indeed, there are yet no signs of change.' His claim that the cost of occupation would be £50 million in 1921 was exaggerated speculation.

Yet Lawrence was accurate in his general assessment of the governance of Iraq:

> It has 450 British executive officers running it, and not a single responsible Mesopotamian. In Turkish days, 70 per cent of the executive civil service was local. Our 80,000 troops there are occupied in police duties, not in guarding the frontiers. They are holding down the people. In Turkish days the two army corps in Mesopotamia were 60 per cent Arab in officers, 95 per cent in other ranks. This deprivation of the privilege of sharing the defence and administration of their country is galling to the educated Mesopotamians. It is true we have increased prosperity – but who cares for that when liberty is in the other scale?[19]

His solution was Arab governance:

> I would make the Arabs do the work. They can. My little experience in helping to set up Feisal showed me that the art of government wants more character than brains... I would make Arabic the Government language. This would impose a reduction of the British staff, and a return to employment of the qualified Arabs.[20]

In addition, Lawrence advocated the formation of an Arab security force, which, in fact, already existed in the form of the Iraq levies.

Lawrence made no mention of the mutiny of one of these units at the start of the revolt. He was also perhaps over-optimistic in his assessment of the future:

> These changes would take 12 months, and we should then hold of Mesopotamia exactly as much (or as little) as we hold of South Africa or Canada. I believe the Arabs in these conditions would be as loyal as anyone in the Empire, and they would not cost us a cent.

Reinforced by Lawrence's outburst, the newspapers and prominent enemies of the Prime Minister, David Lloyd George, attacked what they felt was an expensive and self-defeating approach. Wildly exaggerated estimates of the cost soon followed.[21] The result was a serious impairment of the conduct of the campaign. The CIGS, Field Marshal Sir Henry Wilson, fought hard to get the reinforcements General Haldane needed to secure the country, but the Cabinet was now opposed.[22] When he suggested that reserves could be found by withdrawing the occupation garrison from Constantinople, two Cabinet members threatened to resign. There was an impasse over the future of Mosul too. The CIGS insisted it could not be abandoned lest it encourage further revolt amongst the Kurds.[23] The solution to the manpower crisis was to draw more men from India, but there were limits to this. The demobilization and reorganization after the war left few trained men available, while concurrent unrest in the Punjab, Egypt and Ireland imposed further strain on the numbers that could be brought to Iraq.[24]

The other option was a greater use of technological solutions and there was enthusiasm for 'air policing'.[25] During the course of the revolt, the RAF brought their strength up to 92 aircraft and their bombing missions dropped 100 tons of ordnance in just three months. Eleven aircraft were lost in the fighting, and at least two pilots, who were captured, were tortured and executed by the Iraqis. Nevertheless, aircraft could attack settlements where rebels were concentrated but which were out of reach of ground forces. When air and ground units worked in cooperation, providing surveillance and fire support, the Iraqi rebels were soon defeated.

In an echo of Lawrence's own experience, armoured cars of the Light Armoured Brigade also made an important contribution. Limited by the tactics and relative inexperience of the crews, armoured vehicles nevertheless provided cut-off groups, mobile machine gun platforms for the infantry, and covered the flanks and rear of other forces. At Tuwairij, for example, two armoured cars were rushed ahead of a column to prevent the Iraqis from burning a pontoon bridge, which would delay an assault on Karbala. The two cars single-handedly cut down 200 fighters and dispersed the rest. These actions assisted General Haldane to redeploy troops from the Euphrates, which had been quietened, to new areas of unrest, east of Baghdad. There, fines, mainly in the form of surrendered rifles, were imposed. Recalcitrance was met with the burning of villages and the seizure of livestock. The railway line was repaired and more blockhouses constructed along its length. The nodal points of the irrigation systems were then fortified and garrisoned, which sent an important signal to the local clans about who was in control.

Lawrence became aware that Winston Churchill had been given responsibility for the Iraq question before the announcement that he would be made Colonial Secretary, and also got news that Churchill was in communication with Hugh Trenchard, with plans to have the RAF take over responsibility for Iraq's security, while direct British administration would be confined to the coast. Lawrence met with Trenchard in the spring of 1920, and suggested that an RAF officer should act as both military and political chief of Iraq, but operate out of Cairo, with a second in command, in the form of Ronald Storrs, in Baghdad. Lawrence suggested Iraq should become an Arab state with British political advisors, in other words, an extension of the wartime role he had himself fulfilled. Meanwhile, Churchill believed that the rivalries of the Foreign Office, Colonial Office and India Office had clouded and confused judgements over the Middle East. He advocated the formation of a new, separate Middle East Department, full of bright individuals who could help satisfy the conflicting demands and produce a fresh, workable, and clear solution for the region. In February 1921, Churchill met Lawrence and invited him to join the new combination.[26]

Despite subsequent attempts by Iraqi nationalists to portray the uprising as a 'great, national struggle' and Lawrence's own solution in the letter to *The Times*, the unrest revealed deep fissures within Iraqi society. When Kurds in the north revolted in 1919, their objectives and actions were not aligned with the Arab Sunni and Shia populations in the south. The larger revolt of 1920 had, in fact, been a series of uncoordinated outbreaks. The motives of some groups had been opportunism for material gain; others strove for the ideological fulfilment of a theocracy; still others were secularists hoping to impose a modern form of government consisting entirely of Sunni Arabs. By late October 1920, each of them was defeated. Short of funding and support, and hemmed in by British forces, the leaders finally surrendered Najaf, the last symbolic centre of the uprising. It was a reminder that, if unaided by an external force, and without a guerrilla campaign, uncoordinated groups of fighters stood little chance against a modern army and air force.

The imperative after the revolt was to find a cheaper dispensation that was more acceptable to the Iraqi people. Between 1921 and 1922 Lawrence worked for Churchill at the Colonial Office as an advisor on Arab affairs, and, when Churchill decided to forego the idea of touring Mesopotamia, he endorsed the idea of a conference in Cairo which could bring together the regional actors. The hard work had already been done in London, with examination of all the options. Lawrence had sent a memorandum based on his conversations with Feisal, which gave some idea of what would be acceptable (including the ending of Arab claims to Palestine, the establishment of Trans-Jordan, and a resolution on the Hussein-Saudi conflict over the Nejd).[27] The main idea was to have the British and Indian army garrison in Iraq reduced, with security placed into the hands of the RAF, supported by a British police force of 'exceptional individual quality' and Indian troops selectively recruited.[28] Governance was offered to Feisal, who had been living in London after his ejection from Syria. It was recorded that he 'was very bitter about what he considered was the way in which he had been treated by both the British and the French, and he made some wounding remarks about British character in general'.[29] Churchill was eager to have him instated, although he pressed Sir Percy Cox to tell him whether Feisal would be accepted by the Iraqi people.[30]

Churchill visited the new French President, Alexandre Millerand, to gain French support, and found that 'the French are very ready to be conciliatory and accommodating to us', which he said was because they were 'pretty much in the same position' in Syria as Britain was in Iraq, namely 'sick of pouring out money and men on these newly acquired territories when all their great interests in Africa are denied the funds necessary to develop them'.[31]

The problem in late January 1921 was that Abdullah was no longer prepared to wait for diplomacy. He was agitating for an invasion of

Syria, to recover Damascus for Feisal. His forces were assembled at Amman, prompting French demands that he be turned out.[32] The proposed solution was to tell Abdullah that neither he nor Feisal would be backed by Britain in their respective monarchical positions if they did not desist from their conflict with France. If this position was at odds with Lawrence's views, the subsequent demand for Saud and other Arab chiefs to continue to receive generous financial support, while demanding cuts in the costs of the Iraq garrison, seemed more attuned to him.[33]

Churchill told Curzon at the Foreign Office that he was confident he could 'run' both Saud and Hussein and insist on them avoiding conflict with each other, in part through their subsidies.[34] He could not accept any of the other possible rival candidates to Feisal in Iraq because 'Ibn Saud would plunge the whole country into religious pandemonium ... Sayeb Taleb [is a] man of bad character and untrustworthy, [and Talib al-] Naqib [the former Ottoman governor of Basra] is tottering on [the] brink of the grave.'[35] Lawrence was active in persuading the British authorities to select Feisal to rule Iraq and for Abdullah to become the ruler of Trans-Jordan. He knew both men would need Britain and that would cement the relationship. In fact, he believed both sides needed each other.

Lawrence was posted as the British representative in Trans-Jordan and he persuaded Abdullah to terminate his planned operation against the French, promising that inaction would produce a united Syria 'in just six months'. The threat was that, if he marched north, the Saudis might use the opportunity of his absence to strike against the Hejaz, and, if he did not accept this advice the British would abandon him with the comment 'England has done what it can'.[36] Abdullah agreed to the terms offered.

There was also respite in the conflict between the Hashemites and the Saudis. Having been halted close to Mecca in 1919 by British demands, Ibn Saud turned his attention to continuing the conflict with the Shammar. His operations had gone successfully, but the British wanted this conflict to be terminated too. They wanted to pacify the region and develop its ports, commercial air routes and cities, so that the mandates had a chance to take root. Ibn Saud was offered a large subsidy of £100,000 a year, the same pension being offered to Hussein, in return for a cessation of hostilities. For a few years, Saud accepted the provisions, although he remained implacable against the influx of Jewish settlers into Palestine and refused to accept anything but Arab administration there. In fact, despite unrest in 1921 in Palestine, the policies of its governor, Herbert Samuel, did much to end hostilities between rival Arab and Jewish communities.

Hussein proved more determined.[37] Lawrence, the primary negotiator, tried every method to persuade him to accept the mandate provisions and the arrangement of the regional states as they now stood. Hussein refused, obstructed, and claimed betrayal; Lawrence cajoled, threatened withdrawal of all support, and coaxed with offers of British royal approval.[38] Hussein was unmoved, and, when Lawrence withdrew, he still held out.[39] It was this that left Hussein exposed in 1924 to a renewed Saudi offensive, one which carried the Wahabis into Mecca and Medina.[40] Hussein was driven out of the Hejaz and took refuge in Aqaba, then Cyprus and finally Trans-Jordan, symbolically abdicating in protest.

Lawrence's verdict as he left his post in 1922 was that 'we were quit of the war-time eastern adventure, with clean hands'.[41] The comment has been much criticized, in light of subsequent conflicts in the Middle East.[42] But Lawrence cannot have known what was to come. As things stood, he observed that, finally, the Arab leaders had achieved dignified positions of authority, free of colonial occupation. His war aims had largely been achieved. He opposed the French position in Syria, but he felt Feisal had instead acquired the far more significant region of Iraq, a country with a more promising future ahead of it. Abdullah had taken possession of Trans-Jordan, at the heart of Arabia. Britain's other Arab partners were secure. Even Hussein, for all his truculence, seemed, at the time, to be firm in Mecca. The 'clean hands' were Britain's: it had, in the end, honoured the Arabs who had fought alongside it, and far earlier than it would realize its debt, in political terms, to its Indian, Asian and African colonial subjects.

REFLECTIONS ON GUERRILLA WAR: CORRESPONDENCE WITH LIDDELL HART

Captain Basil Liddell Hart, the influential British military thinker, was undoubtedly enamoured by Lawrence's ideas on war.[43] His advocacy of an 'indirect strategy', over direct, frontal operations, was in part a reaction to the high casualties of the Western Front in the First World War, but it was also the product of conversations and correspondence with Lawrence over some years. Liddell Hart shared Lawrence's belief that distilling historical insights would offer the chance to avoid the disasters in modern war and ensure a more cost-effective route to success. Like Lawrence, he imagined technological solutions in the form of air power and mechanized land forces using manoeuvre at the tactical level and indirect ways and means at the strategic. These ideas were also advocated by J. F. C. Fuller who considered concentrations of air and armoured forces driving deep into enemy territory to destroy their 'nervous system'.[44] The psychological aspects of this were central, since acquiring an advantage demanded moves that were unexpected, and which left the enemy unprepared to meet them.

In the opening of his popular work on strategy, Liddell Hart asserted: 'throughout the ages, effective results in war have rarely been attained unless the approach has had such indirectness as to ensure the opponent's unreadiness to meet it. The indirectness has usually been physical, and always psychological. In strategy, the longest way round is often the shortest way home.'[45]

Guerrilla or irregular warfare seemed to offer one mechanism for the fulfilment of an indirect strategy, but it was an approach that, in later years, Liddell Hart came to realize imposed terrible consequences in the long term. He wrote:

A realisation of the dangerous aftermath of guerrilla warfare came to me in reflection on Lawrence's campaigns in Arabia and our discussion on the subject. My book on those campaigns, an exposition of the theory of guerrilla warfare, was taken as a guide by numerous leaders of commando units and resistance movements in the last war [of 1939–45]... But I was beginning to have doubts – not of its immediate efficacy, but of its long-term effects. It seemed that they could be traced, like a thread, running through the persisting troubles that we, as the Turks' successors, were suffering in the same area where Lawrence had spread the Arab Revolt.[46]

Liddell Hart was therefore concerned that 'these lessons of history were too lightly disregarded by those who planned to promote violent insurrections as part of our war policy'.[47] On the other hand, the 'immediate efficacy' had been sufficient to sustain his ideas on how one should use manoeuvre to create operational advantages. He examined Lawrence's reasoning and then considered how these should be applied to conventional warfare, even if it was 'admittedly an extreme form of the indirect approach'.[48]

He began with the calculus of the two belligerents: 'The Arabs were both more mobile and less able to bear casualties than orthodox armies. The Turks were almost insusceptible to loss of men, but not to loss of material – of which they suffered a scarcity.' To this Liddell Hart then added the question of flexibility: 'Superb at sitting tight in a trench, firing at a directly oncoming target, they were neither adaptable to, nor able to endure the strain of, fluid operations.' In this remark, Liddell Hart was rather dismissing the logistical and transport constraints on the Ottomans, but his observations on the mathematics of the case were largely correct: 'They were trying to hold down a vast area of country with a quantity of men which was not large enough to spread itself in a network of posts over the area [and] they depended on a long and frail line of communications.'[49]

This had been a direct reference to Lawrence's calculation that, to hold down the Arabs, the Ottomans would have needed one post every four square miles, each of 20 men. Lawrence had reasoned that this would require, for the region, 600,000 men and was satisfied that only 100,000 were available. He had written: 'Our success was certain, to be proved by pencil and paper as soon as the proportion of space and number had been learned.'[50] Liddell Hart commented that 'such a calculation, although oversimplified, embodies a general truth'.[51] The problem was that Lawrence predicated the idea on an enemy that was entirely fixed, and he didn't have to consider, in his context, a highly mobile counter-insurgency force.

Liddell Hart also noted that the 'relative morales' of the belligerents mattered, as did the terrain, where urban areas were unfavourable to the guerrilla. Even remote regions could create mixed fortunes for the insurgents, with problems of access and distance from their targets, the most important of which was the population. The objective was always, stated Liddell Hart, 'to produce the enemy's increasing overstretch, physical and moral'.[52] But peripheral borderlands, while offering protection to the guerrillas, could impose the very overstretch and demoralization that they hoped to inflict on their enemies. Liddell Hart made no mention of this exact phenomenon affecting the Arab Revolt in the winter of 1917–18.

He was therefore correct in his assertion that the ratio of space to forces could not be separated from the 'psychological-cum-political factors'. The attitude of the people was the most critical element, not least in intelligence on which their security would depend: 'Guerrilla war', he wrote, 'is waged by the few but dependent on the support of the many.'[53] A combination of a plea 'to national resistance or desire for independence with an appeal to a socially and economically discontent population' was the ideal.

Liddell Hart was less convinced about the idea of guerrilla warfare during the Second World War and the Cold War. It had appealed to Churchill during the Second World War because of his temperament and pugnacious desire to strike back at Hitler's regime in occupied Europe, but also because he 'had been a close associate and admirer of Lawrence'.[54] It was Churchill's desire to practise on a larger scale what Lawrence had demonstrated in a relatively limited theatre in Arabia. Liddell Hart noted that few dared criticize the policy of 'setting Europe ablaze' but his conclusion was that partisan warfare had been 'little more than a nuisance' to the Axis powers, unless they 'coincided with the operations of a strong regular army that was engaging the enemy's front and drawing off his reserves'. This had been precisely the situation in Lawrence's campaign.

Like Lawrence, Liddell Hart speculated that armed insurgency was perhaps no more effective than widespread passive resistance, while armed guerrillas brought more harm to their own country because of reprisals. Interestingly, Liddell Hart noted that guerrillas might even restore morale amongst counter-insurgents in that 'They afforded his troops the opportunity for violent action that is always a relief to the nerves of a garrison in an unfriendly country.'[55] What concerned Liddell Hart was that while patriotic resistance might seem noble, it could impair the long-term recovery of a country. Moreover, guerrilla movements tended to attract 'bad hats', that is, men of a criminal disposition. Lawrence had sought out such men for his personal bodyguard because they owed no loyalty to anyone or anything other than himself. But Liddell Hart saw a strategic consequence in guerrilla warfare that affected detrimentally the cost-benefit calculus of conflict.

Famously, he wrote:

Nations do not wage war for war's sake, but in pursuance of policy.
The military objective is only the means to a political end. Hence the
military objective should be governed by the political objective ...
The objective in war is a better state of peace – even if only from your
own point of view. Hence it is essential to conduct war with constant
regard to the peace you desire.[56]

He believed, like many of his generation, that waging a war that left the
country in a worse state was evidence of a strategic failure, since strategy
was 'the art of distributing and applying military means to fulfill the
ends of policy'.[57]

Liddell Hart's appreciation of Lawrence resonates in the pages of
his work, including his criticism of the mathematical and mechanistic
approaches he saw in Jomini and the other adherents of that doctrinal
genre such as Foch. His understanding of the complex and contested
nature of pre-war French thinking was nevertheless limited, and his
assessment of Foch, who was much-lauded after the war for the Allied
victory in 1918, was therefore critical. In his anthology of axioms by
the commanders of world history, Foch's *Principles of War* are cited
briefly, with the quotation: 'No strategy can henceforth prevail over
that which aims at ensuring tactical results, victory by fighting.
A strategy paving the way to tactical decisions alone: this is the end
we come to in following a study that has produced so many learned
theories.'[58] This thinking, Liddell Hart believed, had been the result
of a misunderstanding stemming back to Clausewitz.[59] The Prussians
had been shocked by the success of the French Revolutionary and
Napoleonic methods of war, and Clausewitz had tried to understand
its driving forces.

The German's conclusion was that the old strategy of manoeuvre
was hopeless against the directness, simplicity, violence and energy of
the French Army. In the late nineteenth century, this interpretation
had surprised French officers, who, while acknowledging Napoleon's
search for decisive battles, had made extensive use of '*manoeuvre sur
les derrieres*', a movement against the enemy's rear. Liddell Hart seized
upon these observations to reinforce his own arguments of how to avoid
the Germanic direct and bloody approach.[60]

His preference was for surprise, manoeuvre, 'the moral plane' (that is, morale and psychological operations), and presenting multiple options for the enemy to induce hesitation, doubt, or the wrong choice of action.[61] He then considered how Lawrence's indirect approach, if time permitted, might be generalizable:

> Its application to the problem of normal warfare is conditioned by the factors of time, space, and force. While it is a quickened and active form of blockade, it is inherently slower to take effect than a strategy of dislocation. Hence, if national conditions make a quick issue imperative the latter appears preferable. But unless the end is sought by an indirect approach, the short cut is likely to prove slower, more costly, and more dangerous than the 'Lawrence' strategy.[62]

Liddell Hart attributed the success against the Ottomans to Allenby's offensive, but claimed a 'significant part' by the Arab forces. He seemed sure that those who discounted Allenby's success on the grounds of casualties suffered or inflicted were in error because 'their scale of values is governed by the dogma of Clausewitz [in] that blood is the price of victory', which is classic Lawrence.[63] On the other hand, Liddell Hart was more certain that the 'decaying morale' of the Ottomans was due in part to the manoeuvres of both Allenby's army and the Arab guerrilla campaign.

The key, he argued, had been mastery of the lines of communications, on which he quoted Napoleon. Cutting the enemy's lines of logistics and communications paralysed the adversary's physical organization, and closing them paralysed its moral organization. To destroy the line of communication meant the paralysis, he argued, of its sensory organization, that is the link between 'brain and body'.[64] This final effect he attributed not to guerrilla operations but to the air force. He explained the RAF had cleared the skies, blinding the German and Ottoman commanders. The bombing of telephone and telegraph nodes at Afule had cut off their ability to communicate. The contribution that Lawrence and his Arab partners had made was to simultaneously sever the railway at Deraa, depriving the Ottomans temporarily of their supply chain and thus compelling them to divert vital reserves to that nodal junction from which three lines radiated. The railway nodes were out of reach of Allenby's army, but Lawrence had created what Liddell

Hart would refer to as a 'strategic barrage' in depth. In the 1940s, this interdiction became an air force task, isolating enemy fighting formations at the front and depriving them of critical combat supplies and munitions. Lawrence predicted, to Liddell Hart, that 'What the Arabs did yesterday the Air Forces could do tomorrow.' He added: 'And in the same way and more swiftly.'[65]

Lawrence aided Liddell Hart's understanding of how to extract the generalizable aspects of the war in the desert of 1916–18 into a general theory. Lawrence had written: 'To provoke the soldiers to battle on my own ground I kept on limiting what I said to irregular warfare. But', he continued, 'for irregular war' one could write 'war of movement in nearly every place, and find the argument fitted as well or ill as it did.'[66] Liddell Hart urged Lawrence to write the entry into *Encyclopaedia Britannica* on guerrilla war and learned of the limited edition of *Seven Pillars*. He made extensive use of Lawrence's thinking, but did not always attribute the ideas to their source.[67]

It was Lawrence's caustic comments that gave Liddell Hart the confidence to adopt a more insistent and sometimes strident tone in his own work. As one biographer noted:

> Liddell Hart ... tended to link this capacity for independent and critical judgement with Lawrence's outspokenness. Lawrence thus served as a model for Liddell Hart to inveigh against two of his bugbears: the mentally cramping effects of military professionalism and the tendency of British soldiers to acquiesce unduly in the hierarchy of seniority.[68]

Lawrence was keen to distance himself from his past life, but passed on his approval for Liddell Hart's approach, noting it was 'a queer experience – like going back, in memory, to school – for by myself ... I had trodden all this road before the war'.[69]

It was also Lawrence who contributed to Liddell Hart's rediscovery of the eighteenth-century military thinkers, in an era before the totalizing ideology of the French revolutionaries and the subsequent desire for a decisive battle that would annihilate the enemy, and, in so doing, cost the societies that waged such war very dearly. It was not all Lawrence's doing, as there was a strong desire to seek alternatives to the costly battles of Europe in 1914–18. Hans Delbrück in Germany,

Sir Julian Corbett in his work on maritime strategy, and J. F. C. Fuller in his thoughts on mechanized warfare had each reached the same deductions. Liddell Hart picked up the theme himself, advocating the psychological as well as the physical dislocation of the enemy. He offered a revision of the standard interpretation of Clausewitz, noting the subtle distinction, that while Clausewitz had advocated 'the employment of battle (perhaps combat would be a better translation) as a means to gain the object of war', Liddell Hart noted that this battle should be brought about 'under the most advantageous circumstances' possible, which meant, in Lawrence's terms, the perfection of strategy would be, sometimes, to 'produce a decision without any fighting'.[70]

Lawrence was aware that Liddell Hart, like himself, was more than a chronicler of the past; he was also an advocate of a particular line of argument. They were aligned because they both felt that the war had not been conducted as economically in lives and resources as it should have been. There was no shortage of determination and will in 1914–18, but they felt that there had been an absence of critical thinking. Lawrence also observed that, across the ages, certain strategic ideas were in fashion and were then corrected by an alternative. He summed this up with a comment in a letter to Liddell Hart in 1928 where he had written:

> A surfeit of the 'hit' school brings on an attack of the 'run' method; and then the pendulum swings back. You, at present, are trying … to put the balance straight after the orgy of the late war. When you succeed (about 1945) your sheep will pass your bounds of discretion, and have to be chivvied back by some later strategist. Back and forward we go.[71]

Liddell Hart made the observation in his own writings, but his search for a general theory of strategy led him to elide over the specific conditions which had given rise to a particular approach in his early work. He also tended to downplay the economic and social constraints of each era, in favour of a purely operational approach, or attributing failure to an erroneous set of decisions.[72] He had a tendency to focus on individual commanders too, which in part explains his hagiography of Lawrence.[73] He did not always appreciate the complex and competing sets of demands that shaped decision-making.

There were plenty of critics of Liddell Hart, and therefore, by extension, of Lawrence's assumptions, at least in the way that Liddell Hart presented them. Spenser Wilkinson, the Chichele Professor in the History of War at Lawrence's own college at Oxford after the war, namely All Souls, disagreed with Liddell Hart's abuse of Clausewitz. The problem is a common one. Many who read Clausewitz do so in order to seek some better way of conducting war, including insights into operational or strategic success. But even the incomplete versions of *On War* that were published, posthumously, were not designed to be used in this way. Clausewitz made extensive use of dialectical methods to explore the philosophical foundations of war, that is, its very essence or '*Natur*'. That said, Clausewitz had set out with the purpose of revealing the insight that would make war understandable. He had rejected a purely theoretical approach and aimed to ground his conclusions on the hard realities of war. The deduction he eventually reached was that decisive action was necessary.

Spenser Wilkinson therefore advocated that 'The war that aims at striking down the enemy by the destruction of his forces is that of a successful State; the war that tries to limit its aims, and therefore its exertions, is that of the defeated.'[74] Wilkinson criticized Liddell Hart and others who argued that the entire Western Front campaign had been a waste of resources, and noted the imperative that had existed to defend France by a sufficient concentration of forces in Western Europe. Wilkinson was critical of some of the decisions that were made in the war, not least in its early stages, but he was not prepared to tolerate the inaccurate and caricatured version presented by Liddell Hart. Professor Azar Gat, in his seminal study of military thought, concludes that Liddell Hart was guilty, like Clausewitz in his own day, of pushing a line of argument very strongly, as a reaction to their immediate experiences: 'The difference between them, of course, was only that one had stood at the dawn of the total war and called on his country for an all-out national effort ... whereas a century later the other witnessed the peaking of total war and preached restraint and a return to manoeuvre.'[75] 'Back and forth', just as Lawrence had put it.

Lawrence had called for 'hard study and brain-work', seeking to apply an appropriate strategy to the context in which he found himself. Liddell Hart was searching for a general theory, and was eager to make use of history to serve that purpose. Here was the fundamental contradiction between these two thinkers on war. It is also a salutary reminder about the instrumentalization of any insights on the conduct of war, and the value of thinking carefully, and critically, about the specific conditions that strategists may encounter.

THE WEIGHT OF REPUTATION

Lowell Thomas's shows on 'Lawrence of Arabia', and Lawrence's desire to escape the publicity, fuelled by the failure to achieve his ambitions, led to his desire to seek a 'monastic' anonymity in the Royal Air Force. He obtained permission to enlist as an aircraftsman under the assumed name of John Hume Ross. The press discovered his subterfuge and played on the subject, until the RAF had Lawrence dismissed. In 1924, Lawrence tried another route. He joined the Royal Tank Regiment at Bovington in Dorset under the name of Thomas Edward Shaw, but he found the return to the army unsatisfactory. In his spare time, he discovered the ruined cottage close to the barracks at Moreton which he subsequently renovated as Cloud's Hill. But he really wanted to return to the RAF, and lobbied a number of prominent public figures to obtain permission.

Lawrence was clearly at a low ebb. In a letter to Edward Garnett, his literary editor, he wrote that his manuscript, *Seven Pillars*, was utterly disappointing: 'what muck, irredeemable, irremediable, the whole thing is! My gloomy view of it deepens each time I have to wade through it.'[76] He felt that a rejection of his request to rejoin the RAF meant 'I'm going to quit: but in my usual comic fashion I'm going to finish the reprint ... before I hop it!' Concerns that Lawrence meant to commit suicide if he didn't fulfil this objective prompted Garnett, George Bernard Shaw, and John Buchan to lobby on his behalf and avoid the potential national scandal of a war hero taking his own life.

As a result, Lawrence rejoined the RAF, and he was stationed in Cranwell, until, the following year, he was posted to India as a clerk.[77] In May 1928, he was sent to the 'brick and barbed wire fort' at Miranshah, in Waziristan on the North-West Frontier with Afghanistan.[78] In July, an American journalist invented a story and submitted it to the *New York World* claiming that Lawrence had disappeared because he was a spy operating in Persia, Yemen and Arabia.[79] The story was not published, but speculation increased when Amir Amanullah, the king of Afghanistan, was violently deposed after years of unpopular Westernizing policies. In December that year, Lawrence's presence close to the Afghan border seemed to suggest that he was involved. A week later, the *Daily Herald* announced that the Afghan authorities had ordered the arrest of Lawrence for espionage, and circulated the rumour that Lawrence was at that moment in Amritsar disguised as a Muslim saint. One man, mistaken for Lawrence, was beaten by a mob.[80]

Stories of British covert action were generating anti-British unrest, despite official Afghan denials about the stories. Amid critical parliamentary questions, the Foreign Secretary, Austen Chamberlain, ordered Lawrence back to Britain. The chances of remaining in the RAF seemed slim, but Lawrence was transferred to work on rescue boats in southern England. Despite his desire to keep a low profile, he continued to correspond with a large number of prominent literary figures, including Robert Graves, Thomas Hardy, Noel Coward and E. M. Forster, and he kept up his own writing habits. Despite another period of depression, Lawrence was eventually transferred to the Marine Aircraft Experimental Establishment at Felixstowe. His final posting was Bridlington, in November 1934, until, as he had planned, he left the RAF in February 1935. He moved into Cloud's Hill in Dorset, and, as he had predicted in 1928, he would 'streak home top-speed' on his favourite Brough motorcycle. Two months after leaving the service, Lawrence was involved in a road accident. He died on 18 May 1935, five days later.

The man was dead, but the legend was not. And Lawrence's ideas were to be invoked in irregular conflicts, from the missions of Special Operations Executive in the Second World War through to those of Special Operations Forces in the Iraq War. But, as with Liddell Hart, this instrumentalization of his thinking was not always as authentic as it could have been.

I5

Instrumentalizing Lawrence's Ideas
in Other Wars

Lawrence's ideas on guerrilla warfare have been considered, extensively cited, and sometimes adopted, since the First World War. Although superseded by other theorists, especially during the Cold War, Lawrence is still regarded as a significant authority in irregular operations. He even features in curricula of professional military education and often reappears in doctrinal publications.

The reason for Lawrence's apotheosis as prophet of guerrilla warfare is well known. His appearance in the innovative and popular film documentary on the Middle East campaign, in Lowell Thomas's 'With Allenby and Lawrence in Arabia', in New York and London in the 1920s turned Lawrence into an international celebrity, and his books confirmed him in more serious literary circles. His popularity immortalized him.

The difficulty, or perhaps the appeal, in the popular endorsement was Lawrence's 'otherness'. What he represented was a quintessential British figure who, to use the derogatory parlance, had 'gone native'. Although a lot closer to the official line than he liked to admit, this cultivation of Lawrence as a maverick emphasized the individualism of both the man and the archetypal guerrilla commander. In this exceptionalism, he seemed to have much in common with many later irregular warfare proponents, including the British commander of the Chindits, Orde Wingate.[1] Lawrence was nevertheless distinct as an advocate, not only of irregular war, but of the diplomacy that was required to convert military action into lasting political change. He was compelled, by force of circumstance, to adopt this approach and in both the conflict and in the peace-making, he was dependent on a particular backdrop, namely the scale and influence of the British Empire and its conventional forces, to achieve his ends. His own efforts were not always successful. Making use of Lawrence in a superficial manner can miss this important aspect of the way in which he operated, his dependencies, and the unique context of the ideas that underpinned his actions.

The potential that irregular forces accompanied by enterprising regular officers had, operating stealthily behind enemy lines, and causing disproportionate strategic effect, was the basis of Winston Churchill's enthusiasm for them in the Second World War. Churchill had seen for himself the damage that commandos could do in the South African War at the turn of the century, and his association with Lawrence reinforced his expectation that Europe could be 'set ablaze' to discomfit the Nazi regime as it occupied the European continent. The individual Churchill looked to in that effort was Colonel (later General) Colin Gubbins.

Gubbins had served on the Western Front in the Great War, but he had also experienced at first hand the effects of Bolshevik subversion during the military mission to Russia. There he noted the absence of continuous fronts, and the key role played by intelligence and propaganda.[2] He went on to serve as an intelligence officer in Ireland during the unrest there, deriving considerable insight into both counter-guerrilla and insurgent operations. He noted, for example, how vulnerable guerrilla fighters were, especially in terms of intercepted communications and documents. He also commented on the threat, and the opportunity, posed by informers and clandestine operatives, particularly those in innocuous occupations.[3] He started to formulate principles, such as the value of mobility, hit-and-run raids, and the need for operational security. Nevertheless, these were early interests, and historian Eunan O'Halpin noted that Ireland was perhaps not the most influential factor in the emergence of Special Operations Executive (SOE). O'Halpin cited Guy Liddell, an MI5 officer, who said the advisory and supporting role of the wartime SOE was based on the Arab Bureau.[4] What we do know is that when war seemed imminent in 1939, Section D of military intelligence and the General Staff (Research) branch were tasked to examine how to conduct partisan warfare and how it might be supported. Under Gubbins' direction, they immediately scoured the historical records, and, while adding the significant development of air power in coercing insurgents in the inter-war years, they paid particular attention to Lawrence's campaign.[5]

Gubbins agreed with Lawrence's idea that the guerrilla must force the enemy to disperse his strength, to protect lines of communications, depots, flanks and detachments.[6] He also endorsed the importance of psychology, both of one's own forces and the population around them. Nevertheless, Gubbins was interested in producing a greater psychological effect on the enemy than a material one. Lawrence had made arguably less specific references to Ottoman soldiers' morale, but Gubbins believed this was a fundamental target. He concluded: 'To inflict damage and death on the enemy and to escape scot-free has an irritant and depressing effect on the enemy's spirit.'[7]

Both Lawrence and Gubbins believed that intelligence, derived from the population, was another crucial element, but this could also be achieved by the public withholding cooperation with the enemy.[8] Gubbins believed that fostering patriotism and ensuring good treatment of the population were essential. This led him to the same conclusion as Lawrence, that the presence of foreign officers, even as advisors, could be problematic. The ideal partisan leader was a local, with all the credibility of being independent. However, he felt there was a requirement that this leader had some military training, and, if not, it would be necessary to appoint serving officers to serve with the guerrillas.[9]

Gubbins diverged from Lawrence in several respects. Where Lawrence had counted on the desert being devoid of an enemy presence, Gubbins assumed that the enemy would hold any occupied territory strongly and this, in turn, meant a greater emphasis on stealth and security. It also meant, contra Lawrence, that the partisan would not necessarily be able to count on an unassailable base. Gubbins had to assume his enemy would deploy a range of counter-measures, and be highly mobile, unlike the largely 'fixed' Ottomans.[10] He believed a modern enemy would make full use of mechanized forces, motorized transport and air power to move rapidly to any threatened point. They would employ counter-ambushes, the interrogation of suspects, infiltration of guerrilla groups, and surveillance of movement and communications.

If guerrillas were driven from their homes, finding a secure base in remote areas seemed imperative, but Gubbins was unsure if this was truly viable. He foresaw immense difficulties in movement, supplies, and other challenges that offset the value of concealment.[11]

Lawrence had tried to keep the Arab guerrillas independent, believing they did not operate well alongside regular forces. He had been able to assume that the Ottomans could never spare the forces necessary to pursue and cordon areas of operation.[12] Gubbins did not think that guerrillas could succeed on their own at all. He saw the value of the Arab forces as Allenby had done, as a phenomenon that could distract the enemy, tie up some of their fighting power, and act as a drain on resources while the 'main effort' was conducted elsewhere. At the end of the campaign, large guerrilla formations, Gubbins believed, would eventually fight 'in conjunction with the operations of regular troops'.[13]

Gubbins saw the future as one where Lawrence's conception of the algebra of space was transformed into the algebra of people: large populations would be used to conceal guerrillas just as the desert had done in 1917–18.[14] But this was a somewhat limited interpretation of Lawrence. It seems clear that Lawrence had a much broader view of the algebra of war, one that encompassed not just territorial space but populations, resources, funds and munitions. Gubbins should be forgiven though, for his objective was to glean as much value as possible from Lawrence's philosophical thinking for the practical business of fighting an imminent, existential threat.

The initial operations of SOE were an attempt to put into practice what had been derived from the past, but, while those actions lie beyond the scope of this book, there were some hard-won lessons to come. SOE operations to Albania in 1940–41, for example, were plagued with difficulties including language, social organization, political conflicts and the problem of reaching any nascent partisan force.[15] Like the first fateful missions of the SAS and OSS, theory could only take the operatives so far. Context was everything.

Paradoxically, a figure one might have assumed to have embraced the theories put forward by Lawrence, rejected them entirely. Orde Wingate, who emerged as a controversial exponent of operations behind enemy lines in South East Asia during the Second World War, was a distant relative of Lawrence, but he deplored the cult status that surrounded him.[16] In Abyssinia, during operations against the Italians, Wingate refused to accept local tribal support unless he was absolutely certain he could rely on their appearance and adherence to orders.[17]

His innovation in Palestine, the Special Night Squads, a Jewish force of patrolling units, was designed to counter guerrillas by employing similar methods, and it was successful in deriving critical intelligence, but the personnel, while drawn in part from the population, were a far cry from Lawrence's model, except insofar as they looked to control particular areas of operation. Wingate was eager to take a practical approach, in contrast to Lawrence's apparent search for the philosophical in war, emphasizing only the value of training, discipline and techniques.

The greatest similarity usually drawn between Lawrence and Wingate is in the deployment of the Chindits, the Long-Range Penetration Group, to South East Asia. While worthy of a comparative study in itself, there are very significant contrasts. The 'guerrilla force' consisted of some trained Burmese troops, but was dominated by British and Indian personnel. Inserted into the highly vegetated interior of the region in 1943, and resupplied by air, the Chindit columns attempted to attack Japanese supply lines or more isolated forces. The conditions were so severe that heavy losses and Japanese pressure reduced what could be achieved. In the second campaign of 1944, Wingate sought to establish fortified bases in strategic locations, from which columns would strike out once again against Japanese logistics and infrastructure. There were also plans to inspire a general uprising amongst the Burmese population, such as the Kachins of the north. Heavy casualties, in part through diseases, Japanese counter-measures, and severe fighting have created controversy about the value of the operations ever since.[18]

ROMANTICIZING GUERRILLA WARFARE DURING THE COLD WAR

The first paradox of the alleged Arab war of 'national' liberation of 1916–18, like those at the close of the era of European empires in Africa and Asia, is that it took place amongst peoples without a sense of national identity or unity.[19] Identities associated with nation states, where they did exist, were imagined, borrowed from European ideologies, created, forged, and propagated in an instrumentalist fashion by more educated vanguards. But, for Lawrence, these nationalist elites were too European: his model was an 'Orientalist' ideal. In many ways, it irritated Lawrence that so many regarded him as a hero when he wished to create a heroic myth about the Arab liberation cause itself.

But Lawrence's leadership role resonated with later revolutionary causes. In many 'liberation' struggles, 'heroic', charismatic and personal leadership mattered, whether it was national, sub-national or transnational. Men like Fidel Castro emphasized a communist revolution for Cuba and Ernesto 'Che' Guevara tried to transcend national agendas with focoism. Kwame Nkrumah sought to build a pan-African consensus from his base in Ghana. Mao became an Asian liberationist icon, and, like Marx and Lenin, largely after his achievements were complete, but he was always most popular in developing countries with a rural majority in the population.

The guerrilla armies they led often had profound political consequences. Armies continued to provide the basis of national identity or the means of governance in 'liberated' states. Indeed, military rule often proved to be the only means left to govern a faction-ridden or ethnically divided state where efforts to build a national identity based on a monarchical head of state, or a representative government, had failed. Many guerrilla movements have been seen as part of an inevitable march of progressive politics. Liberation struggles in the era of decolonization have been attributed with a somewhat romantic reputation largely by the liberated states themselves as they sought to create new national identities and histories. All too often the assumption has been that victory is the default outcome for guerrilla forces, the over-optimistic verdict of many scholars on the political left during the Cold War, and an error which has sometimes deceived even the revolutionary organizations themselves. Under the right circumstances, there have been some dramatic examples of successful insurgencies in the twentieth century, as in the case of China and Cuba, and some where even the Superpowers were forced to concede defeat, such as Vietnam and Afghanistan, but there are also many examples where liberationist guerrillas were defeated or contained.

Guerrillas of liberation movements faced a number of challenges far removed from the confident narrative of 'inevitability', including communal rivalry, faction fighting and a lack of finances. To this we should add the alienation of the majority of the population by violence, difficulty of obtaining weapons, the challenges of resupply or movement, and, frequently, heavy casualties. Historically, guerrillas were often dependent on circumstances of specific terrain, the attitude of the civilian population, the will of the government they opposed, and the determination and skill of the individual guerrilla fighters rather than purely on ideology. Above all, acquiring legitimacy has been a common problem for many insurgent movements.

In his theory of Revolutionary Warfare, Mao, like Lawrence, believed that, since war was an extension of politics, it was the political agenda that should dominate – that is, the appeal to the people. The quality and quantity of revolutionary military strength was, Mao argued, only directly proportional to the political commitment or attitude of the people. Famously, Mao advocated the application of the 'Three Unities', namely 'political activities, first, as applied to the troops; second, as applied to the people; and, third, as applied to the enemy'. He wrote: 'The fundamental problems are: first, spiritual unification of officers and men within the army; second spiritual unification of the army and the people; and, last, destruction of the unity of the enemy.'[20] The similarity with Lawrence's suggested 'arrangement of the minds' of local forces, the population, and the enemy, is uncanny.[21]

Nevertheless, Mao developed his theory in response to specific weaknesses and there is no evidence to show he consulted Lawrence's work.[22] Unable to confront the nationalist Kuomintang army head-on, standing amidst a large, ill-educated rural population, and faced with a vast, pre-industrial society with a weak transport infrastructure, Mao was forced to use indirect methods to turn each of these weaknesses to an advantage: emphasizing the simple, sloganized political education of the masses, trading space for time, and withdrawing into the deep hinterland whenever he was challenged by superior forces to practise a wearing out strategy. After the event, this pragmatism was elevated to 'heroic' status and became the standard approach for guerrillas in rural, less developed countries struggling for national liberation.

In terms of motivation, not all fight selflessly for national liberation. As Lawrence showed, some fight for money, for revenge for the death or displacement of family, or for the recovery of land from the state. Perception is especially important in motivation: what fighters and populations believe to be true can far outweigh the actual truth of their situation. The Sharifians were encouraged by the military presence of Allenby's EEF and believed in their own strength. But for all the praise lavished on their raiding and attritional, 'wearing out', strategy, the mode of warfare they adopted was, in fact, the only option left to them.

Better-equipped armies usually seek to resolve a revolutionary, guerrilla conflict quickly – by forcing the insurgents to give battle and inflicting defeats. The Ottomans had tried to crush the nascent rising in 1916 and may have succeeded had there been no external intervention. British assistance enabled the Sharifian forces to sustain the campaign, and to exploit both time and space. Similarly, Mao, aware that China lent itself to a war of time, space and the infiltration of large and potentially irresistible masses, deliberately set out to prolong war so that the enemy power would gradually tire of the campaign, politically and economically, and seek a resolution. This belief in exhausting the strategic patience of an adversary further reinforced the idea of the 'inevitability' of insurgent victory.

The motivation of revolutionaries who have embarked on a war of liberation may be dominated by pragmatic concerns, but conflicts take on a dynamic of their own. Mounting casualties can make the idea of compromise and reconciliation to a government less attractive. As the numbers of martyrs and the frequency of incidents of heavy-handedness by state security forces accumulate, so the revolutionary cause can deepen and broaden. Lawrence warned, however, that Arab communities would not sustain operations if they lost heavily. Despite his criticism of the direct, bloody approach to war, he did still recognize its necessity.

To increase support, insurgents need to polarize the loyalties of the population and discipline their own side using the rhetorical justification of a national or higher cause. Bernard Fall noted that insurgents had to establish 'a competitive system of control over the population'.[23] 'To do this', he stated, 'they had to kill some of the occupying forces and attack some of the military targets.' 'But', he added, 'above all they had to kill their own people who collaborated with the enemy.' The goal was nevertheless to assert a psychological defeat in the minds of the enemy. As the defence specialist and former Marine Thomas X. Hammes noted: 'They [the insurgents] know they cannot militarily defeat the outside power. Instead, they seek to destroy the outside power's political will so that it gives up and withdraws forces. They seek to do so by causing political, economic, social, and military damage to the target nation.' He reminded his readers that 'You don't outfight the insurgent; you outgovern him.'[24]

After the war, Lawrence advocated more of a general strike or a coup than a war, but he was aware of the disastrous historical track record of protests against the forces of an organized and determined state authority.

The key to Mao's concept of victory was the support of the population and the development of an alternative 'shadow' government. Educating the people by simple political arguments, while exploiting their grievances and claiming to be the sole representative of the people, became the standard approach of guerrilla movements in the twentieth century. Only by being concealed by an actively supportive public, could the guerrilla survive, and thrive, hence Mao's famous reminder: 'A guerrilla is like a fish that swims in the sea of the people.'[25] With overwhelming popular backing, a politically educated population could be drilled in the requirements of a guerilla campaign, and, eventually, this would allow for Mao's third and final phase: the reversion to a conventional war with a 'people's liberation army' that could seize power under the communist party's direction.

General Vo Nguyen Giap, of the North Vietnamese Army, added to Maoist doctrine, stating: 'The aim is to exhaust the enemy forces little by little by small victories, and, at the same time, to maintain and increase our forces.'[26] His contributions to Mao's theory were to seek to gain confidence over the enemy through psychological warfare, and to use terrorism both during and after insurgency to assert power over the population.

But these theoretical conditions are always contextual. Information campaigns can work in the government's favour too. The successive defeat of vulnerable bands of guerrillas may convince the population the insurgents are a lost cause. Acts of terror earn the condemnation of larger audiences, destroy legitimacy, and enable a government to criminalize a guerrilla force. People can change allegiance, mobilized by influencers and opinion leaders, through political crises (which are short term) and emotional-cultural narratives (which are more deep-seated); they may prioritize the protection of family, property and livelihood too, but their actions are often justified through a lens of nationalism, ethnicity, sectarianism, regionalism, history, language, local identities, or informational and associational expectations.[27] In other words, there are a multitude of reasons why the 'inevitability' of guerrilla victory is fallacious. This was also true of Lawrence's campaign, which might indicate just how remarkable his achievements were.

COUNTERING INSURGENCY

Lawrence's ideas on insurgency and partnering with local forces were influential in the United States-led Coalition campaigns in Iraq and Afghanistan after 2001. Determined to avoid the mistakes of the Soviet Union in Afghanistan in the 1980s, where the entire population had been alienated by aggression, the Coalition made a virtue of seeking only to eliminate Al Qaeda, the perpetrators of the 9/11 terrorist outrage. The Afghan population, by contrast, were to be assisted and supported. Development would be introduced, although not by the George W. Bush administration, which claimed it wasn't interested in 'nation-building'. Instead, aid agencies and funding would be donated in generous amounts. Although no one spoke of it at the time, there was nevertheless an analogy here to Lawrence's use of gold to facilitate support. And like Lawrence, this largesse was funnelled through a local political leader. Afghans initially had enormously high expectations about this wealth, but there was also disquiet about the Westerners staying.

In Iraq, the situation was quite different. While Saddam was feared by all, detested by many, and supported by only a few, there was still a strong sense of Iraqi nationalist pride at stake. A sufficiently large number of Iraqi troops had already decided not to fight the Americans in a conventional way, and 'Fedayeen' guerrilla attacks began from the invasion of March 2003, not, as some like to contend, some time afterwards. What fuelled this insurgency was a succession of decisions that caused panic amongst the Sunni majority about the future government of the country. When the US administration decided to abolish the Ba'ath party and dismantle the army, the entire former apparatus of the Iraqi regime took up arms. As their attacks escalated, so the Shia population took the opportunity to defend themselves, and take on the Americans too. Security deteriorated. Criminal gangs emerged to make a profit in kidnapping middle class families or to fuel the fighting. Against this background, and the bewildering variety of violent groups springing up, Coalition troops had to find a solution rapidly. They needed knowledge of the Iraqis, the driving forces of violence, and they needed ways to bring the killing under control as quickly as they could.

Work got underway on a manual of counter-insurgency that could be issued to the troops. There was some opposition from senior American officers, who disliked the idea that an insurgency was developing, since that had the whiff of Vietnam about it, a profound psychological trauma in the US military psyche. The second problem was that existing field manuals tended to examine only what to achieve and not how to operate at the tactical level. A handful of officers, assisted by the US think-tank RAND Corporation, and supported by more sympathetic senior officers such as Generals David Petraeus and James Mattis, opened up the debate on what was working, and, crucially, what was not. Journals associated with the US military hosted forums, workshops and discussions, as did academics like Professor Eliot Cohen of Johns Hopkins University and Frank Hoffman of the National Defense University. In this intensifying debate, T. E. Lawrence was a frequently cited source.

Dave Kilcullen, the former Australian officer who was working in the State Department, emulated 'T. E. Lawrence's article in the *Arab Bulletin* of August 1917' as it was, he said, 'a document with which both I and my readers were very familiar – it was widely read within the counter-insurgency community and was being circulated among the company and platoon commanders in the field in its electronic version.'[28] Kilcullen decided to emulate and update this advice, entitling his version as the '28 Articles'. He acknowledged that Lawrence

> wrote of insurgency and the art of military combat advising ... But I felt that if I organised my article along similar lines, and passed it to my peers in the field as a companion piece with Lawrence's already-circulating article, it would resonate with them and they would readily grasp the allusion.[29]

Within weeks, the article had indeed been circulated widely, reaching many combatants, and there was valuable feedback. Kilcullen's concern was only that some might try to use it as a template, rather than as a guide. He concluded: 'there is no substitute for studying the environment in detail, developing locally tailored solutions, and being prepared to adjust them in an agile way as the situation develops.'[30] Lawrence would have agreed with that sentiment.

Frank Ledwidge, in his coverage of the war in Iraq, was less impressed with the British performance. He noted the lack of knowledge about Iraq as a significant problem that led to the dependence on the doctrines of counter-insurgency. He described some of Kilcullen's '28 Articles' as 'if extracted from a commonplace self-help guide'.[31] This is perhaps to underestimate the sense that men were dying because of ignorance about how to proceed. If nothing else the guidance they received restored some confidence. Ledwidge certainly applauded the use of the past, noting: 'it is always instructive to see the musings of the young Arabist Lawrence referred to, imitated or contained in military reading lists'.[32] He is also brilliant in his searing honesty, and offers a balanced assessment against those who enthused about counter-insurgency as a strategy and a method, rather than a set of tactics.

On the aficionados of counter-insurgency, referred to by the denigrating term 'coindinstas' after the common use of the abbreviation 'COIN', Ledwidge points out the many errors in their assumptions. He notes, for example, the refusal to acknowledge that one cannot easily isolate the people from the insurgents, since, all too often, the people *are* the insurgents.[33] In Afghanistan, for example, local farmers laid improvised explosive devices, and children acted as couriers, observers and, in some cases, fighters and suicide bombers. Ledwidge points out that it doesn't matter how many schools or mosques one builds if the population regard the counter-insurgents as armed foreigners engaged in a process of occupation. He cites Lawrence's criticism of the suppression of the Iraqis in the 1920s.[34] In two phrases applicable beyond his own campaign, Ledwidge related what Lawrence had warned: 'The foreigner and the Christian is not a popular person in Arabia.' Lawrence's verdict was that: 'However friendly and informal the treatment of yourself may be, remember always that your foundations are very sandy ones.'[35]

Once the initial phase of the counter-insurgency was underway, attention turned to reforming an Iraqi security force. Colonel John Nagl, a champion for the doctrine of counter-insurgency who titled his book after Lawrence's expression of how messy counter-insurgency was, explained the appeal: 'What Lawrence gave us was an appreciation of how difficult the task is in understanding that we have to work through our local allies.'[36] There were more citations. Lawrence's injunctions featured in an article by Thomas Ricks, as 'Lessons of Arabia', in the *Washington Post* on 26 November 2004. Lawrence was added to the military curriculum of the United States Army, and one could not escape references to the '27 Articles', especially the oft-cited 15th, which states: 'Do not try to do too much with your own hands. Better the Arabs do it tolerably than that you do it perfectly. It is their war, and you are to help them, not to win it for them.' The unfortunate consequence of this mantra was that it may have created a reluctance to act decisively, lead, or direct local forces when appropriate.

The problem with all doctrinal codes is that they can be applied dogmatically rather than as guidance. A reprint of the '27 Articles' in 2017 was described as: 'a long-forgotten philosophy that constitutes nothing less than an entirely workable blueprint for nation-building in our troubled era'.[37] What we have seen in recent decades is the instrumentalization of Lawrence. His ideas are invoked at moments that seem far outside of their context.[38] Ahead of his '27 Articles' in the *Arab Bulletin*, Lawrence had cautioned:

> The following notes have been expressed in commandment form for greater clarity and to save words. They are, however, only my personal conclusions, arrived at gradually while I worked in the Hejaz and now put on paper as stalking horses for beginners in the Arab armies. They are meant to apply only to Bedu; townspeople or Syrians require totally different treatment. They are of course not suitable to any other person's need, or applicable unchanged in any particular situation.[39]

Clearly, Iraq in 2003–11 was not Arabia in 1917–18. One of the obvious differences was the tactics of Al Qaeda against the Iraqi civilians. To draw the Americans out and to 'discipline' the population, Al Qaeda murdered entire villages. Their objective was to enrage the population by sectarian killings, fulfil their ideological ambitions of annihilating apostasy, and render Iraq ungovernable. Iraqi insurgents were never able to threaten the mobile supply lines of the Coalition either; there was no Hejaz railway or fixed garrisons. In Anbar, after two years of brutal treatment by Abu Zarqawi of Al Qaeda, and several abortive attempts at resistance, the Anbaris aligned with the Coalition. An educated, settled, and urbanized Iraqi population rejected the nomadic and murderous legions of bin Laden.

In Afghanistan, the attempt to push the Kabul government's authority out into the provinces in 2006 stirred up a great deal of local anger, largely because it empowered rivals to the lucrative drug trade of the south-west, deposed existing powerbrokers, and offered an opportunity for the Taliban to assert their narrative as the liberators of Afghanistan. The relatively small numbers of American, British and Canadian forces in southern Afghanistan led to a greater reliance on firepower and air strikes, which fuelled the violence still further. Frank Ledwidge concluded that, by 2009, the Taliban had 95 per cent control of the valuable province of Helmand and most of the Coalition troops were absorbed in guarding bases and routes. A brigade force could only manage a mobile reserve of 168 men, although his figure does not include the air forces. Lawrence appreciated the difficulty that confronts a counter-insurgent force that cannot make use of the local manpower: it is forced to hold physical space which increases its costs and leaves it fixed.

In his work, Ledwidge advocated strongly another of Lawrence's injunctions: a dedicated approach to military education, and not just training. He condemned 'instant knowledge' and encouraged the embrace of civilians, including academics, to develop a more comprehensive picture of any conflict.[40] Above all it is the local view, as Lawrence believed, that matters most. Ledwidge's book was a clarion call to ditch the institutionalized mindset of bureaucracy and military exceptionalism in wars which require a deep understanding of the population, the drivers of the conflict, and, critically, its unique context. This change was prompted when the British Army mentioned Lawrence in its counter-insurgency doctrine and reduced the experience to a handful of 'take-away' memorable components. As a consequence, British personnel, following Lawrence, expected attacks on logistics and communications, and, while protecting the population, the army would have to actively seek out the elusive insurgent. But for the modern counter-insurgent, Lawrence's work suggested the civilian population would be largely uninvolved. Soldiers found it hard to accept the people would be actively supporting the insurgents because they were, in fact, inseparable. They believed that treating civilians well was essential, but even so, they accepted any such conflict would be intelligence-led and therefore painstaking.

Most military personnel accept that Lawrence may be a useful starting point, but he cannot be taken at face value. Nor, indeed, can the guerrilla warfare theories of the Cold War. Thomas X. Hammes, in his analysis of recent irregular warfare, noted:

Today's insurgents do not plan for the Phase III conventional campaigns that were an integral part of Mao's three-phased insurgency. They know they cannot militarily defeat the outside power. Instead, they seek to destroy the outside power's *political will* so that it gives up and withdraws forces. They seek to do so by causing political, economic, social, and military damage to the target nation.[41]

In other words, the modern insurgent targets the civilian population and government that sends its forces into interventionist operations, a phenomenon called 'Fourth Generation Warfare'.

Bringing insurgencies to an end requires not just a military force; it demands a political settlement to which armed forces will contribute. The goal of the guerrilla is to achieve political rather than military success, and consequently de-escalation and a reconfiguration of politics can sometimes subvert the approach of the insurgents. That said, war has its own logic and momentum. Guerrilla wars cannot be stopped only by offering talks. Long-term success requires a military campaign which facilitates the establishment of viable governance and leadership. A government must eventually address the grievances that gave rise to unrest and govern without substantial external support.[42]

Lawrence's ideas have therefore inspired, cautioned, and qualified some military practices since the 1920s. Colonel Gubbins sought to draw on some of Lawrence's approach, but, like Wingate, wisely acknowledged its limitations in a new setting. Lawrence's ideas on guerrilla warfare were to a large extent superseded by the theorists and practitioners of the Cold War. In the early twenty-first century, it was the counter-insurgents who returned to Lawrence's principles for guidance on working with local forces against extremist groups. Not all have been content with this instrumentalization, but there is little doubt Lawrence's thoughts have endured.

16

Rethinking Lawrence and His Ideas on War

The assessment of Lawrence and the revolt might be understood as the two logical elements of his personal contribution and that of the Arab forces themselves. Biographers have focussed on the former: the man and his enigmatic character. There is no doubt that Lawrence was personally courageous, from his early intrepid travels to the daring raids deep behind Ottoman lines in 1918. Despite his obvious individualism and preference for freedom of action, he praised others in *Seven Pillars* and claimed it had been a team effort. He was embarrassed by Lowell Thomas 'booming' him, and he evidently suffered a profound loss of confidence at times, and especially after the war. A deeply flawed man, he was nonetheless an evocative writer. His reclusiveness, not least in the RAF, as a ranker in the army, and periodically at Cloud's Hill, in Dorset, underscored some profound trauma with publicity and his war experiences. Even his portraits show a haunted, troubled image.

From the military point of view, the Arab revolutionaries possessed certain qualities that lent themselves to the campaign that unfolded, but they were also hamstrung by constraints. Lawrence was aware that the Arabs had great mobility, and he noted that a camel-borne force could cover considerable distances, and this range reduced their dependence on scattered water supplies. The untrained Arab forces could, under certain circumstances, fight with enthusiasm and courage, but they often lost heart against fortified Ottoman defences, or when subjected to artillery bombardment and air attack. Their loose formations could disperse into the desert hinterlands, and small groups were more easily concealed in the folds of the landscape. But, by tradition, Arab fighters were reluctant to operate in the lands of other clans, and they were weakened by rivalry and feuding. The gradual regularization and enhanced British support to Arab units assisted them in their operations, but they were still dwarfed, from a purely military perspective, by the British and Ottoman belligerents in the conflict.

Lawrence's contribution was to act as an important link between the Arab forces and the headquarters of the EEF. He was able to convey the role that irregulars could play and offered guidance on the conduct of the operations. He showed the Arabs the tactical advantages of working with British forces, of a demolition campaign, raiding, and the power of mobile firepower in the air and on the ground.

Lawrence and his Arab partners were useful as a means of deception and disruption.[1] Allenby recognized their value in this limited capacity, and facilitated the operations, but never depended upon them. The balance of threat to the Ottomans was always clear. One British officer related his interview with an Ottoman divisional commander who survived the battle of Megiddo: 'The Arabs gave us pin pricks; the British – blows with a sledgehammer.'[2] Ultimately, the revolt would not have been a success without the British and Indian armies, the support of the Royal Air Force or the efforts of the Royal Navy. The Ottomans had demonstrated that they could overpower Arab forces if they caught them, but Lawrence made a virtue of their elusive quality in the vastness of the desert. What he could not overcome was their divisions, and despite his success in encouraging unity around Feisal, it was Arab disunity which sabotaged the achievement of taking Damascus, although outsiders were later blamed.

Lawrence went to great pains to try to demonstrate that Feisal was the most suitable figure to lend coherence to the offensive into Syria from the Hejaz, even to the extent of denigrating other potential leaders. There was some pride in Feisal's achievements, and one biographer calls him 'Feisal the Great', but the accolade rings hollow when tested against his later career: he was unable to dissuade the French from their occupation of Syria; his half measures in compromise garnered little public support there and he was ousted after a failed revolt in 1920; he was then handed the consolation of the monarchy of Iraq, not by his own followers, but by his generous sponsors, the British. Feisal managed a rather unremarkable reign, marred by bad-tempered relationships with his British guardians in Baghdad, but he oversaw the emergence of an independent Iraq. One might say, without Lawrence or the other British advisors, Feisal could never have achieved as much as he did. The Hashemite defeat at the hands of Ibn Saud after the war, after Hussein's refusal to accept the compromises worked out with all the other interested parties, which led to Britain's inability to continue its support, was the final indication that Hussein and his clansmen were dependent on external backers.

Lawrence emphasized the value of Arab forces in order to further the political argument for independence. For him, it was not really their tactical achievements that mattered, but their existence. He wrote to Clayton in August 1917, specifying: 'I don't think that any appreciation of the Arab situation will be of any use to you, unless its author can see for himself the difference between a national rising and a campaign.'[3] He came to see that fighting was the means to give the Arabs political legitimacy. If he demonstrated the military contribution, he could win for them a seat at the peace negotiations. Magnifying their success, their 'triumph', especially the conquest of Damascus, was therefore integral to the cause of national liberation.

Lawrence cannot be faulted for trying or risking all, for what he thought was a just cause. Part romantic, part political pragmatist, Lawrence was guided by a sense of chivalric mission from an imagined past, but he struggled with his own personal failings and weaknesses. In 1918 and 1919 he seemed a rather broken and disappointed man, not least because it appeared the cause he had embraced, the creation of a territory for all Arabs, was unrealizable in the face of particularist interests within the region and the strategic security arrangements preferred in Paris and London.

It suited Lawrence's generation, and many since, to allege betrayal and bad faith by Western leaders, not least because of the seemingly contradictory blueprints they produced during that war. Lawrence saw no contradictions, believing that the Arabs had been promised a territorial reward. Many of the allegations about bad faith though stemmed from Lawrence's own doubts about his role. He never resolved the differences between his identity as a British officer, working within intelligence, his mission to make use of the Arabs as an instrument in a wider strategic plan, and the proximity of the Arabs he was charged to guide. His personal difficulties also came from his sense of collective obligation and the more egocentric desire to seize opportunities thrown up by the war. Yet, in the end, it was the agency of the Arab peoples themselves that determined the divided space of the Middle East region. Lawrence was familiar with the minds of the men in the Near East, but his was a relationship limited by time and the extraordinary pressures of the war.

The project of united Arab independence was not achieved in the period 1916–19, but not because Britain 'betrayed' the Arab cause, as Lawrence had suggested. Lawrence expressed his doubts about the sincerity of his political masters, but he did not have the full range of diplomatic and strategic calculations in his possession, and he was just as critical of Arab 'nationalism'. He knew that Britain had to maintain its interests, and he knew that Britain was also keen to preserve good relations with a number of actors and groups, many of whom had competing or overlapping interests of their own. His reference to Britain emerging with 'clean hands' from the Middle East in 1920 demonstrates that, at that point, he believed the Arabs had achieved the independence, with British protection, he had visualized from the start. He believed strongly that the Hashemites should be rewarded for their part in Britain's war effort. After the Cairo conference, he was convinced that, for all its imperfections, this had been achieved.

This work has been concerned with Lawrence's ideas on war and what he learned from his experience. Of all his insights, there are some that seem enduring, but which are not limited to the obvious axioms about working with local forces and conducting, or countering, insurgency. Mindful of Lawrence's warning that the context of any conflict is absolute and that working towards the most appropriate strategy requires 'intense study', 'concentration', and 'brain work', it is striking that he identified a number of elements, especially in guerrilla warfare, which constitute the essential nature of war. Even if he did not always succeed in applying his 'theory', his energy, pragmatism and determination clearly attracted and inspired others.

A sensible conclusion might be that he was trying to solve a specific problem, which, after the war, he later generalized as a strategic theory. He admitted that the problems and solutions he conceived had originally been thought of 'mainly in terms of the Hejaz'.[4] That said, there were some perennial themes which Lawrence had drawn from his study of history, and which, through the prism of his desire to understand the psychology of his subjects, could be applied generally.

He recognized the value of leadership and urged sustained study of war in all its forms as the means to prepare for the stress, urgency and intensity of decision-making in conflict. His skill as a writer created a memorable mental image of intuition, not least his famous observation that: 'Nine-tenths of tactics were certain enough to be teachable in schools; but the irrational tenth was like the kingfisher flashing across the pool.'[5] He captured the need for the leaders of weaker belligerents to avoid the full retaliatory force of the strong, and, like many of his generation, he condemned the eagerness for direct combat, writing:

> Battles in Arabia were a mistake, since we profited in them only by the ammunition the enemy fired off. Napoleon had said it was rare to find generals willing to fight battles; but the curse of this war was that so few would do anything else. Saxe had told us that irrational battles were the refuges of fools: rather they seemed to me impositions on the side which believed itself weaker, hazards made unavoidable either by lack of land room or by the need to defend a material property dearer than the lives of soldiers.[6]

In his writing, Lawrence also captured the importance of morale, and how fighting personnel can be affected detrimentally by casualties, surprise attacks or setbacks. He believed that having intelligence, knowledge of the environment, and what soldiers call 'situational awareness' gave combatants greater motivation, concluding: 'Morale, if built on knowledge, was broken by ignorance.'[7] He was deeply concerned with this human frailty in war, perhaps because of his awareness of his own vulnerabilities in this regard. He clearly disliked discipline, in the sense of inculcating obedience, but advocated 'arranging minds' and playing on a sense of honour to motivate the fighters and maintain their cohesion. Consequently, he made a plea for the study of psychology in war, the state of mind, and the behaviours that stem from it. He tried to build the confidence and experience of his fighting partners. He made a virtue of elusiveness and the 'silent threat' of the desert to deter and demoralize his enemy. He used this to add to the enemy's exhaustion, not just in a physical sense, but in their spirit.

Winning the population, by constant appeals, was evidently important to the campaign, although Lawrence left this task to Feisal and the Arab leaders: he tried to avoid making it seem that a foreigner was making the request. After the war, Lawrence forecast the power of ideas and their propagation that could be achieved. He famously remarked that the printing press would become the greatest weapon in the arsenal of the modern commander. He believed this form of war was, in essence, 'a war of communications'.[8]

Lawrence placed considerable emphasis, in his theory and practice, on the individual. He referred to his early interest in medieval single combat, but in his contemporary context he believed that the willingness of the individual to fight was critical at the tactical level. He described the Arab fighters as an aggregation of snipers, that is, men who seem to fight alone, with a disproportionate psychological effect on those subjected to their fire. He believed that mass in war was partly a functional requirement, but its greater significance was in its psychological effects.

Yet Lawrence concluded these individual fighters could not stand against regular troops, so their strength lay in their depth and in their ability to remain mobile and concealed. If their enemies tried to pursue them, they would take to their heels and try to disappear into the desert. Air power began to reduce the effectiveness of this technique, but, fortunately for Lawrence, this interdiction came too late in the desert campaign to change its outcome.

Raiding, especially the attacks on the Ottoman military infrastructure, served a number of purposes, both psychological and physical. Lawrence claimed raids kept the Ottomans fixed, tying them up in manpower-intensive but wasteful guard duties. In fact, the Ottoman Army could not spare the men to pursue the Sharifians because they had to prioritize the main fronts, in Palestine, in Mesopotamia, and the Caucasus. There remains some controversy about whether Lawrence's claims that 'extending the Ottoman's flank' and pinning them into Medina were considered wartime aims, or just a consequence of other decisions (including the Ottomans' desire to retain the iconic city of Medina for subsequent peace negotiations). But there is no doubt that Lawrence advocated mobility and manoeuvre to assert an advantage over the Ottoman forces.

The 'war of detachment', where the guerrillas only attacked the fabric of the enemy's infrastructure and not their forces, was only partially successful. There was a calculation to be made about risk and the need for success by engaging isolated Ottoman units or opening routes, such as the one to Aqaba. The ideal, Lawrence claimed, was to fight only as a consequence of accidental encounters, but his actions at Tafila (Wadi Hesa), or Sheikh Sa'ad, suggest that either the practice or the circumstances was different.

The purpose of war, and the way that it had been waged, had clearly varied through history, as Lawrence noted from his earliest studies. He was aware that, in revolutionary war, force was the means to acquire power: the objective was to govern. Revolutionaries nevertheless struggled to acquire legitimacy as much as they fought to acquire geographical control. In the war in the desert, Lawrence knew that certain geographical positions, especially sacred sites, possessed disproportionate influence on the campaign. The Allied and Arab forces could not afford to lose the Red Sea ports, and the Sharifian armies could not give up Mecca. This reduced their ability to strike against the Ottomans, except towards Syria and Palestine. The Ottomans too were unwilling to relinquish Medina. Jerusalem took on political importance for the British government, if not for Allenby, and territorial claims were extended by all the belligerents as they imagined the peace settlement to come. Each of these locations conferred legitimacy.

We might say that Lawrence was more interested in the geography of the mind, that is, the transfer of identity and allegiance from the Ottomans to a new Arab dispensation, in partnership with Great Britain. Honour, a key element in his thinking, was part of this mental geography. But the objective was to secure the cognitive support of the Arabs as the means to gain control of physical space. The sense of dishonour he experienced was that he knew the Hejaz Bedouin, the main core of fighters in 1916–17, could not be expected to form a bureaucratic government. This was not in keeping with their aspirations, culture or political preferences. He felt uncomfortable that these men were being asked to fight for a cause from which they could not be the main beneficiaries. The solution he had in mind was for a more archaic form of government, based on the fealty of the people to their personal monarch. The suspicion that France would acquire Syria, and not accept an Arab authority, worsened his anxieties about the purpose of this war.

It is not just the outcomes of the revolt that make Lawrence memorable. On the conduct of guerrilla war, Lawrence's ideas have been cited repeatedly. Famously, he summed up the essence, as he saw it, in '50 words':

> Granted mobility, security (in the form of denying targets to the enemy), time, and doctrine (the idea to convert every subject to friendliness), victory will rest with the insurgents, for the algebraical factors are in the end decisive, and against them perfections of means and spirit struggle quite in vain.[9]

Above all, it was Lawrence's ability to summarize the essence of war into the three fundamental elements of algebra, bionomics and diathetics, and to emphasize the importance of the mind in particular, which illustrates his value as a military thinker. None of the setbacks he suffered in any way diminishes the extraordinary ride of Lawrence in that war. We should remain conscious of his distinct context, and his flaws, but it is his articulation and advocacy of intense 'brain work' in preparing for conflict and the conduct of war which earns him his place in the history of military affairs. And if we must fight, as he reminded Liddell Hart, with 2,000 years of experience behind us, there are no excuses for not fighting well.

Notes

PREFACE

1 For a full and annotated review of the recent literature, see: Robert Johnson, 'The First World War and the Middle East: A literature review of recent scholarship', *Middle Eastern Studies*, 54(1) (2018), pp. 142–51.

CHAPTER 1

1 Lowell Jackson Thomas, *With Lawrence in Arabia* (London: Hutchinson, 1923), pp. 16–17.

2 Thomas, *With Lawrence*, p. 18.

3 Walter Lacquer, *Guerrilla: A Historical and Critical Study* (London: Weidenfeld and Nicholson, 1977), p. 155.

4 Himmet Umunc, '"A Hope So Transcendent": The Arab Revolt in the Great War and T. E. Lawrence', in Robert Johnson and James Kitchen (eds), *The Great War in the Middle East: A Clash of Empires* (London: Routledge, 2019).

5 See, for example, S. Mousa, *T. E. Lawrence: An Arab View* (London: Oxford University Press, 1966), pp. 72–9.

6 Compare, for example, T. E. Lawrence, *Seven Pillars of Wisdom: A Triumph* (London: Jonathan Cape, 1935), p. 225, with, on the same dates, T. E. Lawrence, *Secret Despatches from Arabia* (London: Golden Cockerel, 1939), p. 111.

7 Richard Aldington, *Lawrence of Arabia: A Biographical Enquiry* (London: Collins, 1969), pp. 210–11.

8 Efraim Karsh and Inari Karsh, 'Myth in the Desert, or Not the Great Arab Revolt', *Middle Eastern Studies*, 33(2) (1997), pp. 267–312.

9 Linda J. Tarver, 'In Wisdom's House: T. E. Lawrence in the Near East', *Journal of Contemporary History*, 13 (July 1978), p. 591.

10 For the writing and publication of *Seven Pillars*, see Jeremy Wilson's essay at: www.telstudies.org/discussion/writings_and_criticism/wilson_7_pillars_1.shtml (accessed June 2018).

11 Elie Kedourie, 'The Real T. E. Lawrence', *Commentary*, 64 (1977), p. 54.

12 See Robert Taber, *War of the Flea* (New York: L. Stuart, 1965), p. 190.

13 Lawrence, *Seven Pillars*, p. 23.

14 Basil Liddell Hart, *T. E. Lawrence: In Arabia and After* (London: Jonathan Cape, 1934), pp. 272–3.

15 Neil Faulkner, *Lawrence of Arabia's War: The Arabs, the British and the Remaking of the Middle East in WWI* (New Haven, CT: Yale University Press, 2017); J. E. Mack, *Prince of Our Disorder: The Life of T. E. Lawrence* (Boston: Little, Brown, 1976); Michael Konda, *Hero: The Life and Legend of Lawrence of Arabia* (London: Aurum Press, 2011); Scott Anderson, *Lawrence in Arabia: War, Deceit, Imperial Folly and the Making of the Modern Middle East* (London: Atlantic Books, 2014). For contemporary views, see Robert Graves, *Lawrence and the Arabs* (London: Jonathan Cape, 1927), and for the epitome of hero-worship, see Liddell Hart, *Lawrence: In Arabia and After*, p. 16.

16 See Jeremy Wilson, *Lawrence of Arabia* (New York: Athenaeum, 1990).

17 Thomas, *With Lawrence*, pp. 180–7.

18 Wilson, *Lawrence of Arabia*, p. 493.

19 See E. M. Forster, cited in Mack, *Prince of Our Disorder*, p. 38.

20 Wilson, *Lawrence of Arabia*, p. 543.

21 Philip Walker, *Behind the Lawrence Legend* (Oxford: Oxford University Press, 2018).

22 Rob Johnson, *The Great War and the Middle East: A Strategic Study* (Oxford: Oxford University Press, 2016).

23 Cyril Falls and A. F. Becke, *Official History: Military Operations, Egypt and Palestine: From June 1917 to the End of the War*, vol. 2, part II, *History of The Great War* (London: HMSO, 1930), pp. 411–21.

24 Johnson, *The Great War and the Middle East*, p. 234. Lawrence made light of the setback, choosing to praise the 'spirit' of the regulars that showed the 'Arabs did not need British stiffening': Lawrence, *Seven Pillars*, p. 520.

25 T. E. Lawrence to Basil Liddell Hart, 26 June 1933, in D. Garnett, *The Letters of Lawrence of Arabia* (London: Jonathan Cape, 1938), pp. 768–9.

26 T. E. Lawrence to Basil Liddell Hart, 26 June 1933, in Garnett, *Letters*, pp. 768–9.

27 T. E. Lawrence to Basil Liddell Hart, 26 June 1933, in Garnett, *Letters*, pp. 768–9.

28 T. E. Lawrence to Basil Liddell Hart, 26 June 1933, in Garnett, *Letters*, pp. 768–9.

29 In the war, Lawrence carried with him a copy of the cheerful Aristophanes.

30 Faulkner, *Lawrence of Arabia's War*, pp. 194–6.

31 M. D. Allen, *The Medievalism of Lawrence of Arabia* (University Park, PA: Pennsylvania State University Press, 1991), pp. 29–33; Faulkner, *Lawrence of Arabia's War*, p. 198.

32 The preliminary elements of this book were written in the same building, which housed my office for four years. In the Research Hall of the Faculty, there is a portrait of T. E. Lawrence as well as papers and artefacts from the school. All Souls was my college for the same period. In Jesus College, Lawrence's undergraduate college, I ran an intensive study for the British military officers who worked in Arabia, Lawrence's descendants. The concluding elements of this book were written in the shadow of St Aldate's, where Lawrence had attended the Boys Brigade before joining the Oxford Officer Training Corps for students.

33 He later claimed he had conceived of a 'new Asia', but we have little contemporary evidence of this. Mack, *Prince of Our Disorder*, p. 37.

34 Mack, *Prince of Our Disorder*, p. 49.

35 Wilson, *Lawrence of Arabia*, p. 45.

36 Wilson, *Lawrence of Arabia*, p. 53.

37 Mack, *Prince of Our Disorder*, pp. 53–5.

38 Charles Doughty, *Travels in Arabia Deserta* (Cambridge: Cambridge University Press, 1888) was by far the most profound influence on Lawrence, not only for its subject, but also the style in which it was written. Lawrence had the work republished after the First World War (by Jonathan Cape, in 1936) and David Hogarth produced a biography of the traveller in 1928.

39 Hew Strachan, centenary lecture of the Chichele Chair in the History of War, University of Oxford, 2009.

40 Wilkinson became a critic of Britain's strategy during the First World War, and he maintained the critique until he died in 1937. His correspondence with Liddell Hart is at King's College London, while his other papers are at the National Army Museum in Chelsea.

41 Spenser Wilkinson, 'The French Army before Napoleon: Lectures delivered before the University of Oxford', pp. 14–16; Spenser Wilkinson, *Government and the War* (London: Constable, 1918).

42 Wilkinson, 'The French Army before Napoleon', pp. 14–16; Wilkinson, *Government and the War*.

43 Thomas, *With Lawrence*, p. 33; Robin Bidwell (ed.), *The Diary Kept by T. E. Lawrence While Travelling in Arabia During 1911* (Reading: Garnet, 1993), pp. 6, 9–10.

44 Mack, *Prince of Our Disorder*, p. 91; Faulkner, *Lawrence of Arabia's War*, p. 32.

45 Charles Edward Callwell, *Small Wars: Their Principles and Practice* (London: HMSO, 1896; 3rd edition, 1906), p. 126.

46 Callwell, citing Sir Garnet Wolseley, in *Small Wars*, p. 40.

47 Callwell, *Small Wars*, p. 130.

48 Callwell, *Small Wars*, p. 136.

49 Callwell, citing Lord Frederick Roberts, in *Small Wars*, p. 141.

50 Callwell, *Small Wars*, p. 141.

51 Callwell, *Small Wars*, p. 144.

52 Callwell, *Small Wars*, p. 35.

53 Hew Strachan, *Carl von Clausewitz's On War: A Biography* (London: Atlantic Monthly Press, 2007); one should note here how unpopular Clausewitz was as a source in British military circles: see the introduction to Carl von Clausewitz, *On War*, trans. J. J. Graham, F. N. Maude (ed.) (London: Routledge and Kegan Paul, 1908), vol. 1, pp. i–vii, and the citation in Hew Strachan, 'Clausewitz and the First World War', *The Journal of Military History* 75 (April 2011), p. 372.

54 Antulio Echevarria II, 'Borrowing from the Master: Uses of Clausewitz in German Military Literature before the Great War', *War in History*, 3 (1996), pp. 274–92.

55 T. H. E. Travers, 'Technology, Tactics and Morale: Jean de Bloch, the Boer War, and British Military Theory, 1900–1914', *Journal of Modern History*, 51 (June 1979), pp. 273, 276–7; Stephen van Evera, 'The Cult of the Offensive and the Origins of the First World War', *International Security*, 9, 1 (1984), pp. 60–1.

56 Clausewitz, *On War*, p. 480.

57 Clausewitz, *On War*, p. 480.

58 Clausewitz, *On War*, p. 482.

59 John Bourne, 'Total War: I' in Charles Townshend (ed.), *The Oxford History of Modern War* (Oxford: Oxford University Press, 2005), p. 118.

60 Jan Bloch, *Is War Now Impossible?* (London: Grant Richards, 1899).

61 Michael Howard, 'Men Against Fire: Expectations of War in 1914', in *International Security*, 9, 1 (Summer 1984), p. 41.

62 Travers, 'Technology, Tactics and Morale', p. 273; Tim H. E. Travers, 'Future Warfare: H. G. Wells and British Military Theory, 1895–1916' in Brian Bond and Ian Roy (eds), *War and Society* (London: Croom Helm, 1975).

63 See the reports of Lt. Col. A. L. Haldane, Colonel Waters and Major Home in *The Russo-Japanese War: Reports from British Officers Attached to the Japanese Forces in the Field*, 3 vols. (London, 1908), 1:73, 2:519, 3:205–15; and *Field Service Regulations, Part 1, Operations* (London:

HMSO, 1909), pp. 107, 111, and 114. J. F. C. Fuller made an appeal to the psychological element in his own pre-war study, Capt. J. F. C. Fuller, 'The Procedure of the Infantry Attack: A Synthesis from a Psychological Standpoint', *JRUSI*, 58 (January 1914), pp. 65–6.

64 H. G. Wells, *The War in the Air* (London: George Bell and Sons, 1908).

65 Azar Gat, *A History of Military Thought* (Oxford: Oxford University Press, 2001), p. 526.

66 In his science fiction, such as *War of the Worlds* (1898), it was, however, the humble microbe that defeated the technologically advanced invading alien civilization.

67 William Carr, *A History of Germany, 1815–1990* (London: Edward Arnold, 1969, reprntd. 1991), p. 167. German investment was considerable. Some 80 per cent of Ottoman war expenditure was paid for by Germany.

68 See, for example, intercepted letter from Bethmann Hollweg [Chancellor of Germany] to the Maharaja of Jodhpur, Chelmsford Papers Mss Eur E 264/52. India Office Records, British Library, London; 'Special Military Resources of the German Empire', Report prepared by the General Staff, February 1912, p. 52, WO 33/579, TNA; Allan Hepburn, *Intrigue: Espionage and Culture* (New Haven, CT: Yale University Press, 2005); S. Hynes, *The Edwardian Turn of Mind* (Princeton, NJ: Princeton University Press, 1975), p. 26.

69 Three million published items were created during the war, covering all the regional languages, and distributed through 25 offices. The project was funded generously and staffed with German academics and military personnel. Hew Strachan, *The First World War, I: To Arms* (Oxford: Oxford University Press, 2001), pp. 695–6, 707–8. For the detail of the alliance and the aspirations behind it, see C. Mühlmann, *Das deutsch-türkische Waffenbündnis im Weltkriege* (Leipzig: Koehler & Amelang, 1940); J. L. Wallach, *Anatomie einer Militärhilfe: Die preußisch-deutschen Militärmissionen in der Türkei 1835–1919* (Düsseldorf: Droste, 1976).

70 Garnett, *Letters*, p. 184; Wilson, *Lawrence of Arabia*, p. 166.

71 Captain Gilbert Clayton was the Director of Intelligence and led this new initiative on the Ottomans, which had formerly been a Foreign Office and War Office responsibility. The Cairo bureau was tasked with acquiring information specifically on the Ottoman threat to Egypt. The personnel included Captain (later Colonel) Stewart Newcombe, Captain George Lloyd, Captain Aubrey Herbert, Lieutenant Leonard Woolley, Lieutenant Hay and 2nd Lieutenant Lawrence. Herbert was focussed on internal security and Ottoman (nationalist) politics, Lloyd on Mesopotamia, Newcombe on collection, Woolley on dissemination. Lawrence was considered a translator.

72 If Lawrence had not moved beyond his desk job in Cairo, or if he had
suffered an early death, it seems likely that history would have forgotten
him. This is precisely what happened to Captain William Henry Irving
Shakespeare (1878–1915), an experienced Arabian traveller who
was killed in action at the battle of Jarrab on 24 January 1915 while
accompanying Ibn Saud's fighters against the forces of Ibn Rashid.
Report on the Najd Mission, 1917–1918, IOR/R/15/1/747, f 25r, and
File E/8, I, Ibn Sa'ud, IOR/R/15/2/31, India Office Records, London.

73 Lawrence already had been in contact with Mesopotamian Arab leaders,
during his mission to negotiate with the Ottomans for the ending of the
siege of Kut. The failure of the talks, and the desperate relief operations
for Kut, meant the capitulation of the British Imperial garrison of the
town. The captive British soldiers were forced into slave labour for
the Berlin–Baghdad railway. Faulkner, *Lawrence of Arabia's War*, p. 92;
Johnson, *The Great War and the Middle East*, pp. 149–50.

CHAPTER 2

1 Ryan Gingeras, *Fall of the Sultanate: The Great War and the End of the
Ottoman Empire, 1908–1922.* (Oxford: Oxford University Press, 2016),
pp. 208–9; Eugene Rogan, *The Fall of the Ottomans* (New York: Basic
Books, 2015), pp. 262–4; Mehmet Beşiki, *The Ottoman Mobilisation of
Manpower in the First World War: Between Volunteerism and Resistance*
(Leiden: Brill, 2012), p. 113.

2 Rogan, *Fall of the Ottomans*, pp. 58–9.

3 Feroz Ahmad, *The Young Turks: The Committee of Union and Progress in
Turkish Politics, 1908–1914* (London: Hurst & Co., 1969).

4 For eye-witness accounts of routine Ottoman brutality, especially by
soldiers towards Ottoman subjects, see Gertrude Bell, *Syria: The Desert
and the Sown* (New York: E. P. Dutton and Co., 1907), pp. 132, 171 and
262; see also Faulkner, *Lawrence of Arabia's War*, p. 184. For accounts of
the mistreatment of Ottoman soldiers by their officers and NCOs, see
R. de Nogales, *Four Years Beneath the Crescent* (London: Charles Scribner's
Sons, 1926), pp. 166, 188 and 189.

5 Ibn al-Hussein, Abdullah, *Memoirs of King Abdullah of Jordan*, edited
by P. Graves (London: Jonathan Cape, 1950), p. 112; Ronald Storrs,
Orientations (London: Readers' Union, 1939), p. 129; Rogan, *Fall of
the Ottomans*, p. 276. Sir Ronald Storrs had served in Cairo as Oriental
Secretary, having previously worked in the Finance Ministry of the
Egyptian government. He was the political officer responsible for liaison
with the British mission in Mesopotamia, but his considerable, and

understated diplomatic skills were often deployed in negotiations with the Hashemites. In 1917 he became the governor of Jerusalem, and then, after the war was appointed, in turn, governor of Cyprus and Northern Rhodesia. He was a pallbearer for Lawrence in 1935, served in the Ministry of Information in the Second World War, and died in 1955, two years after his retirement.

6 Falls and Becke, *Military Operations, Egypt and Palestine*, vol. 2, part II, p. 629.

7 Wilson, *Lawrence of Arabia*, pp. 219–20; Major Sir Hubert Young, *The Independent Arab* (London: John Murray, 1933), p. 271.

8 C. E. Dawn, *From Ottomanism to Arabism: Essays on the Origins of Arab Nationalism* (Urbana: University of Illinois Press, 1973), p. 26; Donald McKale, *War by Revolution* (Kent, OH: Kent State University Press, 1998), p. 75.

9 McKale, *War by Revolution*, p. 75.

10 Rashid commanded about 1,000 retainers, but he could call on a much larger force of irregulars. The Ottomans apparently gave him 12,000 rifles, suggesting a significant force, in return for a supply of camels and livestock. Rashid controlled an area of approximately 500 square miles and held sway over some 35,000 Arabs and 25 important oases. Abdulaziz Ibn Saud possessed a dedicated bodyguard, the Wahabi *Ikhwan*, that rose from 11,000 before the war to some 30,000 men in 1919. In addition, he could call on over 8,000 Bedouin irregulars. Saud's weakness was in armaments, as his men had only 8,000 modern rifles, four machine guns and 12 mountain guns. Most of the army was equipped with antiquated weapons. His strength was in the remoteness of his dominions, mostly out of reach of the Ottoman Army, and by his exercise of power. Peripheral tribes knew that to defy Saud could mean massacre, and the Saudi Emir focussed his wartime efforts on extending and consolidating his area of control, usually at the expense of the Shammar of Hail. R. Lacey, *The Kingdom: Arabia and the House of Saud* (London: Fontana, 1981), pp. 102–6.

11 George McMunn and Cyril Falls, *Official History of the Great War Military Operations, Egypt and Palestine*, vol. I (London: HMSO, 1927), p. 213.

12 Lawrence to C. E. Wilson, 8 January 1917, in Garnett, *Letters*, p. 219.

13 Lacey, *The Kingdom*, p. 57; Faulkner, *Lawrence of Arabia's War*, p. 160.

14 Karsh and Karsh, 'Myth in the Desert, or Not the Great Arab Revolt', pp. 267–312.

15 McMunn and Falls, *Military Operations, Egypt and Palestine*, vol. I, p. 221.

16 Nationalism was not clearly defined. For more details on the various factions and aspirations see Gingeras, *Fall of the Sultanate*, p. 197; Rogan, *Fall of the Ottomans*, pp. 37, 283, 288; George Antonius, *The Arab Awakening* (London: Hamish Hamilton, 1938), p. 191; Faulkner, *Lawrence of Arabia's War*, pp. 180–1.

17 Antonius, *The Arab Awakening*, pp. 152–3; Rogan, *Fall of the Ottomans*, p. 283.

18 J. C. Hurewitz (ed.), *The Middle East and North Africa in World Politics: A Documentary Record* (New Haven, CT: Yale University Press, 1979), vol. II, pp. 46–56.

19 Report of the Committee on Asiatic Turkey, 30 June 1915, CAB 42/3/12, p. 2, TNA; Robert Johnson, 'The de Bunsen Committee and the "Conspiracy" of Sykes-Picot', *Middle Eastern Studies* (March 2018), p. 5.

20 Johnson, 'The de Bunsen Committee', pp. 11–12. Lieutenant Colonel Sir Henry McMahon, of the Indian Army and an Anglo-Irish family, served as High Commissioner for Egypt between 1915 and 1917. He had been the Chief Commissioner of Baluchistan and gave his name to the border between India and China. He served as the foreign secretary to the Government of India until his appointment in Egypt. He resigned when the details of the Sykes-Picot Agreement were published by the Russians in 1917.

21 Rogan, *Fall of the Ottomans*, pp. 282–3.

22 Ronald Storrs noted that 'it may be regarded as certain that he [Hussein] has received no sort of mandate from other [Arab] potentates'. Ronald Storrs to the Foreign Office, 'Communication from the Sherif of Mecca', 20 August 1915 and 4 September 1915, FO 371/2486/125293, TNA; Faulkner, *Lawrence of Arabia's War*, p. 169.

23 Antonius, *The Arab Awakening*, pp. 152–3.

24 Antonius, *The Arab Awakening*, pp. 188–9; Faulkner, *Lawrence of Arabia's War*, p. 183; A. Allawi, *Feisal I of Iraq* (New Haven, CT: Yale University Press, 2014), p. 59.

25 Faulkner, *Lawrence of Arabia's War*, p. 171.

26 Hurewitz, *The Middle East and North Africa in World Politics*, vol. II, pp. 60–4.

27 Johnson, 'The de Bunsen Committee', pp. 19–20.

28 M. Cheetham to Earl Curzon of Kedleston, 9 February 1919, FO 608/97; FO 371 375/1/3, no. 467. TNA; Correspondence between Sir Henry McMahon and the Sharif of Mecca July 1915–March 1916, Cmd 5957 (London, 1939), p. 3; Elie Kedourie, *In the Anglo-Arab Labyrinth: The McMahon-Hussein Correspondence and its Interpretations, 1914–1939*

(Cambridge: Cambridge University Press, 1976); Wingate to Balfour, 25 December 1917, FO 371/3395/12077, TNA; see also Karsh and Karsh, 'Myth in the Desert, or Not the Great Arab Revolt', pp. 289–90; Ali Allawi, *Faisal I of Iraq* (New Haven CT: Yale University Press, 2014), pp. 138–41.

29 President Wilson's Message to Congress, 8 January 1918, Records of the United States' Senate, Senate Records Group 46; Cartographic Records of Proposed Jewish and Syrian States (1919), 1–4, of 65, and Maps of Arabia (1917–1919), 1–6, of 62, Records of the American Commission to Negotiate Peace, RG 256, NARA.

30 Lawrence to the editor of *The Times*, September 1919, in Garnett, *Letters*, no. 113, pp. 281–2.

31 *Memoirs of King Abdullah of Jordan*, p. 136; Djemal Pasha, *Memories of a Turkish Statesman, 1913–1919* (London: Hutchinson, n.d.), p. 215.

32 Faulkner, *Lawrence of Arabia's War*, p. 179.

33 Faulkner, *Lawrence of Arabia's War*, p. 162.

34 McMunn and Falls, *Military Operations, Egypt and Palestine*, vol. I, p. 225. The numbers of active members of the uprising are difficult to determine. The British *Official History* estimated that there may have been as many as 50,000 fighters at the end of the campaign, but this figure would not represent the numbers that could be sustained in the field. The Ottomans were probably closer in their estimate of 15,000 across the Hejaz.

35 Even Lawrence had his doubts. He wrote: 'A British landing and they would scatter'. See Wilson, *Lawrence of Arabia*, pp. 325–6.

36 Faulkner, *Lawrence of Arabia's War*, p. 174. General Sir Reginald Wingate, a Glaswegian artillery officer, had served in the Gordon Relief Expedition (1884–85) and he earned decorations for his active service in the Sudan. He wrote an authoritative account of the phenomenon of Mahdism in 1891 and served in the campaign that brought down the Dervish regime in 1898 under Lord Kitchener's command. He became governor-general of the Sudan in 1899 and helped develop infrastructure there, such that his services were rewarded with an honorary doctorate at Oxford University. During the war, in 1917, he succeeded McMahon as the Governor of Egypt but was blamed for the post-war unrest. He refused to resign, despite the appointment of General Allenby as his successor. He was denied a peerage, and resigned his commission, but he was made a baronet. He died in 1949. He was related to Sir William Dobbie, who served in Egypt and Palestine after the war, and to Orde Wingate, the unorthodox leader of the Special Night Squads in 1936 that protected Zionists in Palestine, and the guerrilla-style Chindit commander of the Second World War.

37 Wilson, *Lawrence of Arabia*, pp. 287–8.

38 Liddell Hart, *T. E. Lawrence: In Arabia and After*, p. 86; James Barr, *Setting the Desert on Fire: T. E. Lawrence and Britain's Secret War in Arabia, 1916–1918* (London: Bloomsbury, 2006), p. 28; *Memoirs of King Abdullah of Jordan*, pp. 147–9; Faulkner, *Lawrence of Arabia's War*, p. 177.

39 Barr, *Setting the Desert on Fire*, p. 28; Faulkner, *Lawrence of Arabia's War*, p. 176.

40 This was certainly the view of the Arab Bureau in Cairo. 'Note on the Conference at Ismailia', 12 September 1916, FO 882/4, TNA.

41 Lawrence, *Seven Pillars*, p. 69; Lawrence to C. E. Wilson, 6 December 1916, in Garnett, *Letters*, 92, p. 211.

42 S. A. El-Edroos, *The Hashemite Arab Army, 1908–1979: An Appreciation and Analysis of Military Operations* (Amman: The Publishing Committee, 1980), pp. 68–74.

43 Lawrence, *Seven Pillars*, p. 80.

44 Colonel Cyril Wilson served alongside the British-Egyptian Army in the reconquest of the Sudan in 1898 and took up positions as governor of various provinces until the outbreak of the Hashemite revolt. He acted as chief negotiator with the Hashemite leaders, and his honesty won support from them and from Lawrence. He protested strongly when he learned of the Sykes-Picot arrangements, arguing for a settlement that rewarded Arab efforts. Philip Walker believed Wilson offered a steadying influence on the Arab Revolt, and was thanked by Wingate in later life for his contribution to the uprising's success.

45 Konrad Morsey, 'T. E. Lawrence: Strategist', in Stephen E. Tabachnick (ed.), *The T. E. Lawrence Puzzle* (Athens, GA: University of Georgia Press, 1984), p. 187.

46 Eliezer Tauber, *The Arab Movements in World War I* (London: Frank Cass, 1993), pp. 102–17; Rogan, *Fall of the Ottomans*, p. 302.

47 Philip Walker, *Behind the Lawrence Legend: The Forgotten Few Who Shaped the Arab Revolt* (Oxford: Oxford University Press, 2018), pp. 31–2, 56–7. Lieutenant Colonel Pierce Joyce, from an Anglo-Irish family. Of Lawrence, he famously noted: 'Lawrence rarely spoke. He merely studied the men around him and when the argument ended, he then dictated his plan of action which was usually adopted and everyone went away satisfied. It was not, as is often supposed, by his individual leadership of hordes of Bedouin that he achieved success but by the wise selection of tribal leaders.'

48 Colonel Stewart Newcombe had served in the South African War and conducted a surveying expedition in Sinai and Negev, a likely invasion route, with Lawrence in 1913–14. He was the leading light in the campaign to destroy and disrupt the Hejaz railway. He was captured in

1917 during the Third Battle of Gaza while leading a detachment deep behind Ottoman lines, but escaped from captivity in Istanbul and went into hiding for the rest of the war. He married his fellow escapee and named their son after Lawrence, his godfather. He acted as pallbearer to Lawrence at his funeral. He died in 1956.

49 Edouard Brémond, *Le Hedjaz dans la Guerre Mondiale* (Paris: Payot, 1931), p. 35; Barr, *Setting the Desert on Fire*, p. 47.

50 Robin Bidwell, 'The Brémond Mission in the Hijaz, 1916–17: A Study in Inter-Allied Co-operation', in Robin Bidwell and Rex Smith (eds), *Arabian and Islamic Studies* (London: Longman, 1983), pp. 182–95.

51 Morsey, 'Lawrence: Strategist', p. 193.

52 Lawrence, *Seven Pillars*, p. 554.

53 McMunn and Falls, *Military Operations, Egypt and Palestine*, vol. I, p. 231.

54 McMunn and Falls, *Military Operations, Egypt and Palestine*, vol. I, p. 233, note 1. The Arab fighters were also unnerved by the reprisals that had been conducted against Arab families around Medina. See Faulkner, *Lawrence of Arabia's War*, p. 178.

55 Lawrence, *Seven Pillars*, p. 129.

56 T. E. Lawrence, 'Military Notes', 26 November 1916, *Secret Despatches from Arabia*, cited in Malcolm Brown, *T. E. Lawrence in War and Peace: An Anthology of the Military Writings of Lawrence of* Arabia (London: Greenhill, 2005), p. 76.

57 Lawrence, 'Military Notes', in Brown, *T. E. Lawrence in War and Peace*, pp. 76–7.

58 Lawrence, 'Military Notes', in Brown, *T. E. Lawrence in War and Peace*, p. 77.

59 Lawrence, 'Military Notes', in Brown, *T. E. Lawrence in War and Peace*, p. 78; Faulkner, *Lawrence of Arabia's War*, p. 206.

60 Lawrence, *Seven Pillars*, p. 130.

61 Lawrence, *Seven Pillars*, p. 134.

62 Lawrence, *Seven Pillars*, pp. 134–5.

63 The near collapse of the Arab force appears in Lawrence, *Seven Pillars*, pp. 127–30. The effect of the naval searchlights is cited on p. 130. Inactivity also affected Feisal: 'With the Northern Army', *Secret Despatches*, 15 February 1917, cited in Brown, *T. E. Lawrence in War and Peace*, p. 99.

64 Lawrence, *Seven Pillars*, p. 130; Wilson, *Lawrence of Arabia*, p. 340.

CHAPTER 3

1 Lawrence, *Seven Pillars*, p. 138; Lawrence to C. E. Wilson, 8 January 1917, in Garnett, *Letters*, 94, pp. 215–16.

2 Lawrence, *Seven Pillars*, p. 138.

3 The Ottoman infrastructure of Arabia was a significant problem. Roads were in poor repair and many were unconsolidated tracks. The railway was therefore a vital element for the carriage of bulk supplies and troop transport. The Ottomans had a special military department for the railways, with some 30,000 personnel. To sustain the lines, there was systematic clearance of woodlands in Palestine, the Yarmouk Valley, and the region south of the Dead Sea, and huge stockpiles of sleepers and rails were created. Faulkner, *Lawrence of Arabia's War*, p. 66.

4 Wilson, *Lawrence of Arabia*, p. 355.

5 Lawrence, *Seven Pillars*, p. 119.

6 Lawrence, *Seven Pillars*, p. 134.

7 Lawrence, *Seven Pillars*, p. 134.

8 Lawrence, diary notes of 5 December 1916, FO 882/6, folio 15; Lawrence, 'Extracts of a Report on Feisal's Operations', 18 November 1916, *Secret Despatches*, cited in Brown, *T. E. Lawrence in War and Peace*, pp. 71–2; Wilson, *Lawrence of Arabia*, p. 337.

9 The state of the Ottoman Army in 1914–16 was certainly mixed. Some formations were well equipped and seasoned by previous conflicts, but mobilization created significant problems. Pay had not been issued for months, food supply was intermittent, and uniforms could not be replaced. The result was that some units took the field in ragged, patched clothing, with troops undernourished, ill-shod or barefoot, and while most carried the new magazine-fed German Mauser rifles, some were armed with converted single-shot Martini-Henry rifles of the 1870s. The German Maxim machine guns were prized, as were the German Krupp 75 mm artillery pieces, and the Austrian mountain guns. The only problem was in ammunition supply, where quantity and quality were inadequate. *Handbook of the Turkish Army* (London: War Office. Intelligence Division, 1916; reproduced by the Imperial War Museum, Dept. of Printed Books, in association with the Battery Press, Nashville, and Articles of War Ltd., 1999).

10 Laila Parsons, *The Commander* (London: Saqi, 2017).

11 Fawzi al-Qawuqji went on to lead an insurgency against the French in Syria in the 1920s and then the 1936 revolt against the British mandate authorities. Later in his career, Qawuqji aligned himself to the Germans in the misguided hope of Nazi support for Arab liberation, before returning to lead the disastrous Arab effort against the nascent state of Israel in 1948. See Rogan, *Fall of the Ottomans*, pp. 299–301; Gingeras, *Fall of the Sultanate*, pp. 214–15; Michael Provence, *The Last Ottoman Generation and the Making of the Modern Middle East* (Cambridge: Cambridge University Press, 2017), p. 243.

12 Gingeras, *Fall of the Sultanate*, pp. 224–5.

13 The Ottoman newspaper *Tanin* reported that Hussein was driven by the desire for gold, not liberation or the Islamic cause, and he and opponents like him would be obliterated. *Tanin*, 3 August 1916, editorial. RG 59, 867.00/789, NARA, cited in Gingeras, *Fall of the Sultanate*, p. 214.

14 Hikmet Ozdemir, *The Ottoman Army 1914–1918: Disease and Death on the Battlefield* (University of Utah, 2008); Faulkner, *Lawrence of Arabia's War*, p. 71.

15 Robert Graves, *Lawrence and the Arabs* (London: Jonathan Cape, 1927; 1936 edn.), pp. 45–6.

16 See, for example, Lawrence, *Seven Pillars*, p. 142; Lawrence to C. E. Wilson, 8 January 1917, in Garnett, *Letters*, pp. 217–8.

17 Lawrence, *Seven Pillars*, p. 104; Scott Anderson, *Lawrence in Arabia* (London: Atlantic, 2013), p. 238.

18 Lawrence, *Seven Pillars*, p. 104.

19 *Arab Bulletin*, 6, 23 June 1916, p. 47; David Fromkin, *A Peace to End All Peace: The Fall of the Ottoman Empire and the Creation of the Modern Middle East* (London: Phoenix Press, 1989), p. 222; Polly Mohs, *Military Intelligence and the Arab Revolt: The First Modern Intelligence War* (London: Routledge, 2007).

20 McMunn and Falls, *Military Operations, Egypt and Palestine*, vol. I, p. 411.

21 Lawrence, 'Military Notes', 26 November 1916, *Secret Despatches*, cited in Brown, *T. E. Lawrence in War and Peace*, p. 76.

22 The Military Writings of Leon Trotsky, vol. II (1919), Problems of Building the Army: I. The Organisation of the Red Army, 'Guerrilla-ism and the Regular Army', https://www.marxists.org/archive/trotsky/1919/military/ch08.htm (accessed 20 July 2018).

23 Robertson to Murray, 16 October 1916, Add 52463, British Library.

24 McMunn and Falls, *Military Operations, Egypt and Palestine*, vol. I, pp. 230, 233–4.

25 Kristian Coates Ulrichsen, *The Logistics and Politics of the British Campaigns in the Middle East, 1914–22* (Basingstoke and New York: Palgrave, 2012).

26 Sir A. Murray to CIGS, 15 February 1916, cited in McMunn and Falls, *Military Operations, Egypt and Palestine*, vol. I, p. 171; Letters of CIGS and Sir A. Murray, 16 October 1916, CAB 44/15, TNA.

27 Kress von Kressenstein noted in his memoirs that 'Eine grössere Expedition' was anticipated, while the Turkish General Staff considered an offensive with seven divisions, specifically 100,000 men in 57 battalions with 23 batteries of guns. Kress von Kressenstein, 'Sinai', p. 21, cited in McMunn and Falls, *Military Operations, Egypt and Palestine*, vol. I, p. 157.

28 W. T. Massey, *The Great War in the Middle East*, pub. as *The Desert Campaigns* (New York: Putnams, 1918; repub. London: Leonaur, 2009), p. 23.

29 Robertson to Murray, 16 October 1916, Add 52463, British Library.

30 Lawrence to Hogarth, 20 April 1915, in Garnett, *Letters*, pp. 196–7.

31 Murray's reluctance to support the Arabs in a secondary theatre was magnified by the episode at Wejh that followed, the last Ottoman-controlled port in the Hejaz. For Lawrence, it demonstrated the value of circling behind the Ottoman port defences, but for the majority of British officers, it reinforced the view that the Arab irregulars were unreliable and militarily ineffective, strengthening their preference to convert them into regular troops, equipped and supported with modern arms. The unreliability of the irregulars, particularly over timings, orders, trust, the distribution of supplies, coordination and what professional officers call 'force protection', were constant and repeated themes in Young's memoir. See Young, *Independent Arab*, pp. 182–6, 189, 208–9.

32 Johnson, *The Great War and the Middle East*, p. 116.

33 McMunn and Falls, *Military Operations, Egypt and Palestine*, vol. I, p. 236.

34 Wilson, *Lawrence of Arabia*, pp. 346–7; Faulkner, *Lawrence of Arabia's War*, p. 213.

35 Gat, *History of Military Thought*, pp. 395 and 411.

36 Lawrence, *Seven Pillars*, p. 131.

37 Lawrence, *Seven Pillars*, p. 132.

38 Erik Lönnroth, *Lawrence of Arabia: A Historical Appreciation* (London: Valentine Mitchell, 1956), p. 31; Morsey, 'Lawrence: Strategist', pp. 196–7.

39 'The Arab Advance on Wejh', 6 February 1917, cited in Brown, *T. E. Lawrence in War and Peace*, p. 91.

40 Lawrence, *Secret Despatches*, p. 111; 'In Sherif Abdullah's Camp, 23 May 1917', cited in Brown, *T. E. Lawrence in War and Peace*, p. 132; Morsey, 'Lawrence: Strategist', pp. 196–7.

41 'A Brief Record of the Advance of the Egyptian Expeditionary Force', cited in Robin Bidwell, 'Queries for Biographers of T. E. Lawrence', *Arabian Studies*, 3 (1977), p. 22. James Barr offers the suggestion that Lawrence was engaged in a campaign to discredit Abdullah and the Medina operations so as to force the British authorities to focus on Palestine and Syria. Barr, *Setting the Desert on Fire*, pp. 118–19.

42 Lawrence, *Secret Despatches*, p. 111; Morsey, 'Lawrence: Strategist', p. 196.

43 Lawrence to C. E. Wilson, 22 December 1916, in Garnett, *Letters*, 93, p. 213.

44 Falls and Becke, *Military Operations, Egypt and Palestine*, vol. 2, part II, p. 396.

45 Balfour to Wingate, 14 May 1917, L/PS/10/609, BL.

46 *Arab Bulletin*, 6, 23 June 1916; see also report of 21 June 1916, in *Arab Bulletin*, 7, 30 June 1916.

47 Lawrence, *Seven Pillars*, p. 133–4.

48 Lawrence, *Seven Pillars*, p. 137.

49 Lawrence, *Seven Pillars*, p. 138.

50 McMunn and Falls, *Military Operations, Egypt and Palestine*, vol. I, p. 237, note 1.

51 Lawrence, *Seven Pillars*, p. 105.

52 Lawrence, *Seven Pillars*, p. 105.

53 Lawrence, *Seven Pillars*, p. 145.

54 For some reason, Lawrence later claimed that the garrison had consisted of only 200 infantry. Lawrence, *Seven Pillars*, p. 162. He claimed the assault had been unnecessary, a 'blunder', perhaps to absolve his Arab comrades of blame for being late.

55 N. N. E. Bray, *Shifting Sands* (London: Unicorn Press, 1934), p. 131.

56 Lawrence, *Seven Pillars*, p. 151.

57 Lawrence, *Seven Pillars*, p. 163. Lawrence did not mention a day lost to celebrations after news of Abdullah's successes. Barr, *Setting the Desert on Fire*, p. 94.

58 Lawrence, *Seven Pillars*, p. 156.

59 Lawrence, *Seven Pillars*, p. 162.

60 Lawrence, *Seven Pillars*, p. 164; Liddell Hart, *Lawrence: In Arabia and After*, p. 138; Wilson, *Lawrence of Arabia*, p. 352; Faulkner, *Lawrence of Arabia's War*, p. 215.

61 It has been suggested that Lawrence had not perhaps grasped the offensive potential of the Arab way of war, but raiding was their preferred style, so this seems difficult to reconcile, especially given his historical knowledge of war in the Middle East. Faulkner, *Lawrence of Arabia's War*, p. 213.

62 Faulkner, *Lawrence of Arabia's War*, p. 216.

63 McMunn and Falls, *Military Operations, Egypt and Palestine*, vol. I, p. 237.

64 Garland, Report, 6 March 1917, FO 882/4, TNA.

65 Walker, *Behind the Lawrence Legend*, p. 80; Mousa, *T. E. Lawrence*, pp. 59–60; Faulkner, *Lawrence of Arabia's War*, p. 216.

66 Lawrence, *Seven Pillars*, p. 114.

67 Lawrence, *Seven Pillars*, p. 115.

68 James Patrick Hynes, *Lawrence of Arabia's Secret Air Force* (Barnsley: Pen and Sword, 2010), p. 15.

69 Lawrence, *Seven Pillars*, p. 115.

70 Faulkner, *Lawrence of Arabia's War*, p. 219.

71 War Cabinet, Minutes, 8 January 1917, CAB 23/1/29, TNA.

72 McMunn and Falls, *Military Operations, Egypt and Palestine*, vol. I, p. 238.

73 McMunn and Falls, *Military Operations, Egypt and Palestine*, vol. I, p. 238.

74 Faulkner, *Lawrence of Arabia's War*, p. 219.

75 Lawrence, *Seven Pillars*, p. 166.

76 Lawrence, *Seven Pillars*, p. 187.

77 Lawrence, *Seven Pillars*, p. 188.

78 For a contrary view that has Lawrence as a 'true Clausewitzian', because of the latter's 'sophisticated use of dialecticism', see Faulkner, *Lawrence of Arabia's War*, p. 220.

79 Lawrence, *Seven Pillars*, p. 189.

80 Lawrence, *Seven Pillars*, p. 190.

CHAPTER 4

1 Lawrence, *Seven Pillars*, p. 193.

2 John Baynes, *Morale: A Study of Men and Courage: The Second Scottish Rifles at the Battle of Neuve Chappelle, 1915* (London: Cassell, 1967).

3 Colonel Ardant du Picq, *Battle Studies: Ancient and Modern Battle* (Paris, 1870), Part I, introduction, i. This complements many of the classic axioms: Napoleon famously attributed the 'moral to the physical as three is to one', and concluded: 'In war, moral factors account for three quarters of the whole; relative material strength accounts for only one quarter.'

4 In this regard, Sun Tzu's *Art of War* is often quoted: In Book III, clause 2, he wrote: 'Hence to fight and conquer in all your battles is not supreme excellence; supreme excellence consists in *breaking the enemy's resistance without fighting*.' [my italics]. This is the Lionel Giles translation (London: Luzac, 1910). There are some discrepancies in translation and meaning which are addressed in Tang Zi Chang, *Principles of Conflict: Recompilation and New English Translation with Annotation of Sun Tzu's 'Art of War'* (San Rafael, CA: TC Press, 1969) and Derek C. Yuen, *Diciphering Sun Tzu: How to Read the Art of War* (Oxford: Oxford University Press, 2014).

5   General Sir Archibald Wavell, *Speaking Generally* (London: Macmillan, 1946), p. 79.

6   Lawrence, *Seven Pillars*, p. 188.

7   Jeremy Wilson, *Lawrence of Arabia: Authorised Biography* (New York: Athenaeum, 1990), p. 272.

8   Napoleon cited by du Picq, *Battle Studies*, p. 121.

9   Lawrence, *Seven Pillars*, p. 192.

10 Konrad Morsey asserted there is no evidence from the documents at the time that Lawrence conceived of a strategy for the Hejaz and Levant. The first appearance of a complete strategy appears in 1920 in his essay 'Evolution of a Revolt', although Morsey pointed out that, as early as 1915, Lawrence had intended to divert the Arabs from the Hejaz towards Syria. The intention, expressed before the outbreak of the revolt, does not constitute a strategy, and it is clear that, in the thinking here, Lawrence was struggling to solve a particular problem. Morsey, 'Lawrence: Strategist', pp. 193–4.

11 Lawrence, *Seven Pillars*, p. 193.

12 Lawrence, *Seven Pillars*, pp. 192, 194–5. Xenophon, the Athenian historian and mercenary soldier of the Ten Thousand, fought under the command of Cyrus and completed a history of the final seven years of the Peloponnesian War, previously documented by Thucydides, in a work entitled *Hellenica* (411–362 BC). Like many Oxford students, Lawrence would have translated Xenophon's Greek because it was considered to be a particularly elegant form.

13 T. E. Lawrence, 'Science of Guerrilla Warfare', *Encyclopaedia Britannica* (1929), strategy and tactics, para.1, p. 950.

14 Lawrence, *Seven Pillars*, p. 114.

15 Lawrence, *Seven Pillars*, p. 114.

16 Lawrence's written reply to Basil Liddell Hart's 'Queries I', *T. E. Lawrence to his Biographer Basil Liddell Hart* (London: Doubleday and Doran and Co., 1938), pp. 50–1; see also Lawrence, *Seven Pillars*, p. 188.

17 This is the method that Professor Bruce Gudmundsson and I have championed in professional military education in recent years.

18 T. E. Lawrence, *Revolt in the Desert* (London: Jonathan Cape, 1926), p. 96.

19 Maurice de Saxe, *Reveries on the Art of War* (New Delhi: Pentagon Press, 2017), p. 121.

20 Clausewitz noted that the moral spirits 'seek to escape from all book-knowledge, for they will neither be brought into numbers nor into classes, and want only to be seen and felt'. From this, Lawrence derived his 'felt elements'. Clausewitz, *On War*, Book III, opening to ch.3.

21 Clausewitz, *On War*, p. 76.

22 Caemmerer was a Prussian staff officer (1845–1911) who wrote a biography of Clausewitz. He was an ensign in the Austro-Prussian War and took part in the battle of Woerth in 1870, during the Franco-Prussian War, where he was awarded the Iron Cross, II class. Between 1876 and 1883, he worked in the General Staff, before returning to Battalion command and later Divisional command appointments. He wrote on military history, including *Explanation of Strategy in the Nineteenth Century* (1904) as *Die Entwicklung der strategischen Wissenschaft im 19. Jahrhundert*. The work which may have appealed to Lawrence was that of the *War of Liberation*, published in 1909: *Geschichte der Befreiungskriege 1813–1815*. Gat, *History of Military Thought*, pp. 380–1. Caemmerer was also highly critical of French pre-war strategic planning. Caemmerer, *Entwicklung der strategischen Wissenschaft*, pp. 230–8.

23 Field Marshal Helmuth Moltke 'the Elder' was the Prussian Chief of the General Staff who commanded the successful campaigns against Austria (1866) and France (1870), which led to the unification of the German states. He was celebrated for his powers of organization and for executing envelopment manoeuvres against his enemies at the theatre, operational, and tactical levels. His emphasis was on encouraging the initiative of his corps commanders, within the parameters of the intent of the overall commander, and he wrote extensively on war and strategy, emphasizing the pragmatism of ways and means. He stressed that flexibility and adaptability in contact with the enemy were essential, and he rejected rigid planning assumptions or the formulaic approach he found in Jomini. Ironically, Moltke had served in the Ottoman Army in the 1840s, and he was the subject of a work by Spenser Wilkinson. Gat, *History of Military Thought*, Book II, ch. 2.

24 Brown, *T. E. Lawrence in War and Peace*, p. 263.

25 Gat, *History of Military Thought*, pp. 382–4. There was also, to some extent, a conservative French reaction to the more assertive republican atmosphere sweeping the country in the years prior to the First World War. Doug Porch has shown that there was not a simplistic division between republicans and the old elite of the army, but a more intellectual division about the relative balance of defensive and offensive postures, the degree to which the emphasis should be on morale or firepower, or manoeuvre and fortifications. See D. Porch, *The March to the Marne: The French Army 1871–1914* (Cambridge: Cambridge University Press, 1981).

26 Stephen van Evera, 'The Cult of the Offensive and the Origins of the First World War', *International Security*, 9, 1 (1984), p. 60; Basil Liddell

Hart, 'French Military Ideas before the First World War' in M. Gilbert (ed.), *A Century of Conflict, 1850–1950* (London: Hamish Hamilton, 1966), pp. 135–48.

27 Jules-Lewis Lewal, *Introduction à la partie positive de la strategie* (Paris, 1892), cited in Gat, *History of Military Thought*, p. 389.

28 See, for example, Captain Georges Gilbert, *La Nouvelle Revue*, 47 1, 15 (1887), pp. 540–6, cited in Gat, *History of Military Thought*, p. 392.

29 Colonel Maillard, lecturer at the war school, summed up the French spirit as: 'the destruction of the enemy is the aim; the offensive is the means'. However, the 'ways' were a detailed application of manoeuvre: advancing dispersed but concentrating to fight; attacking from the line of march; and maintaining a balance between formations such that the army could move in any direction. Henri Bonnal, influential professor of Military History and Strategy, assembled the examples of the Napoleonic campaigns, including the value of feints, deception, diversions and sudden, unexpected manoeuvres. Bonnal believed he had discovered a fundamental weakness in the German method: their emphasis on attacking gave their troops a sense of advantage, but it set a predictable pattern. If France maintained a flexible defence, it could respond successfully to any German offensive. L. Maillard, *Elements de la guerre* (Paris, 1891), cited in Gat, *History of Military Thought*, pp. 389 and 395; Henri Bonnal, *Sadowa: A Study* (London: 1907), pp. 243–4; Gat, *History of Military Thought*, pp. 394–5.

30 Gat shows that Foch later altered his accounts of his views in this period, particularly in his post-war version of *Principles of War* (London, 1920; published in French in 1903). Gat, *History of Military Thought*, p. 403, n. 73.

31 Basil Liddell Hart, *Foch: The Man of Orleans* (London: Eyre and Spottiswoode, 1931), p. 458.

32 E. Carrias, *La pensée militaire française* (Paris: Presses Universities de France, 1960), p. 288.

33 Gat, *History of Military Thought*, p. 404.

34 Gat, *History of Military Thought*, pp. 405, 408.

35 Du Picq, *Battle Studies*, pp. 120–21, 128; Major Francois-Jules-Louis de Grandmaison, *Dressage de l'infanterie* (Paris, 1906), pp. 68, 89; Jack Snyder, *The Ideology of the Offensive* (Ithaca: Cornell, 1984), pp. 57–9. The prevalence of the offensive was taken up in doctrine, such as *Conduite des grandes unites* (Paris, 1913), translated into English as: War Office General Staff, *The Operations of Large Formations* (London, 1914).

36 Brown, *T. E. Lawrence in War and Peace*, p. 272.

37 For influences on Lawrence, as evidenced by his library of books at Cloud's Hill for example, see A. W. Lawrence, *T. E. Lawrence and his Friends* (London: Jonathan Cape, 1937), pp. 476–510; for the influence of the concept of will, through Schopenhauer, and Nietzsche, see Thomas J. O'Donnell, 'The Assertion and Denial of the Romantic Will in Seven Pillars and The Mint', in Stephen E. Tabachnick (ed.), *The T. E. Lawrence Puzzle* (Athens: University of Georgia Press, 1984), pp. 71–95; Gat, *History of Military Thought*, pp. 431–2.

38 T. E. Lawrence to Liddell Hart, 31 March 1929, Liddell Hart Papers 9/13/18, cited in Brian Holden Reid, *British Military Thought* (Lincoln: University of Nebraska Press, 1998), p. 159.

39 T. E. Lawrence, 'The Evolution of a Revolt', *Army Quarterly and Defence Journal* (October 1920), pp. 2–3.

40 Lawrence, 'The Evolution of a Revolt', pp. 2–3.

41 Lawrence, 'The Evolution of a Revolt', p. 3.

42 Lawrence, 'Science of Guerrilla War', para. 5, p. 950.

43 Lawrence, 'The Evolution of a Revolt', p. 4.

44 Lawrence, *Seven Pillars*, p. 193; Ottoman intelligence improved as the campaign unfolded. Barr, *Setting the Desert on Fire*, p. 242.

45 Morsey, 'Lawrence: Strategist', p. 194.

46 Lawrence, *Seven Pillars*, p. 189.

47 Lawrence, 'The Evolution of a Revolt', p. 6; Lawrence, *Seven Pillars*, p. 189.

48 Johnson, *The Great War and the Middle East*, pp. 152 and 171.

49 Lawrence, 'The Evolution of a Revolt', p. 8; Lawrence, *Seven Pillars*, p. 192.

50 Lawrence, *Seven Pillars*, p. 192.

51 Faulkner, *Lawrence of Arabia's War*, p. 371.

52 Lawrence, 'Science of Guerrilla Warfare', strategy and tactics, para. 1.

53 Lawrence, 'Science of Guerrilla Warfare', humanity in battle, para. 3.

54 Lawrence, 'Science of Guerrilla Warfare', strategy and tactics, para. 2.

55 Lawrence, *Revolt in the Desert*, p. 96.

56 Lawrence, 'Science of Guerrilla Warfare', strategy and tactics, para. 3.

57 Lawrence to C. E. Wilson, 22 December 1916, in Garnett, *Letters*, 93, pp. 213–14.

58 Lawrence, *Seven Pillars*, p. 195; Antulio Echevarria, *Clausewitz and Contemporary War* (Oxford: Oxford University Press, 2007), p. 137.

59 Lacquer, *Guerrilla*, p. 403.

60 Robert Asprey, *War in the Shadows: The Guerrilla in History* (London: Macdonald, 1975), p. 164; Werner Halweg, 'Clausewitz and Guerrilla

Warfare' in Michael I. Handel (ed.), *Clausewitz and Modern Strategy* (London: Frank Cass, 1986), pp. 127–33.

61 Clausewitz, *On War*, pp. 92 and 94.

62 Clausewitz, *On War*, p. 183; see also Book III, chapters 3–7, and 10.

63 Lawrence, 'The Evolution of a Revolt', p. 9.

64 Lawrence, 'Science of Guerrilla Warfare', humanity in battle, para. 1.

65 It was not only the Ottomans who feared the desert. In August 1918, the critical shortage of supplies, caused in part by the habit of camel drovers selling their stocks for personal profit, left even the Arab regular troops 'half-mutinous with fear of the desert'. Lawrence, *Seven Pillars*, p. 561.

66 Lawrence, 'The Evolution of a Revolt', p. 11.

67 Lawrence, 'Science of Guerrilla Warfare', the crowd in action, para. 1.

68 Lawrence, *Seven Pillars*, p. 539.

69 Lawrence, *Seven Pillars*, p. 29.

70 Lawrence, *Secret Despatches*, p. 65; 'With the Northern Army', 15 February 1917, cited in Brown, *T. E. Lawrence in War and Peace*, p. 99.

71 'Nationalism Amongst the Tribesmen', 26 November 1916, *Secret Despatches*, cited in Brown, *T. E. Lawrence in War and Peace*, p. 82.

72 Lawrence, 'Science of Guerrilla Warfare', the crowd in action, para. 2.

73 Lawrence, *Seven Pillars*, p. 339.

74 Daniel Ussishkin, *Morale: A Modern British History* (Oxford: Oxford University Press, 2017), p. 75; Hew Strachan, 'Training, Morale, and Modern War', *Journal of Contemporary History*, 41, 2 (2006), pp. 211–27; G. D. Sheffield, *Leadership in the Trenches: Officer-Man Relations, Morale, and Discipline in the British Army in the Era of the First World War* (London: Macmillan, 2000).

75 Young, *Independent Arab*, p. 173.

76 T 1/12249/33669, circa August 1918, Treasury Records, TNA. See also Neil Dearberg, *Desert Anzacs: The Under-Told Story of the Sinai Palestine Campaign 1916–1918* (Glass House Books, 2017), pp. 164–6. Dearberg estimates £20 million, but the methodology for making this calculation is unclear and the partial nature of this text creates some doubt over the figure. Young concluded: 'Lawrence could not have done what he did without the gold, but no one could have done it with ten times the amount.' Young, *Independent Arab*, p. 157.

77 Lawrence, 'The Evolution of a Revolt', p. 19.

78 Lawrence, 'The Evolution of a Revolt', p. 19.

79 Zeine N. Zeine, *The Emergence of Arab Nationalism: With a Background Study of Arab-Turkish Relations in the Near East* (Delmar, NY: Caravan, 1958, 3rd edn, 1976), pp. 106–9 and 116; William Oschenwald, 'Ironic

Origins: Arab Nationalism in the Hijaz, 1882–1914', in Rashid Khalidi, et al. (eds), *The Origins of Arab Nationalism* (New York: Columbia University Press, 1991), pp. 189–96; Fromkin, *A Peace to End All Peace*, p. 221; Himmet Umunc, 'In Pursuit of a Futile Fantasy: A Critique of T. E. Lawrence and the Arab Revolt', paper presented to the XVth Turkish History Congress, 11–15 September 2006, Ankara. I am most grateful to Professor Umunc for permission to cite his paper.

80 *Arab Bulletin*, 12 August 1917, 'The Sherif's Religious Views', cited in Brown, *T. E. Lawrence in War and Peace*, p. 113. Among Lawrence's more interesting observations was Feisal's distaste for the concept of a Caliphate and his ambivalence towards most sects of Islam.

81 'Abdullah and the Akhwan', 24 December 1917, cited in Brown, *T. E. Lawrence in War and Peace*, pp. 156–7. See also the report of 27 January 1918, 'Akhwan Converts', pp. 157–8, which suggests further radicalization.

82 Lawrence, *Seven Pillars*, p. 137.

83 Lawrence, *Seven Pillars*, p. 145.

84 Young, *Independent Arab*, p. 234.

85 Andrew Silke, 'Ferocious Times: The IRA, the RIC, and Britain's Failure in 1919–1921', *Terrorism and Political Violence*, 28, 3 (2016), pp. 417–34.

86 See Charles Townshend, *The British Campaign in Ireland, 1919–1921: The Development of Political and Military Policies* (Oxford: Oxford University Press, 1975); Charles Townshend, *The Republic: The Fight for Irish Independence, 1918–1923* (London: Penguin, 2014).

87 Lawrence to Newcombe, 16 November 1920, cited in Garnett, *Letters*, p. 322.

88 Morsey, 'Lawrence: Strategist', p. 186.

89 Asprey, *War in the Shadows*, p. 288.

90 C. A. Johnson, 'Civilian Loyalties and Guerrilla Conflict', *World Politics* 14 (October 1961), pp. 646–7.

91 Max Boot, *Invisible Armies: An Epic History of Guerrilla Warfare from Ancient Times to the Present* (New York: Liverlight-W. W. Norton & Co., 2013), p. 287.

92 At the outbreak of war, Syria provided 52,000 men, while Amman and Es Salt produced another 5,000 recruits. Approximately a quarter of the Ottoman Army was drawn from the Middle East. See Yücel Yanıkdâg, *Healing the Nation: Prisoners of War, Medicine and Nationalism in Turkey, 1914–1939* (Edinburgh: Edinburgh University Press, 2013), p. 17; Gingeras, *Fall of the Sultanate*, pp. 207–8.

93 Lawrence, 'The Evolution of a Revolt', p. 11.

94 Emmanuel-Auguste-Dieudonné comte de Las Cases, *Journal of the Private Life and Conversations of the Emperor at St Helena*, Volume 4 (London: Henry Colburn, 1824); Rev. James Wood, *Dictionary of Quotations from Ancient and Modern English and Foreign Sources* (London, 1899), p. 567.

95 The exemplar of this effect was produced by the Mongols, who made extensive use of massacres to ensure compliance to their reign of terror and deliberately encouraged the effect by sending ahead of their armies 'agents of influence'. These pathfinders would spread exaggerated stories of the size, strength and destructive capability of the Mongol armies. At the same time, mounted messengers were found and killed, to deprive the enemy of information. Doubt would be allowed to grow and fester in the minds of their adversaries.

96 The remark was made at the height of the Vietnam War, by Hillman Dickenson, 'Master Guerrilla of Araby's Desert', *Army* (August 1967), p. 70.

97 Linda Schatkowski Schilcher, 'The Famine of 1915–1918 in Greater Syria', in John Spagnolo (ed.), *Problems of the Modern Middle East in Historical Perspective: Essays in Honour of Albert Hourani* (Reading: Ithaca Press, 1992), p. 254.

98 Djemal Pasha, *Memories of a Turkish Statesman*, p. 144.

99 See Selahattin Gunay, *Bizi Kimlere Birakap Gidiyorsun Türk: Suriye ve Filistin Anıları* [Who are you going to take us to? Turkish: Syrian and Palestinian memories] (Istanbul: Türkiye İş Bankası Kültür Yayınalrı, 2006), p. 2.

100 TC Genelkurmay Başkanligi [Turkish General Staff], *Birinci Diinya Harbinde Turk Harbi, Vnci Cilt, Qanakkale Cephesi Harekati, Inci Kitap (Haziran 1914–25 Nisan 1915)* [*The Turkish War in the First World War,* 5th edition, Gallipoli Front Operations, Vol. 1 (June 1914–25 April 1915)] (Ankara: Genelkurmay Basimevi, 1993).

CHAPTER 5

1 'Note of a Meeting at the Residency, Cairo, on 12th May 1917', Wingate Papers, W145/6/62-3, Durham University.

2 Johnson, *The Great War and the Middle East*, pp. 212–13; Young, *Independent Arab*, pp. 126–7.

3 Faulkner, *Lawrence of Arabia's War*, p. 258.

4 Lawrence, *Seven Pillars*, pp. 175–6.

5 Lawrence, *Seven Pillars*, p. 177.

6 Rogan, *Fall of the Ottomans*, pp. 335, 396; Gingeras, *Fall of the Sultanate*, p. 215.

7 Lawrence, *Seven Pillars*, p. 178.

8 Lawrence, f. 21, Add Mss 45914, BL.

9 Lawrence, *Seven Pillars*, p. 167.

10 Lawrence, *Seven Pillars*, p. 167.

11 Faulkner, *Lawrence of Arabia's War*, p. 258.

12 Lawrence, *Seven Pillars*, p. 169.

13 Faulkner, *Lawrence of Arabia's War*, p. 105.

14 Maxwell was later appointed the Military Governor of Ireland, after the Easter Rising of 1916, and charged to use the powers of Martial Law. His actions did much to galvanize popular opinion against the British authorities in favour of the Irish revolutionaries. H. de Watteville, 'Sir John Grenfell Maxwell (1859–1929)', *Oxford Dictionary of National Biography* (2004).

15 McMunn and Falls, *Military Operations, Egypt and Palestine*, vol. I, pp. 80–1.

16 McMunn and Falls, *Military Operations, Egypt and Palestine*, vol. I, pp. 80–1.

17 He estimated that a perimeter would be only 40 miles, and by use of a major river, only the crossing points need be held in strength. He therefore concluded that only 80,000–100,000 men would be required. He pointed out that the wastage figures were the same across the Near East, and he saw no reason to contemplate any evacuation. McMunn and Falls, *Military Operations, Egypt and Palestine*, vol. I, p. 81.

18 Wilson, *Lawrence of Arabia*, pp. 170–2.

19 Wilson, *Lawrence of Arabia*, pp. 224–5.

20 Wilson, *Lawrence of Arabia*, p. 178; Faulkner, *Lawrence of Arabia's War*, p. 106.

21 James Barr, *A Line in the Sand* (New York: Simon and Schuster, 2011), p. 17.

22 *Committee of Imperial Defence: Asiatic Turkey, Report of a Committee*, 30 June 1915, CAB 42/3/12, TNA.

23 Correspondence between Sir Henry McMahon and the Sharif of Mecca July 1915–March 1916, Cmd 5957 (London, 1939), p. 3; Kedourie, *In the Anglo-Arab Labyrinth*, Wingate to Balfour, 25 December 1917, FO 371/3395/12077, TNA; see also Karsh and Karsh, 'Myth in the Desert, or Not the Great Arab Revolt', pp. 289–90; Ali Allawi, *Faisal I of Iraq* (New Haven CT: Yale University Press, 2014), pp. 138–41.

24 Lawrence, *Seven Pillars*, p. 168.

25 Lawrence, *Seven Pillars*, introduction.

26 Wilson, *Lawrence of Arabia*, p. 398.

27 Lawrence to Hogarth, 22 March 1915, cited in Garnett, *Letters*, pp. 195–6.

28 Faulkner, *Lawrence of Arabia's War*, p. 263.

29 Lawrence, *Seven Pillars*, p. 180.

30 Wilson, *Lawrence of Arabia*, pp. 667–8.

31 Pocket diary, British Library Add Mss 45983A.

32 Lawrence, notebook, entry 5 June 1917, British Library Add Mss 45915. Text is struck out.

33 Lawrence, *Seven Pillars of Wisdom* (the 'Oxford' text, 1922), folio for ch. 51.

34 Lawrence, *Seven Pillars of Wisdom* (1926, limited publication), reference to 5 June 1917.

35 Lawrence, *Seven Pillars*, p. 275.

36 Karsh and Karsh, 'Myth in the Desert, or Not the Great Arab Revolt', pp. 288, 296; Rogan, *Fall of the Ottomans*, p. 336; Elie Kedourie, *England and the Middle East. The Destruction of the Ottoman Empire 1914–1921* (London: Bowes and Bowes, 1956).

37 Liddell Hart, *Lawrence: In Arabia and After*, p. 192.

38 Lawrence, *Seven Pillars*, p. 221; Newcombe and Garland were frustrated by the lack of support they received from the Arab fighters, and the way that custom interfered with their ideas of military efficiency. Garland, Report, 22 May 1917, FO 686/6 and Newcombe, Report, 4–10 May 1917, FO 686/6, TNA.

39 Barr, *Setting the Desert on Fire*, p. 114.

40 Lawrence, *Seven Pillars*, p. 224.

41 Lawrence, *Seven Pillars*, p. 224.

42 Lawrence, *Seven Pillars*, p. 224.

43 Accounts vary, but it seems it was between 40 and 50 strong.

44 Lawrence, *Seven Pillars*, p. 245.

45 Lawrence, *Seven Pillars* (1922 Oxford), pp. 240–2, cited in Wilson, *Lawrence of Arabia*, p. 406.

46 Lawrence, *Seven Pillars*, pp. 256–7 and 263.

47 Faulkner, *Lawrence of Arabia's War*, p. 270.

48 Lawrence, *Seven Pillars*, pp. 258–9.

49 Faulkner, *Lawrence of Arabia's War*, p. 151.

50 Lawrence, *Seven Pillars*, p. 273.

51 The theoretical underpinning of this robust 'satisficing' of objectives is explained by Yakov Ben Haim as 'info-gap', in *Info-Gap Decision Theory:*

Decisions Under Severe Uncertainty, 2nd edition (London: Academic Press, 2006), and unpublished paper, Robert Johnson and Yakov Ben Haim, 'Defence Planning Under Conditions of Deep Uncertainty: Info-Gap, Robust Decisions and Critical Questions' (2017).

52 Lawrence, *Seven Pillars*, p. 273; For Lawrence's manipulation of Auda's pride see also Young, *Independent Arab*, p. 175.

53 Carlos Marighella, *Minimanual of the Urban Guerrilla*, 'The Seven Sins of the Urban Guerrilla', https://www.marxists.org/archive/marighella-carlos/1969/06/minimanual-urban-guerrilla/ch37.htm (accessed October 2018).

54 Lawrence, *Seven Pillars*, p. 274.

55 Lawrence, *Seven Pillars*, p. 276.

56 Lawrence, *Seven Pillars*, p. 284.

57 Lawrence, *Seven Pillars*, p. 284.

58 Lawrence, *Seven Pillars*, pp. 284–5.

59 Faulkner, *Lawrence of Arabia's War*, p. 272.

60 Lawrence, *Seven Pillars*, p. 285.

61 Lawrence, *Seven Pillars*, p. 291.

62 Lawrence, *Seven Pillars*, p. 293.

63 David Murphy, *The Arab Revolt 1916–1918* (Oxford: Osprey, 2008), p. 49.

64 Karsh and Karsh, 'Myth in the Desert, or Not the Great Arab Revolt', p. 293; see also Rogan, *Fall of the Ottomans*, pp. 339–42.

65 Lawrence, *Seven Pillars*, p. 297.

66 Wilson, *Lawrence of Arabia*, p. 416–17.

67 Wilson, *Lawrence of Arabia*, p. 497.

68 Lawrence, *Seven Pillars*, pp. 298–9.

69 Lawrence, *Seven Pillars*, p. 298.

70 Lawrence, *Seven Pillars*, p. 302.

71 Lawrence, *Seven Pillars*, pp. 302–3; Faulkner, *Lawrence of Arabia's War*, p. 276.

72 Wilson, *Lawrence of Arabia*, p. 417.

73 Lawrence, *Seven Pillars*, p. 306.

74 Lawrence, *Seven Pillars*, p. 307.

75 Lawrence, *Seven Pillars*, p. 308

76 Lawrence, *Seven Pillars*, p. 310.

77 Lawrence, *Seven Pillars*, pp. 310–11.

78 Lawrence, *Seven Pillars*, p. 311.

79 The Ottoman garrison was only 600 strong. McMunn and Falls, *Military Operations, Egypt and Palestine*, vol. I, p. 240.

80 T. E. Lawrence, 'The Occupation of Aqaba, 12 August 1917', in Brown, *Lawrence of Arabia in War and Peace*, pp. 138–9.

CHAPTER 6

1   Falls and Becke, *Military Operations, Egypt and Palestine*, vol. 2, part II, p. 395. He was not alone in this verdict. Colonel Newcombe had already outlined the importance of the taking of Aqaba. Newcombe, Note: 'The Importance of the Capture of Aqaba', 24 May 1917, FO 882/6, TNA.

2   Sir Reginal Wingate to Sir Percy Cox, Baghdad, Telegram 530, 24 July 1917, 'Proposal for the Formation of Irregular warfare Organisation Amongst Arabs', FO 882/6, TNA.

3   'The Occupation of Aqaba', August 1917, FO 882/6, TNA; *Arab Bulletin*, 12 August 1917, 'The Occupation of Akaba', cited in Brown, *T. E. Lawrence in War and Peace*, pp. 137–8, 140.

4   R. A. East India Station to CinC Egypforce, 'Possible Turkish Attempt to Recapture Aqaba', 26 July 1917, FO 882/6, TNA.

5   Lawrence, *Seven Pillars*, p. 321.

6   Philip Chetwode would later rise to Field Marshal, but in the early stages of the war he had fought at Ypres before taking command of 2 Cavalry Division. Transferred to the Middle East, he then assumed command of the Desert Mounted Corps. Sir Harry Chauvel of the Australian Imperial Force commanded the ANZAC Mounted Corps, and was largely responsible for the 'deep battle' operations in the Near East in 1918. His forces seized Damascus ahead of the Arab forces and went on to secure Aleppo.

7   Lawrence, *Seven Pillars*, p. 321.

8   Lawrence, *Seven Pillars*, p. 322.

9   Faulkner, *Lawrence of Arabia's War*, pp. 281–3; Barr, *Setting the Desert on Fire*, p. 174.

10 Lawrence, *Seven Pillars*, p. 324. Gilbert Clayton believed Lawrence was 'invaluable' and his contribution 'enormous', but he would not let him lead the talks. Clayton to Major Pearson, letter, Arab Bureau, 2 March 1917, FO 882/6, folios 203–4, TNA.

11 Colonel Wilson to Colonel Symes, 31 August 1917, FO 882/6, TNA.

12 Barr, *Setting the Desert on Fire*, p. 175.

13 Johnson, *The Great War and the Middle East*, p. 182; Wilson, *Lawrence of Arabia*, p. 437. Cholera added to the difficulties.

14 Barr, *Setting the Desert on Fire*, p. 252.

15 Col. S. F. Newcombe, report, n.d. [*c.* 4/10 May 1917], FO 686/6, part 2, folio 72, and folios 82–4, TNA.

16 Wilson, *Lawrence of Arabia*, p. 420.

17 Allenby, 19 July 1917, 'Arab Forces: Arab co-operation in Hedjaz and Syria', WO 158/634, part 1, TNA.

18 Wilson, *Lawrence of Arabia*, p. 468.

19 Lawrence, *Seven Pillars*, p. 325.

20 Lawrence, *Seven Pillars*, p. 325.

21 *Arab Bulletin*, 24 July 1917, 'The Howeitat and Their Chiefs', cited in Brown, *T. E. Lawrence in War and Peace*, pp. 132–3.

22 Christopher Leclerc, 'French Eye-Witness Accounts of Lawrence and the Arab Revolt', Part 2, *The Journal of the T. E. Lawrence Society*, XX, 2 (2010/11). Auda's descendants sued Columbia Pictures for its portrayal, by Antony Quinn, in the 1960s film *Lawrence of Arabia*: he was characterized as a man driven by money.

23 Lawrence, *Seven Pillars*, p. 327.

24 Lawrence, *Seven Pillars*, pp. 324–5.

25 Lawrence, *Seven Pillars*, p. 328.

26 Matthew Hughes (ed.), *Allenby in Palestine: The Middle East Correspondence of Field Marshal Viscount Allenby* (Stroud: Sutton Publishing, 2004), pp. 36 and 37.

27 Lawrence, *Seven Pillars*, pp. 328–9.

28 Lawrence, *Seven Pillars*, p. 336.

29 Lawrence, *Seven Pillars*, p. 337.

30 Liddell Hart, *Lawrence: In Arabia and After*, p. 218.

31 Lawrence, *Seven Pillars*, p. 337.

32 Lawrence, *Seven Pillars*, p. 338.

33 Joanna Bourke, *An Intimate History of Killing* (London: Granta, 1999), pp. 50, 61–2; see also Joanna Bourke, *Fear: A Cultural History* (London: 2005), p. 199.

34 Lawrence, *Seven Pillars*, p. 385.

35 The first German squadron, no. 300 'Pascha', took part in the Sinai operations under Gerhard Felmy. It was later reinforced, in October 1917, with 301 (Jenin), 302 (Afule), 303 (Jenin) and 304 (a Bavarian unit at Afule) squadrons. This was joined by 305 squadron in February 1918 which was based at Amman and Deraa. The combat squadron known as Jasta I arrived in March 1918, and was based at Amman and Jenin, while Ottoman Squadron 14, with German pilots, was co-located. Squadron 300 was re-allocated to Samakh. Benjamin Z. Kedar, *The Changing Land between the Jordan and the Sea: Aerial Photographs from 1917 to the Present* (Tel Aviv: Yad Ben-Zvi Press, 1999), p. 29.

36 Barr, *Setting the Desert on Fire*, p. 210. Neil Faulkner argues that the 'mere presence of Jafar [al-Askari's] 2000 recruits in training had been

sufficient to deter an Ottoman advance from Abu al Lissan'. This seems highly unlikely and no empirical evidence is provided on this from Ottoman sources, or indeed, any other incident, so we must conclude it was geography and logistics, not the prowess of untrained troops that deterred. Faulkner, *Lawrence of Arabia's War*, p. 371.

37 Djemal to Feisal, November 1917, FO 686/38, TNA.

38 Lawrence, *Seven Pillars*, p. 341.

39 Lawrence, *Seven Pillars*, p. 342; Hynes, *Lawrence of Arabia's Secret Air Force*, pp. 29 and 50.

40 Lawrence, *Seven Pillars*, p. 342.

41 Lawrence, *Seven Pillars*, p. 342. They actually returned to Aqaba and not El Arish.

42 One aircraft was lost. Hynes, *Lawrence of Arabia's Secret Air Force*, p. 52.

43 Lawrence, *Seven Pillars*, p. 343.

44 Lawrence, *Seven Pillars*, p. 349.

45 *Arab Bulletin*, 24 July 1917, 'The Howeitat and Their Chiefs', cited in Brown, *T. E. Lawrence in War and Peace*, pp. 132–3.

46 Lawrence, *Seven Pillars*, p. 353.

47 Lawrence, *Seven Pillars*, p. 354.

48 Faulkner, *Lawrence of Arabia's War*, p. 303.

49 Lawrence, *Seven Pillars*, p. 359.

50 Young, *Independent Arab*, p. 142.

51 H. Prie-Gordon (ed.), *A Brief Record of the Advance of the Egyptian Expeditionary Force under the Command of General Sir Edmund H. H. Allenby, July 1917 to October 1918* (London: HMSO, 1919), n.p.

CHAPTER 7

1 *Arab Bulletin*, 13 May 1917, entry for 28 March 1917, cited in Brown, *T. E. Lawrence in War and Peace*, p. 113.

2 Lawrence, *Seven Pillars*, p. 201.

3 Lawrence, *Seven Pillars*, p. 203; *Arab Bulletin*, 13 May 1917, entry for 29 March 1917, cited in Brown, *T. E. Lawrence in War and Peace*, pp. 114–15.

4 Lawrence, *Seven Pillars*, p. 208.

5 *Arab Bulletin*, 13 May 1917, entry for 5 April 1917, cited in Brown, *T. E. Lawrence in War and Peace*, p. 119.

6 Lawrence, *Seven Pillars*, p. 210. The raid, which had resulted in one dead through a fall, missed tragedy when it blundered into one of its own machine gun teams which opened fire, but hit no one.

7 Lawrence, *Seven Pillars*, p. 211.

8   *Arab Bulletin*, 13 May 1917, entry for 7 April 1917, cited in Brown, *T. E. Lawrence in War and Peace*, pp. 120–1.

9   *Arab Bulletin*, 13 May 1917, entry for 7 April 1917, cited in Brown, *T. E. Lawrence in War and Peace*, p. 121.

10   Lawrence, *Seven Pillars*, pp. 239–40.

11   Lawrence, *Seven Pillars*, p. 361.

12   *Arab Bulletin*, 8 October 1917, 'The Raid at Haret Ammar', entry for 18 September 1917, cited in Brown, *T. E. Lawrence in War and Peace*, p. 148.

13   Lawrence, *Seven Pillars*, p. 365.

14   Lawrence, *Seven Pillars*, p. 366.

15   Faulkner, *Lawrence of Arabia's War*, p. 302.

16   Lawrence, *Seven Pillars*, p. 367; Lawrence had already expressed misgivings about taking on a large force. See *Arab Bulletin*, 8 October 1917, 'The Raid at Haret Ammar', entry for 17 September 1917, cited in Brown, *T. E. Lawrence in War and Peace*, p. 148.

17   Lawrence, *Seven Pillars*, p. 367.

18   *Arab Bulletin*, 8 October 1917, 'The Raid at Haret Ammar', entry for 19 September 1917, cited in Brown, *T. E. Lawrence in War and Peace*, p. 149.

19   Some 20 bodies were found at the point of detonation. The Lewis gun accounted for about 30 more.

20   Faulkner, *Lawrence of Arabia's War*, p. 305.

21   Lawrence, *Seven Pillars*, p. 371.

22   Young expressed concern, on several occasions, that British personnel would be left behind. See Young, *Independent Arab*.

23   Lawrence, *Seven Pillars*, p. 371.

24   In fact, he was later found, having been collected by the Howeitat.

25   Lawrence, *Seven Pillars*, p. 373.

26   *Arab Bulletin*, 8 October 1917, 'The Raid at Haret Ammar', entry for 19 September 1917, cited in Brown, *T. E. Lawrence in War and Peace*, p. 149.

27   Lawrence, *Seven Pillars*, p. 377.

28   Lawrence, *Seven Pillars*, p. 378.

29   Lawrence, *Seven Pillars*, p. 379.

30   Major Lawrence to Brigadier Clayton, 'Raid near Bir esh-Shediyah', 10 October 1917, FO 882/6, TNA; *Arab Bulletin*, 21 October 1917, 'The Raid near Bir esh-Shediyah', cited in Brown, *T. E. Lawrence in War and Peace*, p. 151.

31   *Arab Bulletin*, 21 October 1917, 'The Raid near Bir esh-Shediyah', cited in Brown, *T. E. Lawrence in War and Peace*, p. 152.

32   Lawrence, *Seven Pillars*, p. 380.

33 Lawrence, *Seven Pillars*, p. 380.

34 Falls and Becke, *Military Operations, Egypt and Palestine*, vol. 2, part II, p. 398.

35 Liddell Hart, *Lawrence: In Arabia and After*, p. 235; Mousa, *T. E. Lawrence*, p. 122.

36 The Great Arab Revolt Project [GARP] cited in Faulkner, *Lawrence of Arabia's War*, p. 486.

37 See Faulkner, *Lawrence of Arabia's War*, p. 307.

38 Liddell Hart, *Lawrence: In Arabia and After*, p. 227.

39 Lawrence, *Seven Pillars*, p. 381.

40 Thomas, *With Lawrence*, pp. 182–7.

41 Falls and Becke, *Military Operations, Egypt and Palestine*, vol. 2, part II, p. 401.

42 Falls and Becke, *Military Operations, Egypt and Palestine*, vol. 2, part II, p. 400.

43 Lawrence, *Seven Pillars*, p. 385.

44 Lawrence, *Seven Pillars*, p. 386.

45 For comparative analysis, see Faulkner, *Lawrence of Arabia's War*, p. 317.

46 Wilson, *Lawrence of Arabia*, pp. 452–7.

47 Lawrence, *Seven Pillars*, p. 390.

48 Matthew Hughes, 'Command, Strategy and the Battle for Palestine, 1917', in Ian Beckett (ed.), *1917: Beyond the Western Front* (Leiden: Brill, 2009); Hughes, *Allenby in Palestine*.

49 Hughes, *Allenby in Palestine*, p. 8; Johnson, *The Great War and the Middle East*, p. 192.

50 Robertson to Allenby, secret correspondence, 10 August 1917, WO 158/611, TNA.

51 Falls and Becke, *Military Operations, Egypt and Palestine*, vol. 2, part II, p. 15; David Lloyd George, *War Memoirs* (London: Odhams, 1933), II, pp. 1091–2.

52 Archibald Wavell, *Allenby: A Study in Greatness* (London: 1940), p. 186; John Grigg, *Lloyd George: War Leader* (London: Allen Lane, 2002), p. 150.

53 Robertson to Allenby, 1 August 1917, 8/1/67, Robertson Papers, Liddell Hart Centre for Military Archives, London.

54 For narratives of the battle see Eran Dolev, *Allenby's Military Machine: Life and Death in World War I Palestine* (London: I. B. Tauris, 2007); Michael Mortlock, *The Egyptian Expeditionary Force in World War I* (Jefferson, NC: McFarland, 2011); David R. Woodward, *Hell in the Holy Land: World War I in the Middle East* (Lexington: University of Kentucky, 2006).

55 Falls and Becke, *Military Operations, Egypt and Palestine*, vol. 2, part II, p. 50.
56 Falls and Becke, *Military Operations, Egypt and Palestine*, vol. 2, part II, p. 56.
57 Falls and Becke, *Military Operations, Egypt and Palestine*, vol. 2, part II, p. 60.
58 Falls and Becke, *Military Operations, Egypt and Palestine*, vol. 2, part II, pp. 66–9.
59 Falls and Becke, *Military Operations, Egypt and Palestine*, vol. 2, part II, p. 74.
60 Falls and Becke, *Military Operations, Egypt and Palestine*, vol. 2, part II, pp. 95–101.
61 Falls and Becke, *Military Operations, Egypt and Palestine*, vol. 2, part II, pp. 75, 104, 110.
62 Scott Anderson, *Lawrence in Arabia* (London: Atlantic Books, 2013), p. 381.
63 C. E. Lloyd to Clayton, 20 October 1917, cited in Anderson, *Lawrence in Arabia*. Lloyd recorded Lawrence's intent to have Feisal in power and refuse to negotiate any concessions to France. Lloyd, 'notes', 9/10, Lloyd papers, Churchill College, Cambridge, cited in Barr, *Setting the Desert on Fire*, pp. 186–7.
64 Lawrence wrote: '[he] flatly refused to join with Lloyd and myself into one caravan, for safety'. Lawrence, *Seven Pillars*, p. 396.
65 Lawrence, *Seven Pillars*, p. 399.
66 *Arab Bulletin*, 16 December 1917, 'A Raid', cited in Brown, *T. E. Lawrence in War and Peace*, p. 154.
67 Lawrence, *Seven Pillars*, p. 411.
68 Faulkner, *Lawrence of Arabia's War*, pp. 318–19.
69 Lawrence, *Seven Pillars*, p. 416.
70 *Arab Bulletin*, 16 December 1917, 'A Raid', cited in Brown, *T. E. Lawrence in War and Peace*, p. 154.
71 Falls and Becke, *Military Operations, Egypt and Palestine*, vol. 2, part II, p. 400.
72 *Arab Bulletin*, 16 December 1917, 'A Raid', cited in Brown, *T. E. Lawrence in War and Peace*, p. 154.
73 Lawrence, *Seven Pillars*, p. 423.
74 The Yarmuk bridge that Lawrence had tried to destroy was brought down on 19 June 1946 by the Haganah during the so-called 'night of the bridges'. For the magnitude of the task, see the RAF air photos at AIR 5/1155, TNA.

75 *Arab Bulletin*, 16 December 1917, 'A Raid', cited in Brown, *T. E. Lawrence in War and Peace*, p. 155.

76 Lawrence, *Seven Pillars*, p. 428.

77 Lawrence, *Seven Pillars*, p. 431.

78 *Arab Bulletin*, 16 December 1917, 'A Raid', cited in Brown, *T. E. Lawrence in War and Peace*, p. 155.

79 Lawrence, *Seven Pillars*, p. 432.

80 Lawrence, *Seven Pillars*, p. 437.

81 Lawrence, *Seven Pillars*, p. 441.

82 Philip Knightly and Colin Simpson, *The Secret Lives of Lawrence of Arabia* (London: Nelson, 1969), p. 83.

83 Wilson, *Lawrence of Arabia*, pp. 459–61; Faulkner, *Lawrence of Arabia's War*, p. 322; Jeremy Wilson, 'Lawrence James on the Deraa episode', www.telstudies.org/discussion/rejected_legend/rejected_legend_deraa.shtml (accessed September 2018).

84 Lawrence, *Seven Pillars*, p. 449.

85 Wilson, *Lawrence of Arabia*, p. 447; Anderson, *Lawrence in Arabia*, p. 380.

86 Lawrence, *Seven Pillars*, p. 450.

87 Lawrence, *Seven Pillars*, p. 453.

CHAPTER 8

1 Liddell Hart, *Lawrence: In Arabia and After*, p. 259.

2 Lawrence, *Seven Pillars*, p. 455.

3 Lawrence, *Seven Pillars*, p. 456; Wilson, *Lawrence of Arabia*, pp. 465–6.

4 Falls and Becke, *Military Operations, Egypt and Palestine*, vol. 2, part II, I, pp. 82–3.

5 The Ottomans feared this was a prelude to a general Arab rising. Interestingly, Newcombe later escaped captivity in Istanbul and remained at large until the war's end; Falls and Becke, *Military Operations, Egypt and Palestine*, vol. 2, part II, I, pp. 82–3.

6 Wilson, *Lawrence of Arabia*, pp. 492, 498. The decision was also a result of improved Ottoman intelligence, conceivably through Arabs who were embedded within the Sharifian forces. Memorandum to DMI, 5 January 1918, 148/1. Wingate Papers, Sudan Archive, Durham. See also Akaba [HQ] to Dawnay, 6 January 1918, 'Report on Armoured Car Reconnaissance of Railway Line to Draw Troops from Maan to Help Arabs at Abu Lissal', Joyce Papers, LHCMA, London.

7 Lawrence, *Seven Pillars*, p. 459.

8 Lawrence, *Seven Pillars*, p. 459.

9 Lawrence, *Seven Pillars*, p. 460.

10 Liddell Hart, *Lawrence: In Arabia and After*, p. 263.

11 Faulkner, *Lawrence of Arabia's War*, p. 373.

12 Two died of exposure on the march. Faulkner, *Lawrence of Arabia's War*, p. 373.

13 Lawrence, *Seven Pillars*, p. 471.

14 Lawrence, *Seven Pillars*, p. 471.

15 The weather conditions meant that Zeid had only managed to bring up 100 regulars and two mountain guns. Falls and Becke, *Military Operations, Egypt and Palestine*, vol. 2, part II, p. 402.

16 Lawrence, *Seven Pillars*, p. 474.

17 *Arab Bulletin*, 11 February 1918, 'First Reports from Tafila', cited in Brown, *T. E. Lawrence in War and Peace*, p. 158. Major Lawrence to Brigadier Clayton, 22 December 1917, 'Situation at Tafileh', FO 882/6, TNA.

18 For an alternative account of the action, see Mousa, *T. E. Lawrence*, pp. 132–44. See also *Arab Bulletin*, 18 February 1918, 'The Battle of Seil el-Hasa', cited in Brown, *T. E. Lawrence in War and Peace*, p. 159; Major Lawrence to Brigadier Clayton, 26 January 1918, FO 882/6, TNA.

19 Lawrence, *Seven Pillars*, p. 475.

20 Lawrence, *Seven Pillars*, p. 475.

21 *Arab Bulletin*, 18 February 1918, 'The Battle of Seil el-Hasa', cited in Brown, *T. E. Lawrence in War and Peace*, p. 159.

22 *Arab Bulletin*, 18 February 1918, 'The Battle of Seil el-Hasa', cited in Brown, *T. E. Lawrence in War and Peace*, p. 160.

23 Falls and Becke, *Military Operations, Egypt and Palestine*, vol. 2, part II, p. 403.

24 Mousa, *T. E. Lawrence*, p. 136; Murphy, *Arab Revolt*, p. 62.

25 Lawrence, *Seven Pillars*, p. 479.

26 Falls and Becke, *Military Operations, Egypt and Palestine*, vol. 2, part II, p. 403.

27 Lawrence, *Seven Pillars*, p. 480.

28 Falls and Becke, *Military Operations, Egypt and Palestine*, vol. 2, part II, pp. 403–4.

29 Lawrence, *Seven Pillars*, p. 481. *Arab Bulletin*, 18 February 1918, 'The Battle of Seil el-Hasa', cited in Brown, *T. E. Lawrence in War and Peace*, p. 160.

30 Liddell Hart, *Lawrence: In Arabia and After*, pp. 274–6; Mousa, *T. E. Lawrence*, pp. 136–8; Murphy, *Arab Revolt*, p. 62; Faulkner, *Lawrence of Arabia's War*, pp. 375–7.

31 Lieutenant Colonel Hussein Husni, *Yıldırım*, Part 4, ch. V, cited in Falls and Becke, *Military Operations, Egypt and Palestine*, vol. 2, part II, p. 404.

32 Falls and Becke, *Military Operations, Egypt and Palestine*, vol. 2, part II, p. 404.

33 Lawrence, *Seven Pillars*, p. 482.

34 Murphy, *Arab Revolt*, pp. 64–5.

35 Falls and Becke, *Military Operations, Egypt and Palestine*, vol. 2, part II, p. 404.

36 Barr, *Setting the Desert on Fire*, pp. 225–7.

37 Falls and Becke, *Military Operations, Egypt and Palestine*, vol. 2, part II, p. 405.

38 Lawrence, *Seven Pillars*, p. 482.

39 Lawrence, *Seven Pillars*, p. 484.

40 Wilson, *Lawrence of Arabia*, p. 477.

41 Lawrence, *Seven Pillars*, p. 489.

42 Lawrence, *Seven Pillars*, p. 490.

43 Wilson, *Lawrence of Arabia*, p. 498; see also Lawrence's comment on the typescript of Basil Liddell Hart's, *T. E. Lawrence to his Biographer Basil Liddell-Hart* (London: Doubleday and Doran and Co., 1938), p. 110.

44 Lawrence, *Seven Pillars*, p. 492.

45 Lawrence, *Seven Pillars*, p. 492.

46 Lawrence, *Seven Pillars*, p. 499.

47 Lawrence, *Seven Pillars*, p. 500; Wilson, *Lawrence of Arabia*, p. 480.

48 Wilson, *Lawrence of Arabia*, p. 482.

49 Lawrence, *Seven Pillars*, p. 503. Allenby reported only that: 'The Arabs, led by Lawrence … are an unstable lot.' Allenby to Robertson, 23 February 1918, 7/5/86, Robertson Papers, LHCMA.

50 Lawrence, *Seven Pillars*, p. 504.

51 Lawrence, *Seven Pillars*, p. 225.

52 Rogan, *Fall of the Ottomans*, pp. 339–42; Allawi, *Feisal I*, pp. 108–18 and 120.

53 Lawrence, *Seven Pillars*, p. 504.

54 Lawrence, *Seven Pillars*, p. 504.

55 Wilson, *Lawrence of Arabia*, pp. 477–8; Dawnay's assessments are at A. G. C. Dawnay to Chief of the General Staff, General Headquarters, EEF, 15 February 1918, WO 158 616, TNA.

56 Lawrence, *Seven Pillars*, p. 507.

CHAPTER 9

1 Young, *Independent Arab*, pp. 164, 167.

2 Lawrence, *Seven Pillars*, p. 509.

3 Lawrence, *Seven Pillars*, pp. 224, 339.

4 Lawrence, *Seven Pillars*, p. 339.

5 Lawrence, *Seven Pillars*, p. 510.

6 Lawrence, *Seven Pillars*, p. 510. Lawrence took this line from the Epilogue of James Elroy Flecker, 'The Golden Road to Samarkand' (1913). Lawrence's essay on Flecker was published in 1937. The expression was subsequently adopted by 22 SAS, the British Special Forces Regiment.

7 Lawrence, *Seven Pillars*, p. 339.

8 Lawrence, *Seven Pillars*, p. 511.

9 Lawrence, *Seven Pillars*, p. 340.

10 Lord Charles Moran, *The Anatomy of Courage* (Chiswick: Eyre and Spottiswoode, 1945).

11 Moran suggested that courage could be enhanced by selection based on exclusion; transformation by training and induction to attain *esprit de corps*; discipline based on control from within, or self-control; devotion to the Regiment, a cause, or a religious faith; enhanced status accorded by the individual's community or country; or by being appointed a leader, thereby having to fulfil the expectations of leadership. Moran, *The Anatomy of Courage*.

12 Walker, *Behind the Lawrence Legend*, pp. 223–7.

13 Lawrence, *Seven Pillars*, p. 234.

14 Lawrence, *Seven Pillars*, p. 239.

15 Lawrence, *Seven Pillars*, pp. 219–20.

16 *Arab Bulletin*, August 1917, Memorandum by Major Lawrence, '27 Articles', FO 882/6, TNA.

17 Lawrence, *Seven Pillars*, p. 223.

18 Lawrence, *Seven Pillars*, pp. 465–7.

19 John Alexander, '"Hot Air, Aeroplanes and Arabs": T. E. Lawrence and Air Power', *Air Power Review*, 22, 1 (2019), p. 93; Hynes, *Lawrence of Arabia's Secret Air Force*, pp. 1–5.

20 L. Stein, *The Balfour Declaration* (London, 1961), p. i.

21 The Declaration was not, as later posited, a blueprint for the creation of the state of Israel. Balfour had written only that the British government would help to 'facilitate' an entity they 'viewed with favour'. Johnson, 'The de Bunsen Committee', p. 17.

22 Sykes to Clayton, 22 July 1917, Sykes Papers, Middle East Centre Archive, St Anthony's College, Oxford (hereafter MECA).

23 Sykes to Drummond, 20 July 1917, Sykes Papers, MECA.

24 Clayton to Lawrence, 20 September 1917, Clayton papers 693/12, Sudan Archive, Durham.

25 Sykes, memorandum, 18 July 1917; Sykes to Clayton, 22 July 1917, Sykes Papers, MECA; Barr, *Line in the Sand*, pp. 52–3.

26 Sykes to Wingate, 3 March 1918; see also Sykes to Clayton, 3 March 1918, Sykes Papers, MECA.

27 Rogan, *Fall of the Ottomans*, p. 358; Barr, *Setting the Desert on Fire*, p. 209.

28 *Arab Bulletin*, 1 February 1918, 'Syrian Cross-Currents', cited in Brown, *T. E. Lawrence in War and Peace*, pp. 164, 166.

29 Falls and Becke, *Military Operations, Egypt and Palestine*, vol. 2, part II, p. 409.

30 Hussein was diverting some of his British funding to preparations for operations against Ibn Saud. Barr, *Setting the Desert on Fire*, p. 245.

31 Hogarth to Wingate, 19 January 1918, 148/2, Wingate Papers, Sudan Archive, Durham.

32 Lacey, *The Kingdom*, pp. 147–8.

33 Lawrence, *Seven Pillars*, introduction to Book VIII, p. 506.

CHAPTER 10

1 Lawrence, *Seven Pillars*, p. 514.

2 Lawrence, *Seven Pillars*, p. 514.

3 Lawrence, *Seven Pillars*, p. 514.

4 Lawrence, *Seven Pillars*, p. 517.

5 Wilson, *Lawrence of Arabia*, p. 495; Liddell Hart, *T. E. Lawrence to his Biographer Basil Liddell-Hart* (London: Doubleday and Doran and Co., 1938), p. 166.

6 Rogan, *Fall of the Ottomans*, p. 362.

7 Otto Liman von Sanders, *Five Years in Turkey* (Annapolis: US Naval Institute Press, 1927), p. 211.

8 Falls and Becke, *Military Operations, Egypt and Palestine*, vol. 2, part II, p. 337; Faulkner, *Lawrence of Arabia's War*, pp. 387–9.

9 Liman von Sanders, *Five Years in Turkey*, p. 213.

10 Falls and Becke, *Military Operations, Egypt and Palestine*, vol. 2, part II, p. 346. There were significant massacres of Christians after the withdrawal. Many Arab clans made settlements with the Ottomans to avoid retribution. *Arab Bulletin* 92, 11 June 1918, FO 882/27, TNA.

11 Allenby to Field Marshal Sir Henry Wilson, 6 April 1918, Wilson Papers, HHW2/33A/1, IWM; Allenby to Wigram, 5 May 1918, cited in Hughes, *Allenby in Palestine*, pp. 148–53.

12 Falls and Becke, *Military Operations, Egypt and Palestine*, vol. 2, part II, p. 347.
13 For details of this engagement, see Young, *Independent Arab*, pp. 190–1.
14 The *Arab Bulletin* carried an exaggerated report on the extent of the damage done. *Arab Bulletin* 84, 7 April 1918, FO 882/27, TNA; Barr, *Setting the Desert on Fire*, p. 228.
15 Liddell Hart, *Lawrence: In Arabia and After*, p. 290; Faulkner, *Lawrence of Arabia's War*, p. 390.
16 Half of the Arab regular officers were killed and wounded. Jafar Pasha al-Askari, *A Soldier's Story: The Memoirs of Jafar Pasha al-Askari*, edited by William Facey and Najdat Fathi Safwat (London: Arabian Publishing Ltd, 2003), p. 143.
17 Lawrence, *Seven Pillars*, p. 520.
18 Faulkner, *Lawrence of Arabia's War*, p. 392; Mousa, *T. E. Lawrence*, p. 162; Al-Askari, *A Soldier's Story*, p. 142; Murphy, *Arab Revolt*, p. 66.
19 Lawrence, *Seven Pillars*, p. 521.
20 Lawrence, *Seven Pillars*, p. 522.
21 Lawrence, *Seven Pillars*, p. 523.
22 Wilson, *Lawrence of Arabia*, p. 498.
23 Lawrence to Graves, *T. E. Lawrence to his Biographers Robert Graves and Basil Liddell Hart* (London: Connell and Doubleday Doran, 1963).
24 Lawrence, *Seven Pillars*, p. 524.
25 Young, *Independent Arab*, p. 177.
26 Lloyd George, *War Memoirs*, II, p. 1728.
27 Falls and Becke, *Military Operations, Egypt and Palestine*, vol. 2, part II, p. 411–21.
28 Faulkner, *Lawrence of Arabia's War*, p. 395.
29 Falls and Becke, *Military Operations, Egypt and Palestine*, vol. 2, part II, pp. 375–6.
30 Joyce's report, 31 May 1918, WO 158/634, TNA; 'Testimony of Ibn al Najdawi', 1/Q/8, Joyce Papers, LHCMA.
31 Lawrence, *Seven Pillars*, p. 526.
32 Lawrence, *Seven Pillars*, p. 526.
33 Lawrence, *Seven Pillars*, p. 526.
34 Lawrence, *Seven Pillars*, p. 527.
35 Lawrence, *Seven Pillars*, p. 527; see also Young, *Independent Arab*, pp. 198–9.
36 Young, *Independent Arab*, p. 198.
37 Funding had, however, had a detrimental effect on motivation, as some clans considered themselves wealthy enough to avoid further risk. *Arab Bulletin Supplementary Papers*, 5, FO 882/13, TNA.

38 Dawnay to Joyce, 3 July 1918. 1/264, Joyce Papers, LHCMA.

39 Lawrence, *Seven Pillars*, p. 531.

40 Lawrence, *Seven Pillars*, p. 533.

41 Lawrence, *Seven Pillars*, pp. 533–4; see Bartholomew papers, LHCMA.

CHAPTER 11

1 Erik-Jan Zürcher, 'Little Mehmet in the Desert: The Ottoman Soldier's Experience', in Peter Liddle and Hugh Cecil (eds), *Facing Armageddon: The First World War Experienced* (London: Leo Cooper, 1996), pp. 233–4.

2 See for example: Rafael de Nogales Mèndez, *Four Years beneath the Crescent* (New York; London: C. Scribner's Sons, 1926).

3 Erickson, *Ottoman Army Effectiveness in World War I: A Comparative Study* (London: Routledge, 2007), p. 130. Intelligence Report, General Headquarters, Egyptian Expeditionary Force, 4 July 1918 AWM4 1/8/25. AWM, Canberra.

4 Lawrence, *Seven Pillars*, p. 537.

5 Lawrence, *Seven Pillars*, p. 537.

6 Lawrence, *Seven Pillars*, p. 538.

7 Falls and Becke, *Military Operations, Egypt and Palestine*, vol. 2, part II, pp. 450, 454–5.

8 Lawrence, *Seven Pillars*, p. 538.

9 Robert Vere 'Robin' Buxton (1883–1953) had been at Trinity College Oxford, had played cricket for Middlesex, had served in the Sudan, and then had been commissioned into the West Kent (Queen's Own Yeomanry) in Palestine. After the war, as a director of Martins Bank, he oversaw the financing of *Seven Pillars of Wisdom*.

10 Lawrence, *Seven Pillars*, p. 539.

11 Young, *Independent Arab*, pp. 204, 218–19.

12 Lawrence, *Seven Pillars*, p. 539.

13 Lawrence, *Seven Pillars*, pp. 539–40.

14 Young, *Independent Arab*, p. 245.

15 Young, *Independent Arab*, p. 219.

16 Lawrence, *Seven Pillars*, p. 541.

17 Lawrence, *Seven Pillars*, p. 541.

18 Lawrence, *Seven Pillars*, p. 539.

19 Lawrence, *Seven Pillars*, p. 542.

20 Lawrence, *Seven Pillars*, p. 553.

21 Faulkner, *Lawrence of Arabia's War*, pp. 417–19.

22 'The [aircraft] bombed [the northern redoubt], while the Camel Corps [attacked] from north and east and west … At seven in the morning the

last of the enemy surrendered quietly. We had lost four killed and ten wounded. The Turks lost twenty-one killed, and one hundred and fifty prisoners, with two field-guns and three machine-guns.' Lawrence, *Seven Pillars*, p. 553.

23 Lawrence, *Seven Pillars*, p. 546.

24 Lawrence, *Seven Pillars*, p. 547.

25 Major H. Garland to Colonel C. Wilson, 14 August 1917, FO 882/7, TNA.

26 Major Charles Vickery, 'Arabia and the Hedjaz', *Journal of the Royal Central Asian Society*, 10 (1923), pp. 51–2; Morsey, 'Lawrence: Strategist', p. 192; Major Vickery, Memorandum, 'Policy and Organisation of the British Mission to the Grand Sherif', 2 February 1917, FO 882/6, TNA.

27 Lawrence, *Seven Pillars*, p. 548.

28 Lawrence, *Seven Pillars*, p. 548.

29 John Keegan, *Mask of Command* (London and New York: Penguin, 1987), p. 11.

30 Lawrence, *Seven Pillars*, p. 554.

31 FO 371/ 3881; Wilson, *Lawrence of Arabia*, pp. 470 and 500–1; Faulkner, *Lawrence of Arabia's War*, p. 403; Karsh and Karsh, 'Myth in the Desert, or Not the Great Arab Revolt', pp. 302–3; Barr, *Setting the Desert on Fire*, p. 241.

32 Lawrence, *Seven Pillars*, p. 555.

33 Johnson, 'The de Bunsen Committee', p. 4.

34 Lawrence, *Seven Pillars*, chapter CIII.

CHAPTER 12

1 Lawrence, *Seven Pillars*, p. 558.

2 Lawrence, *Seven Pillars*, p. 568; Falls and Becke, *Military Operations, Egypt and Palestine*, vol. 2, part II, p. 408.

3 Lawrence, *Seven Pillars*, p. 571.

4 Lawrence, *Seven Pillars*, p. 571.

5 Lawrence, *Seven Pillars*, p. 572.

6 Falls and Becke, *Military Operations, Egypt and Palestine*, vol. 2, part II, pp. 408–9; Wilson, *Lawrence of Arabia*, p. 538.

7 Lawrence, *Seven Pillars*, p. 572.

8 Falls and Becke, *Military Operations, Egypt and Palestine*, vol. 2, part I, p. 363.

9 Faulkner, *Lawrence of Arabia's War*, p. 405; Wilson, *Lawrence of Arabia*, pp. 521–3.

10 Lawrence, *Seven Pillars*, p. 576.

11 Lawrence, *Seven Pillars*, p. 577.

12 Lawrence, *Seven Pillars*, p. 577.

13 Lawrence, *Seven Pillars*, p. 578.

14 Lawrence, *Seven Pillars*, p. 579.

15 Lawrence, *Seven Pillars*, p. 582.

16 Falls and Becke, *Military Operations, Egypt and Palestine*, vol. 2, part II, pp. 41–3; Faulkner, *Lawrence of Arabia's War*, p. 135.

17 Liman von Sanders, *Five Years in Turkey*, pp. 265 and 269.

18 Lawrence, *Seven Pillars*, p. 583.

19 Wilson, *Lawrence of Arabia*, p. 526.

20 Lawrence, *Seven Pillars*, p. 584.

21 Lawrence, *Seven Pillars*, p. 584.

22 Lawrence, *Seven Pillars*, pp. 584–5; *Arab Bulletin*, 'The Destruction of the Fourth Army', 22 October 1918, cited in Brown, *T. E. Lawrence in War and Peace*, p. 168.

23 Lawrence, *Seven Pillars*, p. 585.

24 Liddell Hart, *Lawrence: In Arabia and After*, pp. 330–33; Wilson, *Lawrence of Arabia*, pp. 545–6; Faulkner, *Lawrence of Arabia's War*, p. 426.

25 Lawrence, *Seven Pillars*, p. 587; Wilson, *Lawrence of Arabia*, p. 547.

26 Young, *Independent Arab*, p. 217.

27 Lawrence, *Seven Pillars*, p. 588; Faulkner, *Lawrence of Arabia's War*, p. 427.

28 *Arab Bulletin*, 'The Destruction of the Fourth Army', 22 October 1918, cited in Brown, *T. E. Lawrence in War and Peace*, p. 168.

29 Lawrence, *Seven Pillars*, p. 590.

30 Lawrence, *Seven Pillars*, p. 590.

31 Lawrence, *Seven Pillars*, p. 592.

32 Lawrence, *Seven Pillars*, p. 593.

33 Lawrence, *Seven Pillars*, pp. 593–4.

34 Lawrence, *Seven Pillars*, p. 595; Young, *Independent Arab*, p. 222.

35 Young, *Independent Arab*, pp. 221–2.

36 *Arab Bulletin*, 22 October 1918, 'The Destruction of the Fourth Army', cited in Brown, *T. E. Lawrence in War and Peace*, pp. 168–9; Falls and Becke, *Military Operations, Egypt and Palestine*, vol. 2, part II, p. 565.

37 Young, *Independent Arab*, pp. 224–5; A. Kirkbride, *An Awakening* (Tavistock: University Press of Arabia, 1971), p. 69; H. A. Jones, *The War in the Air*, VI, (Oxford: Clarendon Press, 1935), pp. 213–14; Alexander, 'Hot Air, Aeroplanes and Arabs', p. 102.

38 Lawrence, *Seven Pillars*, p. 598.

39 *Arab Bulletin*, 22 October 1918, 'The Destruction of the Fourth Army', cited in Brown, *T. E. Lawrence in War and Peace*, p. 169.

40 Lawrence, *Seven Pillars*, p. 598.

41 Lawrence, *Seven Pillars*, p. 599; Young, *Independent Arab*, p. 227.

42 *Arab Bulletin*, 22 October 1918, 'The Destruction of the Fourth Army', cited in Brown, *T. E. Lawrence in War and Peace*, p. 169.
43 Lawrence, *Seven Pillars*, p. 600.
44 Lawrence, *Seven Pillars*, p. 601.
45 Young, *Independent Arab*, p. 230.
46 Lawrence, *Seven Pillars*, p. 604.
47 Young, *Independent Arab*, p. 231.
48 The *Official History* described the position as a dangerous one, given its exposure to counter-attack. Falls and Becke, *Military Operations, Egypt and Palestine*, vol. 2, part II, p. 565.
49 Lawrence, *Seven Pillars*, p. 605.
50 Young, *Independent Arab*, p. 233.
51 Lawrence, *Seven Pillars*, p. 606; *Arab Bulletin*, 22 October 1918, 'The Destruction of the Fourth Army', cited in Brown, *T. E. Lawrence in War and Peace*, p. 170.
52 Lawrence, *Seven Pillars*, p. 610.
53 Lawrence, *Seven Pillars*, p. 612.
54 Lawrence, *Seven Pillars*, p. 612; Young, *Independent Arab*, p. 235.
55 Young, *Independent Arab*, p. 240.
56 Lawrence, *Seven Pillars*, p. 612; Young, *Independent Arab*, p. 206.
57 Young, *Independent Arab*, pp. 234–5.
58 Lawrence, *Seven Pillars*, p. 616.
59 Lawrence, *Seven Pillars*, p. 618.
60 Falls and Becke, *Military Operations, Egypt and Palestine*, vol. 2, part II, pp. 565–6.
61 Young, *Independent Arab*, pp. 219–20; Jones, *War in the Air*, VI, pp. 229–30.
62 Young, *Independent Arab*, p. 242.
63 Lawrence, *Seven Pillars*, p. 621.
64 *Arab Bulletin*, 22 October 1918, 'The Destruction of the Fourth Army', cited in Brown, *T. E. Lawrence in War and Peace*, pp. 170–71.
65 Lawrence, *Seven Pillars*, p. 622.
66 Lawrence, *Seven Pillars*, p. 622.
67 Young, *Independent Arab*, p. 245.
68 Young, *Independent Arab*, p. 243.

CHAPTER 13

1 Lawrence, *Seven Pillars*, p. 623.
2 *Arab Bulletin*, 22 October 1918, 'The Destruction of the Fourth Army', cited in Brown, *T. E. Lawrence in War and Peace*, p. 171.

3 Lawrence, *Seven Pillars*, p. 623; Falls and Becke, *Military Operations, Egypt and Palestine*, vol. 2, part II, p. 566.

4 Lawrence, *Seven Pillars*, p. 624.

5 Lawrence, *Seven Pillars*, p. 624.

6 Lawrence, *Seven Pillars*, pp. 626–7.

7 Lawrence, *Seven Pillars*, p. 627.

8 Lawrence, *Seven Pillars*, p. 628.

9 Falls and Becke, *Military Operations, Egypt and Palestine*, vol. 2, part II, pp. 566–7.

10 Lawrence, *Seven Pillars*, p. 629; General Sir George Barrow, *The Fire of Life* (London: Hutchinson, n.d.), p. 208.

11 Lawrence, *Seven Pillars*, p. 629; Liddell Hart, *Lawrence: In Arabia and After*, pp. 349–54; Wilson, *Lawrence of Arabia*, p. 556.

12 *Arab Bulletin*, 22 October 1918, 'The Destruction of the Fourth Army', cited in Brown, *T. E. Lawrence in War and Peace*, p. 171.

13 Young, *Independent Arab*, p. 251.

14 Lawrence, *Seven Pillars*, p. 631.

15 Lawrence, *Seven Pillars*, p. 631.

16 Young, *Independent Arab*, p. 251.

17 Lawrence, *Seven Pillars*, p. 633.

18 Wilson, *Lawrence of Arabia*, p. 557.

19 Lawrence, *Seven Pillars*, p. 633; *Arab Bulletin*, 22 October 1918, 'The Destruction of the Fourth Army', cited in Brown, *T. E. Lawrence in War and Peace*, p. 172; Barr, *Setting the Desert on Fire*, p. 272.

20 Lawrence, *Seven Pillars*, p. 633.

21 Lawrence, *Seven Pillars*, pp. 633–4.

22 'The Action of the Enemy' in Falls and Becke, *Military Operations, Egypt and Palestine*, vol. 2, part II, pp. 594–5.

23 Lawrence, *Seven Pillars*, p. 634.

24 Lawrence, *Seven Pillars*, p. 634.

25 Falls and Becke, *Military Operations, Egypt and Palestine*, vol. 2, part II, p. 582.

26 Liddell Hart, *Lawrence: In Arabia and After*, pp. 357–9; Falls and Becke, *Military Operations, Egypt and Palestine*, vol. 2, part II, pp. 129–30; Wilson, *Lawrence of Arabia*, pp. 559–60.

27 Barrow, *Fire of Life*, p. 209. See also his corrections to Robert Graves' myths, p. 210.

28 Young relates that Barrow was appalled by the results of Arab looting and the sense of disorder in the town. Young, *Independent Arab*, p. 252. George Morton Jack also shows that Lawrence was wrong in his own accusations against the Indian Army. See George Morton Jack,

The Indian Empire at War: From Jihad to Victory, the Untold Story of the Indian Army in the First World War (London: Little, Brown, 2018), pp. 480–1.

29 Barrow, *Fire of Life*, p. 211, and footnote.

30 Barrow, *Fire of Life*, p. 211, and footnote.

31 Lawrence, *Seven Pillars*, p. 637.

32 According to the Australian Official History, Australian troops disparaged the Arabs who wanted the troopers to do all the fighting while they did all the looting, cited in Faulkner, *Lawrence of Arabia's War*, p. 446. Falls and Becke, *Military Operations, Egypt and Palestine*, vol. 2, part II, pp. 590–1. A more memorable tribute was from Lawrence to the air force. He concluded: 'The RAF lost four killed. The Turks lost a Corps.' Lawrence, *Revolt in the Desert*, p. 92.

33 Barrow, *Fire of Life*, p. 212.

34 Liman von Sanders, *Five Years in Turkey*, p. 273.

35 Lawrence, *Seven Pillars*, p. 643; Falls and Becke, *Military Operations, Egypt and Palestine*, vol. 2, part II, pp. 113–19.

36 Falls and Becke, *Military Operations, Egypt and Palestine*, vol. 2, part II, p. 567.

37 Faulkner, *Lawrence of Arabia's War*, pp. 452–4.

38 Philip Khoury, *Urban Notables and Arab Nationalism: the Politics of Damascus 1806–1920* (Cambridge, 1983), pp. 76–8.

39 A. Kirkbride, *A Crackle of Thorns* (London: John Murray, 1956), p. 9; W. F. Stirling, *Safety Last* (London, 1953), p. 95, cited in Barr, *Setting the Desert on Fire*, p. 295.

40 For detail on the vast administrative task and lack of resources, see Young, *Independent Arab*, pp. 254–65.

41 Lawrence, *Seven Pillars*, p. 658.

42 Lawrence, *Seven Pillars*, p. 659.

43 Chauvel to Allenby, 22 October 1929, cited in Hughes, *Allenby in Palestine*, pp. 297–300.

44 Allenby concluded, after the war, that Lawrence 'thinks himself a hell of a soldier and loves posturing in the limelight': Barrow, *Fire of Life*, p. 215.

CHAPTER 14

1 See FO 371 4183, TNA; Mousa, *T. E. Lawrence*, p. 227.

2 Garnett, *Letters*, 'Reconstruction of Arabia', 4 November 1918, p. 268.

3 He had told Clayton, after his success at Aqaba, 'I take it no modification of the policy agreed upon in Cairo will be decided upon, without my being given an opportunity of putting forward my views in detail.' Lawrence to Clayton, August 1917, FO 882/7/1, folio 89, TNA.

4 Cabinet Minutes, 20 September 1918, CAB 23/7, no. 475 (3), TNA.

5 There were some difficulties in this regard. The Secretary of State for India, Edwin Montagu, and the India Office, distrusted Lawrence's intentions. The Foreign Office were initially tolerant, eager to keep the Arab representatives on side, but they grew increasingly frustrated with Lawrence and eventually terminated his position at Paris, largely to save the relationship with France. Knightly and Simpson, *The Secret Lives of Lawrence of Arabia*, p. 122.

6 Barbara Walter, *Committing to Peace* (Princeton, NJ: Princeton University Press, 2002), pp. 41, 59–61.

7 Knightly and Simpson, *The Secret Lives of Lawrence of Arabia*, p. 124.

8 The full archive of the King-Crane Commission can be found at http://www2.oberlin.edu/library/digital/king-crane/ (accessed October 2018); Andrew Patrick, *America's Forgotten Middle East Initiative: The King-Crane Commission of 1919* (London: I. B. Tauris, 2015).

9 Foreign Office, private and confidential telegram, to A. Balfour, 17 July 1919, FO 608/92, TNA.

10 Telegram and Minutes, Foreign Office to A. Balfour, 17 July 1919–8 August 1919, FO 608/92, TNA.

11 Garnett, *Letters*, no. 115, Memorandum to the Foreign Office, 15 September 1919, p. 289.

12 See FO 371/4182, TNA.

13 Philip Knightly illustrates how far Harry Philby's perspectives rivalled Lawrence's. Knightly and Simpson, *The Secret Lives of Lawrence of Arabia*, pp. 122 and 133.

14 Garnett, *Letters*, pp. 285–8; Knightly and Simpson, *The Secret Lives of Lawrence of Arabia*, p. 129.

15 Lawrence to D. G. Pearman [undated, 1928], in Garnett, *Letters*, pp. 577–8; Lawrence, Letter to *The Times*, 22 July 1920, cited in Garnett, *Letters*, pp. 306–8.

16 Gertrude Margaret Lowthian Bell, CBE, was a courageous traveller, and, subsequently, a political officer for the British political administration in Iraq. She possessed considerable knowledge of Syria, Mesopotamia, Asia Minor, and Arabia both before the war and after, and knew Lawrence well. She also advocated the establishment of the Hashemite dynasty in Trans-Jordan and Iraq, where she worked to persuade local sheikhs of the value of an Arab monarchy protected by Britain.

17 Aylmer Haldane, *Insurrection in Mesopotamia* (Edinburgh: Blackwood's, 1922); Mark Jacobsen, '"Only by the Sword": British Counter-insurgency in Iraq, 1920', *Small Wars & Insurgencies*, vol. 2, 2 (1991), pp. 323–63.

18 T. E. Lawrence to the editor of *The Times*, 22 July 1920, in Garnett, *Letters*, pp. 306–8. See also Faulkner, *Lawrence of Arabia's War*, p. 96.

19 T. E. Lawrence to the editor of *The Times*, 22 July 1920, in Garnett, *Letters*, pp. 306–8.

20 T. E. Lawrence to the editor of *The Times*, 22 July 1920, in Garnett, *Letters*, pp. 306–8.

21 The actual cost of operations in Iraq was £6 million, not the £40 million claimed by the press.

22 Henry Wilson, 'Palestine and Mesopotamia', printed for Cabinet, 6 May 1920, LG/F/2056/5 and Memorandum by Winston Churchill, circulating and enclosing papers and calling for decision on transfer of Mesopotamia to the Colonial Office (n.d., *c.* May 1920) LG/F/205/6/1, Lloyd George Papers.

23 Keith Jeffrey, *The British Army and the Crisis of Empire, 1918–1922* (Manchester: Manchester University Press, 1984); Keith Jeffrey, *Field Marshal Sir Henry Wilson* (Oxford: Oxford University Press, 2006).

24 Morton Jack, *Indian Empire at War*, p. 498.

25 Although there was a brief consideration of the use of poison gas, the idea was quickly dismissed, for logistical reasons. Lawrence later claimed 'air policing' had been his idea, although he cautioned it was not something that had universal application. Liddell Hart, *T. E. Lawrence to his Biographer Basil Liddell-Hart* (London: Connell and Doubleday Doran, 1963), p. 112. For the advocates and critics, see Alexander, 'Hot Air, Aeroplanes and Arabs', pp. 104–106.

26 Martin Gilbert, *Winston S. Churchill, vol. IV: 1916–1922* (London: William Heinemann, 1975), pp. 510 and 514. Churchill favoured the 'utmost use of mechanical contrivances' to reduce costs in lives and finance. 'Naval, War and Air Estimates', 15 August 1919, WC 616A, CAB 23/15. TNA.

27 Gilbert, *Winston S. Churchill*, pp. 515–6.

28 Gilbert, *Winston S. Churchill*, p. 511.

29 Alan Houghton Broderick, *Near to Greatness: A Life of Earl Winterton* (London: Hutchinson, 1965), cited in Knightly and Simpson, *The Secret Lives of Lawrence of Arabia*, p. 140.

30 FO 686/85, TNA; Gilbert, *Winston S. Churchill*, pp. 511–12.

31 Gilbert, *Winston S. Churchill*, p. 513.

32 Knightly and Simpson, *The Secret Lives of Lawrence of Arabia*, p. 140.

33 Gilbert, *Winston S. Churchill*, pp. 522–3.

34 Gilbert, *Winston S. Churchill*, p. 523.

35 Talib al-Naqib had been the Ottoman governor of Nejd, where he had suppressed tribal raiding, but he was a nationalist and had been granted

the governorship of Basra in 1913 after some misgivings about his loyalty. After the war he opposed the mandate of Iraq, but condemned the revolt of 1920. His antagonism towards Feisal meant he was sent, along with Sayeb Taleb, into exile in Ceylon on the instructions of Gertrude Bell.

36 This conversation is attributed to Lawrence in Abdullah Ibn al-Hussein, *Al-Amali al-Siyasiya* (*Political Dictates*) [original in Arabic] (Amman, 1939), p. 24.

37 Suleiman Mousa, 'A Matter of Principle: King Hussein of the Hijaz and the Arabs of Palestine', *International Journal of Middle East Studies*, 2, 9 (1978), p. 185.

38 Jeddah Report, 20 February 1921, p. 16, FO 686/27, TNA.

39 Faulkner, *Lawrence of Arabia's War*, p. 465.

40 Faulkner, *Lawrence of Arabia's War*, p. 466.

41 Lawrence, *Seven Pillars*, p. 276, Footnote '1919'.

42 Knightly and Simpson, *The Secret Lives of Lawrence of Arabia*, p. 151.

43 Educated at Cambridge, Captain Basil Liddell Hart had joined the King's Own Yorkshire Light Infantry in 1914, and was invalided by concussion injuries caused by shelling in 1915. He returned to serve in the battle of the Somme where he was wounded and gassed. He was posted to write training manuals under General Sir Ivor Maxse. He was eventually invalided out of the British Army in 1924 and became a journalist for *The Daily Telegraph*, and then took up writing on military history with enthusiasm.

44 Gat, *History of Military Thought*, p. 667.

45 Basil Liddell Hart, *Strategy* (London: Faber and Faber, 1954; previously published as *Decisive Wars of History*, 1929), p. 5.

46 Liddell Hart, *Strategy*, p. 369.

47 Liddell Hart, *Strategy*, p. 370. A similar verdict was reached by Sir John Keegan in the Reith Lectures of 1998, 'War and Our World', episode 3, available at: https://www.bbc.co.uk/programmes/p00gw9zf (accessed October 2018).

48 Liddell Hart, *Strategy*, p. 181.

49 Liddell Hart, *Strategy*, p. 181.

50 Liddell Hart, *Strategy*, p. 366.

51 Liddell Hart, *Strategy*, p. 366.

52 Liddell Hart, *Strategy*, p. 366.

53 Liddell Hart, *Strategy*, p. 367.

54 Liddell Hart, *Strategy*, p. 368.

55 Liddell Hart, *Strategy*, pp. 368–9.

56 Liddell Hart, *Strategy*, pp. 338.

57 Liddell Hart, *Strategy*, p. 321; see also J. F. C. Fuller, *The Reformation of War* (London: Hutchinson, 1923), p. 75.

58 Basil Liddell Hart, *The Sword and the Pen* (London: Cassell, 1978), p. 196.

59 Basil Liddell Hart, *The Ghost of Napoleon* (London: Faber and Faber, 1933; New Haven, CT, 1934), p. 133.

60 Liddell Hart made use of Jean Colin's work on Napoleon, as did Spenser Wilkinson. Jean Colin, *L'éducation militaire de Napoleon* (Paris: R. Chapelot et Cie, 1900); Gat, *History of Military Thought*, pp. 670 and 671–2. See also Basil Liddell Hart, *Paris, or the Future of War* (London: Kegan Paul, 1925), pp. 13–22.

61 References to Bourcet, Napoleon and Sherman, see Liddell Hart, *Strategy*, chapters VII, X, and p. 221.

62 Liddell Hart, *Strategy*, p. 182.

63 Liddell Hart, *Strategy*, p. 183.

64 Liddell Hart, *Strategy*, pp. 183–4.

65 Basil Liddell Hart, *Lawrence: In Arabia and After*, p. 438.

66 Lawrence to Liddell Hart, 17 October 1928, in Basil Liddell Hart, *T. E. Lawrence to his Biographer Basil Liddell Hart*, I (London: Faber and Faber, 1938), pp. 3–4; Gat, *History of Military Thought*, p. 673 and note 31.

67 Gat, *History of Military Thought*, p. 674. The *Enclyclopaedia* entry was a joint effort by Liddell Hart and Lawrence. Liddell Hart sent Lawrence the fee for the entry. Basil Liddell Hart, *The Memoirs of Captain Liddell Hart* (London: Cassell, 1965), I, pp. 84–5.

68 Brian Holden Reid, *Studies in British Military Thought* (Lincoln: University of Nebraska Press, 1998), p. 155.

69 Lawrence to Liddell Hart, in Liddell Hart, *T. E. Lawrence to His Biographer Basil Liddell Hart*, I (London: Faber and Faber, 1938), p. 132.

70 Liddell Hart, *Strategy*, pp. 333 and 338–9; Liddell Hart, *Paris, or the Future of War*, pp. 29–33; Lawrence, *Revolt in the Desert*, p. 66; Lawrence, *Seven Pillars*, p. 188; Gat, *History of Military Thought*, pp. 677–9.

71 Lawrence to Liddell Hart, 17 October 1928, in Liddell Hart, *T. E. Lawrence to His Biographer Basil Liddell Hart*, I (London: Faber and Faber, 1938), p. 4; Gat, *History of Military Thought*, p. 682.

72 Gat, *History of Military Thought*, p. 683.

73 Gat, *History of Military Thought*, p. 684; see for example, Liddell Hart, *The Ghost of Napoleon*, pp. 11–13.

74 Spenser Wilkinson, *War and Policy* (London and New York: Dodd, Mead and Company, 1900); Spenser Wilkinson, 'Killing No Murder: An Examination of Some New Theories of War', *Army Quarterly*, 14 (October 1927), which was a response to Liddell Hart's *The Remaking of*

Modern Armies (London: John Murray, 1927); Gat, *History of Military Thought*, p. 691.

75 Gat, *History of Military Thought*, p. 693.

76 Lawrence to Edward Garnett, in Garnett, *Letters*, no. 266, 13 July 1925, pp. 476–7.

77 Lawrence to John Buchan, in Garnett, *Letters*, no. 268, 5 August 1925, p. 478.

78 Lawrence to Johnathan Cape, 30 June 1928, in Garnett, *Letters*, no. 361, p. 613.

79 Garnett, *Letters*, p. 631.

80 Garnett, *Letters*, pp. 632–3.

CHAPTER 15

1 Simon Anglim, *Orde Wingate and the British Army, 1922–44* (London: Pickering and Chatto, 2010); Christopher Sykes, *Orde Wingate: A Biography* (Cleveland and New York: The World Publishing Company, 1959).

2 A. R. B. Linderman, *Rediscovering Irregular Warfare: Colin Gubbins and the Origins of Britain's Special Operations Executive* (Norman, OK: University of Oklahoma Press, 2016), p. 16.

3 Entry 3/2/57, Gubbins papers, IWM, cited in Linderman, *Rediscovering*, p. 28.

4 Eunan O'Halpin, 'The Irish Experience of Insurgency and Counterinsurgency since 1919', in Peter Dennis and Jeffrey Grey (eds), *An Art in Itself: The Theory and Conduct of Small Wars and Insurgencies* (Canberra: AHMP, 2006), p. 71.

5 Gubbins, 'Guerrilla', 5/8, Gubbins papers, IWM.

6 Colin Gubbins, *The Art of Guerrilla Warfare* (Scotts Valley, CA: Create Space Independent Publishing Platform, 2016), 1, p. 1.

7 Gubbins, *The Art of Guerrilla Warfare*, 5, p. 15; Linderman, *Rediscovering*, p. 63.

8 Gubbins, *The Art of Guerrilla Warfare*, 4, p. 12; Linderman, *Rediscovering*, p. 63.

9 Gubbins, *The Art of Guerrilla Warfare*, 7, p. 18.

10 Lawrence, 'Evolution of a Revolt', p. 56; Gubbins, *The Art of Guerrilla Warfare*, 2, p. 5; 15, p. 55.

11 Gubbins, *The Art of Guerrilla Warfare*, 8, p. 25.

12 Lawrence, 'Evolution of a Revolt', p. 69.

13 Gubbins, *The Art of Guerrilla Warfare*, 1, p. 1.

14 Linderman, *Rediscovering*, pp. 66–7.

15 Roderick Bailey, *The Wildest Province: SOE in the Land of the Eagle* (London: Vintage, 2009).

16 Sykes, *Wingate*, p. 33.

17 Sykes, *Wingate*, p. 89.

18 Raymond Callahan, *Wingate in Burma 1942–1945* (London: Davis-Poynter, 1978); Jon Latimer, *Burma: The Forgotten War* (London: John Murray, 2004).

19 'The First World War in the Middle East From an Arab Perspective', broadcast on Al Jezeera, 17 November 2018.

20 Mao Zedong, *On Guerrilla Warfare* (1937), ch. 6.

21 Lawrence, 'Evolution of a Revolt', p. 11; T. E. Lawrence, 'Science of Guerrilla Warfare', the crowd in action, para. 1.

22 In 1968, Colonel James L. Mrazek claimed that Mao had plagiarized Lawrence. However, Francis Grice, who has examined all of Mao's writings, can find no direct link. James L. Mrazek, 'The Philosophy of the Guerrilla Fighter', *Army Quarterly and Defense Journal*, 96 (April 1968), p. 72; Francis Grice, 'The Insurgent Myth of Mao: A Critical Reappraisal of the Chinese Guerrilla Legend', unpublished doctoral dissertation, King's College London (2014).

23 Bernard Fall, 'The Theory and Practice of Insurgency and Counterinsurgency', *Naval War College Review* (April 1965).

24 T. X. Hammes, 'The Way to Win a Guerrilla War', *Calhoun: The NPS Institutional Archive* (November 2006), p. 1. https://core.ac.uk/download/pdf/36733069.pdf (accessed September 2019).

25 Mao Zedong, *Basic Tactics*, Chapter 2, (1937), taken from Sun Tzu.

26 General Vo Nguyen Giap, *People's War, People's Army* (Hanoi: The Gioi Publisher, 1961), p. 48.

27 Stathis Kalyvas, *The Logic of Violence in Civil War* (New York: Cambridge University Press, 2006), pp. 388–90.

28 David Kilcullen, *Counterinsurgency* (London: Hurst & Co., 2010), p. 24.

29 Kilcullen, *Counterinsurgency*, p. 24.

30 Kilcullen, *Counterinsurgency*, pp. 26–7.

31 Frank Ledwidge, *Losing Small Wars* (New Haven: Yale University Press, 2011), p. 166.

32 Ledwidge, *Losing Small Wars*, p. 166.

33 Ledwidge, *Losing Small Wars*, p. 218.

34 Ledwidge, *Losing Small Wars*, pp. 16–17.

35 *Arab Bulletin*, 20 August 1917, II, p. 348; Lawrence, 'Secret Despatches, XXVII', in Brown, *T. E. Lawrence in War and Peace*, p. 144; Mack, *Prince of Our Disorder*; Robert Johnson, *True to Their Salt* (London: Hurst & Co., 2017), p. 421; cited also in Ledwidge, *Losing Small Wars*, p. 166.

36 Alasdair Soussi, 'Lawrence of Arabia, guiding US Army in Iraq and Afghanistan', at: https://www.csmonitor.com/World/2010/0619/Lawrence-of-Arabia-guiding-US-Army-in-Iraq-and-Afghanistan (accessed February 2018). See also Stephen Grey, '"Lawrence of Afghanistan" and the Lost Chance to Win Over the Taliban Fighters', *The Times*, 29 March 2009. John Nagl, *Learning to Eat Soup with a Knife: Counterinsurgency Lessons from Malaya and Vietnam* (University of Chicago Press, 2005).

37 John Hulsman, *Council of Foreign Relations* (New York: Simon and Schuster, 2017), jacket comment.

38 For an interesting exchange on this, see Robert Bateman, 'Lawrence and his Message', 27 April 2008, *Small Wars Journal*, http://smallwarsjournal.com/blog/lawrence-and-his-message (accessed February 2018).

39 *Arab Bulletin*, 20 August 1917, II, p. 347.

40 Ledwidge, *Losing Small Wars*, pp. 234, 235–6, 244.

41 Thomas X. Hammes, 'Dealing With Uncertainty', *Marine Corps Gazette* (November 2005).

42 US Army & Marine Corps Counterinsurgency Field Manual FM 3–24 (Chicago and London: University of Chicago Press, 2007), p. 1.1–1.4, 2.14, 2.33; Kilcullen, *Counterinsurgency*, pp. 149–50.

CHAPTER 16

1 Asprey, *War in the Shadows*, p. 288.

2 General Barrow, cited in Morton Jack, *Indian Empire at War*, p. 482.

3 Lawrence to Clayton, 27 August 1917, FO 882/7, folio 92, TNA.

4 Morsey, 'Lawrence: Strategist', p. 193; Lawrence, *Seven Pillars*, p. 196.

5 Lawrence, *Seven Pillars*, p. 193.

6 Lawrence, *Seven Pillars*, p. 196.

7 Lawrence, *Seven Pillars*, p. 194.

8 Lawrence, 'Science of Guerrilla Warfare', The Exact Science of Guerrilla Warfare, final paragraph.

9 Lawrence, 'Science of Guerrilla Warfare', The Exact Science of Guerrilla Warfare, final paragraph.

List of Abbreviations

AWM	Australian War Memorial, Camberra
BL	British Library, London
CUP	Committee of Union and Progress
EEF	Egyptian Expeditionary Force
IOR	India Office Records, British Library, London
LHCMA	Liddell Hart Centre for Military Archives, London
MECA	Middle East Centre Archive, St Antony's College, Oxford
NARA	National Archives, Washington DC
RAF	Royal Air Force
TNA	The National Archives, Kew, London

Select Bibliography

ARCHIVES

Askerî Tarih ve Stratejik Etüt Başjanliği Arşivi (ATASE) [Archive of the Directorate of Military History and Strategic Studies], Ankara
Harp cerideleri [Military Records of the Ottoman Army] K 526; K 1859; K 2918-2121; K 3920
TC Genelkurmay Başkanligi [Turkish General Staff], *Birinci Diinya Harbinde Turk Harbi, Vnci Cilt, Qanakkale Cephesi Harekati,* Inci Kitap (Haziran 1914–25 Nisan 1915) [*The Turkish War in the First World War,* 5th edition, Gallipoli Front Operations, Vol. 1 (June 1914–25 April 1915)] (Ankara: Genelkurmay Basimevi, 1993).
Türk Harbi, Turkish General Staff, 3 vols, (1965)

Australian War Memorial, Canberra (AWM)
AWM4 General Headquarters, Egyptian Expeditionary Force

Bodleian Library, Oxford
Correspondence and papers of A. W. Lawrence, relating to T. E. Lawrence, 1917–85
Correspondence and papers of T. E. Lawrence, with some related papers, c.1894–1970
MS. Eng. c. 6744 folios relating to the Oxford text of the 1922 edition of *Seven Pillars*

British Library, London (BL)
Add Mss 45915 Lawrence's Notebooks
Add Mss 45983A Lawrence's Pocket Diaries
Add 52463 Robertson/Murray Papers

Cambridge University Library, Cambridge
Lord Hardinge Papers

Churchill Archive, Churchill, Cambridge
Churchill papers

Durham University
Wingate Papers

Imperial War Museum, London (IWM)
IWM 79/48 Papers of General Sir Archibald Murray
IWM 12618 Papers of General Colin Gubbins
IWM 12809 Captured Turkish Documents

India Office Records (IOR), Political and Secret, and Military
    Department Records, British Library, London
L/Mil/7/16624-19656 Military Department Records
L/Mil/7/5/2421-4321 Military Department Records
L/Mil/17 Military Department Records
L/PS/8 Political and Secret Files
R/15 Gulf States: Records of the Bushire, Bahrain, Kuwait, Muscat and
    Trucial States Agencies 1763–1951
    Report on the Najd Mission, 1917–1918, IOR/R/15/1/747, f 251
    Report on Ibn Saud, File E/8, I, Ibn Sa'ud, IOR/R/15/2/31
Mss Eur E 264/52 Chelmsford Papers

King's College London, Liddell Hart Centre for Military Archives
    (LHCMA)
Papers of Basil Liddell Hart
Papers of Lieutenant Colonel Pierce Joyce
Papers of Sir William Robertson

Middle East Centre Archive, St Antony's College, Oxford (MECA)
Sir Edmund Allenby Papers
Sir Mark Sykes Papers
Sir R. Wingate Papers

National Archives and Records Association, College Park, Washington
    DC (NARA)
T-137 Auswärtigen Amt (The Middle East)

T-149 Auswärtigen Amt, NfdO (Information Service for the East)
RG 256 Records of the American Commission to Negotiate Peace)

National Army Museum, Chelsea, London (NAM)
Papers of Spenser Wilkinson

Politisches Archiv des Auswärtigen Amts, Bonn (PA)
Turkei 165 (Arabien)
Weltkrieg Nr.IIg (Unternehmungen und Aufwiegelungen gegen unsere
  Feinde in Ägypten, Syrien und Arabien)
Weltkrieg Nr.IIg Geheim (Ägypten, Syrien und Arabien)

LAWRENCE'S WORK

Lawrence, T. E., 'The Evolution of a Revolt', *Army Quarterly and Defence
  Journal* (October 1920)
Lawrence, T. E., *T. E. Lawrence to his Biographers Robert Graves and
  Basil Liddell Hart* (London: Doubleday and Doran and Co., 1938)
Lawrence, T. E., *Revolt in the Desert* (London: Jonathan Cape, 1926)
Lawrence, T. E., 'Science of Guerrilla War', *Encyclopaedia Britannica* (1929)
Lawrence, T. E., *Secret Despatches from Arabia* (London: Golden Cockerel,
  1939)
Lawrence, T. E., *Seven Pillars of Wisdom: A Triumph* (London: Jonathan
  Cape, 1935)

The National Archives, Kew, London (TNA)
Air 5 Air Ministry Records
CAB 24 War Cabinet
CAB 25 Supreme War Council
CAB 27 War Cabinet Committees
CAB 42/3/12 Committee of Imperial Defence, *Report of the Committee on
  Asiatic Turkey*, 30 June 1915
CAB 44 Correspondence of CIGS, Sir William Robertson
FO 371 Foreign Office (Egypt, Persia, Ottoman Empire)
FO 395 Consular Papers
FO 608 Peace Conference: British Delegation Papers and Correspondence
FO 839 Eastern Conference, Lausanne
FO 882 The Arab Bureau
WO 33 Reports and Miscellaneous
WO 106 Directorate of Military Operations
WO 157 Intelligence Summaries, 1914–21

PUBLISHED WORKS

Abdullah, Ibn al-Hussein, HM King of Jordan, *Al-Amali al-Siyasiya* (*Political Dictates*) [original in Arabic] (Amman: n.p., 1939)

Abdullah, Ibn al-Hussein, HM King of Jordan, *Memoirs of King Abdullah of Jordan* (London: Jonathan Cape, 1950)

Ahmad, Feroz, *The Young Turks: The Committee of Union and Progress in Turkish Politics, 1908–1914* (London: Hurst & Co., 1969)

Akin, Yiğit, *When the War Came Home: The Ottomans' Great War and the Devastation of an Empire* (Stanford, CA: Stanford University Press, 2018)

Al-Askari, Jafar Pasha, *A Soldier's Story*, edited by William Facey and Najdat Fathi Safwat (London: Arabian Publishing Ltd, 2003)

Aldington, Richard, *Lawrence of Arabia: A Biographical Enquiry* (London: Collins, 1969)

Alexander, John, '"Hot Air, Aeroplanes and Arabs": T. E. Lawrence and Air Power', *Air Power Review*, 22, 1 (2019), pp. 88–110

Allawi, A., *Feisal I of Iraq* (New Haven, CT: Yale University Press, 2014)

Allen, M. D., *The Medievalism of Lawrence of Arabia* (University Park, PA: Pennsylvania State University Press, 1991)

Anderson, Scott, *Lawrence in Arabia: War, Deceit, Imperial Folly and the Making of the Modern Middle East* (London: Atlantic Books, 2014)

Anglim, Simon, *Orde Wingate and the British Army, 1922–44* (London: Pickering and Chatto, 2010)

Antonius, George, *The Arab Awakening* (London: Hamish Hamilton, 1938)

Asprey, Robert, *War in the Shadows: The Guerrilla in History* (London: Macdonald, 1975)

Bailey, Roderick, *The Wildest Province: SOE in the Land of the Eagle* (London: Vintage, 2009)

Barr, James, *A Line in the Sand* (New York: Simon and Schuster, 2011)

Barr, James, *Setting the Desert on Fire: T. E. Lawrence and Britain's Secret War in Arabia, 1916–1918* (New York: W. W. Norton, 2008)

Bell, Gertrude, *Syria: The Desert and the Sown* (New York: E. P. Dutton and Co., 1907)

Beşiki, Mehmet, *The Ottoman Mobilisation of Manpower in the First World War: Between Volunteerism and Resistance* (Leiden: Brill, 2012)

Bidwell, Robin (ed.), *The Diary Kept by T. E. Lawrence While Travelling in Arabia During 1911* (Reading: Garnet, 1993)

Bidwell, Robin, 'Queries for Biographers of T. E. Lawrence', *Arabian Studies*, 3 (1977)

Bidwell, Robin, and Rex Smith (eds), *Arabian and Islamic Studies* (London: Longman, 1983)

Biger, Gideon, 'The Turkish Activities in Palestine During World War I Revised', in Yigal Sheffy and Shlaul Shani (eds), *The First World War: Middle Eastern Perspective* (Tel Aviv: Israel Society for Military History, 2000)

Bloch, Jan, *Is War Now Impossible?* (London: Grant Richards, 1899)

Blount, Clive, 'Modern Air Power, Counter-Insiurgency, and Lawrence of Arabia', *Air Power Review*, 13, 2 (2010), pp. 21–32

Bourne, John, 'Total War: I', in Charles Townshend (ed.), *The Oxford History of Modern War* (Oxford: Oxford University Press, 2005)

Brémond, Edouard, *Le Hedjaz dans la Guerre Mondiale* (Paris: Payot, 1931)

Brown, Malcolm (ed.), *Lawrence of Arabia: The Selected Letters* (London: Greenhill, 2005)

Brown, Malcolm, *T. E. Lawrence in War and Peace: An Anthology of the Military Writings of Lawrence of Arabia* (London: Greenhill, 2005)

Caemmerer, Rudolph von, *Die Entwicklung der strategischen Wissenschaft im 19. Jahrhundert* (published in 1904, repubd. Berlin: Severus Verlag, 2010)

Caemmerer, Rudolph von, *Geschichte der Befreiungskriege 1813–1815* [*War of Liberation*] (published in 1909, repubd. Paderborn: Aischines Verlag, 2013)

Callahan, Raymond, *Wingate in Burma 1942–1945* (London: Davis-Poynter, 1978)

Callwell, Charles Edward, *Small Wars: Their Principles and Practice* (London: HMSO, 1896; 3rd edition, 1906)

Carr, William, *A History of Germany, 1815–1990* (London: Edward Arnold, 1969, reprntd. 1991)

Chang, Tang Zi, *Principles of Conflict: Recompilation and New English Translation with Annotation of Sun Tzu's 'Art of War'* (San Rafael, CA: TC Press, 1969)

Colin, Jean, *L'éducation militaire de Napoleon* (Paris: R. Chapelot et Cie, 1900)

Dane, Edmund, *British Campaigns in the Near East*, 2 vols (London: Hodder and Stoughton, 1917–19)

Dawn, C. E., *From Ottomanism to Arabism: Essays on the Origins of Arab Nationalism* (Urbana: University of Illinois Press, 1973)

Dearberg, Neil, *Desert Anzacs: The Under-Told Story of the Sinai Palestine Campaign 1916–1918* (London: Glass House Books (Routledge), 2017)

Djemal Pasha, *Memories of a Turkish Statesman, 1913–1919* (London: Hutchinson, n.d.)

Dolev, Eran, *Allenby's Military Machine: Life and Death in World War I Palestine* (London: I. B. Tauris, 2007)

Doughty, Charles, *Travels in Arabia Deserta* (London: Bowes and Bowes, 1888)

Du Picq, Ardant, *Battle Studies: Ancient and Modern Battle* (Paris: 1870; reprntd. Harrisburg, PA: The Military Service Publishing Company, 1946)

Echevarria II, Antulio, 'Borrowing from the Master: Uses of Clausewitz in German Military Literature before the Great War', *War in History*, 3 (1996), pp. 274–92

Echevarria II, Antulio, *Clausewitz and Contemporary War* (Oxford: Oxford University Press, 2007)

El-Edroos, S. A., *The Hashemite Arab Army, 1908–1979: An Appreciation and Analysis of Military Operations* (Amman: The Publishing Committee, 1980)

Erickson, Edward, *Ottoman Army Effectiveness in World War I: A Comparative Study* (London: Routledge, 2007)

Evera, Stephen van, 'The Cult of the Offensive and the Origins of the First World War', *International Security*, 9, 1 (1984), pp. 58–107

Facey, W., and N. F. Safwat (eds), *The Memoirs of Jafar Pasha al-Askari* (London: Arabian Publishing Ltd, 2003)

Falls, Cyril, and A. F. Becke, *Official History: Military Operations, Egypt and Palestine: From June 1917 to the end of the War*, vol. 2, part II, *History of The Great War* (London: HMSO, 1930)

Faulkner, Neil, *Lawrence of Arabia's War: The Arabs, the British and the Remaking of the Middle East in WWI* (New Haven, CT: Yale University Press, 2017)

Fromkin, David, *A Peace to End All Peace: The Fall of the Ottoman Empire and the Creation of the Modern Middle East* (London: Phoenix Press, 1989)

Fuller, J. F. C., 'The Procedure of the Infantry Attack: A Synthesis from a Psychological Standpoint', *JRUSI*, 58 (January 1914), pp. 65–6

Fuller, J. F. C., *The Reformation of War* (London: Hutchinson, 1923)

Garnett, D., *The Letters of Lawrence of Arabia* (London: Jonathan Cape, 1938)

Gat, Azar, *A History of Military Thought* (Oxford: Oxford University Press, 2001)

Giap, Vo Nguyen, *People's War, People's Army* (Hanoi: The Gioi Publisher, 1961); repubd. https://www.marxists.org/archive/giap/1961-pwpa.pdf

Gilbert, Martin, *Winston S. Churchill, vol. IV: 1916–1922* (London: William Heinemann, 1975)

Gingeras, Ryan, *Fall of the Sultanate: The Great War and the End of the Ottoman Empire, 1908–1922* (Oxford: Oxford University Press, 2016)

Graves, Robert, *Lawrence and the Arabs* (London: Jonathan Cape, 1927; 1936 edn)

Gubbins, Colin, *The Art of Guerrilla Warfare* (Scotts Valley, CA: CreateSpace Independent Publishing Platform, 2016)

Gunay, Selahattin, *Bizi Kimlere Birakap Gidiyorsun Türk: Suriye ve Filistin Anıları [Who are you going to take us to? Turkish: Syrian and Palestinian memories]* (Istanbul: Türkiye İş Bankası Kültür Yayınalrı, 2006)

Haldane, Aylmer, *Insurrection in Mesopotamia* (Edinburgh: Blackwood's, 1922)

Halweg, Werner, 'Clausewitz and Guerrilla Warfare', in Michael I. Handel (ed.), *Clausewitz and Modern Strategy* (London: Frank Cass, 1986)

Handbook of the Turkish Army (London: War Office. Intelligence Division, 1916; reproduced by the Imperial War Museum, Dept. of Printed Books, in association with the Battery Press, Nashville, and Articles of War Ltd., 1999)

Hepburn, Allan, *Intrigue: Espionage and Culture* (New Haven, CT: Yale University Press, 2005)

Holden Reid, Brian, *British Military Thought* (Lincoln: University of Nebraska Press, 1998)

Howard, Michael, 'Men Against Fire: Expectations of War in 1914', in *International Security*, 9, 1 (Summer 1984), pp. 41–57

Hughes, Matthew, *Allenby in Palestine: The Middle East Correspondence of Field Marshal Viscount Allenby June 1917 – October 1919* (Stroud: Sutton Publishing, 2004)

Hughes, Matthew, 'Command, Strategy and the Battle for Palestine, 1917', in Ian Beckett (ed.), *1917: Beyond the Western Front* (Leiden: Brill, 2009)

Hurewitz, J. C. (ed.), *The Middle East and North Africa in World Politics: A Documentary Record*, vol. II (New Haven, CT: Yale Universty Press, 1979)

Hynes, James Patrick, *Lawrence of Arabia's Secret Air Force* (Barnsley: Pen and Sword, 2010)

Hynes, S., *The Edwardian Turn of Mind* (Princeton, NJ: Princeton University Press, 1975)

Jacobsen, Mark, '"Only by the Sword": British Counter-insurgency in Iraq, 1920', *Small Wars & Insurgencies*, 2, 2 (1991), pp. 323–63

Jeffrey, Keith, *The British Army and the Crisis of Empire, 1918–1922* (Manchester: Manchester University Press, 1984)

Jeffrey, Keith, *Field Marshal Sir Henry Wilson* (Oxford: Oxford University Press, 2006)

Johnson, C. A., 'Civilian Loyalties and Guerrilla Conflict', *World Politics*, 14 (October 1961), pp. 646–61

Johnson, Robert, 'The de Bunsen Committee and the "Conspiracy" of Sykes-Picot', *Middle Eastern Studies* (March 2018)

Johnson, Robert, 'The First World War and the Middle East: A Literature Review of Recent Scholarship', *Middle Eastern Studies*, 54, 1 (2018), pp. 142–51

Johnson, Rob, *The Great War and the Middle East* (Oxford: Oxford University Press, 2016)

Jones, H. A., *The War in the Air: Being the Part Played in the Great War by the Royal Air Force*, 5 volumes (Oxford: Clarendon Press, 1935)

Kalyvas, Stathis, *The Logic of Violence in Civil War* (New York: Cambridge University Press, 2006)

Karsh, Efraim, and Inari Karsh, 'Myth in the Desert, or Not the Great Arab Revolt', *Middle Eastern Studies*, 33, 2 (1997), pp. 267–312

Kedar, Benjamin Z., *The Changing Land between the Jordan and the Sea: Aerial Photographs from 1917 to the Present* (Tel Aviv: Yad Ben-Zvi Press, 1999)

Kedourie, Elie, *In the Anglo-Arab Labyrinth: The McMahon-Hussein Correspondence and its Interpretations, 1914–1939* (Cambridge: Cambridge University Press, 1976)

Kedourie, Elie, 'The Real T. E. Lawrence', *Commentary*, 64, 1 (1977), pp. 49–56; with correspondence, 64, 4 (1977), pp. 10–18

Keegan, John, *Mask of Command* (London: Viking, 1987)

Kennedy, Caroline, and Sophia Dingli, 'Lawrence and the Study of War', *The Journal of the T. E. Lawrence Society*, XXIII, 1 (2013), pp. 28–37

Kilcullen, David, *Counterinsurgency* (London: Hurst & Co., 2010)

Kirkbride, A., *An Awakening* (Tavistock: University Press of Arabia, 1971)

Kitchen, James, *The British Imperial Army in the Middle East: Morale and Military Identity in the Sinai and Palestine Campaigns, 1916–1918* (London: Bloomsbury, 2014)

Knightly, Philip, and Colin Simpson, *The Secret Lives of Lawrence of Arabia* (London: Nelson, 1969)

Konda, Michael, *Hero: The Life and Legend of Lawrence of Arabia* (London: Aurum Press, 2011)

Lacey, R., *The Kingdom: Arabia and the House of Saud* (London: Fontana, 1981)

Lacquer, Walter, *Guerrilla: A Historical and Critical Study* (London: Little, Brown, 1976)

Latimer, Jon, *Burma: The Forgotten War* (London: John Murray, 2004)

Leach, Hugh, 'Lawrence's Strategy and Tactics in the Arab Revolt', *Asian Affairs*, 37, 3 (2006), pp. 337–41

Leclerc, Christopher, 'French Eye-Witness Accounts of Lawrence and the Arab Revolt', part 2, *The Journal of the T. E. Lawrence Society*, XX, 2 (2010/11)

Ledwidge, Frank, *Losing Small Wars* (New Haven, CT: Yale University Press, 2011)

Leigh, Bruce, *Lawrence: Warrior and Scholar* (Ticehurst: Tattered Flag Press, 2014)

Liddell Hart, Basil, *Foch: The Man of Orleans* (London: Eyre and Spottiswoode, 1931)

Liddell Hart, Basil, 'French Military Ideas before the First World War', in M. Gilbert (ed.), *A Century of Conflict, 1850–1950* (London: Hamish Hamilton, 1966)

Liddell Hart, Basil, *The Ghost of Napoleon* (London: Faber and Faber, 1933; New Haven, CT: 1934)

Liddell Hart, Basil, *Paris, or the Future of War* (London: Kegan Paul, 1925)

Liddell Hart, Basil, *Strategy* (London: Faber and Faber, 1954; previously published as *Decisive Wars of History*, 1929)

Liddell Hart, Basil, *The Sword and the Pen* (London: Cassell, 1978)

Liddell Hart, Basil, *T. E. Lawrence: In Arabia and After* (London: Jonathan Cape, 1934)

Liddell Hart, Basil, *T. E. Lawrence to his Biographer Basil Liddell Hart* (London: Faber and Faber, 1938)

Liman von Sanders, Otto, *Five Years in Turkey* (Annapolis: US Naval Institute Press, 1927)

Linderman, A. R. B., *Rediscovering Irregular Warfare: Colin Gubbins and the Origins of Britain's Special Operations Executive* (Norman, OK: University of Oklahoma Press, 2016)

Lloyd George, David, *War Memoirs* (London: Odhams, 1933)

Lüdke, Tilman, 'Loyalty, Indifference, Treason: The Ottoman-German Experience in Palestine During World War I', in Yigal Sheffy and Haim Goren Eran Dolev (eds), *Palestine and World War I: Grand Strategy, Military Tactics and Culture in War* (London: I. B. Tauris, 2014)

Mack, J. E., *Prince of Our Disorder: The Life of T. E. Lawrence* (Boston: Little, Brown, 1976)

Marighella, Carlos, *Minimanual of the Urban Guerrilla* (New York, 1969; available at: https://www.marxists.org/archive/marighella-carlos/1969/06/minimanual-urban-guerrilla/index.htm)

Massey, W. T., *The Great War in the Middle East*, published as *The Desert Campaigns* (New York: Putnams, 1918; repubd. London: Leonaur, 2009)

McKale, Donald, *War by Revolution* (Kent, OH: Kent State University Press, 1998)

McMunn, George, and Cyril Falls, *Official History of the Great War: Military Operations, Egypt and Palestine*, vol. I (London: HMSO, 1927)

McQuaid, Kim, *The Real and Assumed Personalities of Famous Men: Rafael de Nogales, T. E. Lawrence and the Birth of the Modern Era, 1914–1937* (London: Gomides Institute, 2010) .

Mohs, Polly, *Military Intelligence and the Arab Revolt: The First Modern Intelligence War* (New York: Routledge, 2007)

Moran, Lord Charles, *The Anatomy of Courage* (Chiswick: Eyre and Spottiswoode, 1945)

Morsey, Konrad, 'T. E. Lawrence: Strategist', in Stephen E. Tabachnick (ed.), *The T. E. Lawrence Puzzle* (Athens, GA: University of Georgia Press, 1984)

Mortlock, Michael, *The Egyptian Expeditionary Force in World War I* (Jefferson, NC: McFarland, 2011)

Morton Jack, George, *The Indian Empire at War: From Jihad to Victory, the Untold Story of the Indian Army in the First World War* (London: Little, Brown, 2018)

Mousa, Suleiman, *al-Haraka al-Arabiyya* [The Arab Movement] (Beirut: Dar al-nahar, 1970)

Mousa, S., *T. E. Lawrence: An Arab View* (Oxford: Oxford University Press, 1966)

Mühlmann, C., *Das deutsch-türkische Waffenbündnis im Weltkriege* (Leipzig: Koehler & Amelang, 1940)

Murphy, David, *The Arab Revolt 1916–1918* (Oxford: Osprey Publishing, 2008)

Nogales, R. de, *Four Years Beneath the Crescent* (London: Charles Scribner's Sons, 1926)

O'Halpin, Eunan, 'The Irish Experience of Insurgency and Counterinsurgency since 1919', in Peter Dennis and Jeffrey Grey (eds), *An Art in Itself: The Theory and Conduct of Small Wars and Insurgencies* (Canberra: AHMP, 2006)

Oschenwald, William, 'Ironic Origins: Arab Nationalism in the Hijaz, 1882–1914', in Rashid Khalidi, et al. (eds), *The Origins of Arab Nationalism* (New York: Columbia University Press, 1991)

Ozdemir, Hikmet, *The Ottoman Army 1914–1918: Disease and Death on the Battlefield* (University of Utah, 2008)

Parsons, Laila, *The Commander* (London: Saqi, 2017)

Peaty, John, 'Palestine', in John Wilson (ed.), *Battlefield Guide, vol.2: The Forgotten Fronts* (Andover: Army Headquarters, 2016)

Prie-Gordon, H. (ed.), *A Brief Record of the Advance of the Egyptian Expeditionary Force under the Command of General Sir Edmund H. H. Allenby, July 1917 to October 1918* (London: HMSO, 1919)

Provence, Michael, *The Last Ottoman Generation and the Making of the Modern Middle East* (Cambridge: Cambridge University Press, 2017)

Rogan, Eugene, *The Fall of the Ottomans* (New York: Basic Books, 2015)

Said, Amin, *al-Thawra al-Arabiyya al-Kubra* [The Great Arab Revolt] (Cairo: Dar al-ilm lil-Malayin, 1934)

Saxe, Maurice de, *Reveries on the Art of War* (repubd. New Delhi: Pentagon Press, 2017)

Schilcher, Linda Schatkowski, 'The Famine of 1915–1918 in Greater Syria', in John Spagnolo (ed.), *Problems of the Modern Middle East in Historical Perspective: Essays in Honour of Albert Hourani* (Reading: Ithaca Press, 1992)

Sheffield, G. D., *Leadership in the Trenches: Officer-Man Relations, Morale, and Discipline in the British Army in the Era of the First World War* (London: Macmillan, 2000)

Silke, Andrew, 'Ferocious Times: The IRA, the RIC, and Britain's Failure in 1919–1921', *Terrorism and Political Violence*, 28, 3 (2016), pp. 417–34

Storrs, Ronald, *Orientations* (London: Readers' Union, 1939)

Strachan, Hew, *Carl von Clausewitz's On War: A Biography* (London: Atlantic Monthly Press, 2007)

Strachan, Hew, 'Clausewitz and the First World War', *The Journal of Military History*, 75 (April 2011), pp. 367–91.

Strachan, Hew, *The First World War, I: To Arms* (Oxford: Oxford University Press, 2001)

Strachan, Hew, 'Training, Morale, and Modern War', *Journal of Contemporary History*, 41, 2 (2006), pp. 211–27

Sykes, Christopher, *Orde Wingate: A Biography* (Cleveland and New York: The World Publishing Company, 1959)

Taber, Robert, *War of the Flea* (New York: L. Stuart, 1965)

Tarver, Linda J., 'In Wisdom's House: T. E. Lawrence in the Near East', *Journal of Contemporary History*, 13 (July 1978), pp. 585–608.

Tauber, Eliezer, *The Arab Movements in World War I* (London: Frank Cass, 1993)

Thomas, Lowell Jackson, *With Lawrence in Arabia* (London: Hutchinson, 1923)

Townshend, Charles, *The British Campaign in Ireland, 1919–1921: The Development of Political and Military Policies* (Oxford: Oxford University Press, 1975)

Townshend, Charles, *The Republic: The Fight for Irish Independence, 1918–1923* (London: Penguin, 2014)

Travers, T. H. E., 'Technology, Tactics and Morale: Jean de Bloch, the Boer War, and British Military Theory, 1900–1914', *Journal of Modern History*, 51 (June 1979), pp. 264–86

Umunc, Himmet, '"A Hope So Transcendent": The Arab Revolt in the Great War and T. E. Lawrence', in Robert Johnson and James Kitchen (eds), *The Great War in the Middle East: A Clash of Empires* (London: Routledge, 2018)

Ussishkin, Daniel, *Morale: A Modern British History* (Oxford: Oxford University Press, 2017)

Walker, Philip, *Behind the Lawrence Legend: The Forgotten Few Who Shaped the Arab Revolt* (Oxford: Oxford University Press, 2018)

Wallach, J. L., *Anatomie einer Militärhilfe: Die preußisch-deutschen Militärmissionen in der Türkei 1835–1919* (Düsseldorf: Droste, 1976)

Walter, Barbara, *Committing to Peace* (Princeton, NJ: Princeton University Press, 2002)

Wavell, General Sir Archibald, *Speaking Generally* (London: Macmillan, 1946)

Wells, H. G., *The War in the Air* (London: George Bell and Sons, 1908)

Wilkinson, Spenser, 'Killing No Murder: An Examination of Some New Theories of War', *Army Quarterly*, 14 (October 1927)

Wilkinson, Spenser, *War and Policy* (New York: Dodd, Mead and Company, 1900)

Wilson, Jeremy, *Lawrence of Arabia: Authorised Biography* (New York: Athenaeum, 1990)

Wilson, Mary C., 'The Hashemites, the Arab Revolt, and Arab Nationalism', in Rashid Khalidi, Lisa Anderson, Muhammad Muslih and Reeva Simon (eds), *The Origins of Arab Nationalism* (New York, 1991)

Woodward, David R., *Hell in the Holy Land: World War I in the Middle East* (Lexington: University of Kentucky, 2006)

Yanıkdağ, Yücel, *Healing the Nation: Prisoners of War, Medicine and Nationalism in Turkey, 1914–1939* (Edinburgh: Edinburgh University Press, 2013)

Yuen, Derek C., *Diciphering Sun Tzu: How to Read the Art of War* (Oxford: Oxford University Press, 2014)

Zeine, Zeine N., *The Emergence of Arab Nationalism: With a Background Study of Arab-Turkish Relations in the Near East* (Delmar, NY: Caravan, 1958, 3rd edn, 1976)

Zürcher, Erik-Jan, 'Little Mehmet in the Desert: The Ottoman Soldier's Experience', in Peter Liddle and Hugh Cecil (eds), *Facing Armageddon: The First World War Experienced* (London: Leo Cooper, 1996)

WEB REFERENCES

Soussi, Alasdair, 'Lawrence of Arabia, guiding US Army in Iraq and
    Afghanistan', https://www.csmonitor.com/World/2010/0619/Lawrence-
    of-Arabia-guiding-US-Army-in-Iraq-and-Afghanistan (accessed February
    2018)

Bateman, Robert, 'Lawrence and his Message', 27 April 2008, *Small Wars
    Journal*, http://smallwarsjournal.com/blog/lawrence-and-his-message
    (accessed February 2018)

Index

References to maps are in **bold**; references to notes are indicated by n.